# An Introduction to Television Studies

Praise for the first edition:

'A wonderfully ambitious and clear introduction to television studies for the undergraduate reader.'
Gill Branston, University of Cardiff, and co-author of *The Media Student's Book*

'An excellent introduction to television studies, with helpful accounts of key concepts tied to some engaging discussions of recent shows.'
David Gauntlett, University of Bournemouth and author of *Media, Gender and Identity*

'I have no doubt that this work will become a must for all students wishing to study the new and growing discipline of television studies.'
Paul Rixon, University of Surrey, Roehampton

'. . . destined to feature prominently on every television student's preparatory reading wish-list.'
Deborah Jermyn, University of Surrey, Roehampton and co-editor of *Understanding Reality Television*

In this comprehensive textbook, newly updated for its second edition, Jonathan Bignell provides students with a framework for understanding the key concepts and main approaches to Television Studies, including audience research, television history and broadcasting policy, and the analytical study of individual programmes.
    Features for the second edition include:

- a glossary of key terms
- key terms defined in margins
- suggestions for further reading at the end of each chapter
- activities for use in class or as assignments
- new and updated case studies discussing advertisements such as the Guinness 'Surfer' ad, approaches to news reporting, television scheduling, and programmes such as *Big Brother* and *Wife Swap*.

Individual chapters address: studying television, television histories, television cultures, television texts and narratives, television and genre, television production, postmodern television, television realities, television representation, television you can't see, shaping audiences, television in everyday life.

**Jonathan Bignell** is Professor of Television and Film at the University of Reading. He is the author of *Media Semiotics: An Introduction, Big Brother: Reality TV in the Twenty-first Century* and *Postmodern Media Culture*, and co-author of *The Television Handbook*. He is the editor of *Writing and Cinema*, and joint editor of *Popular Television Drama* and *British Television Drama: Past, Present and Future*.

# An Introduction to Television Studies

*Second edition*

Jonathan Bignell

Routledge
Taylor & Francis Group

LONDON AND NEW YORK

First published 2004
by Routledge
2 Park Square, Milton Park, Abingdon, Oxon OX14 4RN

Simultaneously published in the USA and Canada
by Routledge
270 Madison Ave, New York, NY 10016

Second edition published 2008

Routledge is an imprint of the Taylor & Francis Group, an informa business

© 2004, 2008 Jonathan Bignell

Typeset in Akzidenz Grotesk by
Keystroke, 28 High Street, Tettenhall, Wolverhampton
Printed and bound in Great Britain by
The Cromwell Press, Trowbridge, Wiltshire

*British Library Cataloguing in Publication Data*
A catalogue record for this book is available from the British Library

*Library of Congress Cataloging in Publication Data*
Bignell, Jonathan.
An introduction to television studies / Jonathan Bignell. – 2nd ed.
p. cm.
Includes bibliographical references and index.
1. Television broadcasting. 2. Television. I. Title.
PN1992.5.B48 2007
791.45–dc22
2007007147

ISBN10: 0–415–41917–4 (hbk)
ISBN10: 0–415–41918–2 (pbk)

ISBN13: 978–0–415–41917–8 (hbk)
ISBN13: 978–0–415–41918–5 (pbk)

# Contents

# Illustrations

The above were reproduced with kind permission. While every effort has been made to trace copyright holders and obtain permission, this has not been possible in all cases. Any omissions brought to our attention will be remedied in future editions.

# Acknowledgements

I would like to thank my colleagues at the University of Reading and at Royal Holloway University of London who have assisted in shaping my approach to Television Studies, and whose expertise has suggested material, activities and further reading in some of the chapters of the book. The wider community of scholars in Television Studies also deserve my thanks, not only for the work explicitly acknowledged and referenced in the text but also for the wealth of ideas that I have encountered over the last two decades of studying and writing about television. I am grateful to the undergraduate and postgraduate students I have worked with over the years, because discussions with them have often prompted new ways of thinking and new problems to grapple with. During the preparation of both editions of this book I received invaluable feedback from anonymous readers of draft material, and I have benefited from the expertise and enthusiasm of the editorial staff at Routledge. Finally, as always, I acknowledge the support and love of Lib Taylor, to whom the book is dedicated.

# Introduction

## Using this book

This book is an introduction to Television Studies, aimed especially at those who are new to the study of the medium at college and university level. It describes some of the critical approaches to television that have become widely accepted in the subject. It also explains and makes use of key concepts in Television Studies that every student needs to know about. The book re-evaluates the terms and ideas that have been significant in studying television, and tests out their limits, drawing attention to the strengths and weaknesses in the ways in which television has been studied up to now. So it draws together a collection of concepts and critical languages that are sometimes quite diverse, or even contradictory, and suggests how there are some ways of thinking about television that are more fruitful than others. Television Studies is a new, dynamic and rapidly changing field of work, as the next section explains. This makes the task of the student of television an open-ended and exciting one, and the book also aims to convey some of this energy and diversity in its organisation and layout.

This book outlines significant strands of critical work in the field, and provides worked-through case study examples of how critical approaches can be applied to actual problems, programmes and issues. It encourages active learning by including many activities which can form the basis of classroom discussion or written assignments. The book is organised into short chapters, suitable for use as preparatory reading for class study, or as follow-up reading to support classroom debate. Significant terms are highlighted in **bold** in the text when they are doing important work in the discussion. A definition of the highlighted term appears in the margin next to its first appearance in a chapter, and these definitions can also be found in alphabetical order in the glossary of key terms at the end of the book. In this Introduction key terms are highlighted in bold though their definitions do not appear in the margin. The terms I have highlighted in this way are those that seem to require a specific definition. Some of them are part of the critical terminology of the academic discipline of Television Studies or one of the areas of research that has fed into the field. Some of them are terms used in the television industry in Britain or the USA to describe an aspect of how television technology works, or how programme-making and **broadcasting** are carried out. Some terms are more widely known and are part of non-professional language, but seem to me to need a precise definition so that they can be understood and used accurately by readers and students of television. Readers of this book will already know some terms, will have heard but not understood others, and will be introduced to others that I hope will enrich their capacity to talk and write about television.

Each chapter ends with a short list of suggested further reading. The books, essays and articles chosen are often those that have been quoted, but there are also some other books listed that deal with the topics covered in the chapter. There is great insight to be gained from noting how other voices have expressed ideas that I have written about here, and especially so if another writer has an alternative or even opposed attitude to a subject. Like any academic subject, Television Studies is diverse and evolving, and there are strongly held and articulately presented points of view within it that differ greatly in aims, assumptions, emphases and conclusions. Approaches to Television Studies are not a set of tools, but more like a group of different languages. They do not translate neatly one into another, and each defines its world in rather different ways. The book is concerned with the most commonly studied theoretical issues in television courses. The major differences between courses of study are in their focus on one or two of the following areas:

- analytical study of television programmes as **texts**
- the television industry as an institution and its production practices and organisation
- television in contemporary culture and the **sociological** study of audiences
- television history and developments in broadcasting policy.

This book provides introductory explanation, evaluation and routes for further study in each of these areas. I aim to show why these approaches have a significant role in Television Studies, to encourage students to participate in debates within and between these approaches, and to gain an understanding of the strengths and weaknesses of particular theoretical models for studying television.

In each chapter the reader will discover references to work by others who have contributed to Television Studies, and these references can be followed up in the Select Bibliography at the end of the book. Indeed, the Select Bibliography can itself be a useful tool for looking at the range of the subject, and exploring sources for independent work. In a single volume it is impossible for me to note all of the significant ideas in the sources I have used, and readers have many opportunities to build on the brief discussions of existing research that I have included here by reading the source texts that I have cited. Indeed, the many directions that such further work can take indicate the comparative newness and potential of Television Studies, and I hope that readers of this book will be encouraged to make their own contributions to the subject by identifying the gaps, new directions and even contradictions opened up in these pages.

## Television Studies

The academic study of television has had little interest in valuing one programme or kind of television over another. Yet in the ways people talk about television, these evaluative issues are high on the agenda. What might it mean to say that a programme (or a channel, or an evening's viewing) is 'good'? **Quality**, or 'good', television is an informal category that often separates prestigious dramas, documentaries, art films and **adaptations** from the rest, from 'popular' television. Attaching the label 'quality' involves assigning cultural importance to programmes or kinds of television that have acquired a valued position in **culture**, rather like theatre's distinctions between 'serious' theatre and musicals or pantomime. There is a social and cultural framework which enables the study of some television to carry value, and the programmes or kinds of television labelled as 'quality' to carry value in a way that popular television does not. The academic subject of Television Studies has taken popular television seriously, because it is the television most people watch most of the time. This is despite the common criticism in the press, and sometimes in the television industry itself, that popular television is unimportant, 'just' commercial, and lacking in artistic value.

Television Studies has tried to define how the medium communicates, and this has involved distinguishing between television communication and the media of cinema or radio, for example. But it has used methodologies for describing and analysing television texts that come from disciplines including Film Studies (see Chapter 4), methods of discussing audiences and television institutions that come from sociology, and ways of describing the development of television that amount to different histories of the medium. Charlotte Brunsdon (1998b: 96) has summarised this by explaining that

> much of the literature of television studies could be characterised as attempting to formulate accounts of the specificity of television, often using comparison with, on the one hand, radio (broadcast, liveness, civic address), and on the other, cinema (moving pictures, fantasy), with particular attention . . . to debate about the nature of the television text and the television audience.

Because television includes so many different programmes, channels and ways of addressing its audiences even at one point in time in a single geographical region, it has proved very difficult for critics and commentators to produce useful general insights into the medium. This is even more the case once the history of the medium and its variations across countries and regions of the world are considered (see Chapter 2).

Early predictions (in the 1930s, for instance) of what television would be emphasised its liveness, its ability to present to a mass audience images of what was happening in the real world. Commentators remarked on television's inability to compete with cinema as entertainment and therefore expected the medium to focus on information and **actuality**. These early thoughts conditioned the ways in which **realism**, connection to the contemporary and uneasiness about bringing controversial visions into the home were played out. The connection of television technology to immediacy (television as a means of relaying something that would have happened anyway) predisposes it to linear real-time progress, and the claim to report the real world (see Chapter 8). Film has been theorised in terms of space (what can be seen on the space of the screen), and this has led to theories about how individual film spectators **identify** with the usually fictional characters and **points of view** offered for spectators to see. Some of these ways of thinking from studying film have been deployed in Television Studies to explain how viewers make sense of the television medium. On the other hand, television has also been theorised in terms of time. Television consists of a **flow** of audio-visual material that, although divided up into programmes, runs on across a period of time without empty gaps in between. Brunsdon (1998b: 105–6) has noted that: 'Television is, for the most part, made as programmes or runs of programmes: series, serials and mini-series. However this is not necessarily how television is watched . . . It is precisely this possible "drifting" through an evening's viewing that has come to seem . . . one of the unique features of television watching.' Rather than anticipating and wishing for the end of an individual film **narrative**, the television viewer is usually drawn into and out of a flow of material that does not come to a decisive end.

The experience of watching television occurs in a dimension of time where little end-points (like the ends of programmes) keep occurring, but where viewers are always aware that something new is about to take the place of what they have just been watching. Television Studies has tried to address this situation by looking not only at individual programmes but also at the ways they link together. These links might be in terms of the similarities of one programme with another, where shared features of a **genre** tell us something about the persistence of some kinds of storytelling, sets of issues or ideas being explored or the **conventions** to which the makers of programmes adhere (see Chapter 5). The links might also be in the planning and organisation of a period of viewing, for example an evening's television **schedule** on a certain channel. Planning a schedule to include variety, yet also a continuity of interest that might keep a viewer tuned to a single channel, can tell us a lot about how an idea of the viewing audience and its interests drives the organisation of television and assumptions about how television is used and enjoyed. The links between programmes in a schedule are the responsibility of the institutions that broadcast them, and looking at how television institutions work has been important to Television Studies' understanding of the medium's role as an industrial product (see Chapter 6), made and organised in different ways in different parts of the world.

Television has no dominant **global** form; it is always local. Even though television programmes and formats are distributed globally, its local forms are different (see Chapter 3). This can be seen immediately in the difference between **commercial television** in the USA and the British tradition, which has a strong civic, '**public service**' character. In Britain there has always been a tension between taking television's responsibility to society seriously and regarding television as entertainment for a consumer. So although television has been regarded as the medium most appropriate to the way we live now in Western societies, to the extent that it has been described as '**postmodern**' (see Chapter 7), it is not the same throughout the world; nor does it lack a history that has shaped its present form in each society. The contexts that the organisation of television in particular places offers to Television Studies are important because they draw attention to the fact that television does not have to take the form that it does in the places with which we might be familiar. There is no necessity about the fact that in Britain, for example, there are television channels funded by advertising and **sponsorship**, and others funded by a **licence fee** that is in effect a tax on the ownership of television sets.

The ways in which television connects with the character of the society where it is watched raise the issue of the social significance of what television represents. The questions of what is represented, in what ways and with what possible effects have been considered in Television Studies with particular attention to the representation of groups who are relatively lacking in social power (see Chapter 9). This kind of study can illuminate the active contribution of television to the ways that viewers understand and experience their social environments, as well as how television reflects that environment to them. As well as looking at what can be seen and heard in the medium of television, how it is organised in different parts of the world and its relationship with the ways of thinking and experiencing the world in social contexts, Television Studies pays attention to the audiences of television and how they interact with the medium. This involves noting which programmes and kinds of programme are watched the most, using information that television institutions themselves collect in statistical form (see Chapter 11). But it also involves undertaking independent studies where groups of viewers are asked by Television Studies researchers about their attitudes to what they watch, and how their television viewing fits into their life experience and their sense of who they are (see Chapter 12). Research on audiences attempts to engage with how viewers make sense of television, and how it is important (or perhaps unimportant) to them. In this way Television Studies aims to break down the boundaries between the academic agendas that it has developed for specialised work on the medium and the place of watching television in the lives of non-specialist viewers for whom television can function in a range of ways among other routines and everyday experiences.

## The organisation of chapters

### Studying Television

The first chapter sketches out the topics of study and critical approaches which can be found in academic Television Studies, noting its significant emphases and exclusions. Television Studies in Britain and the USA, for example, most usually addresses **broadcast** television in the English-speaking world. One dominant strand is the detailed **textual analysis** of programmes, with a preference for popular programmes in **serial** and **series** form, concentrating on dramatic, **documentary** and news programmes. This derives from the tradition in academic work of studying content and form in detail. It also reflects the dominance of English-language programmes in the world television market. There are other kinds of television to mention, however, which stimulate thinking about what television can include: trailers, commercials and channel **idents**, for instance. Television can now be viewed on computer screens, competing with games or text, and is viewed in a different position and often in a different room from the traditional household television set. This chapter considers different understandings of what television is, and how Television Studies approaches are based on assumptions about the television text, the form of its transmission and who is watching where and when. The chapter includes a case study comparing and contrasting representations of television viewing in the 1950s and the 2000s, showing how the medium has been thought about in different ways at different times.

### Television Histories

This chapter describes and analyses the different approaches to the evolution of television from the 1930s to the 1990s in Britain, comparing and contrasting these with historical approaches to television in other countries, especially the USA. This involves discussion of state **regulation** of television, the increasing proliferation of channels and the introduction of non-**terrestrial** satellite broadcasting systems, competition and commerce. Part of the different historical shape of television around the world comes from distinct and different understandings of the television audience, perceived as a market of consumers or as a public whose needs television should serve. The chapter aims to introduce the subject of television history, with regard to the changing social place of television in society, changes in television institutions and changing conceptions of the television audience and the nature of television viewing. The range of approaches to television history in the chapter provides different selections of landmark developments and landmark programmes, for example according to whether the focus is on technology, institutions or audience issues. The chapter explains a range of historical approaches, in order to show how television history can be written in many different ways. The case study at the end of the chapter explores one aspect of television's likely future, as new technologies allow viewers to compose their own viewing **schedules** and selections of programmes from huge databases from which viewers can download their choices, or have their personal video recorders make choices for them.

## Television Cultures

This chapter looks at the competing ways of analysing television institutions, and the significance of national and international **cultures** of television broadcasting. It explains and discusses patterns of commercial and **public service** broadcasting, and debates about whether television contributes to **media imperialism**. This leads to a discussion of television **globalisation**, comparing and contrasting ways of thinking about television as a market and an industry with political implications. Television in the developed world is still largely organised on national lines, but the increasing significance of international flows from West to East and North to South has been hotly debated. The chapter refers to inequalities in production funding and the role of imported programming in national television cultures. The focus of the chapter is on the theories which propose that television institutions both embody and transmit **ideologies** because of their ownership, and their relationships with national broadcasting cultures. The chapter finishes with a case study of the ways in which popular Brazilian drama serials, the 'telenovelas', have been used as an example in debates about the politics of global television.

## Television Texts and Television Narratives

This chapter evaluates the theoretical approaches that have considered television programmes as '**texts**' that can be studied in close detail to reveal how their meanings are made. The techniques for undertaking this kind of close analysis, deriving from the methodologies of **semiotics**, are explained. This includes methodologies for analysing **narrative**, the relationships between programmes across a period of television viewing, and ways of thinking about the relations between image and sound. While this way of working can be very powerful, the chapter also considers what it leaves out, such as television's institutional context and history, and the relationships between actual viewers and programmes. The question of who or what is the maker of television's meanings, in other words the question of **authorship**, is also considered in the chapter, and it explores different **genres** of television and how they can be studied. The case study in this chapter takes a single television commercial and conducts a close analysis of its images and sounds, showing how textual and narrative approaches to television can be used in practice.

## Television and Genre

This chapter focuses on the significance of **genre** in television, showing how genres are relatively stable, but also how genres mix and change over time. It addresses the distinctions made by academics and broadcasting companies between, for example, fact and fiction, drama and documentary, series and serial. The chapter explains theories of genre, and tests them in relation to a range of programmes, some of which have mixed or uncertain genre. The effects of the **flow** of television viewing for audiences, and channel hopping, are introduced since understandings of genre depend not only on how programmes themselves work but on how they are watched. The chapter ends with a case study in which programmes on an apparently similar topic, but in different genres and television forms, are compared and contrasted. The related but different examples of the television police series and the true crime **actuality** programme are used to discuss this question.

## Television Production

This chapter discusses the production practices and technologies which are used in bringing programmes to the screen, including the **pitching**, production planning, production scheduling, shooting and post-production of programmes. It gives an account of the professional culture of television production in different kinds of broadcasting environment and in different **genres** and forms of programme. The chapter aims to provide a critical understanding of the television industry as a profession. This includes such issues as the **conventions** of lighting, camerawork and editing, and the significance of sound, music and graphics. Attention is paid to developments in technology, such as non-linear editing, and the different kinds of equipment used in programme-making. The chapter discusses the institutional organisation and technology of television, and encourages readers to gain an understanding of the production process. The chapter includes a case study of the Avid editing system, noting how the design and operation of the system carries assumptions about the role of the programme-maker, and discussing the opportunities and constraints which the system allows or imposes.

## Postmodern Television

**Postmodernism** has been an important concept in Television Studies in recent years, and the several meanings of the term are discussed and explained in this chapter. Postmodernism can refer to the interrelationships between one programme or television form and others, and the **pastiche** or imitation of existing television forms. Theories of postmodernism also deal with how the television of the present represents a break with the past, or, on the other hand, an irreverent return to past forms. In some of the work in postmodernist theory, the present is regarded as a distinctive new phase in human culture, and this related meaning of the term is also explained in the chapter. As a relatively new mass medium, addressed to a broad popular audience, television has been regarded by some theorists as a postmodern medium because it focuses so much on the present. The chapter explores the politics of postmodernism and what is at stake in using this approach as a way of describing the media **cultures** of developed societies. The global and local characteristics of contemporary television are also part of describing television as postmodern, and the chapter ends with a case study of MTV, which has been claimed as postmodern both in its style and form, and in its global organisation.

## Television Realities

This chapter focuses on the ways in which questions of **realism** can be addressed in Television Studies. This includes looking at what realism might mean in different programme genres, and the conventions used in various kinds of **documentary** and factual programmes. Television has a strong tradition of showing its viewers images of reality, using live footage and **actuality** in such diverse forms as news, documentary, **docusoap** and public access television. The chapter debates the different understandings of reality and realism in television, and how kinds of realism are achieved. As well as dealing with television forms which are centred on representations of reality, the chapter considers the realist conventions in fictional programmes, and the crossovers between documentary modes and other television forms (such as docusoap and '**reality TV**'). The chapter contains a case study of the use of actuality footage in news coverage, and the conventions for representing immediate live events.

## Television Representation

This chapter looks at how television criticism has dealt with the representation of certain groups in society. In particular it discusses the significance of representations of people belonging to different races, and the issue of **gender** representation on television. The chapter outlines the different methods adopted in Television Studies for approaching these issues, including content analysis, identifying stereotypes and debates over bias and objectivity. Television broadcasting is closely connected to the worlds of public affairs and democratic debate, where creating fair and accurate representations of different kinds of people has been a matter of concern for a long time. In this context television has participated in setting up and also changing the cultural norms that underlie how members of society think about themselves and about people who seem different to them. The portrayal of particular groups is discussed in the chapter, with attention to differences across television forms and genres. The chapter concludes with a case study of the representation of women in the popular factual series *Wife Swap*, and some of the critical arguments advanced about this programme.

## Television You Can't See

This chapter is about **censorship** and **regulation**, with particular attention paid to broadcasters' assumptions about the audience and what viewers should not see or would like not to see on television. This includes an account of the main principles of broadcasting regulation in Britain, with brief references to other television cultures. The chapter discusses the assumptions about the protection of vulnerable groups (such as children) which are embedded in broadcasting regulations, and the attitudes to such issues as nudity and homosexuality which are addressed in television regulations. A significant aspect of the issue of what can and cannot be shown is the way in which television institutions and programme-makers censor themselves, and why and how they do this. The chapter also explains the regulation of programme content at moments of political and military tension, and the effect of a perception by broadcasters of public concern. The chapter ends with a case study of the British television coverage of the war in Iraq (still current as this edition was completed in 2007), focusing on the problems posed by the attempts in television news to cover this conflict 'fairly' and within the constraints of regulation and censorship.

## Shaping Audiences

This chapter analyses the methods of understanding audiences, and of seeking to control their television viewing behaviour, which are used by television institutions. The methods used by British and US broadcasters to gather information about television viewers are explained in the context of a discussion of the underlying assumptions about viewers and the television medium which accompany them. The chapter introduces the different industry and academic approaches to audiences, and their implications. The identification of **niche audiences** in today's multichannel environment and the ever-increasing drive for reliable information in order to predict audience behaviour have led to a greater interest by broadcasters in fragmented, specific viewing groups and viewing practices. This mirrors the emphasis in academic audience research on highly specific studies of audience behaviour and people's responses to television. The discussion of understandings of audience is placed in the context of how broadcasters try to attract and hold audiences, especially through the ways they **schedule** programmes. The chapter concludes with a case study of television scheduling which develops these issues in more specific detail.

## Television in Everyday Life

This chapter discusses the different kinds of academic audience research, referring to important studies conducted in the 1980s and 1990s, and debating their critical significance. Much of this work is concerned with highly individual responses to popular programmes. This kind of work represents a significant shift from thinking of the audience as something shaped by the ways a programme addresses its viewers, and has been very important in changing the ways television is studied. But working with small samples of viewers and focusing on popular television (such as **soap**

**opera**) raise questions about how to apply the conclusions of this recent audience research to other television **genres**. The chapter addresses issues connected with the activity or 'agency' of viewers, the role of academic television audience researchers and the ways that audiences make and **resist** the meanings of television programmes. The relationship of television to other aspects of media interaction and everyday life is also discussed. The chapter ends with a case study of academic work on soap opera, discussing the shifts in methodology and critical stance which have been adopted in this field, and explaining the changing relationships between **feminist** Television Studies and conceptions of the viewer.

## Further reading

Allen, R. (ed.), *Channels of Discourse, Reassembled: Television and Contemporary Criticism* (London: Routledge, 1992).

Brunsdon, C., 'What is the television of television studies?', in C. Geraghty and D. Lusted (eds), *The Television Studies Book* (London: Arnold, 1998), pp. 95–113.

Burton, G., *Talking Television: An Introduction to the Study of Television* (London: Arnold, 2000).

Corner, J., *Critical Ideas in Television Studies* (Oxford: Clarendon, 1999).

Fiske, J., *Television Culture* (London: Routledge, 1992).

Geraghty, C. and D. Lusted (eds), *The Television Studies Book* (London: Arnold, 1998).

Goodwin, A. and G. Whannel (eds), *Understanding Television* (London: Routledge, 1990).

McQueen, D., *Television: A Media Student's Guide* (London: Arnold, 1998).

Mullan, B., *Consuming Television* (Oxford: Blackwell, 1997).

Newcomb, H., 'The development of television studies', in J. Wasko (ed.), *A Companion to Television* (Malden, Mass., and Oxford: Blackwell, 2005), pp. 15–28.

Selby, K. and R. Cowdery, *How to Study Television* (Basingstoke: Macmillan, 1995).

Wasko, J., 'Introduction', in J. Wasko (ed.), *A Companion to Television* (Malden, Mass., and Oxford: Blackwell, 2005), pp. 1–8.

# Studying Television

# Studying Television

## Introduction

This chapter briefly maps out the topics of study and introduces some of the critical approaches which can be found in academic Television Studies today, with emphasis on the approaches used in Britain and the United States. By doing this, the chapter aims to provide an overview of the kinds of question which students of television should carry with them as they use this book. Each of the chapters in the remainder of this book focuses on a particular aspect of the study of television, picking up the concerns and ways of thinking about television which are introduced here. The discipline of Television Studies is a relatively new academic subject, and in its short history the questions which have been asked about television, and the answers which researchers have discovered, have changed in interesting ways. Television Studies, like all academic subjects, is in a continual process of development. This is partly because researchers discover new information and respond to changes in what is happening in television in the present. Television Studies also changes because, as ways of thinking about television are discussed and their strengths and weaknesses discovered, new questions and problems in understanding television are found. One of the aims of this book is to involve readers in the debates and disagreements about television which animate Television Studies.

## Broadcast television

broadcasting
the transmission of
signals from a central
source which can be
received by
dispersed receivers
over a large
geographical area.

Television Studies focuses on **broadcast** television. Both television and radio are broadcast by sending out signals either over the air (which are received by aerials or receiving dishes) or along cables embedded in the ground. Many different signals may be available to be received at any one time, like the signals which carry the programmes of several different television channels. But all the television receivers tuned into a signal will receive the same programme at the same time. The emphasis on broadcasting means that some of the material which we might see on a television screen is not part of the topic of Television Studies because it is not broadcast. Non-broadcast television includes surveillance video made by retailers and police, for example. This material is not designed for broadcast, though it is sometimes included in broadcast programmes. For instance, *Crimewatch* might broadcast extracts from surveillance video in order to show a crime being committed and to identify the perpetrator so that television viewers can provide information to help catch the offender. Other non-broadcast material made by members of the public also looks like television, for example wedding videos and video of family holidays. These programmes are often watched on television screens (by plugging the camera into a television set, or by buying the wedding photographer's edited version of the wedding and watching it on television) but they are rarely discussed in Television Studies because they are not broadcast. But some television programmes use extracts from these domestic video programmes for comic purposes (in *America's Funniest Home Videos*, for example). Interestingly, both surveillance video and domestic video which are broadcast in television programmes change their meaning once they are put in a broadcast context. What was private becomes public when it is broadcast. The fascination of '**reality TV**' programmes such as *Big Brother* derives partly from this contrast between the usually private and intrusive material caught by surveillance or amateur cameras and the very public broadcasting of the material on television.

reality TV programmes where the unscripted behaviour of 'ordinary people' is the focus of interest.

---

### ACTIVITY 1.1

What is it about television that might make it seem unworthy of serious study? How would you respond to such criticisms?

---

Specialised kinds of non-broadcast television are also made for screening in particular venues, but again they are rarely discussed in Television Studies because of the subject's concentration on material which is transmitted from a central source to a large and unspecified audience. Since the 1960s visual artists have incorporated live or recorded video into artworks, to be seen in a gallery space, but the different

Figure 1.1  Metropolitan Police CCTV still of an attack on Wayne Miller, who was sleeping rough in a doorway in Leake Street, London, 29 October 2004. © EMPICS/ Metropolitan Police

art video the use of video technology in artistic work intended for gallery exhibition.

avant-garde work aiming to challenge the norms and conventions of its medium, and the group of people making such work.

documentary a form aiming to record actual events, often with an explanatory purpose or to analyse and debate an issue.

schedule the arrangement of programmes, advertisements and other material into a sequential order within a certain period of time, such as an evening, day or week

connotations the term used in semiotic analysis for the meanings that are associated with a particular sign or combination of signs.

location of viewing, and the different ways of watching (standing up rather than sitting down, in a gallery rather than in the home), make **art video** different from television. Occasionally these art videos might be screened in a late-night compilation of **avant-garde** works, or as part of a television **documentary**, but like wedding videos these films change their meaning once they are transmitted to a different kind of audience as part of the day's broadcast television **schedule**. At some large public events, such as football matches or rock concerts, live video is shown on big screens, but this is not television because of the specialised venue and non-broadcast transmission of the pictures. But one of the conventions of pop videos, such as those shown on the MTV or VH1 broadcast television channels, is to recreate the kinds of images which are projected at concerts, by using mist and lighting effects, and footage of the band apparently playing their instruments on a stage. Broadcast television borrows the conventions of non-broadcast video in order to communicate the excitement of being at a live performance.

Studying television nearly always involves studying broadcast television. There are some kinds of material which is live or recorded, seen on screens, captured by television cameras, and shown to an audience, which is not television as Television Studies has come to define it. So Television Studies gets a grip on the things which it studies partly by excluding some kinds of audio-visual material. But even though these other kinds of material, called video or non-broadcast television, do not fall into the category of television as it is used in this book and in Television Studies, they are sometimes broadcast. Some of the distinguishing features of music television (MTV) or 'reality TV', for example, come from the ways in which they draw on non-broadcast television or video and make use of the **connotations** which they carry, such as

- privacy
- performance, or
- evidence.

The greatest challenge to Television Studies' theoretical approaches to studying television is about to be the distribution of programmes to different kinds of screen and to locations other than the home. As this book was being completed in early 2007 some indications of this changed future for television were emerging. The computer company Apple launched an iPod in the USA with the capability to down-load episodes of some popular programmes, such as *Lost* and *Desperate Housewives*, for the payment of a small fee. This arrangement is like downloading music from the company's iTunes website, so potential users will already be familiar with the principle and more likely to adopt it. But the small screens on these portable devices may not offer enough picture definition and clarity to make downloadable television attractive to watch, and an existing service that enables users to download short extracts from programmes onto mobile phones has not proved very successful. On the other hand, the BBC, Channel 4 and the American conglomerate AOL–Time Warner, for example, are beginning to offer television programmes that can be downloaded onto a home computer. Although this way of watching television has yet to become widespread, the assumptions that television is watched on a television set rather than a computer, and that programmes are broadcast at a set time in a schedule, may be about to be overturned.

## 'Our' television?

Almost all the examples of television which are discussed in this book were made and broadcast in the English-speaking world, and most of the books which are used in courses in Television Studies in Britain refer to British and American television. One of the reasons for this is that English-language television programmes are exported around the world to many other countries whose national language is not English, where they are shown either with **subtitled** dialogue or with a **dubbed** soundtrack in another language, spoken by actors from the country in which the programme is broadcast. This issue is discussed further in Chapter 3, where television around the world is considered. Television advertisements are also sometimes shown in several different countries, with the same visual images but with a soundtrack made in another language. People in Britain are notoriously resistant to watching television programmes in languages other than English, and are unwilling to read subtitles translating foreign-language dialogue. But this is relatively unusual:

- In Poland imported foreign-language programmes have the dialogue of all the speakers (whether young or old, male or female) read in Polish by a single actor.
- In France British and American programmes are usually shown with dubbed dialogue in French.
- In the Netherlands British and American programmes are shown with Dutch subtitles.

The experience of watching television in Britain is relatively unusual, in that almost all programmes on the terrestrial channels – BBC1, BBC2, ITV1, Channel 4 and Five – are in English, originating in Britain, America or Australia, the latter two being countries with which Britain has had a historical 'special relationship'. The situation is different in other countries, where imported television from Britain or America is immediately marked as different because of its dubbed or subtitled dialogue. In countries where there are several commonly spoken languages television is broadcast in each of these languages.

- In Singapore there are television channels in English, Chinese and Malay.
- In the United States there are channels in English and Spanish.

The sense of what 'our' television might be is different in these countries, and the experience of familiarity would be different to the experience in Britain. Television has aimed to represent a relatively unified **culture** in Britain, though its division into the nations of England and Scotland, together with the principality of Wales and the province of Northern Ireland, means that television also has a regional character. The further, related division of terrestrial television broadcasting into regional areas (the south-west of England, the Midlands and East Anglia, for example) which offer some distinctive programmes to their local audiences makes this situation more marked. The issue of belonging to a region, nation or country complicates the assumption that British television can be referred to as a national television culture. Furthermore, since Britain is a multicultural society, there are channels aimed at people from an overseas background and in languages other than English, such as channels in Chinese and the languages of the Indian subcontinent. The proliferation

**subtitle**  written text appearing on the television screen, normally to translate speech in a foreign language.

**dubbing**  replacing the original speech in a programme, advertisement, etc. with speech added later, often to translate speech in a foreign language.

**culture**  the shared attitudes, ways of life and assumptions of a group of people.

of channels in recent years has permitted the development of new television services aimed at British people from specific ethnic backgrounds. Zee TV began broadcasting in 1995 and targets its programmes at British Asian viewers, as does the B4Utv channel, which screens Bollywood films from the Indian subcontinent, and several other channels that specialise in Asian celebrity features and sports reports. Greek Cypriots in Britain are the target audience for Hellenic TV, and households equipped with cable television or a satellite dish are able to receive programmes from broadcasters transmitting from Cyprus and Greece. The Phoenix Chinese Channel was launched in 1999 and shows programmes for Chinese communities around the world on five different channels which are themed around different kinds of content, such as entertainment, news and films. The unity and diversity of contemporary television matches the forces of unification and diversification that are at work in 'our' society, and raise questions about who 'we' might be.

## Studying programmes

An important component of many courses in Television Studies is the study of particular television programmes. Particular programmes might be chosen for study in each week of a course, and there are several reasons for this. Television Studies emerged in the 1970s and 1980s out of three ways of writing about television:

● the reviewing of programmes in newspapers and magazines (see Caughie 1984)
● the criticism of programmes as works of art (like literature texts)
● and the **sociology** of culture (see Brunsdon 1998b).

**sociology** the academic study of society, aiming to describe and explain aspects of life in that society.

Journalists' reviews and literary criticism focus on television programmes as **texts**, where the method of discussing them is to study closely their structure, characters and themes, in a similar way to the study of literature and drama. The advantage for the students and teachers who adopt this way of studying television is that there is an example accessible to the class, who can watch and rewatch the programme, and focus on selected moments in it. By closely analysing a programme it can be discovered how the programme is structured and how it creates its meanings by using images and sound in certain ways; critical arguments about the programme can be tested and proved by referring back to a concrete example.

**text** an object such as a television programme, film or poem, considered as a network of meaningful signs that can be analysed and interpreted.

Studying television by analysing programmes is useful for setting up categories and making distinctions between programmes. Making distinctions is good way of discovering the rules and **conventions** which the makers of programmes use, and which television viewers learn to recognise, in order to make meaning in the television medium. Even in the 1970s Television Studies books addressing television programmes as texts recognised the significance of the mixed formal and informal **registers** in programmes, and the connections these might have to television's address to its audience and television's relationship with social values. For John Fiske and John Hartley, writing in 1978, the discourse of television was made up of a mixture of what they called 'literate' and 'oral' codes. By this they meant that television programmes have 'literate' components shared with written texts and relatively high-status forms of written communication, since they are 'narrative, sequential, abstract, univocal, "consistent"'. Yet, in addition, television texts have

**conventions** the frameworks and procedures used to make or interpret texts.

**register** a term in the study of language for the kinds of speech or writing used to represent a particular kind of idea or to address a certain audience.

features which are more similar to the informal communication of spoken language, in anecdotes, folk tales or popular songs, in that they are also 'dramatic, episodic, concrete, social, dialectical' (Fiske and Hartley 1978: 125). The literate codes of television underlie the novelistic narrative structures and linear explanatory forms of programmes, and can be regarded as reflecting the unifying and official language of social power, which imposes an ordered view of the world and a system of values and regulations on society.

On the other hand, Fiske and Hartley saw the 'oral' features of television as deriving from the organic culture of people's own communities and everyday lives, and in some ways as a representation of people's vigorous **popular culture**. In the context of Television Studies' critique of the forces of social control, and its valuation of ordinary people and their world-views, the oral mode of television was regarded as a vital and **progressive** element in the dynamic mixture of the literate and oral modes in television. Television's oral mode seemed to possess radical potential as the vision of a lost social communication, a free speech by the mass audience which restores a lost unity to ordinary people. So, although this analysis rests on the interpretation of television texts, it gestures towards Television Studies' increasing desire to validate the ordinary viewer, popular culture and the contribution of television audiences to the meanings apparently fixed immutably in television programmes. But there are also several drawbacks to this approach, which mean that the study of programmes as texts misses what seem to be important aspects of television. In broadcasting, television also includes trailers, advertisements and channel **idents**. It can often happen that several minutes in each hour of broadcasting are taken up by these kinds of television, but they are not programmes and are not often studied. Nevertheless, it could be argued that trailers for forthcoming programmes have important functions:

- They inform the audience about what will be available to watch in the future.
- They shape the viewer's expectations about what a future programme will be like.
- They offer suggestions why it might be interesting and enjoyable.

Since television advertisements are the means of gaining income for many television broadcasters, who charge fees to advertisers to screen them, it could be argued that they are more significant to what television is than the programmes which they interrupt. Television advertisements cost much more per minute of screen-time to make than programmes, and they are often innovative, memorable and amusing. The density and speed of information and meaning in television commercials make them rewarding objects of study, and show the conventions by which images and sounds can be put together in the television medium. Since our society is one where desiring, buying and owning products are important to our sense of identity and our place in society, it is also illuminating to see how products are brought to our attention in television advertisements, so studying them may also tell us much about how our society works. Channel idents are also moments of television which are frequently repeated and familiar, giving a **brand** identity to television broadcasters, like advertisements for the broadcaster, and they too are worthy of study. So it is not only programmes which can be analysed in Television Studies, though programmes have been the core of syllabuses in the subject for many years.

**popular culture** the texts created by ordinary people (as opposed to an elite group) or created for them, and the ways these are used.

**progressive** encouraging positive change or progress, usually implying progress towards fairer and more equal ways of organising society.

**idents** the symbols representing production companies, television channels, etc., often comprising graphics or animations.

**brand recognition** the ability of audiences to recognise the distinctive identity of a product, service or institution and the values and meanings associated with it.

Studying programmes closely as single texts also has the disadvantage of separating a programme from its place in the schedule of the day in which it was broadcast. Although there are some television programmes which viewers might select and view with special attention ('must see' programmes), this kind of viewing is relatively unusual. Television is most often watched as a sequence of programmes, ads, trailers, etc., and of course viewers also switch channels, sometimes part-way through a programme, and their level of attention may vary considerably from moment to moment and programme to programme. Indeed, within programmes, high-points or turning-points are included by programme-makers where breaks for advertisements are to be included. This is done to encourage viewers to stay on the same channel to find out what the consequences or developments will be once the programme returns after the break. The two consequences of studying programmes as individual units relate to the important Television Studies concept of **'flow'** (Williams 1974). Selecting individual programmes for study means extracting them from the flow of material of which they are a part, and which might have important effects on their meaning. For example, a news programme including items about rising petrol prices might be followed by a commercial break including ads for new cars, and then the programme *Fifth Gear*, where new cars are reviewed and motoring issues are discussed. While each programme or ad might be interesting to analyse in itself, more meanings relating to speed, pollution, road safety or **masculine** bravado might arise because of the connections between the programmes and ads in this television flow.

Part of the textual study of television is an interest in **authorship**, in who the authors of television programmes are and what the intended meanings of their work might be. There is a historical context for this approach, which arose in the 1960s when the expansion of the television industry allowed opportunities for younger, working-class, university-educated men and women to enter the industry. Rejecting the seemingly staid and conservative values of their predecessors, and picking up on the interest in working people and ordinary lives which were being explored in the film and theatre of the time, these people aimed for a **'committed'** form of television. 'Committed' meant committed to an agenda of social change, where television programmes might be a force to change society in a more equal and tolerant direction. Thus, the textual analysis of television programmes still carries a legacy of identifying which programmes might be 'progressive' and socially challenging, versus identifying programmes which perpetuate formerly dominant social conventions and support the **status quo**. British television drama has been especially important to Television Studies' discussion of committed and progressive television, because the legacy of cultural value which theatre and literature have has been attached to authored dramatic works on television.

In Britain television was established in the 1930s by the same broadcaster, the BBC, which operated all the radio broadcasting. Both radio and television have been required by their legal constitutions to fulfil a **public service** role. Public service television aims to:

- provide programmes which are educative or improving
- offer a range of different kinds of programme at different levels of accessibility
- engage audiences in the significant events and issues occurring in the present.

**flow** the ways in which programmes, advertisements, etc. follow one another in an unbroken sequence across the day or part of the day, and the experience of watching the sequence of programmes, advertisements, trailers, etc.

**masculine** having characteristics associated with the cultural role of men, not women.

**authorship** the question of who an author is, the role of the author as creator and the significance of the author's input into the material being studied.

**committed** a term used in the study of the politics of culture, implying that a person or a text has a commitment to positive and progressive social change.

**status quo** the ways in which culture and society are currently organised.

**public service** in television, the provision of a mix of programmes that inform, educate and entertain in ways that encourage the betterment of audiences and society in general.

Since literature and drama are also considered to be educative and improving, it is authored dramatic television work which has often featured as the ground for debates about the quality of television in Britain and whether the public service commitment is being fulfilled. Graham Murdoch (1980: 25) wrote, in an early theoretical essay on this subject, 'The promotion of authorship and creativity lies at the heart of the broadcasters' presentation of themselves as guarantors of cultural diversity and patrons of the contemporary arts, elements which are central to their claims to responsibility and public service.' Television drama has been regarded as the most culturally prestigious part of broadcast output, and it is expensive, and often prominently scheduled, trailed and advertised. Its high profile has made it the subject of hype and controversy, orchestrated by the broadcasters themselves, the press or concerned groups (such as MediaWatch) which represent viewers' interests.

Authored drama has also been one of the main forms of television exported to other countries (for example, to the *Masterpiece Theatre* slot on US **public television**). There were and still are debates about public service television, seen either as:

- an old-fashioned and monolithic system which prevents change, or as
- a space in which television that challenges commercial values and aspires to artistic **quality** might find an audience.

In this context, the analysis of television programmes provides the grounds for valuing one programme over another, as more or less conducive of social change, or more or less worthy of consideration as a creative statement. A further reason for this focus on authored television drama and its connection to Literary and Drama Studies is that in the early years of television broadcasting in Britain – just before and after the Second World War – many TV plays were adaptations of theatre plays or extracts from them, sometimes using the same cast as productions being staged in London's West End. But a drawback of this concern for television drama as if it were literature or written drama is a neglect of the importance of performers and performances in television. Although Film Studies has for many years had a critical interest in stardom and stars, Television Studies has not often remembered the significance of how actors and television **personalities** affect the meanings which television programmes may have (Caughie 2000).

The fact that a television play or **serial** can be considered as a self-contained text, written by an author, made this television form especially significant for researchers studying television from this perspective. Although there were some early studies of television (Williams 1968; Newcomb 1974) which discussed popular programmes such as **soap opera**, writing about television focused on the high-profile programmes regarded as 'quality television'. But Television Studies has in the last decade or so moved away from the close study of fictional programmes (although this is still an important part of the subject) and considered other topics. Part of the reason for this is that Television Studies has established itself by breaking away from the study of literature and drama, so that the methods of textual criticism increasingly appear to be drawn from subjects outside of Television Studies itself. Rather than studying high-profile television fiction by authors whose names become nationally known (such as Lynda La Plante and Andrew Davies), Television Studies academics have discussed programmes which fall solidly into **genres** (such as soap opera and

**public television** television funded by government or by private supporters, rather than solely by advertising.

**quality** in television, kinds of programme that are perceived as more expensively produced and, especially, more culturally worthwhile than other programmes.

**personalities** people appearing on television who are recognised by audiences as celebrities with a media image and public status beyond the role they play in a particular programme.

**serial** a television form where a developing narrative unfolds across a sequence of separate episodes.

**soap opera** a continuing drama serial involving a large number of characters in a specific location, focusing on relationships, emotions and reversals of fortune.

**genre** a type of programme. Programmes of the same genre have shared characteristics.

police fiction) and whose authors work in teams or groups and are little known outside the television industry. These are also the programmes which attract the largest audiences, and can be described as 'popular' rather than 'elite' culture.

---

### ACTIVITY 1.2

Look at the articles in current listings magazines. Are any of the articles about the authors of television programmes? If so, what kinds of programmes are these? If not, which personalities are associated with the programmes, and why?

---

## Television and society

Unlike cinema, television has always placed emphasis on the witnessing of events in the real world. When television began, all of its programmes were live, because the technology to record television signals had not been invented. The thrill of watching television in its early days, and still occasionally now, is to see and hear representations of events, people and places distant from the viewer. Indeed, the word 'television' literally means 'seeing from afar'. On one hand, television gives viewers access to the world with immediacy and credibility, because television technology appears to transcribe or reproduce faithfully what is seen and heard. The ability of television to disseminate information widely, beyond the local and personal experience of its viewers, can be argued to broaden the experience and awareness of the television audience. The political effects of this might be for television to assist national institutions in involving citizens in social and political debate, so that television enhances public debate and participation in democratic decision-making. Television broadcasting might therefore contribute to the '**public sphere**': to discussion and thought about issues which concern the direction of society as a whole, and have bearing on the lives of most people. On the other hand, television can present only selected images and sounds, chosen by someone else, and present them according to the conventions of storytelling and reporting which are established by television institutions and legal regulations. In a sense, television takes over the job of relating the viewer to the world around them, and separates the viewer from their experience of reality. The political consequences of television from this point of view are negative. If television experiences the world on its audience's behalf, and substitutes mediated and partial versions of information and understanding for the authentic experience of people, then its effect is to dissuade people from involvement in discussion and debate. The television viewer might be disempowered and alone, with discussion and participation simulated by television rather than enabled by it. Watching the political question-and-answer programme *Question Time* or the commentaries by experts in current affairs programmes might allow viewers to feel involved in debates when they are not. From this point of view, television viewing reproduces the apparent passivity of consumers and spectators, turning its audience into '**couch potatoes**', and encourages it to continue.

Social science research in Television Studies considers how television has a role in reproducing the patterns of values and the divisions between groups and **classes**

**public sphere**
the world of politics, economic affairs and national and international events, as opposed to the 'private sphere' of domestic life.

**couch potatoes**
a derogatory term for television viewers supposedly sitting motionless at home watching television passively and indiscriminately.

**class** a section of society defined by their relationship to economic activity, whether as workers (the working class) or possessors of economic power (the bourgoisie), for example.

Figure 1.2  A forensic officer walks next to the wreckage of a double decker bus at Tavistock Square in central London on Thursday, 7 July 2005. Photo by Sang Tan. © EMPICS

of people in society; in other words, how television represents and affects the social order. Part of this research concerns how television adopts the 'public speech' of institutions such as:

● Parliament
● academia
● the judicial system.

Social science is concerned with how this contrasts with adoptions of 'private speech' such as:

● gossip
● everyday talk
● the language of subcultural groups, such as football fans and youth subcultures.

By investigating these aspects of television, it can be seen how television gives different kinds of value and legitimacy to different facets of social life, and separates or unites people. Since television is controlled by institutions, and governed by laws, questions of the **regulation** and ownership of television are also addressed by this strand of research. Social science research considers television as a form of mass communication, in relation to sociological and political issues rather than studies of textuality or the form of programmes. Because of their interest in the relations of social groups to each other, and the place of television in communicating social values and attitudes, researchers tend to discuss popular genres such as television sports programmes, or kinds of content (especially violence and social disorder) represented in different kinds of programmes.

regulation the control of television institutions by laws, codes of practice or guidelines.

The ways in which broadcasting is organised in different nations are surprisingly varied, and it is important to study broadcasting cultures in comparison and contrast to each other. Although it might seem that American television is the dominant norm because of the worldwide export of such programmes as the drama *CSI*, about police forensic scientists, or the pre-school children's programme *Sesame Street*, the conventions, laws and assumptions about television vary in different countries because of the different evolution of television broadcasting and different conceptions of the nature and function of television. In Britain, for instance, broadcasting (first on radio) began as a monopoly business entrusted in 1922 to the British Broadcasting Company (a commercial organisation), paralleling the monopoly control over the supply of water and electricity in the Victorian period. Radio, and television when it appeared in the 1930s, was considered as if it were drinking water, on tap, which could be run by a national company as long as it was kept clean and available to everyone equally (Caughie 2000). Only later did commercial television and competition appear, and even now there is a strong body of opinion in Britain that television must be taken seriously and must fulfil its moral responsibility to an audience of citizens. In America, by contrast, television quickly developed as a form of commercial business, where the requirements of advertisers and the need for local relay stations to make profits from the programmes supplied by programme-makers have driven the development of television. To put this distinction crudely, there is a debate between two sets of assumptions about television:

- television should provide resources to answer people's needs and raise cultural standards, or
- television should give people what the majority seem to want and what makes the most profit.

Television Studies has engaged frequently in this debate, most often by taking the perhaps impossible compromise position that broadcasting should be a public service but that it should not impose the cultural standards of the few upon a majority whose 'popular' tastes should not be denigrated.

The background to this position in Television Studies is closely bound up with the changes in how broadcasters have conceived of their audiences. The BBC shifted its conception of its role from an initial aim to train its audience to understand and enjoy more 'quality' programmes, with 'worthwhile' levels of intellectual content and sophistication, requiring sustained and attentive viewing (Ang 1991). When the arrival of ITV introduced **commercial television** to Britain in 1955, the high **ratings** for the new channel forced the BBC to compete against such popular **formats** as imported American drama series and quizzes. Since the 1950s, the conception of the audience as consumers able to exercise a free choice has become increasingly dominant in British broadcasting, and this both reflects and supports the view of society which has come to be familiar and natural today. Rather than thinking of British society as if it were a pyramid with a small cultural elite at the top, with sophisticated tastes, and a broad base of ordinary viewers underneath preferring undemanding entertainment, the image of society has changed to one of overlapping and scattered sets of viewers, or **'niche audiences'**, who have changing and diverse preferences across many genres, forms and levels of complexity. Broadcasters no longer attempt to lead the nation to the top of the cultural pyramid,

**commercial television** television funded by the sale of advertising time or sponsorship of programmes.

**ratings** the number of viewers estimated to have watched certain programmes, as compared to the numbers watching other programmes.

**format** the blueprint for a programme, including its setting, main characters, genre, form and main themes.

**niche audiences** particular groups of viewers defined by age group, gender or economic status, for example, who may be the target audience for a programme.

Figure 1.3 Watching television. Photograph courtesy of Powerstock.

but instead reflect what they believe to be the demands of contemporary society. The audience is conceived as a collection of diverse and autonomous individuals whose viewing habits and interests are hard to discover and predict, and who can be as fickle as the consumers surveyed by **market research**.

The role of the academic discipline of Television Studies in political debates about the direction of television in Britain has always been rather peripheral. When the subject focused on making distinctions between progressive and conservative texts in the 1960s and 1970s, and valuing the progressive ones, the highly theoretical arguments about the form and meanings of programmes were largely inaccessible to readerships outside the lecturers and students who engaged in them. Despite the often-repeated claim that programmes could empower audiences to think in challenging and radical ways about their own lives and cultures, Television Studies had little engagement with programme-makers and policy-makers. The discipline of **Cultural Studies**, pioneered in Britain in the 1970s at the University of Birmingham, recognises the significance of popular television and studies how television contributes to the assumptions and attitudes of sectors of society, a set of ideas and emotions described as a '**structure of feeling**'. Key work in this field includes the books by Raymond Williams (1974) and John Ellis (1982), whose interest was in the flows of programmes in the television schedule, and how viewers rarely watch programmes singly but instead as part of flow of programmes and commercials over a period of hours. Viewers also switch from one programme or channel to another, composing their own 'text' of television from these segments which does not exhibit the bounded and unified qualities which derive from thinking of television as a series of whole, individual texts to be analysed singly. In the 1980s the issue of the progressiveness of particular television texts was overtaken by interests in audiences, and how real viewers gained pleasure from their viewing

**market research**
the collection of information about consumers and their preferences, used to identify products that can be sold to consumers likely to buy them.

**Cultural Studies**
the academic discipline devoted to studying culture, involving work on texts, institutions, audiences and economic contexts.

**structure of feeling**
the assumptions, attitudes and ideas prevalent in a society, arising from the ideologies underpinning that society.

(Morley 1980). This approach began to transfer to the USA in the 1980s, and is evident in the work of Lawrence Grossberg (Grossberg *et al.* 1992). While still a political debate, because there could be progressive or conservative kinds of pleasure, this phase in Television Studies refused to identify some programmes as good and some as bad, preferring to value the different kinds of pleasure which different audience groups might gain from programmes. The **commissioners** and **producers** of programmes, let alone actors, politicians or journalists, have always made distinctions between good and bad programmes, in terms of their popularity, cost as compared to profit or the social status of their majority audience.

The sophisticated arguments which led to the refusal to judge quality in Television Studies meant that academic criticism has been largely unable to engage in the debates about television which can be seen expressed in different contexts, including:

- newspapers
- parliamentary debates
- broadcasters' policy documents.

Therefore, the issues which still concern viewers and commentators, such as the effects of violence in programmes, whether there is more or less 'quality television' than there used to be and the standards of **taste and decency** in television, often remain absent from the books and articles written and read by Television Studies academics and students. So although Television Studies is crucially about the relationships between television and society, the topic can often seem to be debated in a vacuum.

> **ACTIVITY 1.3**
>
> Which kinds of television programme, on which channels, do you think are aimed at a family audience? How do you know?

## Television audiences

Because of the variety of the different kinds of programme and advertisement which television broadcasts, television as a medium appears to offer an almost unlimited range of information and entertainment. The different genres of programme, and the range of factual and fictional output on television channels, appear to offer vast choice and to address the needs and desires of different viewers. This is even more evident in recent years with the emergence of themed channels on **digital television**, which focus, for example, on:

- sport
- films
- science

---

**commissioning** the process by which an idea for a programme is selected to go into production.

**producer** the person working for a television institution who is responsible for the budget, planning and making of a television programme or series of programmes.

**taste and decency** conformity to the standards of good taste and acceptable language and behaviour represented on television, as required by regulations.

**digital television** television pictures and sound encoded into the ones and zeros of electronic data. Digital signals can also be sent back down cables by viewers, making possible interaction with television programmes.

- drama
- comedy
- shopping
- lifestyle.

Television companies are especially interested in who is watching which kinds of programme, when and why. Television broadcasters have always referred to audiences in order to back up their claims to give the public what it seems to want, to set the level of fees charged to advertisers and as an indication of which forms and genres of programme seem to 'work'. The BBC's two terrestrial channels are funded by a **licence fee** which must be paid by all owners of television sets. The ITV channel, and the newer terrestrial channels Channel 4 and Five gain their income from charges made to advertisers to screen their advertisements. The various digital channels available by satellite and cable are funded partly by **subscription** charges and partly by advertising, with the exception of the BBC's digital channels, which are free to their viewers. In each case information about audience size and composition is highly significant to broadcasters.

Broadcasters funded by commercial advertising need to attract audiences for their advertisers, and broadcasters funded by the licence fee need to justify the compulsory payment of that licence fee by attracting large audiences. The competition between channels is measured by audience size (the ratings, calculated by multiplying the audience sizes in a representative sample of viewers), and by the proportion of the total available audience watching one channel rather than another (**audience share**). The methods of audience research used in the television industry derive from the methods used to identify new markets for consumer products, to survey current users of products and to measure the sales and reactions to products of all kinds, from washing powder to brands of lager. The academic disciplines of the social sciences, such as sociology and **anthropology**, have a related interest in television audiences. But rather than finding out about audiences in order to target or maximise viewers in the interests of increasing profits for broadcasters, academic audience researchers seek to understand how television viewing fits into people's cultural life, and how pleasure, knowledge and opportunities for social interaction (but also boredom, anger and dissatisfaction) in television arise. The methods used to gain this information include:

- questionnaires
- interviews
- **focus groups**.

The strand of work in Television Studies called '**uses and gratifications**' research describes the uses and pleasures which audiences derive from television, by focusing on how and why people use television. This approach is in contrast to the study of television's **effects** on its viewers (such as making them more violent, or more informed about science, for example) in that studies of effects regard audiences as passive vessels waiting to be filled up by television messages. Uses and gratifications research shows how television is used as an information source, as entertainment and as a resource for constructing the viewer's sense of identity, often by identifying himself or herself as a member of a group. The drawback of this kind of work,

**licence fee**
an annual payment by all owners of television sets, which is the main source of income for the BBC.

**subscription**
payment to a television broadcaster in exchange for the opportunity to view programmes on certain channels that are otherwise blocked.

**audience share** the percentage of viewers estimated to have watched one channel as opposed to another channel broadcasting at the same time.

**anthropology** the study of humankind, including the evolution of humans and the different kinds of human society existing in different times and places.

**focus groups** small groups of selected people representing larger social groupings, such as people of a certain age group, gender or economic status, who take part in discussions about a topic chosen for investigation.

**uses and gratifications**
a theoretical approach that assumes people engage in an activity because it provides them with a benefit of some kind.

**effects**
measurable outcomes produced by watching television, such as becoming more violent or adopting a certain opinion.

however, is that it can neglect the specificity of the television programmes which viewers actually watch.

Academic audience researchers have been especially interested in understanding the ways television fits into the lives of people whose relatively unequal social position has led the programmes they watch to be denigrated, and their reactions to television belittled. When Television Studies researchers sought to analyse the politics of programme texts they tended to mean how programmes dealt with 'national issues' such as law and order, work and political viewpoints, associated with the predominantly male spokespersons and leaders in party politics, trade unions and business. The **feminist** movement argued that 'the personal is political', meaning that people's private concerns with family life, shopping or relationships also had political implications, and these areas of life were associated with women. So feminist Television Studies took an interest both in programmes which represented the **'private sphere'** of life, meaning the usually private goings on in the home, and in the place of television in the lives of ordinary people, especially women. In particular, feminist academics studying television audiences have directed attention to the often-despised genre of soap opera, and have explored in detail the ways in which women viewers watched television in the real circumstances of their own homes (Brunsdon *et al.* 1997). Indeed, the home is an important site of audience research in Television Studies, since television is usually watched there and it has been associated with domesticity.

feminism the political and theoretical thinking which in different ways considers the roles of women and femininity in society and culture, often with the aim of critiquing current roles and changing them for the better.

private sphere the domestic world of the home, family and personal life.

---

**ACTIVITY 1.4**

Feminist television theorists conducted important work on soap opera as a 'women's genre'. Which other television forms might be of interest to feminist television theorists, and why?

---

One of the shifts which has taken place in television culture over the twentieth and twenty-first centuries has been the massive expansion of television ownership. Just a small proportion of homes in a few areas of the country had television in the 1930–50 period, but presently households may own several televisions, as well as personal computers which can receive broadcast television. From being a collective experience shared with family, friends and neighbours, watching television may take place simultaneously in different rooms in the same household, individually by members of the same family. How people of different age groups, genders and daily routines use television in the home is a subject of interest to audience researchers seeking to discover how television integrates into the fabric of present-day life. The underlying impulse behind these studies of the television audience derives from two related concerns. One is the left-wing political view that the interests and enthusiasms of ordinary people in society have been neglected by a tradition of focusing in academic studies on the high-brow cultural products which seem closest to the elite forms of art. The consequence of this view is that programmes sometimes regarded as low brow, trashy and 'mere entertainment' suddenly become the ones which are worthy of study. The second related view is that a great weight of condemnation has been levelled against popular entertainment television by journalistic criticism, professionals within the television industry and earlier generations of academics. Television Studies academics have regarded themselves as rescuing this popular television from its low status and relative invisibility, arguing that what is popular is not necessarily unimportant, simply commercial product or lacking in artistic complexity. It had been argued that popular television distracted its audience of 'couch potatoes', offering them 'chewing gum for the eyes'. But by showing an interest in audiences and the programmes which most ordinary viewers watch Television Studies attempted to understand the processes of how television engages its audiences in ways which the audience finds satisfying and valuable, rather than simply dismissing ordinary viewers' apparently shallow enthusiasms. With the pendulum of critical interest shifting in the direction of audience studies, popular programmes and relatively inattentive viewing, however, Television Studies unfortunately lost sight of the programmes which are watched with concentration and intensity (such as 'quality drama') until quite recently.

A particular strand of audience research which places special emphasis on what viewers have to say about their relationships with television is the approach called television **ethnography**. Ethnographic studies draw on the methods of the discipline of anthropology, in gathering information through close and often lengthy interactions with small samples of viewers (Lull 1988b). Whereas both mass communications research in Television Studies and the television industry have thought of audiences as homogeneous masses whose reactions and interests are broadly the same, and have investigated them by quantitative methods such as counting audience sizes, ethnographic audience research focuses on smaller-scale groupings, selected by a factor such as locality, gender, age group or social class. The problem which ethnography faces is the challenge of selecting some information relevant to the research question while leaving out most of the responses that viewers give to the researcher's questions, and rearranging or 'translating' research information into a wider context which illuminates how television works as a medium (Geraghty 1998). The political project of granting legitimacy to ordinary viewers, their interests and pleasures, as well as involving them directly in Television Studies research as respondents to ethnographic researchers' questions, leads to the claim that audiences are active makers of meaning and negotiators with the television they watch. This celebration of the active audience is most associated with the work of John Fiske (1992c, 1994) and with a body of research on television **fan culture**. Television fans (such as *Star Trek* fans or *Doctor Who* fans) use programmes as the central resource for activities including:

**ethnography**
the detailed study of how people live, conducted by observing behaviour and talking to selected individuals about their attitudes and activities.

**fan culture** the activities of groups of fans, as distinct from 'ordinary' viewers.

- constructing social networks
- setting up social and commercial events (such as conventions)
- creating new texts (such as songs, fanzines or amateur written fiction).

So studies of fan audiences such as the essays in Lisa Lewis's collection (1991) show how some television viewers take hold of television and transform it into their own cultural text, and it is argued that all television viewers, though to a lesser extent than fans, make their own meanings and social relationships out of television. Fans and audiences in general appear to resist swallowing whole the meanings which television programmes may have, and instead they take and reshape the aspects of

**resistance** the ways in which audiences make meaning from television programmes that are counter to the meanings that are thought to be intended, or that are discovered by close analysis.

**active audience** television audiences regarded not as passive consumers of meanings but as negotiating meanings for themselves that are often resistant to those meanings that are intended or that are discovered by close analysis.

programmes which make sense and offer opportunities to them. However, in the context of Television Studies' continuing interest in the politics of watching television, there is little evidence that these **resistant** and **active audience** practices relate to broader questions of politics in society, around campaigns for a better deal for women or working-class people, for instance (Morris 1988). Nevertheless, the dramatic turn of Television Studies towards the audience can be seen, as David Morley (1992) has argued, as a necessary counter to the hitherto dominant tradition of textual interpretative research.

## ACTIVITY 1.5

In what ways do particular television forms lend themselves to some approaches in Television Studies more than others: for example, television news to sociological study? What kinds of television have not appeared in your list of television forms and approaches to them?

## ACTIVITY 1.6

List methods of study which Television Studies might involve. How many of these might appear in studies of another medium? Why is this?

## ACTIVITY 1.7

What problems might be associated with ethnographic study of television audience groups different from those to which you belong – children, for example? How might you deal with these problems?

## Case study:   television past and present

Early predictions in the 1930s of what television would be emphasised its liveness, and its consequent ability to present images of what was happening in the real world to a mass audience. There was little sense that the new medium would compete with cinema as an entertainment medium, because of:

● the small size of early television screens
● their poor definition of pictures and sound, and
● the location of the television set in the home.

It seemed that the role of television would be to bring information to its audience, and to relay images and sounds of events actually happening in distant places. These early thoughts conditioned the makers of television to think of the medium in terms of **realism**, since television would reflect society to itself in the present. Television would focus on the contemporary, and as a new technology, having a television was associated with being modern and engaged in the growing technological sophistication of Britain's industrial society. At the same time there were concerns about television's intrusiveness, because of the uneasiness or even shock which viewers might feel when the box in the corner had access to their private domestic space.

The emphasis on liveness, on seeing things as they happen, made drama and performance important to the first television schedules (Caughie 2000). Plays performed live were fixed points in the BBC's evening television schedules and were very popular, as was a television version of the variety show, where singers, comedians, magicians and other performers from the theatre, music-hall and radio shows of the time did their acts. There were some British films on television, but very few Hollywood films because the Hollywood studios would not allow television broadcasters to screen them, for fear of competition with the cinema as a dominant medium for entertainment. Plays were performed live in the television studio, and could also be relayed live from a London theatre. So the function of television seemed to be to relay the live occasion of a performance (including one made for television) rather than to find programme forms which were different from what audiences might experience in other media, such as radio, music hall or theatre. British television began broadcasting in 1936 to tiny audiences, but even by 1950 the television audience for the single broadcast channel in Britain, the BBC, was only about 300,000. Television was available only in London and the Midlands, and viewers paid a two-pound licence fee covering both television and radio sets. Programmes were broadcast each weekday morning and every afternoon, but stopped in the early evening so that children could be put to bed. They then began again at 8.00 p.m. (after the closedown period known as 'the toddler's truce' was over) and there was no set closedown time, since **outside broadcasts** of sporting events, for instance, could extend the day's viewing hours. On a typical day in 1950, nine hours of television were broadcast in total.

There was a widespread anxiety that watching television might disrupt family routines and waste people's time, especially if it was too entertaining. Writing in the *BBC Year Book 1951* (an annual collection of reports and essays about the doings of the BBC over the year), Ivor Brown (1951: 17) responded to this concern by arguing that 'People who view do not stop going to the play or the films or the cricket-match. Television, at two pounds a year for a whole household and friends, does not, after the initial purchase, seriously affect the family's allotment of cash to fun and games.' Brown was somewhat on the defensive, protecting television from the accusation that people had to make a choice between staying in to watch their expensive new television sets or going out and doing something more healthy instead. It is important to notice too that Brown considers the television audience to be 'household and friends', a collective audience rather than a lone viewer in front of the screen. For most people the experience of watching television was collective, and they gathered in friends' and neighbours' houses to watch television as an event in itself. So, rather than being a distraction from other ways of spending time, or a means of filling dead time, the television set could be a magnet around which social interaction could take place.

In the years following the end of the Second World War in 1945 a relatively prosperous middle class was living in the expanding suburbs around Britain's major cities, and it was these people who could most easily afford the time and expense of watching television. The new

**realism** the aim for representations to reproduce reality faithfully, and the ways in which this is done.

**outside broadcast** the television transmission of outdoor events such as sport or ceremonial occasions, using equipment set up in advance for the purpose. Abbreviated as OB.

*continued*

Figure 1.4 Television rehearsals at Alexandra Palace, 1946. Photograph courtesy of the National Museum of Photography, Film & Television/Society Picture Library.

suburban semi-detached houses offered people more private space than they had ever had before (larger rooms, more bedrooms and big gardens, for example), but also potential loneliness in the recently created suburban estates populated by people who were strangers to each other, and intensely conscious of the social status they and those around them possessed. Ivor Brown (1951: 17) saw television as a remedy for these problems: 'In the suburb, television is plainly acting as a cohesive force.' Owners of television sets invited people round to watch their televisions, to show them off, to make friends, and to enjoy being an audience for programmes:

> That friends and neighbours should come in to watch makes for better audiences, especially in the case of comedy and light shows . . . The more viewers, in the case of comedy, the more they enjoy themselves, since to be a member of an audience is quite a different thing from sitting aloof at a dress-rehearsal, as all theatre people know. So my guess is that, as television expands, it will begin to collect little group-audiences. So it will become a new factor in social life.
>
> (Brown 1951: 17)

The television of the 1950s was aimed at community and family. Television sets were placed near the fire in the family living room, and being warm and cosy together suited the communal experience of watching television as a family group. Families with television sets engaged in social talk that was given new interest by the television programmes they could watch together.

This has to be seen in the context of the BBC's public service ideals, which were to encourage people to expose themselves to a range of programmes, some of them requiring concentration and an aim of self-improvement.

Ivor Brown (1951: 19), thinking of watching television as a rather special event, thought that it would support the raising of cultural standards among viewers: 'The BBC has long advocated, I think, selective listening to sound radio, instead of the vague tap-running which is destructive of taste and leaves its public wayward instead of critical. Television curtails the tap, and makes of viewing a planned and intelligent exercise.' This conception of television is probably very different from the ways most people think of television viewing now. Brown (1951: 19) was concerned about the directions that viewing might take: 'What I most dread for the future is television available at all hours and the coming of the portable plug-in TV set which will destroy the isolation and concentration now imposed by the fixing of the mechanism in one corner of the room.' His worries about the invention of the portable television were not only that it would lead to more distracted viewing but that the television would follow viewers around the house to different rooms, breaking up the collectivity and sociability which television involved.

The proliferation of televisions in contemporary homes means that it is common for different age groups and genders within the home to view different programmes in different rooms in different ways. The other domestic technologies such as video games, uses of computers for internet surfing and email and leisure communication by text messaging and telephone rival the television as the centre of home leisure and the collective experience of television viewing. The current explosion in the number of available channels on digital television also means that different individuals or groupings in the household can watch entirely different programmes from each other, on different television sets in different rooms. Nostalgia for family television can be seen in the sitcom *The Royle Family*, where family members and their neighbours gather in front of the television. As in the 1950s, the television forms the focus of a communal experience in *The Royle Family*, though the watching of the programmes is very much secondary to the cohesive force of the television set itself as the centrepiece around which people gather. A major question for broadcasters, for Television Studies researchers and for all kinds of commentators on the British media is how digital television will change television culture.

British digital multi-channel television began to develop slowly. In the first six months of 2000 the rate of increase in digital subscribers was 53 per cent, but in 2001 the increase fell to 10 per cent, suggesting that the 30 per cent of British households who were connected at that time were those who were keen on the new technology, and that the mass of the British audience were not attracted by digital services. In a government survey only 25 per cent of British households said they expected to connect to digital television by 2006, the earliest date that the government said it would cease **terrestrial** broadcasts using the existing **analogue** transmission system. In homes connected to digital television, average viewers watch only eight to twelve of the dozens of channels available, and the **interactive** services and email through the television set which digital connection offers seemed less attractive to households than home computers that run these services more quickly and more cheaply. Now that dozens or hundreds of channels are available, the size of the audience watching each channel can potentially be a very small fraction of the total. It was unclear how channels would support the cost of producing programmes watched by such small audiences. Some income was clawed back by the paid channels offering films and sport, but the prospect of paying for content was the main reason why the majority of households had not connected

**terrestrial** broadcasting from a ground-based transmission system, as opposed to broadcasting via satellite.

**analogue** broadcasting signals in waves of varying frequency. Analogue signals require greater space or 'bandwidth' than digital signals, and do not allow interactive response from viewers.

**interactive** offering the opportunity for viewers to respond to what is broadcast, by sending signals back to the broadcaster (along a cable or phone line, for example).

*continued*

Figure 1.5 *The Royle Family.* © ITV Granada

to digital television. However, the government committed itself to digital television, primarily so that it can sell the unused analogue frequency spectrums then left over to communications companies who will use them for mobile telephone services. In September 2001 the Minister for Culture, Media and Sport approved BBC plans for two new digital channels, BBC3 and BBC4 (superseding BBC Choice and BBC Knowledge). BBC3 is targeted at under-twenty-fives, including series and serials initially budgeted at £70,000–£230,000 per half-hour, thus matching the **budgets** of BBC2 drama and some cheaper BBC1 programmes. The plan was that drama would no longer appear on BBC2 in much proportion, leaving that channel to address the over-thirty-five audience with factual and arts programmes, though at the risk of losing audience share to Channel 4, BBC2's major competitor. BBC4 is based around the content provided on BBC2 and also BBC Radios 3 and 4, featuring arts, music and culture programmes. Just as Channel 4 has done with E4 and More4, its digital channels, programmes premiere on digital to attract audiences, and may then migrate to terrestrial channels if successful. But the overall aim is to provide recognisable branded channels from terrestrial broadcasters on non-subscription digital channels, thus increasing the chances of bigger digital audiences.

The new date for switching off analogue television transmission is 2012, though different parts of Britain are due to become digital-only at different times. The schedule for switching off terrestrial television was announced in 2007, listing television regions from the far south-west of England northwards, as:

- Westcountry 2009
- West 2010
- Meridian 2012

**budget** the money allocated to the making of a particular programme or series of programmes, which is controlled by the producer.

- London 2012
- Anglia 2011
- Central 2011
- Wales 2009–10
- Granada 2009
- Yorkshire 2011
- Tyne Tees 2012
- Border 2008–9
- Scottish TV Central 2010
- Scottish TV North 2010
- Ulster 2012

Digital television now looks set to become very widespread before switch-off, due in large measure to the success of the Freeview transmission system which offers the mainstream television channels (BBC1, BBC2, ITV1, Channel 4 and Five), and also about fifty other channels, via a roof aerial. The media regulator **Ofcom** publishes a regular report on the communications market, and in 2006 it announced that 73 per cent of homes in the UK had digital television. Freeview is free, apart from the modest cost of a **set-top decoder box**. Satellite and cable services like Sky also offer multi-channel digital viewing for a small monthly charge, but the BBC is at the forefront of this digital revolution, offering all its existing radio and television channels, plus the new ones like BBC3 and BBC4, to Freeview viewers. The BBC has said that it is part of its role to offer 'public value' by enabling almost everyone in Britain to receive its services without direct payment, reflecting the traditional public service broadcasting principles of offering a wide range of different kinds of programme to as many people as possible, to suit the needs and desires of the whole nation. Of course, the BBC will also be in a better position to defend itself in the new digital environment if it is a key player rather than part of a superseded kind of analogue television culture. It is important to the survival of the concept of public service broadcasting that the BBC has appealing programme content and a trusted brand as Britain becomes a fully digital TV nation.

Television in Britain seems to be at a turning-point which is interestingly similar to that in the early 1950s, when the small audiences and single broadcaster of the time were about to be transformed by new channels, much greater television set ownership and new ways of thinking about audiences. David Liddiment, then head of ITV, spoke at the 2001 Edinburgh Television Festival and said:

> Numbers now seem to be the only universal measure for excellence we have: how many, how much, how often. We are losing sight of the innate value of programmes in our fixation on the successes that can be measured by profit, profile or performance. The relentless quest to find out what viewers want and then give it to them has made for sameness as we all seek to engineer the same schedule.
>
> (quoted in Brown and Wells 2001: 3)

The issues of how television is delivered, how it is watched, financed and organised into schedules and channels are matters of major concern to broadcasters, government and cultural commentators. New ways of delivering programmes over the internet for downloading onto computers, and delivering extracts from programmes for viewing on mobile phones, require viewers and television institutions to think in new ways about producing programmes,

**Ofcom** the Office of Communications, a government body responsible for regulating television and other communications media in Britain.

**set-top box** the electronic decoding equipment connected to home television sets that allows access to digital television signals.

*continued*

scheduling them, addressing audiences, and financing the making of television. The television landscape has changed enormously in the last fifty years, and more important changes are happening right now. Studying television in the early twenty-first century is a demanding but important part of understanding culture and society in the past, present and future.

## SUMMARY OF KEY POINTS

- Television Studies focuses on broadcast television, but new ways of delivering television to viewers are now appearing.
- Television has aimed to represent relatively unified cultures, though it also has regional and ethnic characteristics.
- British television has an important emphasis on public service functions, and representing society to itself.
- Television Studies has emphasised the study of particular programmes.
- The flow of programming, and audiences' experience of this flow, is a way of distinguishing television viewing from that of other media, such as cinema.
- The study of audiences and their response to television has become increasingly significant, both to television institutions and to theorists of television.

## Further reading

Ang, I., *Desperately Seeking the Audience* (London: Routledge, 1991).

Brunsdon, C., J. D'Acci and L. Spigel, 'Introduction', in C. Brunsdon, J. D'Acci, and L. Spigel (eds), *Feminist Television Criticism: A Reader* (Oxford: Oxford University Press, 1997), pp. 1–16.

Caughie, J., 'Television criticism: a discourse in search of an object', *Screen*, 25:4–5 (1984), pp. 109–20.

Corner, J., *Critical Ideas in Television Studies* (Oxford: Clarendon, 1999).

Ellis, J., *Visible Fictions: Cinema, Television, Video* (London: Routledge & Kegan Paul, 1982).

Fiske, J., *Media Matters* (Minneapolis: University of Minnesota Press, 1994).

—— *Television Culture* (London: Routledge, 1992).

Fiske, J. and J. Hartley, *Reading Television* (London: Methuen, 1978).

Franklin, B. (ed.), *British Television Policy: A Reader* (London: Routledge, 2001).

Geraghty, C., 'Audiences and "ethnography": questions of practice', in C. Geraghty and D. Lusted (eds), *The Television Studies Book* (London: Arnold, 1998), pp. 141–57.

Goodwin, A. and G. Whannel (eds), *Understanding Television* (London: Routledge, 1990).

Grossberg, L., C. Nelson and P. Treichler, with L. Baughman and J. Macgregor Wise (eds), *Cultural Studies* (New York: Routledge, 1992).

Jancovich, M. and J. Lyons (eds), *Quality Popular Television: Cult TV, the Industry and the Fans* (London: BFI, 2005).

Jermyn, D. and S. Holmes, 'The audience is dead; long live the audience!: interactivity, "telephilia", and the contemporary television audience', *Critical Studies in Television*, 1:1 (2006), pp. 49–57.

Lewis, L. (ed.), *The Adoring Audience: Fan Culture and Popular Media* (London: Routledge, 1991).

Lull, J., 'Critical response: the audience as nuisance', *Critical Studies in Mass Communication*, 5 (1988), pp. 239–43.

Morley, D., *Television, Audiences and Cultural Studies* (London: Routledge, 1992).

—— The *'Nationwide' Audience* (London: BFI, 1980).

Morris, M., 'Banality in cultural studies', *Block*, 14 (1988), pp. 15–25.

Murdoch, G., 'Authorship and organization', *Screen Education*, 35 (1980), pp. 19–34.

Newcomb, H., *TV: The Most Popular Art* (New York: Anchor, 1974).

Wasko, J. (ed.), *A Companion to Television* (Malden, Mass., and Oxford: Blackwell, 2005).

Williams, R., *Television, Technology and Cultural Form* (London: Collins, 1974).

# Television Histories

2

# Television Histories

## Introduction

This chapter discusses ways of approaching the history of television, focusing on Britain, but also comparing and contrasting with other countries. Television Studies has historically focused on television in national contexts. But the assumption that programmes would be viewed and discussed by a significant proportion of a national population is now proving less secure than before. The three factors that have given rise to this change in the nature of television are:

- the proliferation of channels
- the presence of several television sets in a single household
- the increasing control of television production and distribution by corporations and institutions whose activities cross national boundaries.

So it is important in thinking about television now to understand that many of the theoretical and critical approaches to the medium derive from a television history that is undergoing significant change. While the methods of analysis proposed by Television Studies in the past remain significant and useful, it is crucial to pay attention to the present and the possibilities for television that are being shaped for the future. Although this chapter aims to provide information about some moments in the development and change in television across the period from the 1930s to about 1990, it is concerned less with providing a consistent story and a set of key facts than with how the history of television can be approached critically. This is because the historical study of any subject involves making assumptions and value judgements about what is important, how links between events and processes are explained, and what the implications of a history might be. History is always a process of narration, which makes sense by including some pieces of information and excluding others, by linking causes and effects, and by implying a direction to the ways that events unfold. So this chapter does tell parts of several stories but suggests that the history of television can be told in many alternative ways.

## Collecting the evidence

Histories of television face numerous problems in relation to the evidence on which they are based. Relatively inexpensive videocassette recording became available only in the early 1980s. Until that time, studying television from the past relied on gaining access to the archives of material held by television broadcasting institutions themselves. Only in the last two decades or so could students and academics studying television collect examples to work on easily. Even today, when massive libraries of videotape and, increasingly, collections of better-quality DVD can be assembled by interested individuals, by academic institutions or in national archives, it is difficult to know how these resources should be used. When there is plenty of stored television from the past to look at, what principles should be brought to bear in order to decide what to study? Perhaps whole days or even weeks of the output of a particular channel or channels should be studied. Perhaps programmes of a similar **genre** broadcast on different channels should be collected, having decided how the boundaries of a genre should be defined. Perhaps the most popular programmes in a given month or a year should be analysed, on the basis of the audience **ratings** that show which programmes were watched by the most people. Perhaps all the programmes shown by all the channels at a certain time, such as on Friday evenings, should be compared and contrasted with each other. Perhaps it is not programmes at all that should be a focus of interest, but the television advertisements, links and trailers that connect them, since these are the stitches which hold a **flow** of television together as an object for study.

Writing a history of television over the last twenty years or so looks easy, since it is not so difficult to gather evidence, but paradoxically this produces the problem that there is simply too much that could be investigated. To write the history of earlier decades of television is difficult in other ways. Some broadcasting organisations, such as the BBC and Granada in Britain, have maintained archives of programmes on tape or film. But these are far from complete. A few programmes were recorded on film from the 1930s, and more programmes were recorded on videotape after its invention in the late 1950s. However, the purpose of recording programmes was not primarily to preserve them for future television students and scholars, but rather:

- to train staff in how to produce, direct and shoot television
- to make recorded repeats possible
- to make programmes available for export.

Often, such practical difficulties as lack of storage space meant that institutions such as the BBC found it too expensive and difficult to keep sizeable programme archives. Tapes and film copies were simply thrown away, or expensive videotape was reused for some immediately useful purpose. The technologies to record programmes on film or videotape were attractive to television institutions because they made it easier to make programmes. Film inserts could be used during live broadcasts, and videotape made special effects much easier to achieve than during a live recording. So the copies of programmes that can be found in broadcasters' archives represent a fragmentary patchwork that was not intended as an objective record or even as a collection of television programmes that could sum up a decade or a channel's output. A further difficulty is that where programmes were preserved they were usually those that had acquired some status and importance. There are few existing copies of light entertainment programmes made before the 1960s, since news programmes, documentaries and some high-profile drama were thought much more useful to preserve.

**genre** a type of programme. Programmes of the same genre have shared characteristics.

**ratings** the number of viewers estimated to have watched certain programmes, as compared to the numbers watching other programmes.

**flow** the ways in which programmes, advertisements, etc. follow one another in an unbroken sequence across the day or part of the day, and the experience of watching the sequence of programmes, advertisements, trailers, etc.

## ACTIVITY 2.1

Consider what the following terms might mean in the writing of a history (you could use this chapter and the Further Reading at the end to research how the terms could apply to television history, or simply think about the meanings of these terms themselves):

| | |
|---|---|
| Evolution | Invention |
| Turning-points | Cultural history |
| Evidence | National history |
| Progress | International history |

Contemporary Television Studies has focused on the study of programmes in their original audio-visual form. So this section has so far considered the writing of television history in terms of the possibilities of watching television programmes as they were broadcast in some earlier time. Other kinds of history writing can be undertaken by using other kinds of evidence, and some of the recent historical work on television uses written sources to gain an understanding of the television of the past. For example, looking back at the pages of the BBC's listings magazine *Radio Times*, or ITV's *TV Times*, can be instructive in understanding how programmes and programme **schedules** were offered and advertised to their audiences. These magazines also contain features such as interviews with actors and **producers**, and articles by journalistic commentators. They can reveal much about the attitudes to television that were assumed, and the balance between information, education and entertainment in the television of particular periods. These listings publications also contain letters pages with viewers' questions, comments and evaluations of programmes. Although they are hardly representative, these sources give a partial snapshot of the ways that viewers established a relationship with broadcasters, and reveal some of the attitudes to programmes that might have been significant in a particular period.

The archives of broadcasting institutions, especially the BBC, also contain some records of viewer responses to programmes. Some producers kept the letters that viewers wrote to them about programmes, and broadcasters have always engaged in audience research. The BBC had an audience research department which did similar things to what **focus groups** do now by gathering information by questionnaire and interview in order to gauge what viewers like or dislike, and what they approve of or do not approve of about programmes. As well as raw numerical information about audience sizes, these sources provide another glimpse of how people responded to the television they watched in the past. In broadcasters' archives there are also numerous paper records about the making of programmes. The BBC in particular has maintained extensive archives of letters, memos, reports and policy documents that give insight into how and why programmes were made. So the issue of evidence in television history is complex, since it involves these questions:

- What are the different kinds of evidence available about television in the past?

**schedule**
the arrangement of programmes, advertisements and other material into a sequential order within a certain period of time, such as an evening, day or week.

**producer**
the person working for a television institution who is responsible for the budget, planning and making of a television programme or series of programmes.

**focus groups** small groups of selected people representing larger social groupings, such as people of a certain age group, gender or economic status, who take part in discussions about a topic chosen for investigation.

- How does the selection of evidence make some kinds of history writing possible, and others extremely difficult?
- How does one kind of evidence (such as recordings of programmes) relate to other kinds (such as broadcasters' archives or commercial printed publications)?
- How can the attitudes and responses of audiences be reconstructed, and what do they tell us?
- How have television institutions' attitudes to their programmes shaped the evidence available?

As John Caughie (2000) has argued, the inability to record early television supports the view that television is ephemeral by nature, and in the academic discipline of Television Studies there is still a relative lack of concern with television history. As far as television programming itself is concerned, the versions of television's own past that are aired from time to time (in reruns of old black-and-white programmes, compilation programmes of old television advertisements or brief clips from old programmes in quiz shows) are almost always presented in a humorous context. Television from the past is used like a family photo album: it invites the audience to be amazed, embarrassed and amused by what happened in history. Until very recently, television from the past was something to make fun of rather than to appreciate on its own terms. British television and its audiences are sophisticated and complex, and their awareness of growing up with television can be seen in the programmes which celebrate and deride that history. Programmes such as Channel 4's *Hundred Greatest TV Moments* represent television's memory of itself, and the audience's fondness for programmes of the past, but the history of television which appears on television is almost exclusively told in terms of memorable programmes, and is often made the subject of comedy. Television in Britain still seems unable to

Figure 2.1  *Porridge*. Fulton Mackay, Ronnie Barker and Richard Beckinsale. Courtesy of BBC Photograph Library.

take its own history seriously (in comparison to television coverage of other histories, such as those of architecture or cinema). This is despite the increased demand for programme content on the increased number of contemporary channels, which makes the repeating of past programmes a notable feature of the schedules. With the proliferation of new channels, there is some economic value in the archives of old programmes that broadcasters have preserved. The BBC has gained income from its vast library of old programmes, by making business deals with the American cable and satellite company Flextech and the media corporation Pearson in 1995, for example, to screen programmes from its archives. The export of new BBC programmes, another source of revenue, was also made possible by links with the American Discovery Channel in 1996 and the start of BBC World transmitting programmes internationally. The pay channel UK Gold, showing repeated programmes, has now been joined by BBC3 and BBC4, which offer themed programmes aimed at certain audiences. BBC4 is unusual in having a special team of producers who make the *Time Shift* series of documentaries about television history and also screen examples of 'classic' programmes on the channel.

Even presenting television from the past as something to laugh at shows how important television is to the shared memories and experiences of generations of viewers, and for **culture** in general. While television as a medium has always placed great emphasis on the current moment, partly because live broadcasting has been so significant throughout the development of the medium, both the television industry and the discipline of Television Studies have begun to show an awareness of the significance of television history.

**culture** the shared attitudes, ways of life and assumptions of a group of people.

---

### *Cathy Come Home*: the most repeated television play

*Cathy Come Home* was written by Jeremy Sandford (a journalist and radio and television dramatist), directed by Ken Loach, and produced by Tony Garnett. It was broadcast on BBC1 in the *Wednesday Play* series on 16 November 1966 and attracted an audience of ten million. It is the most frequently repeated television drama ever, having been shown again in 1967, 1968, 1976, 1993 and on its fortieth anniversary in 2006. Rather than aiming for the well-formed studio drama whose conventions derived from the theatre, Garnett and Loach adopted the apparent untidiness and immediacy of documentary. Plays such as *Cathy Come Home* told fictional stories, but used them to make sense of the realistically observed world. Rather than maintaining a consistent relationship of the viewer to the drama, the documentary techniques in *Cathy Come Home* offer the viewer a range of points of view on her story. The drama follows her as she arrives in London from the provinces, meets her husband and starts a family. But things go wrong when her husband is injured at work, and the greater part of the play concerns the family's slide into homelessness, the break-up of the marriage and the inability of welfare services to provide for their needs. Sometimes the camera observes Cathy from a distance, or a voice-over will contextualise her situation and provide information. But in other sequences a hand-held camera is close up with Cathy and encourages the viewer to share her experience in emotional terms. The overall effect of the play is to dramatise the separation between officials or institutions and the human experience of being homeless, poor and powerless.

Figure 2.2 *Cathy Come Home*, 1966. Sean King as Sean, Ray Brooks as Reg, Stephen King as Stephen and Carol White as Cathy. Courtesy of BBC Photograph Library.

## ACTIVITY 2.2

Analyse the pages of a television listings publication for one day or one week, to find programmes that were made more than a decade ago. On which channels do you find these? What kinds of programmes are they? When are they screened? Who do you think is expected to watch them?

## Inventing television technologies

The history of television can be thought of in terms of the progressive improvement of technology. From the earliest mechanical devices for broadcasting pictures, through the invention of magnetic tape to transmit pre-recorded material, to the invention of **cable television** and **satellite** transmission, it might seem that the history of television is driven by technological innovation. But technical innovations require the resources of large organisations, and the will to implement technologies in applications which can be sold to a public. They require the stimulation of demand for the technologies, and a framework of **regulation** and law to govern their implementation. So technologies cannot be seen as in themselves the drivers of the development of television. For example, the level of satellite dish ownership rose to five million homes in 1996, largely because of the exclusive rights to football matches which Sky Television had bought using money gained from its majority shareholder Rupert Murdoch's non-television media interests. The recognition of a potential market, and programme content that can be sold to this market, is a precondition for the successful introduction of a new television technology.

The idea of television goes back to the late nineteenth century, when after radio had been invented it seemed a natural next step to transmit pictures to accompany sound. Scientists across the developed world were aware that the way to transmit pictures would be to find a way of breaking down a camera's visual image into tiny areas of black, white and shades of grey. These tiny areas could be reassembled on a television screen in order to reproduce the original image as a series of tiny dots. The principle is the same as the way that newspaper photographs were transmitted by telephone wires from the beginning of the 1900s, by decomposing an image into clusters of larger or smaller black dots, producing areas of darker or lighter space which together added up to the shades and outlines of a photograph.

The discovery of the chemical element selenium enabled this vision of television to seem closer, since a bank of selenium sensors in an electronic camera would turn the different amounts of light falling on them into different strengths of electrical current. If the changing signals for each tiny selenium receptor were sent to a receiver, the changing light and dark of a television picture would result. Inventors in Britain, Russia and Germany worked on different methods of scanning images with selenium sensors in the years before and after 1900, but without perfecting a workable system. The British inventor John Logie Baird, and engineers at the Marconi EMI Company, worked separately on competing systems of television broadcasting in the 1920s, with government and BBC support given to Baird. British television formally began on 2 November 1936, trying out both the Baird and Marconi systems and broadcasting to only about three hundred receivers in the London area.

**cable television** originally called Community Antenna Television (CATV). Transmission of television signals along cables in the ground.

**satellite television** television signals beamed from a ground transmitter to a stationary satellite that broadcasts the signal to a specific area (called the 'footprint') below it.

**regulation** the control of television institutions by laws, codes of practice or guidelines.

---

### ACTIVITY 2.3

Do some research into what happened when John Logie Baird's and Marconi EMI's television systems were tested in Britain. What were the strengths and weaknesses of each system? If you think the best system 'won', what made it the best, and for whom?

Figure 2.3  John Logie Baird with his experimental television receiver, 1926. Photograph
courtesy of National Museum of Photography, Film & Television/Science and
Society Picture Library

## Television institutions

Television today is a centralised business. Large corporations and institutions
own the equipment and facilities to make television programmes, and these are
distributed from central transmission sources to the huge number of receiving
aerials or cable television ports that serve the homes of the television audience.
So production and distribution involve a small number of powerful and centralised
organisations, whereas reception is differentiated and distributed across a very broad
and relatively powerless constituency of viewers.

Television did not need to develop in this way. In the late nineteenth century,
commentators speculated about television technologies which would be more like
telephone systems (Gripsrud 1998: 20–1). People equipped with small and conveni-
ent television recording devices were imagined making and sending pictures and
sound to domestic receivers. Television might have been much more personal,
unregulated and cheaper to make than it is now. Another way of putting this alternative development of television would be to say that television could have been
a popular medium, in the sense that it could have been made as well as received by
the viewers themselves, and the making of television could have been embedded
within their own lives. Instead, television became big business, where national
governments co-operated to set up technical standards to control the mass production of television equipment. A professional community of highly trained technicians
and production staff undertook the making of programmes.

The government and BBC gave no serious consideration to advertising as a means of support when the work of John Logie Baird was being completed in Britain, and plans for a television service were actively developed. The thinking behind the organisation of the BBC as a semi-autonomous public corporation was inherited from the late Victorian corporations which had **monopolies** to provide services such as gas, electricity and water. Their control of supply and freedom from competition were granted in exchange for a remit to operate for the public good. The BBC took seriously its aims to raise the standards of the entire national audience in terms of sophistication of taste, intellectual appetite and levels of knowledge: television as **public service** broadcasting. In the United States big corporations such as RCA and General Electric took over the work on the development of television equipment during the 1920s. This was an important development, in that it was not the government, the Hollywood film studios or individual entrepreneurs who took television forward but the industrial combines behind the production of radio equipment. Television in the USA would be modelled on the organisation of radio broadcasting, rather than the cinema industry or the public services, and in the late 1920s experimental television broadcasts were made in New York, Boston and Chicago, backed by electronics manufacturers hoping to sell the television sets to receive them. The radio broadcasters NBC and CBS were promoting television and could supply programmes to broadcast. American television, like radio, would use national **networks** supplying programmes to local stations which paid to broadcast them, gaining income from commercials and the **sponsorship** of programmes. By the time America entered the Second World War in 1941, the regulator, the **Federal Communications Commission (FCC)**, had licensed thirty-two commercial television stations, broadcasting to the few thousand owners of television sets in America's largest cities.

In the very different television culture of China, the history, purposes and institutions of television are interesting to compare and contrast with the those of the United States and Britain. Broadcasting in China was established by the ruling Communist Party that took power in 1949 as a means to disseminate government policy, news and entertainment sanctioned by the state. Television began in 1958 with one station in Beijing, the capital city, then expanded slowly, with only thirty stations in operation by 1970, based in cities and unable to reach the whole population. After 1976, though, television grew faster than any other communications medium in the country, with over six hundred transmitting stations by 1995. In addition to these terrestrial transmitters, eleven million Chinese people could receive satellite television signals, and 1,800 cable systems were operating. The institutions of television in China have been closely controlled by the government, and the prospect of Chinese people watching programmes and channels made abroad or beamed to them by satellites operated by foreign corporations has led to the licensing of cable television systems and largely unsuccessful attempts to ban the use of satellite dishes. The historical basis of this suspicion of commercial and foreign television in China comes from the principles set out by the revolutionary leader Mao Zedong, who argued that the purposes of broadcasting were:

- to publicise the decisions made by the ruling Communist Party
- to educate the population
- to establish a channel of communication between the party and the people.

**monopoly** control over the provision of a service or product by one institution or business.

**public service** in television, the provision of a mix of programmes that inform, educate and entertain in ways that encourage the betterment of audiences and society in general.

**network** a television institution that transmits programmes through local or regional broadcasting stations that are owned by or affiliated to that institution.

**sponsorship** the funding of programmes or channels by businesses, whose names are usually prominently displayed in the programmes or channels as a means of advertising.

**Federal Communications Commission (FCC)** the government body in the USA which regulates the operations and output of television companies and other broadcasters.

In practice, however, ownership of satellite dishes is common, and services beamed by satellite, notably StarTV, carry channels such as MTV and CNN. The history of television in China can be framed as a gradual movement from state control, with an emphasis on information, political programming and entertainment programmes based on state-approved national values, to increasing commercialisation and diversity. This historical narrative is explored further in the following chapter, where the current state of television around the world in national and international contexts is discussed. But here this brief reference to China shows how the political and cultural histories of a country can take widely different forms as they affect the establishment and development of television.

In Britain the **Annan Committee** report of 1977 called into question the role of television broadcasters as moral and intellectual leaders of society. Instead, television was increasingly considered as a market in which providers of programmes would give their publics what they seemed to want. With three channels and the prospect of a fourth, it no longer seemed necessary for each channel to expose the audience to the full range of both 'accessible' and 'difficult' programmes. The 1970s marked the beginnings of the notion that some channels would direct their resources to some types of programme more than others, leaving viewers to choose the programmes which catered for their existing tastes. Thus, the role of television institutions underwent gradual change across the decades, and conceptions of the purposes of television and its relationship with its audiences developed with different emphases. The history of television involves placing the production and distribution of television in a context informed by the cultural pressures on governments, television institutions and audiences, all of which affect each other. The launch in 1982 of Britain's fourth **terrestrial** channel, Channel 4, was the result of a combination of inherited and traditional views of broadcasting and the new imperatives of the 1979 Conservative government and its allies. From the past came a commitment to **public service**, to educational and cultural programmes, and to programmes for minority audiences. But Conservative policies in the 1980s attempted to introduce the principles of the market into all aspects of British life. So Channel 4 bought programmes from independent programme-makers, who were forced to compete with each other for commissions, and the channel itself made no significant investment in production facilities or training. Its funding derived from advertising revenue through a levy on the ITV companies, which sold advertising time on Channel 4 in their regions, and was therefore reliant on the buoyancy of the British economy.

The Broadcasting Act of 1980 which established Channel 4 required it to 'encourage innovation and experiment in the form and content of programmes'. The first chief executive was Jeremy Isaacs, who led the channel's investment in films for domestic and foreign television screening as well as cinema release. There were programmes for British Asian viewers, and members of trade unions, while in Wales the companion channel S4C (Sianel Pedwar Cymru) broadcast Welsh-language programmes. Channel 4 was required by the Broadcasting Act to provide 'a distinctive service', but attracted criticism for its 'bad language' and alleged left-wing political bias.

The first night of Channel 4 was on Tuesday, 2 November 1982. The programme schedule ran from 4.45 p.m. to 11.50 p.m., with the two most popular programmes being its new **soap opera**, *Brookside* (4.1 million viewers), and the first specially

**Annan Committee** a committee reporting in 1977 to the British government on the future of broadcasting. It supported public service broadcasting, the funding of the BBC by licence fee, and the planned introduction of a fourth television channel.

**terrestrial** broadcasting from a ground-based transmission system, as opposed to broadcasting via satellite.

**soap opera** a continuing drama serial involving a large number of characters in a specific location, focusing on relationships, emotions and reversals of fortune.

commissioned television film for the channel, *Film on Four: Walter* (3.75 million viewers), directed by Stephen Frears. These audiences were low by comparison with the traditional channels, with the highest-rated programme in November 1982 being *Coronation Street* on ITV, with 15.7 million viewers. But Channel 4 introduced significant changes to several programme forms, as well as opening up the **independent production** sector in Britain. *Brookside* was the first British soap opera to be made entirely on location, on a new estate in Liverpool. *Channel 4 News* (made by ITN) was Britain's first hour-long news programme, and set high standards for news analysis. One of Channel 4's aims was to export programmes in order to maximise revenue, and financing film-length dramas for television which could be sold to foreign broadcasters was one way of achieving this. In the 1980s the channel began to release its films in cinemas, as a way of raising their profile and creating publicity before their television transmission. Channel 4 entered the art cinema market with these films, and the distinction between the television film and the cinema film became increasingly blurred. However, with the increased cost of making films to cinematic standards (of length, star quality and production value), fewer films could be made.

> ## ACTIVITY 2.4
>
> Examine the programme schedules on Channel 4 today. Which programmes seem to be aimed at minority audiences? Which audiences, and why?

## Professional cultures in a 'golden age'

The technology to record television pictures and sound was introduced in Britain slowly in the 1950s, and both BBC and ITV made use of it for training purposes, but rarely for transmitting programmes made and recorded on tape. Instead, the medium of film was the preferred method of recording programmes for preservation, for foreign sale or for brief sequences (such as film shot on exterior locations) that would be played into programmes transmitted live from a television studio. It was expensive to transfer programmes shot on film to tape, to buy the tape itself, to store it and to buy and maintain the machines which performed this task. This meant that television programmes that used tape were more expensive to make. The people working in television were also required to become expert and professional in new ways once tape and film became as significant as live broadcasting. The mastery of these technologies led to the development of highly trained and specialist personnel with specific tasks to perform in the production process, with fewer of the attitudes of the enthusiastic upper-middle-class amateur which had previously marked many of the personnel in television.

By the 1960s the increase in broadcasting hours and the presence of three television channels in Britain changed the culture of television production, by moving away from the pioneering amateurism which characterised the early years. The first producers and **directors** in the 1930s and 1940s had some of the open-

*independent production companies* businesses making television programmes which can be sold to television networks that transmit and distribute them.

*director* the person responsible for the creative process of turning a script or idea into a finished programme, by working with a technical crew, performers and an editor.

mindedness, but also some of the blinkered cosiness, of a public school or university drama society as they made up television as they went along. The professionalism and large scale of television production in the 1960s and thereafter encouraged programmes to be made more like an industrial product. Professional writers and directors, most of whose working time was spent in television, worked according to consistent schedules and guidelines, and developed skills, professional codes of conduct and shared expectations. In the 1960s and 1970s producers commissioned programmes, ran the production process, including selecting the directors and technical staff, and oversaw projects to completion. They came to have an authorial role, and were also relatively free from the interference of department heads and television executives.

Television's 'golden age' in Britain – the late 1950s to the 1970s – has gained this label because it was a period when the **status quo** changed. New values were being put in place, and inherited traditions were confronted by new forms and new pressures. It is important to recognise that professional workers in the television industry do not live in a separate cultural world from the rest of society, and ideas circulating among people of similar interests, social class and educational background influence the ways in which these people conceive of their role. In Britain popular books of the 1950s and 1960s by left-wing intellectuals such as Richard Hoggart, Raymond Williams, Stuart Hall and E. P. Thompson encouraged the belief that **culture** (television, radio, popular music, home decoration and sport, for example) was significant in shaping people's **class** position and personal identity, and that these cultural activities were connected to the economics of British society. These theories derived in part from **Marxist** thinking, which argues that the forms of everyday life derive from the ways in which people are positioned as workers in, or owners of, the industries and businesses that produce the wealth of the nation. For these writers, the improvement of social structures and everyday conditions of existence could come about through changing people's relationships to work and wealth, but also through debate and struggles for change in culture itself. To change television might also change society, and the influence of this view was seen in **realistic** (and often pessimistic) drama series such as *Z Cars* (a police series), and controversial **satire** programmes such as *That Was the Week that Was*, which challenged conventions of television and also the representations of British society.

These ideas were familiar to the new generation of school-leavers and university graduates emerging in the late 1950s and early 1960s, often people from working-class backgrounds who had been given the opportunity to gain a good education through scholarships and the expansion of universities. These people were often resistant to the elitism, conservatism and traditionalism which had dominated the Establishment (the civil service, the BBC, the churches, universities and the law) in the past. Television was a young medium, and some of these people saw opportunities to carry forward their radical ideas in the television industry. Vigorous and authentic television seemed to entail the bringing onto the screen and into the TV business people from working-class backgrounds, from outside the stodgy south-east of England. In drama a new kind of realism was needed to reflect the lives of ordinary people beyond London and the Home Counties, and television documentaries could present the different regions and social classes of the nation to the television audience. Television producers, directors and writers were often resistant to the bureaucracy of the television companies, and rejected the stoical and

**status quo** the ways in which culture and society are currently organised.

**class** a section of society defined by their relationship to economic activity, whether as workers (the working class) or possessors of economic power (the bourgeoisie), for example.

**Marxism** the political and economic theories associated with the German nineteenth-century theorist Karl Marx, who described and critiqued capitalist societies and proposed communism as a revolutionary alternative.

**realism** the aim for representations to reproduce reality faithfully, and the ways this is done.

**satire** a mode of critical commentary about society or an aspect of it, using humour to attack people or ideas.

committed a term
used in the study of
the politics of culture,
implying that a
person or a text has a
commitment to
positive and
progressive social
change.

progressive
encouraging positive
change or progress,
usually implying
progress towards
fairer and more equal
ways of organising
society.

popular culture the
texts created by
ordinary people (as
opposed to an elite
group) or created for
them, and the ways
these are used.

outsourcing
obtaining services
from an independent
business rather than
from within a
television institution,
usually as a means of
cutting costs.

submissive attitudes to authority which characterised the older generation which had lived through the Second World War.

The attitudes of these people committed to changing society by changing its culture were evident in the programmes they made, but also in ways of thinking and writing about television that would inform the beginnings of Television Studies. In what became known as '**committed** criticism', writers condemned the status quo and sought both to praise radical television (as well as film and literary works) and to find ways of representing which critiqued the present and offered new and **progressive** ways of thinking. For committed critics, it was important to take the **popular culture** enjoyed by ordinary people seriously, but also to discriminate wisely between what was valuable and what was deadening or worthless. One effect of this was to continue the suspicion of American popular culture (rock 'n' roll music, Hollywood cinema and comics, for instance), which had been gaining audiences and making money with the recognition of a new social group – the teenager. In many television fictions of the 1950s and 1960s isolated young outsider figures, often moving between social classes, struggle to find authentic personal meaning in their apparently absurd and empty lives. The independent outsider and rebel was always male, however, and the heroic vigour of the 1960s hero is often opposed to the entrapping seductiveness of marriage and family represented by women.

In more recent times the culture of television professionals in Britain has changed because of the structural changes made to the television industry as a result of new broadcasting regulations imposed by government, and new working practices introduced by television executives. The BBC reduced its staff by seven thousand between 1986 and 1990, for example, and since the 1980s the use of temporary contracts and the **outsourcing** of production to independent producers, and the introduction of an internal market at the BBC, have shifted decision-making powers from programme-makers to schedulers and commissioners, and made the career paths of programme-makers much less stable. The effect of this market-like situation is that the producer, who commissions and oversees the making of television programmes, becomes a powerful figure, at the expense of the writer and director, because the producer is answerable to the demands of the television institution for audiences and cost-effectiveness. When John Birt led the BBC in the 1990s the sweeping changes he introduced weakened the independence of the producer by centralising power in London and giving more control to commissioners, schedulers and controllers. The same process has affected the commercial channels. The BBC sold off many of its programme production and technical facilities in the early 1990s, and increased the proportion of programmes commissioned from independent producers rather than made in-house. It increasingly resembles Channel 4 as a commissioning rather than programme-making organisation.

## Reception contexts

Television is now watched in the private space of the home, but in the early days of British broadcasting this was by no means the dominant way that viewers experienced the new medium. Philip Corrigan (1990) discovered that in 1937, the year after BBC television broadcasting started, there were more than a hundred public venues for watching television. These included railway stations, restaurants and department stores. Audiences of up to a hundred people could gather to watch television pictures collectively. In the United States a similar situation was evident in the 1930s, and for a short time television looked like a possible competitor for cinema as a medium of public entertainment experienced in buildings set aside for watching (J. Allen 1983). The Nazi government in Germany in the 1930s was interested partly in the propaganda value of television broadcasting, and partly in competing with the large American corporations that were investing in television production and sets. The Olympic Games of 1936 in Berlin were a stimulus to German television, and broadcasts were received not in individual homes but in viewing rooms established in cities. Once again, television was being thought of as a medium for collective viewing of pictures and sound relayed live from major public events. Some of the buildings in which German television broadcasts were watched could hold audiences of four hundred people. But industrial corporations in Germany had considerable political influence during the Nazi era, so their plans to develop domestic television sets to be watched in individual homes, and thus to develop a consumer market for those sets, meant that these public screenings would give way to domestic viewing once the Second World War began in 1939 (Uricchio 1989).

When the pattern of centralised production and dispersed individual reception of television stabilised as the norm after the Second World War, the form of television that we know in Western countries today had been established. There are two sometimes conflicting results of this pattern. First, central control of production and private individual reception set up a structure that matches the democratic organisation of the developed societies, such as those of Europe and the United States. When governments have a direct role in broadcasting, or set up a legal framework of ownership and regulation for private, autonomous institutions to make television, there is a basis for universal access to information and culture that might promote a fairer society. Mass populations, watching television in their own homes with members of their families, could be supplied with the information and ideas they need to participate in a national or regional society. Informed viewers would be given the resources to take part in political and social debates, and to vote in elections on the basis of a level playing field of information about the issues at stake. The centralised production of television and its dispersed reception suit the concept of public service broadcasting as it has developed in Britain and other European countries quite well. Although there is a more questionable side to this issue, since government propaganda and the manipulation of audiences could also be a part of this broadcasting landscape, the structure of broadcasting as we know it is associated with attempts to raise the cultural, educational and social standards of societies.

The second result of centralised production and dispersed reception of television is its connection with the culture of the home. Standards of living and proportions of surplus income available for investment in leisure and entertainment rose steadily throughout the twentieth century in the industrial nations of the Western world. People's houses were not only places to live but places where consumer goods could be accumulated, and new patterns of domestic leisure could develop. Commentators in the 1940s and 1950s in Britain were concerned about how television might prove a disruptive force in the home, disturbing the family routines of eating, conversation and children's bedtimes. To watch could be regarded as a waste of time (compared to reading, doing jobs around the house or engaging in conversation), especially if television was focused on entertainment. However, for most viewers, the experience of watching was not the solitary experience it often is today. Because only a small proportion of homes had invested in the new and expensive technology, most viewing was collective as people gathered in friends' and neighbours' houses to watch programmes. Watching television was a social event in its own right, and in some respects helped to form communities. This was especially the case in the newly built suburbs of the major cities in which people had chosen to locate themselves after leaving the close-knit but overcrowded Victorian housing of older towns and city centres. Separated by the hedges and front gardens of their new semi-detached houses, the residents were able to socialise and display their relative wealth and status to their neighbours by holding informal gatherings around their televisions.

The television set became an important part of the culture of the home as prices fell through the 1950s and they could be acquired not only by the affluent middle classes but increasingly by everyone. It became a central feature of the household living room, often positioned next to the fireplace, where families would gather in the evening both to keep warm (in the age before central heating) and to share the entertainment experiences offered to them by the broadcasters. As well as experiencing entertainment outside the home – at the cinema or the pub, for example – people could now increasingly take their leisure indoors with their friends and families. Radio had already fulfilled a similar function, but as the mass ownership of television sets extended in the 1950s in Europe and the United States the home became the primary site of leisure and consumerism.

Overall, then, the pattern of television broadcasting that dominated the twentieth century and continues into the twenty-first century was neither natural nor necessary. But it suited the developing forms of society characterised by these key features:

● the promotion of democracy and citizenship
● participation in a modern consumer society
● the centrality of the home as the location of private leisure and family life
● access by government and industry to private space and private life.

The significance of this narrative of television history is that it is a cultural history: it emphasises the ways in which television became embedded in people's lives according to the places they lived, the social classes to which they belonged and the expectations about home, work and leisure that they held.

## Programmes and forms

Writing the history of television by choosing significant programmes to exemplify a year, decade or longer period clearly raises some problems. The shape of the narrative of television history that this produces is strongly determined by the choice of the examples used to back it up. Since television in Britain has a public service function, one way of demonstrating this historical tradition is to note the events that television has covered in order to bring a national audience together as members of a common culture. Ceremonies, state occasions and major sporting events are examples that support this view of television history. When the BBC was Britain's only television broadcaster (from 1936 to 1955), it emphasised the live broadcasting of events of this kind from the start, and set up **outside broadcast** units to cover the coronation of King George VI in 1937, the annual Wimbledon tennis championships and the Armistice Day ceremony, for example. British writers in the 1930s who predicted the future of television emphasised its ability to relay such events live across the country, thus keeping people in touch with what was happening beyond their immediate experience and neighbourhood. It was felt that television would not compete with cinema as entertainment because of its domestic setting and lack of a sense of occasion, and would therefore focus on information.

It was in the 1950s that what we would now describe as 'mass audiences' for television began in Britain. But television sets were still expensive, costing more than eighty pounds in the early 1950s, equivalent to about eight weeks' wages for the average employed man. Nevertheless, between 1952 and 1959 in Britain the number of combined television and radio licences increased from 2.1 million to 10 million. The single television programme with the greatest effect on creating this wider ownership of television sets was the live coverage of the coronation of Queen Elizabeth II in 1953. Again, a live event relayed by television suits the construction of a certain kind of history. This history regards television as a medium preoccupied with the present, and with live coverage. Furthermore, the coronation is another example of a television event that addresses a national public (and an international one since in the 1950s Britain still had extensive contacts with and responsibilities for countries that had formed part of its empire). Televised events such as the coronation connect television viewing with the formation of a national culture defined in part by its relationship with the royal family, heritage, tradition and ceremonial. More than twenty years later, the wedding of Princess Anne and Captain Mark Philips in 1974 was broadcast live, and seen by an audience of around twenty-five million, representing about half of the UK population. Television also covered the wedding of Prince Charles and Lady Diana Spencer in July 1981, showing five and a half hours of live coverage on both BBC and ITV. In the UK thirty-nine million viewers watched live, and it was broadcast live to seventy-four countries. The BBC used about sixty cameras, including twelve in St Paul's Cathedral.

**outside broadcast** the television transmission of outdoor events such as sport or ceremonial occasions, using equipment set up in advance for the purpose. Abbreviated as OB.

---

**ACTIVITY 2.5**

Look through magazines (such as Sunday newspaper magazines, style magazines or consumer electronics magazines) to find advertisements for recent television equipment, such as flat-panel television sets, DVD recorders and players, and digital television receivers. What similarities can you find in the ways these are advertised and the potential consumers to whom the advertisements seem to be addressed?

---

Independent **commercial television** began broadcasting on 22 September 1955, available first only in the London region but expanding to nearly all the country over the next six years. Many influential figures resisted ITV, including the BBC director-general John Reith, who compared commercial television to bubonic plague, and concern was fuelled by the American commercial television coverage of the

**commercial television** television funded by the sale of advertising time or sponsorship of programmes.

coronation in 1953, when messages from programme sponsors frequently inter-rupted the Westminster Abbey service. But the Conservative government was keen to break the BBC monopoly and passed the Television Bill of 1954, which set up the **Independent Television Authority (ITA)**, though the Bill revealed its concern for the lowering of standards which commercial television might entail. It was to be 'predominantly British in tone and style and of high quality, and nothing was to be included which offended against good taste or decency or which was likely to incite to crime or to lead to disorder or to be offensive to public feeling' (Vahimagi, 1994: 28). The desire to preserve a national television culture and its protection from the commercialism and triviality associated with another broadcasting culture (that of the United States) can be inferred from this wording. In a history of television, this tentativeness about the start of ITV is evidence of an anxiety about what British television as a whole might become.

The first night on ITV began with a gala including speeches from the Lord Mayor of London, the **Postmaster General** and Sir Kenneth Clark, chairman of the ITA. The evening was very much in the mould of the BBC: the presenter was Leslie Mitchell, who had worked for the BBC and presented *its* opening night in 1936. The **variety** performers on the first night, such as Harry Secombe and Billy Cotton, had regularly appeared on the BBC, and subsequent programming that night consisted of extracts from theatre plays and a boxing match, and concluded with a discussion of the latest London fashions shown at the Mayfair Hotel. Each broadcast day ended with the playing of the national anthem.

Commercial television was organised in regions, with each part of the country having its own broadcasting provider. The BBC was also divided into regions for television production and broadcasting, just as its radio services had been. Each regional company made programmes specifically for its local audience, and also offered programmes to the national network.

Viewers who could receive the new commercial channel (and initially this was by no means everyone in Britain) were immediately keen on ITV, and in 1957 those who could get both BBC and ITV watched the latter two-thirds of the time. In December 1955, for example, 84 per cent of viewers with access to ITV watched its variety programme *Sunday Night at the London Palladium*. Both ITV and BBC channels used popular formats, such as quiz shows, one-off dramas, variety and adventure series, to attract their audiences, with ITV generally catering for more popular tastes. The BBC's audience fell, and it responded by increasing its broadcast hours from forty-one per week to fifty and introducing its first **soap opera**, *The Grove Family*. This was broadcast in weekly fifteen-minute episodes and centred on a suburban middle-class family. It attracted a deluge of approving letters and created massive press coverage. The 1950s also witnessed the emergence of the television **personality**, with familiar figures such as the on-screen announcers Sylvia Peters, Mary Malcolm and McDonald Hobley on the BBC, and the hosts of popular pro-grammes such as the television cook Philip Harben, gardener Fred Streeter, Annette Mills on the children's programme *Muffin the Mule*, and Armand and Michaela Dennis in wildlife programmes filmed around the world.

The reasons why genres of television programmes are created and become significantly popular are varied and complex, so looking at the programmes with the largest audiences in a particular year can be misleading as well as informative. In the boxes below, the ten most popular programmes in Britain from four different

**Independent Television Authority (ITA)** the official body set up to regulate commercial television in Britain.

**Postmaster General** the person appointed by government to regulate communications institutions such as the Post Office, radio and television.

**variety programmes** entertainment programmes containing a mix of material, such as songs and comedy sketches.

**personalities** people appearing on television who are recognised by audiences as celebrities with a media image and public status beyond the role they play in a particular programme.

years are listed, measuring popularity according to the size of audience calculated by broadcasters' audience research figures. Some of the critical points that could be made about what these lists reveal are suggested after them, together with some issues that complicate possible interpretations of the meaning of the figures.

## The ten most popular programmes in March 1958

The ten most popular programmes in March 1958 were all on ITV. At this time audience sizes were measured in millions of homes, though of course the number of viewers in each home could vary widely. *Emergency Ward 10* appears twice in the list because two of its episodes in March made the top ten programmes.

1   *Take Your Pick* (game show, 4.1 million homes)
2   *The Army Game* (sitcom, 4.1m)
3   *Armchair Theatre* (one-off drama, 3.8m)
4   *Emergency Ward 10* (soap opera, 3.8m)
5   *Sunday Night at the London Palladium* (variety show, 3.7m)
6   *Double Your Money* (game show, 3.6m)
7   *TV Playhouse* (one-off drama, 3.6m)
8   *Emergency Ward 10* (3.5m)
9   *Shadow Squad* (thriller series, 3.1m)
10  *Play of the Week* (one-off drama, 3.1m).

## The ten most popular programmes in September 1964

The ten most popular programmes in September 1964 were all shown on ITV. Audience sizes were still measured in millions of viewing homes, where of course the number of people viewing could vary considerably. *Coronation Street* and *Emergency Ward 10* appear twice in this list because two episodes from each series made the top ten programmes.

1   *Coronation Street* (soap opera, 8.1 million homes)
2   *Coronation Street* (7.8m)
3   *No Hiding Place* (drama series, 7.8m)
4   *Sunday Palladium* (variety show, 7.4m)
5   *Emergency Ward 10* (soap opera, 7.2m)
6   *Emergency Ward 10* (7.0m)
7   *Take Your Pick* (game show, 6.9m)
8   *Love Story* (drama series, 6.8m)
9   *Drama 64* (one-off drama, 6.8m)
10  *Double Your Money* (game show, 6.7m).

## The ten most popular programmes in November 1974

Audience sizes were still measured in millions of homes. Both *Coronation Street* and *Crossroads* appear twice in this list because different episodes of each of them gained large audiences during the month.

1   *Bless this House* (ITV sitcom, 8.6 million homes)
2   *Coronation Street* (ITV soap opera, 7.8m)
3   *Man About the House* (ITV sitcom, 7.8m)
4   *The Generation Game* (BBC game show, 7.5m)
5   *Coronation Street* (ITV soap opera, 7.4m)
6   *Crossroads* (ITV soap opera, 7.4m)
7   *Crossroads* (ITV soap opera, 7.4m)
8   *Upstairs Downstairs* (ITV drama series, 7.3m)
9   *Jennie* (ITV drama series, 7.2m)
10  *Opportunity Knocks* (ITV game show, 7.1m)

## The ten most popular programmes in November 1984

Audiences are now measured in millions of viewers.

1   *Coronation Street* (ITV soap opera, 19.0m)
2   *Give Us a Clue* (ITV game show, 15.5m)
3   *Tenko* (BBC drama serial, 15.3m)
4   *Just Good Friends* (BBC sitcom, 15.1m)
5   *Crossroads* (ITV soap opera, 14.8m)
6   *Name That Tune* (ITV game show, 14.6m)
7   *Dallas* (BBC imported US soap opera, 14.6m)
8   *Hi-De-Hi* (BBC sitcom, 14.5m)
9   *Play Your Cards Right* (ITV game show, 14.5m)
10  *Surprise Surprise* (ITV light entertainment, 13.7m).

**format** the blueprint for a programme, including its setting, main characters, genre, form and main themes.

**adaptation** transferring a novel, theatre play, poem, etc. from its original medium into another medium, such as television.

As Andrew Crisell (1997: 84) has written, 'commercial television was set up as an extension of the public service concept . . . The ITA required the contractors to inform, educate and entertain – to produce programmes of balance, quality and variety'. But, when ITV began broadcasting, the pace and style of British television changed somewhat because in order to compete with the BBC the new channel showed imported American programmes and used American **formats**, as in the action drama series *The Adventures of Robin Hood* and *The Count of Monte Cristo*. In this competitive environment research into audience sizes and preferences became more significant, and television viewers began to be seen as consumers seeking entertainment. Nevertheless, ITV followed the BBC in making **adaptations** of theatre plays, and dramas from Europe translated into English, as well as the populist quizzes and variety shows which ITV is credited with bringing to prominence. Looking at the lists above, though, it seems that ITV had considerable success in attracting large audiences by broadcasting programmes in the forms that are still considered today to be popular entertainment, such as soap operas and game shows.

It is important to remember that these programme forms on ITV were designed to deliver audiences to advertisers, who had paid to screen commercials between programme segments. The formation of large audiences for popular programmes was necessary to the profitability of the ITV companies. On its first night, 170,000 sets were able to receive ITV, and, of these, 100,000 were tuned to the channel, while a quarter of households watched BBC instead. The first ITV commercial break was at 8.12 p.m. during the first evening's variety programme, and there were twenty-three commercials that night in total. Advertisers paid about £1,500 for a slot, a 50 per cent premium above normal rates, and demand led to a ballot to select those ads which would be accommodated. The products advertised were similar to those of today: toothpaste, tyres, drinking chocolate, soap, cars and breakfast cereal. Advertisements were not allowed to concern politics or religion, and had to conform to the standards of good taste overseen by two committees. They could appear only in '**natural breaks**' of up to six minutes per hour, and there had to be a two-minute interval between an advertisement and any appearance by a member of the royal family, state occasion, church service or royal ceremony.

The lists above show that light entertainment programmes such as game shows and sitcoms, as well as long-running **series** and **serials**, have become the mainstay of the output of terrestrial channels. Costs are reduced by using the same crew, performers, sets, costumes and studios for each episode, and series and serials can be sold to overseas broadcasters in ready-made packages of programmes. One of the effects of this is to marginalise programmes which are less conventional in form, or more challenging in social and political content. The promise that a continuing series or serial has of holding on to an audience for the duration of the programme's run offers the prospect of a consistent group of viewers whose **demographic** appeal and/or large size may be attractive to advertisers. Genre television (such as soap opera, police or hospital drama, and game shows) is attractive to television executives because a popular generic programme has a brand identity. In the same way as casting a known television personality or performer, the recognition and familiarity of the forms and **conventions** of the programmes provide both security and appeal. Generic television also provides a sense of control and ownership to the audience, who have a stake in the programmes rather than simply being offered another new product to consume. As well as being constrained by repetition, genre allows for innovation within and between genres, and programmes gain large audiences by manipulating conventions in new ways. Generic categories are no longer separate, and such new formats as **docusoaps**, hospital thrillers and soap–drama feed off the rich history and audience knowledge of television to mix realism with **reflexivity**. Thus, the BBC's soap opera *EastEnders* continues the British tradition of addressing contemporary social issues, while also casting Barbara Windsor as a Cockney pub landlady to draw on her associations with 1960s saucy seaside comedy in the *Carry On* comedy films.

**natural break** a vague term meaning a point at which a programme can be interrupted without causing undue disruption to the ongoing flow.

**series** a television form where each programme has a different story or topic, though settings, main characters and performers remain the same.

**serial** a television form where a developing narrative unfolds across a sequence of separate episodes.

**demography** the study of population, and the groupings of people (demographic groups) within the whole population.

**conventions** the frameworks and procedures used to make or interpret texts.

**docusoap** a television form combining documentary's depiction of non-actors in ordinary situations with soap opera's continuing narratives about selected characters.

**reflexivity** a text's reflection on its own status as a text, for example drawing attention to generic conventions, or revealing the technologies used to make a programme.

### ACTIVITY 2.6

Look in more detail at the lists of the ten most popular programmes presented above. What are the similarities and differences you find between the lists? What might these similarities and differences contribute to a history of British television?

### Case study: 'Me TV'

*personal video recorder (PVR)*
a device that records digital television onto a microchip for storage and replay, and can automatically record programmes it thinks the viewer will enjoy.

Domestic television technologies cannot in themselves be regarded as the motors of change in the history or future of television, as this chapter has discussed. Technologies become marketable and attractive to purchasers because of the possibilities they offer in extending existing ways of using television, and their ability to lead practices of viewing in new directions. They also have to be integrated into the institutional and structural arrangements which shape how television is made, broadcast and financially supported. This case study considers how the new technology of the digital video recorder (also known as the **personal video recorder** or **PVR**) is changing current ways of watching television and ways in which television broadcasters and producers might make it.

*set-top box*
the electronic decoding equipment connected to home television sets that allows access to digital television signals.

In 2000 two digital video-recorder products – TiVo and ReplayTV – were introduced. These are **set-top boxes** which look rather like video recorders or the decoder boxes used to bring cable and satellite television to the television screen. Both were introduced to the American market first and then became available in Britain, posing a challenge to the extrapolation of trends towards commercially supported television that the history of the medium seems to imply. TiVo and ReplayTV, and the next generation of similar recorders, like the SkyPlus digital recorder, can record digitally and store programmes under the control of the viewer (like a videotape recorder) but also automatically build up a profile of the user on the basis of the programmes he or she has watched or recorded in the past. The machine will then trawl through the many channels available through digital television broadcasting or cable, and store programmes selectively according either to the user's instructions or to the machine's own expectations of what the viewer *might* want. This capability has been called the beginning of 'Me TV' – in other words the creation of a repertoire of programmes tailored to the desires of the individual viewer. Its implications are significant for both television viewers and broadcasters. It is possible to time-shift any programme and watch it at a different time to its original broadcast, and to record several programmes simultaneously. It is therefore possible never to watch television as it is scheduled at all, but simply to instruct the machine to create a menu of programmes which can be seen at any time. Some of these machines can also be programmed to omit commercials or to skip through them at high speed. Obviously, for channels which generate their income from advertising (as almost all channels do in the USA and as the majority of non-BBC channels do in Britain), this threatens to reduce their resources dramatically, because advertisers pay fees according to the numbers of viewers expected to watch their commercials.

From the perspectives of Television Studies and its accounts of the history of television, this development questions some of the trends identified in this chapter and supports others, changing the possible direction of the history of television in significant ways. This chapter has noted the change from a paternalistic notion of the viewer as a member of a collective national audience to the notion of the viewer as increasingly an individual consumer, offered multiple choices of television content by a proliferating number of channels. Rather than supervising the viewer's cultural education towards 'better' taste and informed citizenship, television institutions increasingly either offer mixed programme schedules which attempt to satisfy perceived desires and capture audiences through entertainment, or diversify their offerings into themed channels which offer related programme types to small **niche audiences**. Digital video recorders promise a future in which the identities of channels and the interest in and loyalty to the programming character of channels become largely irrelevant to television viewers. From among the hundreds of digital channels available now, the digital video recorder would become an agent for the viewer, taking over at least some of the work of programme selection for him or her. The channel on which a programme is broadcast, and the time at which it is broadcast, would become irrelevant since there would be no distinction as far as the viewer is concerned between programmes being broadcast 'live' and those which are recorded. Television would cease to consist of 'must-see' programmes when large audiences view the same live broadcast at the same time, except perhaps in rare times of crisis, such as the terrorist attack on the World Trade Center in New York in 2001. The heritage of liveness and the conception of the audience as a mass or series of masses would cease to apply. Viewer choice, along the lines of the almost infinite choice available to online internet shoppers today, would be taken to a dramatic extreme.

The response to digital video recorders among American television producers was one of anxiety or even panic, since US television culture is almost exclusively funded by the advertising which digital recorders can eliminate for their users. However, virtual digital advertising is one response which is currently being tried, and which may prove widespread in the future. Rather than screening commercials separated from programme content, advertisers are able to buy virtual product placement. This entails the insertion of logos, products or posters created in digital form into the camera shots of programmes. For example, a scene in which characters stand in a city street might have poster hoardings, or a soft-drink dispensing machine, inserted into the background of the shot as an advertisement for the soft drink. This technique was pioneered in the American CBS News programme's coverage of the millennium celebrations in New York's Times Square in 2000, where a large logo for the rival NBC television network was digitally 'pasted out' of the pictures broadcast by CBS. Virtual hoardings are already inserted digitally into pitch-side advertising barriers in some American sports coverage. So the distinctions between advertising and programme content, and between 'live' images and virtually enhanced ones, are eroded in order to preserve the links between programme production funding and commercial advertising in American television.

Current predictions are that by 2010, 30 per cent of British households will have a **PVR**. In homes equipped with a PVR, viewers watch commercial channels more than BBC, but 77 per cent of PVR users now skip the advertisements in the programmes they record. Research by companies involved in selling television advertising slots shows that PVR users watch more television, enjoy it more and watch it more attentively. They are less distracted because they can pause programmes even during their broadcast, and return to the same point when they have finished the activity that interrupted their viewing. PVRs, audience fragmentation due to increase in the number of channels now available, and the increased take-up of subscription channels that are not funded by advertising may lead to the gradual demise of advertising-supported **terrestrial** channels such as ITV, Channel 4 and Five. This is the background to **Ofcom**'s proposal in 2004 to set up a Public Service Publisher Fund that would be used to support **public service** programming in the absence of advertising-based

**niche audiences** particular groups of viewers defined by age group, gender or economic status, for example, who may be the target audience for a programme.

Ofcom  the Office of Communications, a government body responsible for regulating television and other communications media in Britain.

*continued*

money to fund public service programmes that might attract few viewers. Recent research undertaken by the media research company PHD Group (Alps 2004) suggests that there will be a decline in advertisement 'impacts' (the number of times a viewer will see a thirty-second advertisement during a period of viewing) by between 6 and 12 per cent by 2010, because PVRs and subscription channels enable viewers not to come across advertisements at all or to skip through them. However, the same research shows that viewers skip advertisements they have seen before (normally the frequently shown ones for low-value products like washing powder) but stop skipping in order to watch less frequently shown advertisements for more expensive items and for **brands** that invest a lot of money in elaborate advertisements. Viewers also praise the entertainment value of some advertisements and both choose to watch them and remember them. The increase in programme sponsorship also enables advertisers to reach viewers during programme time rather than in commercial breaks, as does the product placement of brands and products within programmes. Advertisers want viewers who are likely to pay attention to advertisements which occur in programmes they watch intensely and to the sponsorship sequences attached to the programme.

The future of television may involve challenges to the current expectation that television images are records of an environment which actually existed in front of the camera, and the expectation that programme content and advertising are identifiably different. But drawing on the account of television history in this chapter, which stresses the power of television institutions to shape viewing practices at the same time as being attentive in responding to apparent viewer desires, it is also important to note the continuity between present and future which American broadcasters show in their response to the digital video recorder. For, rather than considering different ways of organising television along non-advertising-supported lines, the broadcasters attempt to use another aspect of current and future television technology to address the challenge posed by digital video recorders. Just as the digital video recorder uses digital technology to alter viewing habits and television's relationship to the viewer, so advertisers are able to use digital editing technology to insert advertising into programmes in new ways. The economic structure of television in commercially funded systems maintains itself by this means, demonstrating the inertia and power of institutional relationships between programme funding, broadcasting and consumer culture.

**brand recognition**
the ability of audiences to recognise the distinctive identity of a product, service or institution and the values and meanings associated with it.

## ACTIVITY 2.7

How do the issues around the personal video recorder mentioned in the case study rely on ideas about the historical development of television that have been discussed earlier in this chapter and in other sources?

## SUMMARY OF KEY POINTS

- The history of television can be told in many different ways, depending on which evidence is selected and how it is approached.
- The evidence for writing television history includes audio-visual records of programmes, and also printed sources and archival documents.
- Television institutions have rarely preserved historical material, though new opportunities for repeating programmes of the past are changing this situation.
- The invention of television and the development of television institutions need not have happened in the ways they did.
- The political, economic and cultural conditions in which television developed affect the ways it is made, watched and organised.
- The future of television will be affected by technologies, institutions, regulations and the expectations of audiences.


## Further reading

Allen, J., 'The social matrix of television: invention in the United States', in E. A. Kaplan (ed.), *Regarding Television: Critical Approaches – An Anthology* (Los Angeles, Calif.: AFI, 1983), pp. 109–19.

Bignell, J., S. Lacey and M. Macmurraugh-Kavanagh (eds), *British Television Drama: Past, Present and Future* (Basingstoke: Palgrave, 2000).

Born, G., *Uncertain Vision: Birt, Dyke and the Reinvention of the BBC* (London: Vintage, 2005).

Brunsdon, C., 'What is the television of television studies?', in C. Geraghty and D. Lusted (eds), *The Television Studies Book* (London: Arnold, 1998), pp. 95–113.

Bryant, S., *The Television Heritage: Television Archiving Now and in an Uncertain Future* (London: BFI, 1989).

Caughie, J., *Television Drama: Realism, Modernism, and British Culture* (Oxford: Oxford University Press, 2000).

Cooke, L., *British Television Drama: A History* (London: BFI, 2003).

Corner, J., *Critical Ideas in Television Studies* (Oxford: Clarendon, 1999).

—— (ed.), *Popular Television in Britain* (London: BFI, 1991).

Corrigan, P., 'On the difficulty of being sociological (historical materialist) in the study of television: the "moment" of English television, 1936–1939', in T. Syvertsen (ed.), *1992 and after: Nordic Television in Transition* (Bergen: University of Bergen, 1990), pp. 130–60.

Crisell, A., *An Introductory History of British Broadcasting* (London: Routledge, 1997).

Franklin, B. (ed.), *British Television Policy: A Reader* (London: Routledge, 2001).

Gripsrud, J. 'Television, broadcasting, flow: key metaphors in TV theory', in C. Geraghty and D. Lusted (eds), *The Television Studies Book* (London: Arnold, 1998), pp. 17–32.

Harvey, S., 'Channel 4 television from Annan to Grade', in S. Hood (ed.), *Behind the Screens* (London: Lawrence & Wishart, 1994), pp. 102–29.

Hill, J. and M. McLoone (eds), *Big Picture Small Screen: The Relations between Film and Television* (Luton: University of Luton Press, 1997).

Hollingsworth, M. and R. Norton-Taylor, *Blacklist: The Inside Story of Political Vetting* (London, Hogarth, 1988).

Hood, S. (ed.), *Behind the Screens: The Structure of British Television in the Nineties* (London: Lawrence & Wishart, 1994).

Johnson, C. and R. Turnock (eds), *ITV Cultures: Independent Television over Fifty Years* (London: Open University Press, 2005).

Lacey, S., *Tony Garnett* (Manchester: Manchester University Press, 2007).

Mackay, H. and T. O'Sullivan (eds), *The Media Reader: Continuity and Transformation* (London: Sage, 1999).

Nichols, B., *Introduction to Documentary* (Bloomington, Ind.: Indiana University Press, 2001).

O'Sullivan, T., 'Television, memories and cultures of viewing 1950–65', in J. Corner (ed.), *Popular Television in Britain: Studies in Cultural History* (London: BFI, 1991), pp. 159–81.

Scannell, P., 'Television and history', in J. Wasko (ed.), *A Companion to Television* (Malden, Mass., and Oxford: Blackwell, 2005), pp. 51–66.

—— 'Public service broadcasting: the history of a concept', in A. Goodwin and G. Whannel (eds), *Understanding Television* (London: Routledge, 1990), pp. 11–29.

Smith, A., *Television: An International History*, second edition (Oxford: Oxford University Press, 1998).

Uricchio, W., 'Rituals of reception, patterns of neglect: Nazi television and its postwar representation', *Wide Angle*, 11:1 (1989), pp. 48–66.

Wayne, M., *Dissident Voices: The Politics of Television and Cultural Change* (London: Pluto, 1998).

Whitehouse, M., *Cleaning up TV: From Protest to Participation* (London: Blandford, 1967).

Winston, B., *Media Technology and Society: A History* (London: Routledge, 1998).

# Television Cultures

**3**

# Television Cultures

## Introduction

This chapter deals with theories of television institutions that analyse how the making and distribution of programmes take place in the present. It looks at British patterns of commercial and **public service** broadcasting, and places these in the context of American and European television. Television in the developed world is still largely organised on national lines, but the increasing significance of international flows from West to East and North to South has been hotly debated, so any discussion of television today needs to take account of the social and political significance of how transnational and national cultures of broadcasting work in relation to each other. What is at issue is the degree to which the meanings of television are dependent on the kinds of institutions which make and broadcast it, and the conclusions which can be drawn from studying television in terms of its ownership, organisation and spread around the world. There are inequalities in production funding, and different roles of domestic and imported programming in national television cultures, and this chapter refers to television in the less developed world to explain how theorists of television have understood these inequalities.

One of the most significant theories for explaining how television is organised today is that of **globalisation**. This can refer to the phenomenon whereby some programmes or **genres** of television have spread across different nations and cultures, so that the television schedules of different countries can seem surprisingly familiar. One way of explaining this is to use the concept of **media imperialism**, in which it is argued that 'world patterns of communication flow, both in density and in direction, mirror the system of domination in the economic and political order' (Sinclair *et al.* 1999: 173). A second aspect of globalisation is the power of corporations which are relatively independent of nation-states, and broadcast by satellite into several countries or regions. Theorists of television have debated whether globally broadcast programmes and global television corporations have brought new opportunities and freedoms, or whether they have imposed a deadening uniformity on the diverse cultures of the world. An important question which underlies this debate is whether television institutions both embody and transmit **ideological** 'messages' which are the result of their ownership, their relationship to national broadcasting **regulations** and their adoption of particular cultural values. As Chris Barker (1997: 27) notes, the term 'global television' 'implies all the various configurations of public and commercial television which are regulated, funded and viewed within the boundaries of nation-states and/or language communities'.

This chapter provides an account of the critical models which can be employed to evaluate these issues, and the divergent conclusions that have been and could be drawn from them.

## British television in global contexts

Britain is relatively unusual in global terms because its major broadcasting organisations mainly show programmes made in their own country. Some British programmes are also sold to many overseas countries:

- The BBC's new *Doctor Who* has been sold to twenty-eight countries, including Australia, Canada, France, Germany, Israel, Italy, New Zealand, Sweden, Thailand, and the Sci-Fi channel in the USA.
- The natural history series *Planet Earth* has been sold to Australia, Canada, Italy, South Africa and Spain.
- The comedy series *The Office* had been broadcast in eighty countries by 2006.
- The children's programme *Teletubbies* has been sold to Australia, Estonia, Israel, New Zealand, Portugal and the USA, and has a regular audience of over five million in China.

BBC Worldwide, the commercial arm of the BBC which distributes both BBC and other British programmes overseas, has invested in two new programmes by *Teletubbies'* creators Ragdoll Productions in the expectation of further success.

Nevertheless, American television far exceeds British television or television from any other European country in export revenue and coverage. According to a feature article in the *Radio Times* listings magazine (Eden 2006), the most popular programme in the world is the American drama series about police crime-scene investigators *CSI: Miami*. In the list of most viewed programmes around the world, compiled by comparing charts from most of the world's countries, American programmes – including *Lost*, *Desperate Housewives*, *The Simpsons*, *CSI* and *Without a Trace* – dominate. While British programmes are relatively successful as exports, partly because of the importance of the English language as a shared language for business around the world, British television is made primarily for a domestic UK audience.

### ACTIVITY 3.1

Are there any programmes in this week's British television listings that will be broadcast with foreign dialogue translated in subtitles? Whom do you think these programmes are targeting?

### ACTIVITY 3.2

Which British programmes do you think are least suitable for foreign sale? Why is this?

Figure 3.1 *Teletubbies* © BBC/Ragdoll

**audience share** the percentage of viewers estimated to have watched one channel as opposed to another channel broadcasting at the same time.

**subscription** payment to a television broadcaster in exchange for the opportunity to view programmes on certain channels that are otherwise blocked.

**free-to-air** television programming for which viewers make no direct payment.

**Ofcom** the Office of Communications, a government body responsible for regulating television and other communications media in Britain.

**digital television** television pictures and sound encoded into the ones and zeros of electronic data. Digital signals can also be sent back down cables by viewers, making possible interaction with television programmes.

There are nearly twenty-four million households with televisions in Britain, representing all but a tiny percentage of the total households in the country, and the average British person watches about three and a half hours of television per day. When this viewing is divided between channels, BBC1 and ITV1 have **audience shares** of about 22 per cent each, with BBC2 and Channel 4 gaining equal shares of about 10 per cent each and Five about 6 per cent, leaving about 30 per cent of the audience divided between the many channels available only via Freeview, cable or satellite. In 2005, 3.3 million British homes had cable television, while 7.3 million homes were **subscribers** to satellite television services. In comparison to the USA, where cable television has been spectacularly successful, British people seem unwilling to exchange a television culture based on **free-to-air** high-quality programmes for the promise of increased choice which both cable and satellite bring. However, in 2005, **Ofcom** figures showed that 62 per cent of British households had **digital television**. About one-fifth of British homes were getting digital television through the Freeview system that receives television signals through a rooftop aerial, and this means of accessing more channels seems suited to British people's preference for free-to-air television. Cable and satellite television in Britain have continued to grow in significance but at a slow rate. It is very expensive to set up cable networks because of the physical work of wiring up streets and houses across the country, and cable providers borrowed massive sums from banks on the promise of future profits. Since the take-up of cable television is still small, and the introduction of digital television promises hundreds of channels which do not have to be delivered by cable, there are serious questions to be asked about the future profitability of cable in Britain. Satellite television has been more successful at introducing the concept of payment for television channels with mixed content (such as Sky 1) and the concept of direct payment for specific special programmes (such as championship boxing matches).

Digital television enables broadcasters to extend **pay-per-view** television because there are hundreds of channels available on which to stream programmes for which viewers might be prepared to pay. However, the availability of hundreds or even thousands of television channels does not mean that there are very many channels offering mixed programme schedules like those currently offered by **terrestrial** broadcasters. One reason for this is that the television services are owned by a small number of large corporations which offer similar services. Owners of the transmission equipment (the satellites and cable networks on which programmes are carried) make the most profit by providing at least some of the content, so the big firms owning production facilities are also often involved in mergers or joint agreements with the companies which distribute television. The experience of multi-channel television in other countries, such as the USA, shows that an average viewer watches only eight or ten channels with some regularity, and there is little benefit to broadcasters in duplicating services across more channels than this. So the remaining digital capacity can be devoted to pay-per-view movies and subscription channels in which a large range of films or other attractive programmes are available with staggered start times, such as on the Sky movie channels. It is possible to view a film starting at 8.00, 8.30, 9.00 and so on, with one channel devoted to each different screening. Channels are also devoted to shopping services, sports and particular kinds of pop music.

The availability of multi-channel television in developed countries such as Britain has the effect of diminishing audiences for the terrestrial channels as hundreds of new channels split the audience. For commercial channels such as ITV and Five, the splitting of the audience threatens their income from advertisements, since smaller audiences mean less revenue from advertisers unless especially valuable sections of the audience (such as employed childless people in their twenties with surplus income) can be targeted by their programmes. Falling audiences for non-commercial network terrestrial television channels such as Britain's BBC pose a threat to their right to funding, since they cannot expect viewers to pay television **licence fees** if they are rarely watching BBC programmes. But to try to grab audiences back by imitating the programme **formats** and audience address of commercial television programmes causes another problem for such channels since duplicating the programme forms of their rivals means they have no claim to being an essential alternative to commercial television. The BBC has responded to this by capitalising on their high **brand recognition** internationally to produce the global news and current affairs channel BBC World. This was set up in 1991, and was backed in 1996 by joint deals made with the American TCI subsidiary Flextech and the Discovery Channel to make and distribute BBC World programmes. But the 'objectivity' which is so much a part of BBC News's brand image has been a double-edged sword in some respects. The BBC faced exclusion from the Chinese and Saudi Arabian television markets because its reporting offended their governments.

While the sale of programmes to other national broadcasters and diversification into global channels are useful ways for broadcasters to consolidate their position in the international television market place, it is also possible to sell the *idea* of a programme, its format, rather than the programme itself. This process involves the

**pay-per-view**
specific television programmes (such as sports events or films) offered to subscribers on payment of a fixed one-off fee.

**terrestrial**
broadcasting from a ground-based transmission system, as opposed to broadcasting via satellite.

**licence fee** an annual payment by all owners of television sets, which is the main source of income for the BBC.

**format** the blueprint for a programme, including its setting, main characters, genre, form and main themes.

**brand recognition** the ability of audiences to recognise the distinctive identity of a product, service or institution and the values and meanings associated with it.

sale of a programme idea and its narrative structure, character relationships and setting, often including the scripts for batches of episodes. So, rather than buying tapes of the original programme itself, overseas broadcasters acquire the template or set of instructions which enable them to remake the programme using their own facilities, performers and native language and locations. *Strictly Come Dancing*, for example, had been made in twenty-seven countries by 2006, using the same format as in Britain but with local contestants, judges and presenters. The overseas versions were shown in Germany, Spain, Poland and Russia, and the US version, *Dancing with the Stars*, drew the largest audience for an entertainment programme on the ABC network in 2005–6. But programmes whose formats gained large audiences in one country do not always succeed in another. The US sitcom *The Golden Girls* was tried in Britain (on ITV), using scripts from the US version with small adjustments for the British context. The idea of remaking the programme must have seemed attractive to producers, since the US version had already been a staple part of Channel 4's prime-time schedule. However, although the cast of the remake included well-known British comedy actresses, the programme was a commercial and critical failure and was cancelled after just six weeks. *Married for Life* was a British version of the successful US sitcom *Married . . . with Children*, which ran for over two hundred episodes in America, but the ITV show was cancelled after only one series. Nevertheless, some television companies specialise in the development and sale of formats, and there have been spectacular successes. The company Action Time creates formats for quiz programmes, and has sold these formats widely in Britain and abroad, while the Dutch company Endemol developed *Big Brother*, and its vast audiences in Holland were paralleled by the commercial success of the programme when the format was subsequently sold around the world.

---

## ACTIVITY 3.3

Look at the closing credits of a selection of current programmes to see which are co-productions with overseas companies. What are the common features of the co-productions you find?

---

## Global television

The term globalisation has several possible meanings. It can refer to:

- products of global corporations, whether these are concrete products like shoes or textual products like television programmes.
- the distribution system which circulates these products, like the global network of transmission satellites used by television broadcasters.
- the consumers of products distributed in this way, the global audiences.

Theorists of television have emphasised that at the levels of production, distribution and consumption it is possible for the significance of global television to change, and argue that globalisation is not a natural and unstoppable process. In production, global television corporations can be restrained by national or local laws and regulations which make them operate differently in different places. Global distribution networks may transmit the same television programme over a very wide area, but the ways in which the programme is received (by whom, how, and the significance of receiving global television in a particular society) will be different in different contexts. John Sinclair and his fellow authors (Sinclair *et al.* 1999: 176) explain that 'Although US programmes might lead the world in their transportability across cultural boundaries, and even manage to dominate schedules on some channels in particular countries, they are rarely the most popular programmes where viewers have a reasonable menu of locally produced programmes to choose from.' So the theory of globalisation in Television Studies is a way of addressing both processes which homogenise television and those which reduce differences, but also a way of addressing processes of differentiation. Furthermore, globalisation theory brings together approaches to television which concern economic, institutional, textual and reception practices.

One of the ways of approaching television globalisation is to consider it as part of **postmodernism**. The American theorist Fredric Jameson uses the term 'postmodernism' to refer to the ways in which cultural products (such as television programmes) as well as physical products (such as bananas) have become part of the global **capitalist** economy. Jameson's political background is in **Marxism**, and therefore he emphasises how the economic basis of capitalism affects television and media culture, and how the production and reception of television carry on the same principles of inequality and consumerism which are found in other aspects of contemporary commerce. When we analyse television programmes, Jameson argues, they turn out to carry the political **ideologies** of contemporary capitalist culture.

As an example of how this theory works, consider the background to the comedy-drama series *Ugly Betty*, shown on Channel 4 in 2007, and the meanings which underlie its **narratives**. The series was made by the American production company Ventarosa in partnership with Touchstone Television, which is owned by the Disney Corporation. It is based on a telenovela made for Colombian television titled *Yo soy Betty, la fea* ('I am Betty, the ugly one'), in which an unattractive, working-class young woman manages to get a job at a top fashion magazine, and despite being ridiculed by its beautiful but bitchy employees makes herself indispensable to the magazine's success. *Ugly Betty* adapts the Colombian narrative into an American setting in New York, casting America Ferrera as Betty in heavy make-up which includes braces on her teeth, thick glasses and very unfashionable clothes. Whereas the original telenovela was shot on videotape, relatively inexpensively, *Ugly Betty* is shot on the visually richer medium of film, and combines elements of drama, comedy, social comment and mystery in an ongoing storyline involving a conspiracy by the magazine's supposedly dead former editor and Betty's father's risk of being exposed as an illegal immigrant. The series is a combination of American and Latin American television forms within the same programme, and is produced by an American corporation for a Western television audience. Indeed, it is a running joke in the series that Betty's family, who are Latin American, like to watch telenovelas with Spanish dialogue in which a melodramatic and ridiculous story is told about a woman working as a maid in a wealthy household who has inappropriate romantic relationships with its family members and even a priest. The woman

**postmodernism**
the most recent phase of capitalist culture, the aesthetic forms and styles associated with it, and the theoretical approaches developed to understand it.

**capitalism**  the organisation of an economy around the private ownership of accumulated wealth, involving the exploitation of labour to produce profit that creates such wealth.

**Marxism**  the political and economic theories associated with the German nineteenth-century theorist Karl Marx, who described and critiqued capitalist societies and proposed communism as a revolutionary alternative.

**narrative**  an ordered sequence of images and sound that tells a fictional or factual story.

playing the maid in the programme-within-the-programme is Selma Hayek, *Ugly Betty*'s producer, herself a former telenovela actress. So a product which has its origins in the culture of Colombia recycles and adds to its antecedents, with an eye to international sales. After a successful debut on the ABC network, *Ugly Betty* has been sold to other countries' television channels, and in early 2007 these included:

- in Europe: Britain, Ireland, Norway, Sweden, Finland, Greece and Spain
- outside Europe: New Zealand, Australia, Fiji, Malaysia, Singapore, Hong Kong and Canada.

**textual analysis**
a critical approach which seeks to understand a television text's meanings by undertaking detailed analysis of its image and sound components, and the relationships between those components.

It is at this point that a **textual analysis** of the programme can illuminate the underlying subtextual meanings of the series, to show how it might resonate with current concerns and problems which might be recognised by its audience in many developed societies. It could be argued that *Ugly Betty* is successful because it responds to the current cultural concern with the roles of women in the workplace, and especially the idea that women may need to be attractive to men as well as competent at their jobs in order to gain acceptance. Among other things, *Ugly Betty* is about the pressure to be both attractive and successful in the world of work, though it makes this issue a subject for comedy as well as for serious comment. Indeed, when Channel 4 made trailers in advance of the British screening of the series, they placed seemingly attractive female models around a swimming pool, but a camera movement reveals another model emerging from the pool in Betty's glasses, and then, as the models smile at the camera, it is clear that they are all wearing braces on their teeth. So an ideological analysis of *Ugly Betty* as a globalised cultural product would emphasise how it engages with questions of gender and identity (what are the expectations about women today, and how can women deal with a world in which these expectations might disempower them?) and tries to resolve them in a fictional form.

At the end of 2006, the ABC network initiated a campaign entitled 'Be Ugly 07', which aimed to draw attention to the social pressure on women to conform to images of beauty appearing in the media. The television series' potential for export to many other countries suggests that these issues are relevant to a much wider audience than the USA alone, but *Ugly Betty* addresses them by making them the subject of entertaining comedy and by staging the world of fashion and glamour in a very visually attractive way. There are numerous conventionally beautiful actresses (and actors) in the series, costumes sourced from real high-fashion designers, and both designers and models appearing in the programme in minor roles as themselves.

## Cultural imperialism

One of the problems when conducting an analysis such as that of *Ugly Betty* is that it can seem that one programme which is seen by different audiences around the world has the same meanings and significance wherever and by whomever it is watched. In the 1980s, when these questions were taken up by a number of theorists of television, it was particularly striking that American programmes were the ones most exported beyond their own borders, and seen by the largest worldwide audiences. In a famous study, television research by Tamar Liebes and Elihu Katz (1990) found that viewers of the 1980s American soap opera *Dallas* in different national cultures understood it in very different ways. They chose to study viewers of *Dallas* because it had been exported to a large number of nations, and had been seen as an indication that the future of television would be an increasing global homogeneity of programmes dominated by glossy American dramas. But, perhaps surprisingly, *Dallas*'s representation of the 'American dream' of financial success and personal happiness was understood by Jewish members of a kibbutz in Israel as proof that money does *not* bring happiness. By contrast, members of a North African co-operative thought that *Dallas* proved how money rescues people from everyday problems. Russian Jews who had recently arrived in Israel from the Soviet system believed that *Dallas* was a subtle critique of capitalism which unconsciously exposed its contradictions. So Liebes and Katz's study showed that, contrary to many people's expectations at the time, the meanings of television programmes are understood in relation to the cultural environment and expectations of viewers, and are not injected like a pernicious drug into the cultures where they are watched.

Sinclair and his fellow authors (Sinclair *et al.* 1999: 183) noted that 'there tends to be a more distanced realm of "pure entertainment" within which US programmes are processed – as markers of modish modernity, as a "spectacular" world – compared to more culturally specific responses made to domestic and other sources'. In the 1950s and 1960s the theory of **cultural imperialism** was developed by such theorists as Herbert Schiller and versions of this theory were used to discuss the global export of Western, and especially American, television. It was this cultural imperialist model of global television that Liebes and Katz's (1990) study reacted against. Imperialism refers to the building of empires by European nations, especially during the nineteenth century in Africa and Asia. The purpose of empire was to secure natural resources and trade routes in order to feed the industrialising European nations and to provide markets for the goods produced in their factories, but by the end of the Second World War these empires were being dismantled. Cultural imperialism refers to the similar process by which Western nations exercise cultural power over less developed countries, rather than exercising the military, legal and trading power which empire involved. According to this argument, the export of cut-price television programmes (as well as cinema films, pop music and other cultural goods) promotes the commercial interests of Western corporations, especially American ones, and thus supports the political and military interests of the West. By means of the images of affluent Western lifestyles portrayed in television programmes, consumer culture is spread across regions and populations which increasingly aspire to the Western products and expectations which their meagre resources make it difficult for them to acquire.

The crudest forms of this cultural imperialism thesis, which simply proclaim that the world is being Americanised, pay too little attention to the specifics of the local and national organisation of television consumption. They also ignore the flows of television within regions, based for instance on the legacy of the languages of the former empires, which make possible the exchange of programmes in Spanish among the countries of Latin America. There are regional television flows as well as global ones, and sometimes these regional flows allow for reversals of the more common North to South and West to East trade in television, as in the export of telenovelas from Latin America to Europe (see the case study at the end of this chapter). The Colombian telenovela on which *Ugly Betty* was based, for example, was remade in

**cultural imperialism** the critical argument that powerful nations and regions (especially those of the Western world) dominate less developed nations and regions by exporting values and ideologies.

many countries in which the original format of storylines and characters was retained but adjusted to the local language and setting. These versions were:

- *El amor no es como lo pintan* (Mexico, 2000)
- *Jassi Jaissi Koi Nahin* (India, 2003)
- *Esti Ha'mechoeret* (Israel, 2003)
- *Verliebt in Berlin* (Germany, 2005)
- *Ne rodis' krasivoy* (Russia, 2005)
- *La fea más bella* (Mexico, 2006)
- *Lotte* (Netherlands, 2006)
- *Yo soy Bea* (Spain, 2006)
- *Maria, i Asximi* (Greece, 2007)

In the early twenty-first century a small number of international corporations (such as General Electric, which owns the broadcaster NBC, and Sony) control the manufacture of television equipment, the making of programmes and related media interests such as film studios and magazine publishing. This **vertical integration** represents not cultural imperialism by a nation but a form of corporate imperialism. Most of the world's largest media corporations are US owned, and have financial interests in a wide variety of products. They also make deals with smaller companies (such as the makers of fast food or toys) to create interrelated promotions, advertising and sales opportunities. Although many people are aware of the importance of multinational companies and global business, the sheer extent and interconnectedness of the modern economy, and its dependence on television and other media as channels of communication and trade, are often underestimated.

**vertical integration**
the control by media institutions of all levels of a business, from the production of products to their distribution and means of reception.

## The big seven media corporations

This list shows some of the main holdings of seven of the world's biggest television-owning corporations in 2004, with emphasis on television operations relevant to Britain.

- General Electric: NBC network (USA), Telemundo network (USA), European channels including Sci-Fi (UK), CNBC Europe, 13ème Rue (France), 13th Street (Germany), Calle 13 (Spain), Studio Universal (Germany, Italy), Universal (Latin America), CNBC Asia, and more than fifteen cable television channels in the USA.
- Time Warner: WB network (USA); and television channels including HBO (Home Box Office) (USA), Court TV (USA), Cartoon Network (Europe, USA, Latin America, Asia), Turner Classic Movies (TCM) (USA, Europe, Asia, Latin America), Cable News Network (CNN) (USA, Europe, Asia, Latin America).
- Walt Disney: ABC network (USA); Touchstone Television, Buena Vista Television, Walt Disney Television (US television production companies); television channels in the USA and Europe including ESPN, Disney, A&E, History Channel, Biography Channel, Lifetime and E!.

- News Corporation: Fox network (USA), Star TV (satellite television, Asia), Fox film, sport and news channels (USA); and channels available internationally including FX and National Geographic; part owner of British Sky Broadcasting and its Sky channels.
- Bertelsmann: owns RTL Group, which operates thirty-four European television stations and produces programmes in forty countries; European television channels including Five (UK), RTL9 (France), RTL 4 and 5 (Netherlands), Yorin (Netherlands), RTL TVi, Club RTL, Plug TV (Belgium), RTL Télé Lëtzebuerg, BCE, Den 2.RTL, ENEX (Luxembourg), RTL Televizija (Croatia), Antena 3 (Spain), RTL Klub (Hungary).
- CBS: CBS network, UPN network and Showtime network (all USA); and channels available internationally including Showtime and Movie Channel.
- Viacom: Channels available internationally including MTV, Nickelodeon, VH1, Comedy Central, Paramount Comedy and TMF (The Music Factory).

---

## ACTIVITY 3.4

How would you find out who owns the television networks or channels you watch? Why is this information difficult to find by watching television?

---

The countries with the highest proportion of domestically produced television are the United States, Britain, Brazil and Japan, followed by Canada and Australia, which are able to use imports to top up a largely domestic production base. But most of the nations of South America, Africa and Asia have small television industries, insufficient revenue to make many programmes and depend on imports to fill 50 per cent or more of their schedules. The national television networks of Brazil and Mexico, for example, have the funding and facilities to make many of their own programmes, but television broadcasters in the developing world find it much less expensive to buy American or British television than to make their own. Episodes of US television series from several years ago can be acquired by broadcasters in the developing world for just a few hundred dollars, as part of a package of programmes. The production costs of these programmes have, of course, already been more than covered by showing them in the domestic American market, so that the money made from the export of older series is pure profit for the **networks** which sell them. The much higher production values and the aura of sophistication which often surrounds imported television in non-Western countries means that sectors of the television audience which are attractive to advertisers (such as employed young people with surplus income to spend on consumer goods) may be more likely to watch them. This not only has the effect of marginalising the products of the domestic television industry, reducing its chances of expansion, but fills the most popular broadcasting slots with Western programmes in which commercials advertising Western consumer products often appear. Even if crude Americanisation is not the result of this, consumerisation and the reinforcement of Western values may be.

**network** a television institution that transmits programmes through local or regional broadcasting stations that are owned by or affiliated to that institution.

---

### ACTIVITY 3.5

In what ways might television programmes originating in Western television cultures and exported to the developing world and television advertisements for consumer products associated with affluent Western lifestyles share similar ideologies and ways of addressing audiences?

---

## News, nations and the 'New World Order'

news value
the degree of
significance
attributed to a news
story, where items
with high news value
are deemed most
significant to the
audience.

actuality footage
television pictures
representing an event
that was filmed live.
The term usually
refers to pictures of
news events.

The ways of producing television news are similar in cultures other than Britain because the ways in which professional broadcasters do their work, and the ways they give **news value** to certain kinds of story, are held in common by the journalists of many nations and television institutions. Globalisation in television news can be regarded either positively or negatively (Gurevitch 1991). Technologies such as satellite broadcasting allow large and diverse audiences access to television news and live **actuality footage** of events such as the Olympic Games to be made available around the world. This provides possibilities for openness and democratic access to information which have never been available before. On the other hand, footage such as this has to conform to a version of news value which makes these events seem of global importance, and once they have been broadcast the events necessarily acquire global significance. Globalisation can be regarded negatively as the monopoly control of information by a few multinational broadcasters who impose Western news values across the world so that local cultures are drowned out by them. The increase in the quantity of television news which is available makes the activities of news broadcasters in hierarchising and explaining news more significant, because, with more news, the audience is assumed to need increased guidance and support in understanding it. The effect of this is to make the form of news simpler and regularised (reports are short, story structures simple), so that the difference between the news events that are reported is diminished. The conventions which organise news stories predominate over the information which those conventions are used to communicate. But even if control of television networks is concentrated in the hands of a few broadcasters, this does not mean that audiences will simply accept the ideological meanings carried in their news programmes. Global television news needs to be analysed also by looking at how global and international news broadcasting is organised, and how it is understood by audiences.

In the modern world the media contribute to new ways of thinking about time, space and people's relationships with the world around them. Since information circulates around the globe across the different time-zones in which people live, the local time and the sense of people's familiar space can be understood as partial and local variations within a global, international time and space. The activities of people in their local area can be seen in the contexts of international and global problems and opportunities, where traditional and historic ways of understanding oneself, one's community or nation are overlaid or even replaced by globally dominant ways of thinking. Television enables its audience to witness events in different places occurring in the local times of different nations and cultures. For example, international news broadcasts by **CNN** transmitted images of the 1991 Gulf War and the terrorist attacks on New York and Washington in 2001 around the world, images of the apparently comfortable lives and abundant consumer goods were beamed into the countries of the Eastern Bloc and aided the populations' desire for political change, and images representing Western culture, such as satellite broadcasting of MTV, stimulated change in the Soviet Union in the late 1980s. For Chris Barker (1997: 230),

> television on a global scale has the capacity to contribute to democracy (via the principles of diversity and solidarity) through its range of representations, genres, arguments and information. However, the vision of television as a diverse and plural public sphere is seriously compromised by its almost complete penetration by the interest-based messages and images of consumerism.

The international flow of television and its disruption of local cultures can be regarded as politically progressive, though the immediate impact of television has often been to intensify conflicts.

**CNN** Cable News Network, the first international satellite news channel, operating from the United States.

---

## ACTIVITY 3.6

Which kinds of events have been worthy of global broadcasting? What are the common features of these events?

---

Complete news programmes are broadcast by satellite by the American institution CNN, which broadcasts to about 130 countries with content in major regional languages (such as Spanish in Latin America), and Britain's Sky News and BBC World. The selection of news stories on national television networks around the world and the structure and form of news broadcasting are influenced by CNN because its global coverage and broadcasting have the effect of bringing its selection of stories to the attention of national broadcasters. CNN can also affect the events which are being reported as news, since coverage of events almost live on CNN can have the effect of altering the progress of a news event, for example by alerting officials to the perception of their actions abroad, or by attracting demonstrators to attend a protest which CNN is covering. However, it would be mistaken to claim that CNN (or any other global broadcaster, such as BBC World) has direct effects on shaping events or attitudes to them. Apart from the important theoretical insight in Television Studies that television's effects need to be considered within institutional, legal and cultural constraints which delimit and redirect them, there are specific restrictions on the gathering of news and the accessibility of global television news. Attempts to manage global news broadcast journalists by national politicians is common, in order to influence the representation of events outside a particular country where a global television news broadcaster is gathering news. The influence of global broadcasters is limited also by the fact that their programmes are in English and/or the languages spoken by the affluent elites who are attractive to advertisers, so that only a relatively privileged sector of many societies has access to the global news channels broadcasting via satellite or cable.

## BBC World

BBC World was launched in 1991 as BBC World Service Television. It draws on the global recognition of BBC Radio's World Service and uses the radio service's 250 correspondents and 57 regional bureaux, as well as BBC Television's studios, technicians and reporters, already stationed around the world. The scale of this operation makes the BBC the world's largest news-gathering organisation. Half of BBC World's twenty-four hours of television consists of news programmes, each half an hour in length, and the other half is BBC current affairs, factual and entertainment programmes.

BBC World is the biggest rival to the American CNN network, and has a contrasting style. Rather than emphasising breaking news and live broadcast of unfolding events, BBC World is based on the journalistic comment on news which its correspondents and reporters can offer, and the very diverse international coverage which it can provide by using the World Service's expert staff.

The twenty-four-hour broadcasts began to be beamed by the AsiaSat satellite, through an agreement with Hong Kong's Star TV, and in 1992 the service reached three continents, constituting 80 per cent of the world's population. By the end of 1992 the channel was being watched in six million homes and was especially welcomed in Asian countries such as India and Taiwan where broadcasting was dominated by national government-run channels. The Star TV satellite signal also carried an entertainment channel (with mainly American programmes), sports, music video and Mandarin-language programmes, making buying satellite dishes attractive for viewers wanting not only BBC World but also the satellite's other signals. Soon deals had been negotiated for BBC World to be broadcast by satellite to the Middle East, Africa, Europe, Russia, Canada, Japan and Latin America. The channel was the first to offer simultaneous translation of its English-language news programmes into regional languages, soon followed by its rival, CNN. In 1993, however, the global media owner Rupert Murdoch bought a controlling interest in Star TV and challenged BBC World's access to the Middle East, where his own Sky News network planned to begin a news service. In the subsequent arguments China blocked all satellite signals, denying any global broadcaster access to its 4.8 million satellite television-owning households and damaging BBC World's expansion.

**iconic sign** in semiotics, a sign which resembles its referent. Photographs, for example, contain iconic signs resembling the objects they represent.

Sources of television news are perceived as unequal by television viewers, with some regarded as more reliable than others, and news tends to flow from North to South and from West to East. Such a situation provides fuel for arguments that global television news exacerbates the gap between the West and other regions of the world where news seems to happen, and the insulation of television news from the lives of its viewers. There is a paradox in the increasing quantity and speed of international television news. Television, with its focus on liveness, and the showing of actualities from distant places, draws on Western culture's belief in the power of photographic images to bear witness to real events (the **iconicity** of photography), so that seeing something happen on television news claims the immediacy and veracity of fact. But at the same time the proliferation of representations of realities

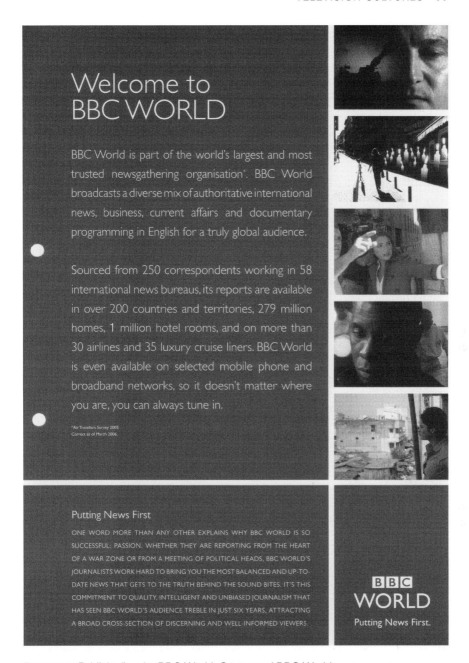

Figure 3.2 Publicity flyer for BBC World. Courtesy of BBC World.

on television news distances what the viewer sees from his or her own physical every-day experience. It was because of this sense of separation and unreality that the French theorist Jean Baudrillard (1991) proclaimed that the 1991 Gulf War was unreal, a **simulation** produced by television news because it was experienced only as images except by the few people who fought in it. Viewers who can afford

simulation
a representation that mirrors an aspect of reality so perfectly that it takes the place of the reality it aims to reproduce.

access to numerous news sources (cable and satellite television channels, for example, but also internet news and email news services) will enjoy greater diversity and quantity of news, but will be further separated from the experience of news events than people who do not have access to so much information. It has often been claimed that the world is divided not only into the rich and the poor but increasingly into the information-rich and the information-poor. Television contributes to the creation of the '**information society**', in which Baudrillard has argued that for the information-rich West there is only **spectacle** in this information and no content. However, such sweeping theories are limited to generalisations about the West and largely to Western television audiences. The blanket coverage of the terrorist attacks on American landmarks in September 2001, when hijacked airliners were flown into the World Trade Center in New York and the Pentagon in Washington, with great loss of life, raises questions about global news and reality. Were these events 'more real' because they were shown almost live around the world to millions of viewers, or 'less real' because the events were so quickly accommodated into the formats and routines of news broadcasting?

Television news broadcasters, it is argued, contain and exchange news in a closed circuit among themselves, producing a global news market which homogenises news. Evidence for this view includes the fact that television news footage is offered to broadcasters by **news agencies** such as Eurovision and Asiavision, and is accessed by British news broadcasters through the European Broadcasting Union (EBU). Six times a day, satellite links exchange news footage between Eurovision and Asiavision, for example. As well as using these mechanisms for exchanging news footage, news broadcasters have set up exchange agreements with news broadcasters in other countries. The BBC, for example, has an exchange agreement with the American ABC network. Satellite technology enables the international news agencies, such as Visnews and Worldwide Television Network, to operate twenty-four hours a day, sending both raw footage and complete news packages to national and regional broadcasters. Because of the different languages of television broadcasting in different nations, the news agencies mainly distribute images without commentary. This makes it more likely that their news footage will be perceived as objective by news editors, and this impression is reinforced by the neutrally phrased written material which the agencies provide with the footage to explain what their pictures denote. The agency footage can have a range of meanings attached to it by the voiceover commentaries which individual news broadcasters add.

Among the proliferation of television channels in recent years some of the new ones address audiences who have been dissatisfied with competitors and are most likely to produce **negotiated readings** of mainstream television. The international television channel Al Jazeera was launched in 1996 and initially broadcast only in Arabic from Qatar, funded by that country's ruling emir. Its aim was to offer a new kind of journalism to audiences in the Middle East, following Western norms by reporting opposing views instead of the official news agendas and opinions of government sources in the region. But despite this aim for objectivity and neutrality, the channel repeatedly annoyed Western governments, especially that of the USA, by broadcasting videotape messages sent to it by the anti-Western Islamic organisation al-Qaeda. These videotapes featured Osama Bin Laden, widely regarded as the terrorist leader behind al-Qaeda and the instigator of numerous attacks on Western targets, including the destruction of the World Trade Center in 2001.

---

**information society**
a contemporary, highly developed culture (especially Western culture) where the production and exchange of information are more significant than conventional industrial production.

**spectacle**
a fascinating image which draws attention to its immediate surface meanings and offers visual pleasure for its own sake.

**news agency**
a media institution that gathers news reports and distributes them to its customers (who include television news broadcasters).

**negotiated reading**
a viewer interpretation of a television text where the viewer understands meaning in relation to his or her own knowledge and experience, rather than simply accepting the meaning proposed by the text.

During the Afghan War in 2001 two American 'smart' bombs destroyed the channel's office in Kabul, though this was said to have been an accident; and during the invasion of Iraq in 2003, US missiles hit its office in Baghdad, killing a journalist.

Al Jazeera started a new English-language channel in 2006, Al Jazeera International, attracting prominent British and other non-Arab journalists to present its programmes. The former BBC news correspondent Rageh Omaar, for example, presents *Witness*, in which non-professional commentators (rather than academics or expert analysts) give first-hand accounts of news stories from around the world. The veteran presenter, interviewer and producer Sir David Frost hosts an hour of interviews and discussions with major world leaders and commentators. The opportunity to follow stories that have not received much coverage in existing national and international news, or have been covered from a predominantly Western point of view, is the main attraction of Al Jazeera to both its audiences and its journalists. But the perception that the channel is unlike CNN or BBC World in this respect also meant that some of its presenters and reporters were cautious about its links with political and religious movements attacking the Western powers. The controversial reputation of Al Jazeera in the West led Frost to check with British and American officials that the channel did not have links with al-Qaeda, for example (Whitaker 2006).

Al Jazeera employs over two hundred staff from thirty national backgrounds in its news team, which it claims will permit reporters with local knowledge to offer new perspectives on news stories. The agenda is to avoid the categorisation of news according to the stereotypes of Western-based channels, so that items from Africa, for example, will not be driven by the narratives about famine, Aids and war which have often dominated coverage of the continent. The programme schedule of the channel is timed to match the time-zones of its viewers, so that over one twenty-four-hour period, moving East to West, it broadcasts for four hours from Kuala Lumpur, eleven hours from Doha, five hours from London and four hours from Washington.

As well as offering English-speaking audiences new kinds of coverage, and a new *balance* of coverage that favours the developing world and non-Western nations, the channel expects to attract audiences from Muslim backgrounds who cannot speak Arabic but are interested in the non-Western perspectives of its journalists and may be **resistant** to coverage of news on Western channels such as CNN. To connect with this large audience is an important economic drive for the channel, since its aim to operate with an agenda different from the established channels like BBC World and CNN could be compromised by the cost, difficulty or unpopularity of being different. If enough viewers watch the new channel, income from advertising and subscriptions to its services will be sufficient to sustain it in the future. There are 1.2 billion Muslims in the potential global audience, but only about 240 million of them speak Arabic. Some of these non-Arabic speakers will be well-educated viewers who could form the core target for the advertising carried on Al Jazeera International.

The channel is initially available free of charge to viewers via cable and satellite, and broadband streaming on the internet is likely to follow. In Britain, it is carried by Sky, and when it launched at the end of 2006, Al Jazeera International hoped to find viewers in about eight million British households. With greater resistance to the channel's brand image in the USA – because of its screening of news footage

**resistance** the ways in which audiences make meaning from television programmes that is counter to the meanings thought to be intended, or that are discovered by close analysis.

and videotape contributions associated with terrorist attacks and resistance to US military action – it seems likely that Al Jazeera International may not penetrate deeply into the American television audience. However, it may be of interest to the large number of US viewers who are dissatisfied with the insular and largely patriotic news programming offered by US-based television networks and US-owned international television services. Already, according to Al Jazeera's press releases, the largest number of visitors to its English-language website are from the USA.

## The global and local interrelationship

On an average day in 1990, 2.5 billion people in more than 160 countries watched 750 million television sets. Four years later, another 100 million households had acquired televisions. The continuing growth in television ownership is happening most quickly in the developing countries of Africa, Asia and Central America, but there are still great differences between the wealthier and less wealthy countries of the world in the availability of television to their populations. Balnaves *et al.* (2001: 14) divided the world into least developed, developing and developed countries, then compared the number of television sets per thousand people in 1970 and 1997.

|      | *Least developed countries* | *Developing countries* | *Developed countries* |
|------|------------------------------|-------------------------|------------------------|
| 1970 | 0.5                          | 9.9                     | 263                    |
| 1997 | 23.0                         | 157.0                   | 548                    |

More recent figures were collected in 2003 and are now available on the internet in the *CIA World Fact Book*. The countries with the largest numbers of television sets per thousand people were:

- Bermuda: 1010 TV sets
- Monaco: 771 TV sets
- USA: 741 TV sets
- Malta: 703 TV sets
- Japan: 679 TV sets

The countries with fewest television sets per thousand people were:

- The Gambia: 3.1 TV sets
- Tanzania: 2.8 TV sets
- Comoros: 1.5 TV sets
- Chad: 1.0 TV set
- Eritrea: 0.2 TV sets

Some of these nations have very low levels of infrastructure (no electricity in rural areas, for example) and average incomes too low for people to buy televisions, so they have been ignored until recently by the global media corporations and the global brands which might support programme content with advertising. In this context it is important to consider not only what people watch, or even which organisations bring television to the viewer, but what the physical presence of a television within a household means to people in a developing country where TV ownership is not universal.

Viewers' experience of television is partly determined by their social positions in society, and differences between audiences are significant within cultures and nations as well as between them. Research by Leal (1990) on the role of television in the lives of a Brazilian working-class family, for example, showed how the uses of the television in the household, and the programmes watched on it, were affected by and had effects on the family's sense of social identity. The family had recently arrived in the city from a rural background. They kept portrait photographs on top of the television, commemorating previous generations and relatives who had migrated to distant parts of Brazil. Tucked into the picture-frames were the passport-size photographs of relatives who had also moved to the city. The assembly of pictures brought together the family's past and its urban present. The **telenovelas** which the family watched on television were dramas set in the city, and the television set, its programmes and the objects around it formed a complex set of negotiations with the family's past and the present, the country and the city, the household's family members and their absent relatives and friends. The television set was a key object among an ensemble of objects which all carried meanings for the family. These meanings were in their different ways associated with bridging gaps between past and present, country and city, household and community. The meanings of television in the household Leal studied were clearly different from the meanings of television in the lives of more affluent middle-class Brazilian landowners, for example. The study of television in this **anthropological** sense can show how it is not just programmes which are significant to television's place in global culture but the embedding of television as a cultural practice, a set of physical objects and a way of understanding one's identity and community.

The global dominance of Western television can easily seem to paper over local and regional differences. Western television theorists are sometimes beguiled by the presence of television familiar to them which is found outside its original cultural contexts. But the fact that Western television seems to be, or seems about to be, everywhere, and appears culturally powerful everywhere, might just reinforce the prejudice that only Western television is worth discussing in arguments about globalisation, whereas really the interrelations of Western with local and regional cultures need to be understood. The relationship between place and television culture is complex, and global television and global television corporations make local and regional differences more, not less, important. Local television cultures find their identities alongside or by resisting the globalisation of television, so that the dominance of global television becomes important to the production of local television. Local, in this connection, can also importantly mean regional, in that television cultures cross national boundaries to include speakers of the same language (like Spanish in much of Latin America, and in the states of the USA with large Spanish-speaking populations) or audiences which share similar cultural assumptions and ideologies (like the audiences in many nations of the Middle East who have shared Islamic beliefs).

The processes of globalisation are open to regulation by individual nations, rather than being an autonomous and unstoppable process, and global markets are regu-

**telenovela**
a fictional, continuing melodrama on television that lasts for a specific number of episodes. Telenovelas are particularly associated with South American television.

**anthropology**
the study of humankind, including the evolution of humans and the different kinds of human society existing in different times and places.

quota a proportion
of television
programming, such
as a proportion of
programmes made in
a particular nation.

free market
a television market
place where factors
such as quotas and
regulations do not
restrict the free
operation of
economic 'laws'
of supply and
demand.

deregulation
the removal of legal
restrictions or
guidelines that
regulate the
economics of the
television industry or
the standards which
programmes must
adhere to.

lated by contracts and by international and national laws. But the world organisations which oversee international television agreements generally support the lowering of national restrictions and **quotas**, because they seek to create a global **free market** economy in communications. The World Trade Organisation, the International Monetary Fund and regional agreements such as the North American Free Trade Agreement and the European Free Trade Association provide support for cross-border television exchanges which are based on the principles of unrestricted commercial exchange. The apparently free and uncontrollable television market is not a natural fact and depends on the taking of political decisions about **deregulation** and competition in television by nation-states and groupings of states. The European Parliament issued the Television Without Frontiers Directive in 1989, for example, which insists that the majority of programming in member states must originate from within that state. The directive has been periodically updated and modified since its creation, taking account of new developments in technology, and has gradually weakened its requirements to allow a more commercial market approach to television in Europe. Countries and regional groupings of countries tend both to deregulate and to encourage globalisation, but also introduce further regulation to protect their societies against it. However, in the global television landscape the concepts of society and nation are diminishing in usefulness. As the philosopher Anthony Giddens (1990) has argued, the concept of society as a unit bounded in time and space loses its force when, for example, live television news or sporting events confuse the sense of time and space by broadcasting across time-zones. Television also brings new ways of understanding space – like the notion of a global 'war on terrorism' or a New World Order, for example, which change people's sense of their place in the world. Because television broadcasts such a range of images of culture – like versions of what youth and age, domesticity, work and gender might mean – global television provides the possibility of reflecting on local cultures. Global television provides resources for people to think about themselves and their social environment, in the same ways that local or national television does. Sinclair and his fellow authors (Sinclair *et al.* 1999: 187) give this example:

> An Egyptian immigrant in Britain, for example, might think of herself as a Glaswegian when she watches her local Scottish channel, a British resident when she switches over to the BBC, an Islamic Arab expatriate in Europe when she tunes in to the satellite service from the Middle East, and a world citizen when she channel surfs on to CNN.

People around the world negotiate their sense of place, time and community in relation to local, regional and global television cultures, and they do this by borrowing from or resisting ways of thinking and living shown on the screen.

---

**ACTIVITY 3.7**

What are the main arguments for and against the influence of television globalisation? Which side of the debate do you find most persuasive, and why?

# Case study:   the Brazilian telenovela

There are about 450 million people in Latin America, and 85 per cent of its households had television sets at the end of the 1990s. About 15 per cent of households had cable or satellite television. Because of this growing television market, Western global media corporations have interests in Latin American broadcasting. Brazil itself has a population of over 160 million, and its population's output per person exceeds those of Poland and Russia, making the country an attractive market for advertisers. But Brazil is something of an exception to the global media imperialism thesis, since although its national television networks import nearly 40 per cent of their programmes, its most popular programmes are domestically made continuing dramas, the telenovelas. Brazil is a former colony of Portugal, its national language is Portuguese and it retains links with its former European master. The major broadcaster in Brazil is TV Globo, a commercial channel which has a 70 per cent share of the television audience. TV Globo is the fourth-largest **commercial television** network in the world (behind the three major US television networks), and in 2007 the television stations which were **affiliated** to it and contracted to broadcast Globo's programmes in their territories could reach 97 per cent of the country's population. There is minimal public service broadcasting in Brazil, such as educational or factual programming, and broadcasters are closely tied to the interests of politicians running the country's political parties. Many of Brazil's politicians are personally wealthy, and have significant financial stakes in broadcasting companies.

Historically, Brazilian television signifies modernity and social status, since the first television stations in the 1950s were set up in the major cities of Rio de Janeiro and São Paulo despite the rural character of much of the country, and the relatively expensive television sets were first owned by the affluent middle classes, whose lifestyles mimicked those of the United States. This American influence extended to the involvement of the American television technology producers General Electric and RCA, which supplied the broadcasting equipment. The telenovelas on Brazilian television continue this urban and Americanised trend, since they are predominantly set in urban locations, and feature performers drawn from the theatre, film and television elites based in Rio de Janeiro. The programmes themselves must also be considered in relation to the advertisements which are broadcast in and around them, in the **prime-time** evening slots which they occupy. Because of the large audiences which telenovelas attract in comparison to other genres of Brazilian programming, there are a larger number of commercials in them than in other programmes. Furthermore, the setting of telenovela stories among relatively affluent urban families means that consumer culture features as the milieu of the characters, whose costumes, domestic appliances and other possessions mirror the products advertised in the commercial breaks.

Telenovelas are structured differently from either conventional Western drama **serials** or **soap operas**. Unlike the latter, they come to a conclusion after about six months of a slowly unfolding story, though they feature the domestic and emotional narratives and complex complications of relationships which are the focus of soap opera. But telenovelas are often based on popular Brazilian literature, and are therefore somewhat similar to the extended multi-episode adaptations of novels which are seen on British and other Western nations' television. Similarly, telenovela episodes are usually broadcast in one-hour slots, thus aligning them with serial drama in other countries, in contrast to the normal half-hour duration of soap opera episodes.

Brazilian television in some ways supports the conclusions of a report for the United Nations Educational, Scientific and Cultural Organisation (UNESCO), which in 1977 set up a body

**commercial television** television funded by the sale of advertising time or sponsorship of programmes.

**affiliates** local television stations (normally in the USA) that have made agreements (affiliations) with a network to broadcast programmes offered by that network rather than another.

**prime time** the part of a day's television schedule when the greatest number of viewers may be watching, normally the mid-evening period.

**serial** a television form in which a developing narrative unfolds across a sequence of separate episodes.

**soap opera** a continuing drama serial involving a large number of characters in a specific location, focusing on relationships, emotions and reversals of fortune.

*continued*

called the International Commission for the Study of Communication Problems to investigate inequalities in the world's media economy. The commission's report on the issue, called *Many Voices, One World* (also known as the MacBride Report, after the commission's chairman), was released by UNESCO in 1980 and argued for the independence of less wealthy nations from the global influence of Western communications businesses. It recommended the setting up of a 'New World Information and Communication Order' in which cultural imperialism by the Northern and Western nations would be discontinued in the same way that imperialism itself had been largely dismantled. If Brazil could attain a largely independent broadcasting culture, it was argued, then other nations could, too. However, the principle of the New World Information and Communication Order was strongly resisted by the USA and the UK, who withdrew their financial support for UNESCO for several years because of its sponsorship of the report.

The argument that cultural imperialism had reached a turning-point was supported by the export of Brazilian telenovelas to the countries of Southern Europe, where the related languages and cultures of the Spanish and Portuguese nations offered easier integration of telenovelas with existing television representations and expectations. Similarly, the large Spanish-speaking population of the USA has enabled Mexico's television producers to export their Spanish-language programmes to specialist American networks serving Hispanic Americans by cable and satellite. On the other hand, Brazilian television's dependence on favour from ruling political parties and politicians meant that it was always careful to avoid reporting news which might challenge the authority of a government which terrorised the population and tortured dissidents during decades of rule by military dictators. From this perspective, Brazilian television might be independent of Western cultural imperialism but it might nevertheless be considered a form for perpetuating an internal imperialism within Brazil. By providing the population with a diet of entertainment and reassuring propaganda, Brazilian television can be regarded as a block on the development of democratic culture, public political debate and improved standards of cultural and educational attainment in the country.

Furthermore, since Brazil (and Mexico) is a much more financially powerful and prodigious producer of programmes than neighbouring countries in the Latin American region, the export of its programmes to its neighbours is as significant as its export of programmes to Europe and the USA. This regional flow of programmes from Brazil to other Latin American countries complicates the simple arguments that television flows from Northern and Western nations to Eastern and Southern nations, and that this flow is being resisted by some programmes moving in the opposite direction. Instead, regional television flows seem to represent the building to maturity of television cultures of relative power and powerlessness within continents and linguistic areas.

The legacy of the **media imperialism** argument is that it is not American programmes nor American television owners which perpetuate regressive kinds of television organisation. American programmes do not always dominate the schedules of countries with less developed television cultures, and, even if they did, it has not been proved that these programmes simply transmit American values to their audiences. Similarly, many American television programme-making companies are not owned solely or at all by American individuals or corporations, and the ownership of television broadcasting institutions in other parts of the world is more likely to be through a combined deal between global media corporations and local or regional interests.

But one aspect of the media imperialism thesis which does remain valid is that the American system of television organisation has been successfully exported to many of the world's national broadcasters. This trend tends to increase as deregulation and liberalisation of television markets advance with the collapse of rigid state broadcasting controls in formerly authoritarian societies. The financing of television by advertising, as in Brazil, where audiences are targeted by particular types of programme in order to deliver them to advertisers, is an American model which has become increasingly common. The American model of the competition between broadcasting channels affiliated to major network or cable and satellite providers is also adopted in nations which have their own indigenous television production bases, like Brazil.

The case of Brazilian telenovelas therefore provides evidence against cruder forms of the cultural imperialism thesis, but draws attention to the global spread of Western (and specifically American) forms of television organisation. It also shows how a distinctive regional television form can develop in response to the history and culture of a particular society, but spread by television export to both relatively similar and dissimilar television regions.

## SUMMARY OF KEY POINTS

- Studying television today involves understanding how national and international television cultures work in relation to each other, in the context of globalisation.
- The media imperialism thesis has argued that political values are communicated when television programmes and television institutions spread around the world.
- New technologies, especially satellite transmission, have made possible greater exchange of television across the world, mainly from developed countries to less developed ones.
- The effects of television globalisation can be both progressive and regressive.
- Local audiences' understanding of global television can be different, so that the meanings of programmes change according to where they are seen.
- Individual viewers understand their identities in relation to the television they watch, and think of themselves in different ways according to the diverse ways that television addresses them.

## Further reading

Alleyne, M., *News Revolution: Political and Economic Decisions about Global Information* (Basingstoke: Macmillan, 1997).

Balnaves, M., J. Donald and S. Hemelryk Donald, *The Global Media Atlas* (London: BFI, 2001).

Barker, C., *Global Television: An Introduction* (Oxford: Blackwell, 1997).

Bignell, J., *Postmodern Media Culture* (Edinburgh: Edinburgh University Press, 2000).

Boyd-Barrett, O. and T. Rantanen, *The Globalization of News* (London: Sage, 1998).

Bruhn Jensen, K. (ed.), *News of the World: World Cultures Look at Television News* (London: Routledge, 1998).

Calabrese, A., 'The trade in television news', in J. Wasko (ed.), *A Companion to Television* (Malden, Mass., and Oxford: Blackwell, 2005), pp. 270–90.

Corner, J., *Critical Ideas in Television Studies* (Oxford: Clarendon, 1999).

Dahlgren, P., *Television and the Public Sphere* (London: Sage, 1995).

Dajani, N., 'Television in the Arab East', in J. Wasko (ed.), *A Companion to Television* (Malden, Mass., and Oxford: Blackwell, 2005), pp. 580–601.

Dowmunt, T. (ed.), *Channels of Resistance: Global Television and Local Empowerment* (London: BFI, 1993).

Drummond, P. and R. Patterson (eds), *Television and its Audience: International Research Perspectives* (London: BFI, 1988).

Gurevitch, M., 'The globalization of electronic journalism', in J. Curran and M. Gurevitch (eds), *Mass Media and Society* (London: Edward Arnold, 1991), pp. 178–93.

Herman, E. and R. McChesney, *The Global Media: The New Missionaries of Global Capitalism* (London: Cassell, 1997).

Leal, O., 'Popular taste and erudite repertoire: the place and space of television in Brazil', *Cultural Studies*, 4:1 (1990), pp. 19–29.

Liebes, T. and E. Katz, *The Export of Meaning: Cross-cultural Readings of 'Dallas'* (New York: Oxford University Press, 1990).

Lull, J. (ed.), *World Families Watch Television* (London: Sage, 1988).

Mackay, H. and T. O'Sullivan (eds), *The Media Reader: Continuity and Transformation* (London: Sage, 1999).

Sinclair, J., E. Jacka and S. Cunningham, 'New patterns in global television', in P. Marris and S. Thornham (eds), *The Media Reader* (Edinburgh: Edinburgh University Press, 1999), pp.170–90.

—— (eds), *Peripheral Vision: New Patterns in Global Television* (Oxford: Oxford University Press, 1996).

Sinclair, J., 'Latin American commercial television: "primitive capitalism"', in J. Wasko (ed.), *A Companion to Television* (Malden, Mass., and Oxford: Blackwell, 2005), pp. 503–20.

Sreberny-Mohammadi, A. with K. Nordenstreng, R. Stevenson and F. Ugboajah (eds), *Foreign News in the Media: International Reporting in 29 Countries* (Paris: UNESCO, 1985).

Thussu, K. D. (ed.), *Electronic Empires: Global Media and Local Resistance* (London: Arnold, 1998).

Zhou, Y. and Z. Guo, 'Television in China: history, political economy, and ideology', in J. Wasko (ed.), *A Companion to Television* (Malden, Mass., and Oxford: Blackwell, 2005), pp. 521–39.

# Television Texts and Television Narratives

# Television Texts and Television Narratives

## Introduction

This chapter evaluates theoretical frameworks for studying television programmes, advertisements, etc. as '**texts**', including methodologies for analysing **narrative**, **intertextual** relations between programmes in a **flow** of different programmes, and **semiotic** approaches to relations between image and sound. These textual approaches are placed in the context of Television Studies in the 1970s and early 1980s, where they developed, which was underpinned by the assemblage of **psycho-analytic**, semiotic and materialist approaches. Rather than being devised specifically for the study of television, these ideas began in the discipline of Film Studies. Textual approaches to television are powerful ways of discussing the meanings made of television by viewers, but they also have some drawbacks. They tend to focus on textual detail at the expense of institutional context and history, and to neglect the ways in which television is understood by audiences. The issues to think about here are:

- how meanings can exist 'in' television texts
- how meanings might depend on relationships between viewers and texts
- how knowledge of production context and history 'outside' the text might affect the meanings which television texts have.

The chapter ranges widely across different television genres and forms, showing how textual approaches to television can explain how meanings are made in them, where these meanings come from and how they might be understood critically. There is a case study at the end of the chapter which shows how semiotic and narrative analysis can be used to study a recent television commercial in some detail.

## The language of television

**Semiotic** approaches to television, as to any other kind of meaning-making activity in society, begin by identifying the different kinds of **sign** which convey meaning in the medium. The principle of semiotic analysis is to begin from the assumption that television has a 'language' which producers and audiences of television have learned to use. The twentieth-century founder of semiotics, the Swiss linguistics professor Ferdinand de Saussure, regarded spoken language as the most fundamental of human meaning-making practices, and argued that all other media could be understood analogously with spoken language. He sought to explain the functioning of spoken language at a particular point in time, describing the system of language as *langue* and any instance of language use as *parole* (which means 'speech' in French). The

---

**text** an object, such as a television programme, film or poem, considered as a network of meaningful signs that can be analysed and interpreted.

**narrative** an ordered sequence of images and sound that tells a fictional or factual story.

**intertextuality** how one text draws on the meanings of another by referring to it, by allusion, quotation or parody, for example.

**flow** the ways that programmes, advertisements, etc. follow one another in an unbroken sequence across the day or part of the day, and the experience of watching the sequence of programmes, advertisements, trailers, etc.

**semiotics** the study of signs and their meanings, initially developed for the study of spoken language, and now used also to study the visual and aural 'languages' of other media, such as television.

**psychoanalysis** the study of human mental life, including not only conscious thoughts, wishes and fears but unconscious ones. Psychoanalysis is an analytical and theoretical set of ideas as well as a therapeutic treatment.

**sign** in semiotics, something which communicates meaning, such as a word, an image or a sound.

'language' of television would be the whole body of conventions and rules for conveying meaning in the medium, while a particular shot or sequence of television would be an instance of *parole*, an example of this system in use.

The language of television consists of visual and aural signs. Television's visual signs include all the images and graphics which are seen on the screen. Aural signs consist of the speech, sound and music which television produces. All of the visual signs on the television screen are two-dimensional, appearing on the flat surface of the screen. Many of television's visual signs closely resemble the people, things and places which they represent in both fictional and non-fictional programmes. Signs which resemble their object in this way are called **iconic signs**, to distinguish them from signs which themselves have no necessary relationship to what they signify. The word 'cat', for example, is a **symbolic sign**, meaning that the letters on the page or the sound of the spoken word 'cat' is arbitrarily used in English to signify a particular type of furry four-legged animal. A television image of a cat, however, closely resembles the real cat which it represents, and is thus an iconic sign. The conventions of representation in television most often rely on the iconic nature of television images to convey an impression of **realism** whereby viewers accept that the television image **denotes** people, places or cats, for example, which exist in the real world. But this acceptance of the realism of television's denotative signs is reliant on the conventions of composition, perspective and framing which are so embedded in Western culture that the two-dimensional image seems simply to convey three-dimensional reality. The power of these conventions can be seen when television represents objects which do not exist in the real world, such as the spacecraft in science-fiction series like *Star Trek* and *Doctor Who*. Often the images of these spacecraft are not images of real objects, or even models, but are created entirely by **computer generated imaging (CGI)**. Yet, because the images of them obey the conventions which audiences recognise from the language of television, viewers can both recognise what they are and accept them as if they were real. These conventions include:

- perspective
- proportion
- light and shade
- shot composition.

Semiotics therefore has a particular interest in such conventions, called **codes**, which govern how signs are used in conventional ways to represent or denote believable worlds.

Television signs which denote speech, the ambient noises of a represented environment or the music accompanying a visual sequence are also used according to codes in the language of television. The analysis of television using semiotic methods has tended to focus more on image than sound, but sound is important to the viewer's relationship with what is on the screen. Television screens are relatively small, and watching programmes often competes with other activities in the same room (such as talking, eating or doing the ironing). In order to grab the viewer's attention, sound is used to call the viewer to take notice of the programme. This is very noticeable in television news programmes, which are punctuated with loud brass music to draw the attention of the viewer, as well as to connote the importance of

**iconic sign** in semiotics, a sign which resembles its referent. Photographs, for example, contain iconic signs resembling the objects they represent.

**symbolic sign** in semiotics, a sign which is connected arbitrarily to its referent rather than because the sign resembles its referent. For example, a photograph of a cat resembles it, whereas the word 'cat' does not: the latter is a symbolic sign.

**realism** the aim for representations to reproduce reality faithfully, and the ways this is done.

**denotation** in semiotics, the function of signs to portray or refer to something in the real world.

**computer generated imaging (CGI)** the creation of images by programming computers with mathematical equations that can generate realistic two-dimensional pictures.

**code** in semiotics, a system or set of rules that shapes how signs can be used, and therefore how meanings can be made and understood.

news as a programme genre. Music and sound effects in television programmes are signs which direct the viewer how to respond emotionally to the significance of the programme or the action denoted in it. Codes of recording, editing and processing intervene between the sound on the set or in the studio and the sound which emanates from the loudspeakers in the television set. Sound recordists on **location**, or sound mixers in the studio, follow conventional codes in setting the levels of sound, and the relative volume of one sound versus another. The distance of a speaker from the camera, for example, might be signified by the loudness or quietness of her speech, while the relative volumes of background music and speech will nearly always be adjusted to allow speech to have priority. Although television images and sounds are often iconic and denotative, seeming simply to convey what the camera and sound-recording equipment have captured, these signs have been processed through the various professional norms, industry practices and conventions of meaning-making that have been consciously or unconsciously adopted by both the makers and audiences of television. These ways of working and ways of understanding are among the codes which structure the language of television.

## Connotations and codes

The iconic and arbitrary signs in the language of television are often presented simply as denoting an object, place or person. But signs rarely simply denote something, since they are produced and understood in a cultural context which enriches them with much more meaning than this. Signs' cultural associations and connections are called **connotations**. For example, the head-on shots of newsreaders, wearing smart clothes, seated behind desks in news programmes not only denote the presenter in a studio but have connotations of authority, seriousness and formality which derive from the connotations of desks, office clothes and head-on address to the camera. These connotations derive partly from social codes which are in circulation in British society, but also from television codes of news programmes which have been conventionalised over time. Newsreaders speak in a neutral and even tone, which is itself a sign connoting the objectivity and authority of both the newsreader and the news organisation which he or she represents. They are usually shot in medium **close-up**, full face, under neutral lighting. This code conventionally positions the newsreader as a mediator of events, who addresses the audience and connects them with the news organisation's reporters, and with the people who are the subjects of the news. The mediator functions as a bridge between the domestic world of the viewer and the public worlds of news. Even though news programmes on Five have used newsreaders sitting on desks with their scripts in their hands to connote a degree of informality (suitable for the relatively new entertainment-based channel), the desk, the clothes and the head-on address to camera remain because they are such integral parts of the coding of news programmes.

Television news programmes use music with loud major chords played on brass instruments in their **title sequences**, and these signs carry connotations of importance, dignity and drama. These title sequences also feature computer graphics in fast-moving sequences, **syntagms** in semiotic terminology, connoting technological sophistication. The function of title sequences in television news programmes is to establish the status of news as significant and authoritative, but also to differentiate

**location** any place in which television images are shot, except inside a television studio.

**connotations** the term used in semiotic analysis for the meanings that are associated with a particular sign or combination of signs.

**close-up** a camera shot where the frame is filled by the face of a person or a detail of a face. Close-ups may also show details of an object or place.

**title sequence** the sequence at the opening of a television programme in which the programme title and performers' names may appear along with other information, accompanied by images, sound and music introducing the programme.

**syntagm** in semiotics, a linked sequence of signs existing at a certain point in time. Written or spoken sentences and television sequences are examples of syntagms.

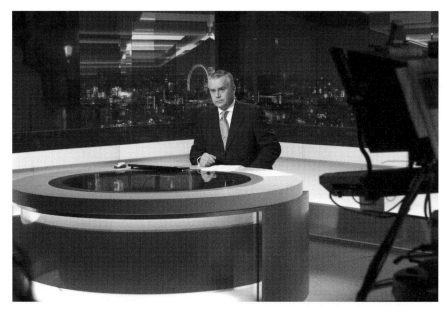

Figure 4.1 Huw Edwards as he prepares to present the *Ten O'Clock News* © BBC

one channel's news programme from another, providing '**brand recognition**'. The title sequences of news programmes, like the title sequences of all television programmes, share many of the functions of television commercials, in differentiating products which are very similar and endowing them with connotations supporting a familiar identity. Title sequences are sequences of signs which collectively signify boundaries between one part of the continual **flow** of television broadcasting and the rest of it.

It is important to remember that the meanings of television images and sounds are not naturally attached to signs. The pleasure and understanding which viewers gain from television often depend on the significance of how signs relate to each other in a particular context, and it is often misleading to carry over the connotations of a sign in one context into another. In the long-running police drama series *Inspector Morse*, for example, Morse drove a burgundy Jaguar Mark II saloon. In combination with the connotations of Morse's affection for real ale, codes of politeness and love of opera, the car had connotations of tradition, 'classicness' and Britishness. By contrast, in the police series of the 1970s (such as *The Sweeney*, in which the Morse actor John Thaw played a main character), Jaguar Mark II saloons were often driven by gangsters and had connotations of the criminal underworld, the glamour of crime and bravado.

In analysing a television programme semiotically, signs gain their meanings in two contrasting ways:

- by their similarity with other signs in the same programme
- by their difference from these surrounding signs.

Television relies on its viewers' often unconscious knowledge of codes and their ability to decode signs and their connotations, and assemble them into meaningful scenes, sequences and stories.

**brand recognition**
the ability of audiences to recognise the distinctive identity of a product, service or institution and the values and meanings associated with it.

Television broadcasters' aim is to keep the viewer watching by assembling verbal
and visual signs in ways which are entertaining or informative, but different kinds
of programme achieve this in different ways. In other words, television **genres** have
their own codes and conventions which enable viewers to recognise and expect
particular kinds of meaning and pleasure. While many genres of television use very
**long shots** (VLS) at the beginning of scenes and sequences to establish a physical
location, **close-up** (CU) is often used to denote emotion signified by performers'
facial expressions in soap opera. In general, the greater the genre's emphasis on
emotional reaction, the greater the proportion of close-up shots. But while close-
up is a signifier of performance in the language of television, and seems highly
dramatic, the shot length in soap operas and other emotionally focused dramas is
relatively long. Shots are held for quite a long time in order to observe characters'
reactions to each other, whereas in action dramas, such as police or hospital programmes, there is less close-up and shorter shot length. Codes of shot composition
can also be used differently in different television genres. Static composition (where
the camera is still) allows space to contemplate the performances in a soap opera,
for example, whereas dynamic composition (moving camera) is used in police and
hospital dramas such as *NYPD Blue* and *ER*, which focus on disorientation and
disorder, and seem to capture action as it is 'naturally' occurring. Even colour can
function as a sign in television programmes: for example, the US sitcom *Frasier*
connotes the warm and comfortable environment of middle-class Seattle with
yellow, red and brown, while other programmes (such as *Waking the Dead*) use the
conventionally colder colours of blue, grey and black to signify a more threatening
and uncertain environment. In the different versions of *CSI*, the mainly yellow tones
of *CSI: Miami* signify its sunny resort location, whereas *CSI: New York* uses brown
colours for the colder and older urban environment of that city. The connotations
of signs in the codes of shot type, shot length and colour are meaningful because of
their use in particular genres of programme, in relation to other signs in the
programme and in contrast to comparable or different programmes.

## Narrative structures

**Binary oppositions** underlie the narrative structures of many television programmes, for example oppositions between **masculine** and **feminine**, or young and
old. An example of a narrative structure found in different kinds of television science
fiction is the use of binary oppositions between human and animal, and human and
machine. Machines are rigid, in opposition to the flesh and bone of organic creatures,
and are represented as determined, focused and disciplined, in opposition to human
and animal tendencies to appetite and excess. These oppositions are set out and
mixed together in the narratives of *Star Trek: The Next Generation*, for example:

- Captain Picard is a human, but his position as captain of the starship *Enterprise*
  makes him disciplined, almost machine-like.
- Lieutenant Commander Worf is a Klingon, a race known for its excessive
  aggression and 'barbarian' behaviour, which aligns him with animal traits of
  excess and indiscipline that he has to control.
- Lieutenant Commander Data is an android, a machine, but his ambition is to
  become human, organic and, to some extent, undisciplined.

**BCU**
Big close-up

**MLS**
Medium long shot

**CU**
Close-up

**LS**
Long shot

**MCU**
Medium close-up

**VLS**
Very long shot

**MS**
Medium shot or Mid-shot

Figure 4.2  Shot sizes. Photographs
courtesy of Jeremy Orlebar.

Storylines in *Star Trek: The Next Generation* often concern these conflicts between opposed animal, human and machine traits in the characters: for example, when Captain Picard is captured by the Borg, an aggressive cyborg race who exaggerate Picard's machine-like self-control and insert mechanical technologies into his organic body. Data featured in episodes where he was able to experience human emotions, such as anger and humour, and had to cope with these unruly passions. Oppositions like these between human and animal, or human and machine, are the underlying system of relationships and conflicts which give structure and meaning to narratives, though they are often less obvious than those in *Star Trek*.

Thinking of narratives as sets of relations between terms which are opposed or similar is useful in understanding how narrative works in television. The tradition in British sitcoms, for example, is to oppose:

- Masculinity/femininity
- Work/domesticity
- Rationality/emotionalism
- Intolerance/tolerance

Humour derives from contrasting these values when they are each embodied in a character, and also from aligning a character who might be expected to represent one side of the binary with the other side. For example, Victor Meldrew in *One Foot in the Grave* was masculine and intolerant, but was made redundant from his job and put in an enforced domestic setting that is conventionally regarded as feminine. This offered numerous opportunities to create comedy from his sense of being 'out of place'. *Frasier* adds to this by setting up oppositions between sophistication and crudeness, youth and age, so that Frasier's and his brother Niles's sophistication and relative youth can be contrasted with their father's crudeness and elderliness.

The simplified character positions in sitcoms are too excessive to be '**realistic**' because it is important to the comedy for a character's place in a system of binary oppositions to be clear in contrast to that of another character. Sitcom narrative works through setting up oppositions and connections, which by the end of an episode have been laid to rest. The movement of sitcom narrative keeps repeating and developing incompatibilities and compatibilities, playing on the established position of each character in the system of binaries. But the audience's pleasure partly derives from the anticipation that these conflicts will be resolved satisfactorily. The audience needs to recognise the narrative codes of sitcom and the stakes of the binary oppositions in order to accept the surprising reversals and conflicts which the narrative requires. The interruption of laughter and close-ups held on the performers' facial expressions are important generic signs and narrative turning-points in sitcom. At these points the viewer is invited to recognise the high point of a conflict or reversal among the binary oppositions, and measure its effect on the characters by reading their expressions. The bursts of laughter in the narrative set out the rhythm and pattern in each scene, and punctuate the narrative with stopping-points around which the action turns. This rhythm of stops and starts keeps confirming the position laid out for the viewer to make sense of the narrative and find it funny. The studio audience's laughter confirms the position of the viewer by representing an audience which shares the viewer's expected reaction. The collective audience laughing on the soundtrack is a representative of the viewer at home, and occupies a mediating position between the performance of the sitcom and the television audience watching singly or in small groups, where laughing out loud is often embarrassing. The noisy studio audience allows the viewer access to a kind of excessive response which is itself pleasurable, and can be enjoyed at second hand by the viewer at home.

---

**ACTIVITY 4.1**

Write down the binary oppositions and structural patterns which underlie a sitcom you have seen. How many other sitcoms can you list which share some or all of these structures?

---

Television news consists of narrative reports, and can be analysed as narrative to discover how priorities and assumptions shared by news broadcasters form a code determining which reports have greatest significance within the bulletin. The reports with the highest **news value** appear near the beginning of the bulletin (in the same way as the front pages of newspapers present the stories that have the highest news value to readers). News bulletins on commercial channels are interspersed with commercials, so each segment of the programme contains its own hierarchy of news reports. The ranking of reports according to their news value shows how the representation of reality offered by television news is not a **denotation** of events but a narrative mediated by the signs and codes of news television. Binary oppositions – such as those between crime and law, left-wing and right-wing opinions, and home and abroad – are the basis for news narrative. Television news both shapes and reflects the dominant commonsense assumptions about what is significant, since by definition what is deemed significant is what makes the news. News narrative contributes to the process of constructing a commonsense climate of opinion through which audiences perceive their reality. Therefore, television news shares with other news media (such as newspapers and radio news) the **ideological** function of naturalising the assumption that the day-to-day occurrences in the public arenas of politics, business and international affairs are the most important aspects of the daily affairs of a society.

Within this field of newsworthy aspects of contemporary life, binary oppositions are again an underlying structure which enables broadcasters and viewers to make sense of the news. News programmes seek to connote **balance** and objectivity by giving approximately equal time to conflicting parties and interested groups who comment on the events narrated in news stories. But balance and objectivity are defined in relation to commonsense assumptions held consensually in society, and these views are naturalised ideological positions. The definition of the norm is a cultural construct and will therefore shift according to the current balance of power. Some decades ago, for example, the social ownership of major industries and institutions such as the railway system and the telephone network was part of a norm which interviewers and politicians accepted as the usual state of things. After the **privatisation** of these industries and services, however, this view is no longer the norm, and it surfaces only rarely in television news, and then as an unlikely

**news value** the degree of significance attributed to a news story, where items with high news value are deemed most significant to the audience.

**ideology** the set of beliefs, attitudes and assumptions arising from the economic and class divisions in a culture, underlying the ways of life accepted as normal in that culture.

**balance** the requirement in television news and current affairs to present both sides of an argument or issue.

**privatisation** the policy of placing industries or institutions in the hands of privately owned businesses, rather than state ownership.
**serial** a television form where a developing narrative unfolds across a sequence of separate episodes.

possibility. News narrative, despite its commitment to balance and objectivity, measures this balance and objectivity against the currently dominant ideologies in society, which occupy an apparently neutral position.

Television news deals with the potentially infinite meanings of events by narrating them in conventional subject categories, and conventional narrative codes, such as 'foreign news' and 'business news'. These divisions reflect the institutional divisions in news broadcasting organisations, where reporters work in teams of specialist staff. Some news programmes title news stories with captions on the screen next to the news presenter, and these captions connote both the specificity of each news story, which is different from the one before or after it, and the connection between a particular story and others in the same category. The effect of using this code is to restrict the narrative frameworks which are available for representing the story. Despite the wide-ranging effects and relevance which one news story might have, placing reports in coded categories restricts the viewer's capacity to make connections between one news report and another in a different category, or to bring an alternative narrative structure to bear in understanding the news events.

---

**ACTIVITY 4.2**

How do the narratives of news programmes use oppositions between 'us' and 'them', 'powerful' and 'less powerful', to reinforce conceptions of social authority and legitimacy?

---

**ACTIVITY 4.3**

Analyses of television news have demonstrated the ideological distortions of news. Would it be possible to create television news that is free of ideology?

---

The significance of the codes which viewers are invited to bring to bear on programmes can be seen in the case of programmes which use codes deriving from more than one form and genre of television narrative. Television fiction is now rarely seen in the form of single, one-off programmes, being increasingly made in episodic forms resembling the **serial**. These consist of a developing story divided into several parts, and television soap opera is a special case of the serial form where the end of the story is infinitely deferred. The series form denotes programmes in which the settings and characters do not change or develop, but where new stories involving the continuing characters and setting are presented in each episode. Contemporary television programmes now frequently combine the single setting and new stories in each episode, which are features of the series form, with developing characters and stories episode to episode, as in serials. Robin Nelson (1997) has coined the term 'flexi-narrative' to denote fiction like this which adopts the short sequences of action and rapid editing which occur in television advertisements, along with the develop-

**serial** a television form where a developing narrative unfolds across a sequence of separate episodes.

ing characters and stories found in television soap opera, and the new stories in each episode which are found in television series. The flexi-narrative form is a case of the combination of television forms, but similar mixing and borrowing can be seen within and between television genres.

The hospital drama series *ER* is a flexi-narrative, whose mix of generic components was designed to appeal to American audiences for whom the interruption of commercials into programmes seems to lead to channel-hopping or **zapping** and loss of involvement in ongoing narrative. Bob Mullan (1997: 60) reports that the novelist and creator of *ER* Michael Crichton believed that American viewers 'are incapable of watching television for any length of time unless it is a "news reality" programme like *The Cops* or a courtroom drama like the O. J. Simpson trial. The only way forward, he believes, is to make drama more dramatic than the news and reality programmes.' The narrative of *ER* is patterned to include periodic bursts of rapid action interspersed with more leisurely character development, and the programme as a whole is segmented into a large number of relatively short scenes. The longer and slower scenes of character interaction draw on the conventions of soap opera, in which reaction by one character to events in the life of another is represented by frequent close-up, emotional cues provided by music and an emphasis on the viewer's memory of past events in the characters' lives to enrich what is happening in the narrative present. By contrast, the shorter scenes of rapid activity, usually when the doctors are responding to the arrival of a seriously injured person, use rapid hand-held camera shots, **whip-pans** and fast editing. In these scenes the dialogue of characters overlaps, and the noises made by medical equipment accompanied by hectic, percussive music add to the sense of urgency and confusion. These action sequences use conventions deriving from **observational documentary** or news footage of action caught on the run by the camera, but add dramatic music and complex sound found in action drama series, such as police shows.

**zapping** hopping rapidly from channel to channel while watching television, using a remote control (a 'zapper').

**whip-pan** a very rapid panning shot from one point to another.

**observational documentary** a documentary form in which the programme-maker aims to observe neutrally what would have happened even if he or she had not been present.

## Narrative functions

The theory of narrative has recognised that although the components of narrative are often relatively simple, and organised into binary oppositions and relationships of difference and similarity, there is much in narratives which does not have an obvious functional purpose. Lots of material appears to be redundant. Redundancy consists of the inclusion in the narrative of a number of signs which have a contextual or supporting role. These signs are unremarked, but deepen the consistency and believability of the narrative. They provide texture and tone for the audience. Details of setting, costume, much of the detail of dialogue and some of the narrative action are likely to be redundant from the point of view of getting across the story itself. But in programmes which claim to be **realistic**, redundancy has the crucial effect of embedding the story in a fully realised world. Furthermore, one of the ways in which narratives can be most pleasurable and interesting is when the relationship between redundancy and functional narrative components is changed in the course of the story. In detective narratives and whodunits, for example, an apparently redundant detail which seemed simply to lend texture to the fictional world might turn out to be a crucial clue. In science-fiction television redundancy is crucial to establishing a futuristic environment as realistic, in the sense that it has the detail and texture for it to be believable. News programmes are full of apparently redundant information and visual detail, but here, too, semiotics and narrative theory are useful in showing how redundant information actually fulfils important functions in shaping the meanings of news reports.

Television news has to deal with events which are by definition new each day, and to do this it has powerful codes for giving shape and meaning to reports. These reports make use of four narrative functions (Hartley 1982: 118–19):

- framing
- focusing
- realising
- closing.

Framing is the activity of establishing the news topic, usually done by the mediating figure of the newsreader, who invokes the narrative code in which the report will be presented. For example, political news is usually coded as adversarial. Although mediators such as news presenters speak in a neutral **register** and establish themselves and the news broadcasting organisation as neutral too, the effect of this is to make the setting-up of the narrative code appear invisible to viewers: it seems to arise from the news itself rather than from how it is being presented. Focusing refers to the opening out of the news report into further detail, conveyed by reporters and correspondents who speak for the news broadcasting institution (Hartley (1982: 110–11) calls them 'institutional voices'). The institutional voices develop the narrative by providing background information, explaining what is at stake in the news event, and introducing comment and **actuality footage** which illustrate this. The interviews, film reports and comments by people involved in the news event are part of the function known as realising, whereby authenticity and evidence of the news event and reactions to it from interested individuals and groups are presented. The availability of actuality footage gives important added value to news reports because it is crucial to the narrative function of realising the story. But although actuality footage might seem to be the dominant type of sign in television news programmes, its visual signs never appear without accompanying **voice-over** commentary. While it is possible for visual sequences to narrate on their own, the multiple meanings which images always have can be contained and directed by the reporter's institutional voice on the soundtrack. Realisation therefore tends to confirm the work of the news reporters' framing and focusing activities. Moving out of the news studio to focus and realise news stories allows room for the visual and aural signs in the programme to differ from and affect the news presenter's framing activities. For instance, the connotations of the signs of situation in news programmes have significant empowering or disempowering effects on the meanings of news reports. The authority of the newsreaders and commentators in the studio can contrast with the much less empowering presence of a member of the public in the street, or a reporter struggling to speak over the voices of a crowd, for example. Closing refers to the way that a news report moves towards a condensed encapsulation of the report, likely to be repeated in the closing headlines of the news programme, and which presents the **preferred reading** of the report. Closure might involve discounting some of the points of view on the news event which have been represented in the report, or repeating the point of view already connoted by the

**register** a term in the study of language for the kinds of speech or writing used to represent a particular kind of idea or to address a certain audience.

**actuality footage** television pictures representing an event that was filmed live. The term usually refers to pictures of news events.

**voice-over** speech accompanying visual images but not presumed to derive from the same place or time as the images.

**preferred reading** an interpretation of a text that seems to be the one most encouraged by the text; the 'correct' interpretation.

frame or focus. This movement towards closure is confirmed at the end of reports, but the report as a whole will involve it throughout.

## Identification

First of all, television viewers can make sense of television only by taking up a position in relation to it, constituting themselves as an audience. What the audience is watching has to seem to be 'for them', and a relationship may then be constructed with it (whether this relationship to television is marked by pleasure, boredom, anger or frustration). So narrative depends on a shifting pattern of **identification** between the viewer and the programme. Viewers can identify with both fictional and non-fictional performers but also distance themselves from a performer (in order to find him or her funny, for instance, in a sitcom). Viewers can also identify with the studio audience denoted by laughter on the soundtrack (in sitcoms and chat shows, for example), taking up a shared position in relation to what the studio audience and home audience have seen. Narrative requires the shifting of the viewer's position into and out of the television programme, and a rhythm of identification and disavowal of identification. But the positioning and repositioning of the viewer as an audience member might succeed or fail for individual viewers in different programmes or parts of the same programme. Narrative lays out positions for its viewers, offering signs and codes which invite the viewers to make sense of and enjoy what they see and hear, but whether viewers actually occupy the position of being-an-audience, and how they inhabit this position, depends on the many variables which compose each viewer's social and psychological identity.

> **identification** a term deriving from psychoanalytic theories of cinema, which describes the viewer's conscious or unconscious wish to take the place of someone or something in a television text.

> **ACTIVITY 4.4**
>
> In what ways does audience positioning serve to keep viewers watching programmes? What might happen if audience positioning ceases to work for viewers?

Clearly, viewers are not often conscious of the relationships which they take up moment by moment with television, and for this reason television theorists have drawn on **psychoanalytic** models of how people relate to representations. This theory draws on the work of the French psychoanalyst Jacques Lacan, who modified the insights of Sigmund Freud, the originator of psychoanalysis. Lacan argued that human beings begin to differentiate themselves from the world around them, and to have a sense of self and other people at a stage of development he called the 'Mirror Stage'. Initially, the human infant feels undifferentiated from its surroundings, and its feelings and needs are not located within a self which exists independently. The first moment of difference comes when the infant perceives an image of itself (in a mirror, hence 'Mirror Stage'). This image appears more complete, co-ordinated and unified than the reality of its own immature body. Lacan proclaimed that this relationship with the mirror image is the beginning of identification: 'We have only to understand the mirror stage as an identification . . . namely, the transformation that takes place in the subject when he assumes an image' (Lacan 1977: 2). Because the image is other to the self, the moment of perceiving it separates individual subjectivity and what is outside it, other to it. For ever afterwards, the human **subject** is defined in relation to what it is not, to further images of itself and others, and to the surrounding world beyond its own body. The pleasure of seeing images and others brings with it the awareness of absence, that 'I' am not 'you', 'he' or 'she'. Narrative offers numerous images of other people, places and things, and keeps repeating the pleasurable moment of identifying with others which the viewer is not, and the displeasure of recognising otherness forever beyond him or her. Wanting to watch television is part of the viewer's desire for the other, which narrative keeps displacing on to the next moment in the succession of images and sounds which it presents. Television images are always framed, with what the viewer sees always being part of a larger possible view of which only a part can be seen. The movement of the camera to reveal new spaces and the cutting between one point of view and another keep offering new others with which to identify, and offering to satisfy new desires for mirroring relationships between self and other.

This psychoanalytic account of pleasure in watching television has therefore argued that there are several identifications which viewers make from moment to moment. The first of these is an identification with the television medium, as something which delivers images of otherness that promise to satisfy viewers' desire to see and imagine themselves in the place of the other. There are also identifications with all the figures who are presented on the screen, the performers who stand in for the viewer and play out the roles which the viewer might desire to play for himself or herself. There are identifications throughout television narratives with the fictional and non-fictional worlds presented in them, just as in a daydream or fantasy we might imagine worlds where we play all the parts in a fictional story. Narrative texts are constructed from a network of looks: relationships between the looks of the people on screen, the look of the camera and the viewer's look. The movement of television narrative in this way is analogous to daydream fantasies which allow for identifications with different people and things (imagining being a person, a car, a bird, etc.), including identifications with different **gender** roles. All the possible roles in the narrative are available to the viewing subject: he or she can imagine being either the subject or object of a look, and can even occupy a position outside the scene, looking on from a spectator's point of view. The importance of an analogy with fantasy is that the disjuncture of looks and positions in its scenarios appears parallel to the way that television narrative cuts and juxtaposes different shots, different camera looks. Television narrative holds back complete knowledge and total vision to the viewer, thereby maintaining the desire to keep on looking. The desires to look and hear are experienced through the viewer's relations with a set of signs and codes which offer meanings to him or her. Television narratives work by closing down the many divergent identifications and understandings of the programme, and binding them into coherence. This psychoanalytic model offers a very complex understanding of the processes of watching television, whereby it can be understood in terms of mobile processes of making sense, experiencing pleasure and displeasure, and giving and withholding interest.

Nevertheless, there are some difficulties with this model. The small size of the television screen and its presence as a domestic object among the furnishings of a room may diminish the importance of imagined identifications compared to the

**subject** in psychoanalysis, the term for the individual self whose identity has both conscious and unconscious components.

**gender** the social and cultural division of people into masculine and feminine individuals. This is different from sex, which refers to the biological difference between male and female bodies.

experience of watching in a cinema, for example. The psychoanalytic approach described here was developed originally for understanding film spectatorship, where film viewers are much more likely to be immersed in narratives. The dark space of the cinema, the large size of the screen and the choice to place oneself in the position of a viewer among an audience of other viewers all militate in favour of much greater involvement in film than viewers often experience watching television. The television theorist John Ellis (1982: 137) pointed out this distinction by describing the viewer's look at television as a 'glance', rather than the concentrated 'gaze' of the film spectator:

> The gaze implies a concentration of the spectator's activity into that of looking, the glance implies that no extraordinary effort is being invested in the activity of looking. The very terms we habitually use to designate the person who watches TV or the cinema screen tend to indicate this difference. The cinema-looker is a spectator: caught by the projection yet separate from its illusion. The TV-looker is a viewer, casting a lazy eye over the proceedings, keeping an eye on events, or, as the slightly archaic designation had it, 'looking in'.

In response to this distinction, television theorists have increasingly moved away from psychoanalytic accounts of television viewing, and instead examined how television narratives offer audience positions for viewers who may be often disengaged glancers rather than immersed spectators. Television uses a range of narrating figures to address the viewer directly, audiences within programmes with whom the viewer is invited to identify, and representative figures who take the place of the ordinary viewer at home. Each of these strategies of viewer involvement contributes to hooking the viewer into television narratives and encouraging the kinds of immersive identification that psychoanalytic theory has explained.

## Television narrators

An obvious question to ask about the meanings of television programmes is: from where do they originate? Are meanings put there by the person responsible for the programme's **authorship**, are they the result of how signs, codes and narrative structures work in a text, or are they constructed through the individual choices of viewers, for example? In earlier decades of British television the promotion of television authors enabled TV executives to rebuff the accusation that television is without value, and TV scriptwriters were compared with theatre dramatists, novelists or poets. But the consequence of this has been the mistaken view that the meanings of television programmes are universally shared by all viewers, and are the result of the creator's individual genius and personal vision. The meanings of television are not universal but local (as the differences between, for example, British and American understandings of **quality** and relevance show) and are produced within the conventions and moral and cultural values of their time. Authors always negotiate with the other practitioners in the making of television (**directors**, **producers**, designers and script editors, for instance) and are not free to mastermind a unique vision of their own.

authorship the question of who an author is, the role of the author as creator and the significance of the author's input into the material being studied.

quality in television, kinds of programme that are perceived as more expensively produced and, especially, more culturally worthwhile than other programmes.

director the person responsible for the creative process of turning a script or idea into a finished programme, by working with a technical crew, performers and an editor.

producer the person working for a television institution who is responsible for the budget, planning and making of a television programme or series of programmes.

But within the television industry particular authors have been elevated to high status and publicised for reasons of claiming prestige and attracting audiences. An author can function as a brand, a familiar name which alerts the audience to styles and themes that the writer has explored in the past, and distinguishes the programme from the **flow** of the schedule around it. The marketing of authors as brands occurred in the 1990s and 2000s with dramas by Lynda La Plante, for example (*Prime Suspect*, *Trial and Retribution*), and classic novel **adaptations** by Andrew Davies (*Pride and Prejudice*, *Emma*, *Bleak House*). A few producers have also occupied this authorial branding role, such as Tony Garnett (*This Life*, *Lillies*) and the Americans Steven Bochco (*NYPD Blue*, *Commander in Chief*) and Jerry Bruckheimer (*CSI*, *Without a Trace*). More popular generic drama, such as the police series or hospital drama, is often authored in a collaborative way, using a pool of writers, and is rarely attached to the name of an author. But if television, even in its most 'literary' form of drama, does not consist of 'messages' put there by an author, there is often the sense in watching television that there is an agency communicating with the viewer. As Sarah Kozloff (1992: 78) explains: 'The "implied author" of a television show . . . is not a flesh-and-blood person but rather a textual construct, the viewer's sense of the organizing force behind the world of the show.' This agency behind narrative appears through the various forms of **narration** used in television.

Analysing narrative requires the distinction between story and **discourse**. Story is the set of events which are represented. They could potentially be told in any order (chronologically or in **flashback**, for example) and with any emphasis. Discourse is the narrating process which puts story events in an order, with a shape and direction. In any medium, someone or something must be doing the storytelling for the audience, on its behalf, and this agency is the narrator, whether it is a voice, an on-screen performer or simply the agency which viewers reconstruct as the force which controls the arrangement of camera shots, sound and music that deliver the story to them. Some fictional and non-fictional programmes have **voice-over** narrators throughout, or in particular sequences. *Star Trek: The Next Generation* begins with the familiar scene-setting narration for the programme as a whole, beginning with the 'Captain's log' where a voice-over narrates the setting and situation at the start of each episode's story, and this is followed by the narration at the start of the **title sequence**, beginning 'Space, the final frontier . . .' Narration can sometimes be found in the title songs of programmes, and series such as *ER* may open with voice-over reminding the audience of scenes in a previous programme explained by the phrase 'Previously, on *ER* . . .' A few drama programmes include a voice-over narrator or an on-screen narrator within scenes, as in *Desperate Housewives*. Non-fiction programmes such as wildlife programmes, history programmes such as *Time Team*, commercials, cooking programmes and '**reality TV**' programmes such as *Big Brother* and *Survivor* all have narrators. In these the function of the narrator is to establish a link between the audience and the programme narrative, by inviting the viewer to involve himself or herself in the ongoing progress of the story. Although some programmes make the function of narration explicit in these ways, all television narratives rely on the more complex narration which is made up of camera shots in a narrative progression, often with music helping to link shots together into sequences and to give them an emotional point of view. Sarah Kozloff (1992: 79) notes that 'Music, in film and in television, is a key channel through which the voiceless narrating agency "speaks" to the viewer.' The viewer

**adaptation** transferring a novel, theatre play, poem, etc. from its original medium into another medium, such as television.

**narration** the process of telling a story through image and sound. Narration can also refer to the spoken text accompanying television images.

**discourse** a particular use of language for a certain purpose in a certain context (such as academic discourse or poetic discourse), and similarly in television, a particular usage of television's audio-visual 'language' (news programme discourse or nature documentary discourse, for instance).

**flashback** a television sequence marked as representing events that happened in a time previous to the programme's present.

**reality TV** programmes where the unscripted behaviour of 'ordinary people' is the focus of interest.

is aligned with **point of view shots** of characters or performers, alternating with apparently neutral points of view which observe the represented space and the people in it. The performers in television fiction behave as if the viewer is absent, making it more evident that the camera is the agency conveying their actions to the audience, whereas factual programmes perhaps make narration less obvious because the camera appears more to be a neutral observer. But in each case there is an implied narrator composed from the different camera points of view which have been edited together to form the narrative as a whole.

The significance of narration is partly that the viewer is necessarily positioned by the changing sequence of camera shots, the words of on-screen or off-screen narrators and the accompanying music in programmes and advertisements. The position of the viewer is the place to which all of them are directed and from where they can make sense as a coherent whole. Television viewers, when they constitute themselves as an audience and answer television's call to join a community of viewers, are making an **identification** with the audience position laid out for them by the signs, codes and narrative structures of the programme or advertisement. In other words the television viewer has occupied the role laid out for him or her by the broadcaster, which is doing the looking on his or her behalf. It is often hard to specify what this institutional narrator is, whether, for instance, it is the production team which has designed and made the programme, or the channel on which it is broadcast. Indeed, both of these vague collective agencies seem to make claims to be the overall narrators of programmes by virtue of the credits and **copyright** ownership information in the end titles of programmes, and by the channel **idents** and logos which appear between programmes and, in the case of some channels, are superimposed in the corner of the screen throughout them. In any case the most overarching kind of narrator might be the channel on which programmes are broadcast, since the flow of the period of viewing, no matter how diverse the types of programmes and advertisements which it includes, is held together as a unity by the narrating voice of the off-screen announcers who connect programmes with each other. They are also narrators, saying, for example, 'Join us after the break, where Neela is having a bad day in tonight's episode of *ER*.' This narrating discourse is striking in the fact that it makes explicit the hailing function of television to call on an individual viewer to become part of a collective audience ('join us'), an audience which is conjured up by that address to it.

## Signs of the viewer

The television medium brings distant events and uncommon sights, such as the exotic animals of wildlife programmes, or distant events recorded for news programmes, into the private arena of the home. Television has always framed its appeal as a medium on its ability to bring what is different, strange and interesting into the viewer's familiar and domestic world. In this sense television seems to bridge the gap between public and private, outside and inside. The means of connecting the two, such as by using narrators or representatives of the viewer, are therefore particularly significant to gaining a sense of television's image of itself. But the paradox is that the more television programmes use textual means to include viewers in worlds beyond their own experience, the greater the chance of simultaneously

**point of view shot** a camera shot where the camera is placed in, or close to, the position from where a previously seen character might look.

**copyright** the legal right of ownership over written, visual or aural material, including the prohibition on copying this material without permission from its owner.

**idents** the symbols representing production companies, television channels, etc., often comprising graphics or animations.

revealing the viewer's own disempowerment and non-involvement. Watching a wildlife programme about the imminent extinction of the tiger might raise viewers' awareness and concern, but might also be a substitute for doing anything about the situation. Broadcasters are concerned to provide a sense of activity and involvement for viewers, whether as part of the **public service** function to show and support initiatives in society or as part of a commercial imperative to encourage consumption of products and services. In either case the ways in which programmes address and position viewers are important subjects of study. Television is a domestic technology, embedded in the home among other technological devices, such as radios, computers and stereo systems. These technologies, and the activities which come from them, compete for attention. Television calls for viewers to take up membership of an audience sharing an experience with millions of unseen others, and thus join in an imaginary community watching the same thing. This call to belong, and to share the values and experiences of a particular social group or even a whole nation, is parallel to the way in which the French philosopher Louis Althusser (1971) explained the important media theoretical concept of **ideology**. This is a structure is which people are addressed as particular kinds of subject, and take up a position laid out for them by this call, along with the values inherent in the position to which they are called. People become individual **subjects**, subject to ideological values and constituted as subjects by ideology.

The inclusion of viewers in programmes, whether literally or by hollowing out a position for them in the discourse of the programme, is complex in daytime talk shows such as *The Jeremy Kyle Show* and *Trisha Goddard*. There is a hierarchy of figures, presided over by the host, including professional 'experts', such as doctors and therapists, guest members of the public, the studio audience and the viewers. The role of the host is to mediate between these categories, by representing the viewer's imagined questions and concerns. Television viewers, along with the studio audience, are invited to evaluate the behaviour and opinions of the speakers, so that the position laid out for the viewer is to identify with any or all the speakers, but especially with the studio audience, who are the viewer's representatives. Occasionally television viewers are able to participate in the programme by phoning in, and can adopt a confessional discourse and describe their own experiences, or adopt the position of an expert in order to evaluate other participants in the programme. Although phone-ins appear to empower and involve these viewers, the **codes** and connotations of their appearance have disempowering effects. How long they can speak, being heard but not being seen, and being directed by the host, are all means of controlling who can speak, how and in which discursive code. The discourses adopted by speakers from home or among the studio audience tend to match those of the programme as a whole, for example by appealing to personal experience as proof of an opinion, or presenting statistical or institutional information in the discursive code of 'objective' professional advice. Talk-show narrative is a series of confrontations between different discourses, each appealing to one of several kinds of authority and legitimacy. The role of the host is to arrange these different discourses into a sequence, acting as a mediating narrator working on behalf of the audience and claiming to represent its concerns.

Television commercials often contain characters representing the viewer, usually someone addressed by an on-screen or off-screen narrator about a difficulty which can be solved by a product (like a household cleaner which will remove stubborn

**public service** in television, the provision of a mix of programmes that inform, educate and entertain in ways that encourage the betterment of audiences and society in general.

**ACTIVITY 4.5**

Use an analysis of your own background and experience to explain why you find a particular programme frustrating. What kinds of audience positioning are you resisting?

stains). The use of viewers' representatives enables the relationship of the producer and consumer to be dramatised as a person-to-person interaction, and to provide the product with a concrete setting in the household environment. A variant on this structure is the common use of viewer representatives in car commercials, featuring drivers whose representation attempts both to mirror the viewer and also to include an aspirational element (a younger, richer, more attractive version of the target consumer). The narrative function of viewer representatives, therefore, whether they are studio audiences, talk-show hosts or characters in commercials, is to mediate between the viewer and the representation in the programme or commercial. The viewer is invited to identify with his or her representative, and to take up the position laid out by the signs and codes of the programme or advertisement. The viewer is invited to constitute himself or herself as part of an audience, becoming the one to whom the text is addressed.

This becoming-audience for the viewer is enhanced by possibilities for **interaction** with programmes and commercials. Comedy programmes invite laughter, television commercials offer puzzles or jokes which the viewer is invited to figure out, and both commercials and programmes provide telephone numbers and websites which offer further information, special offers or competitions. Television shopping channels are, of course, entirely predicated on this interaction, since the viewer is explicitly addressed as a potential buyer of the products shown on screen. Television sports coverage is constructed in order to invite the viewer's involvement through offering patterns of reaction to the sport directed by the commentator. Studio comment by invited sports experts (former players, managers, sports journalists, etc.) focuses on discourses of evaluation and prediction, and aims to invite the viewer to engage in speculation and judgement in a similar way. This imaginary dialogue between the viewer and the programme therefore lays out codes in which the viewer's response should take place. In sports television, for example, singing football songs and throwing cans of beer at the screen are not expected, whereas knowledgeable debate and respect for the rules and conduct of the game are. The use of slow-motion replays in sports programmes is a further means of presenting and encouraging this kind of rational and evaluative critique.

**interactive** offering the opportunity for viewers to respond to what is broadcast, by sending signals back to the broadcaster (along a cable or phone line, for example).

The discussion of signs, codes, functions and narration in this chapter has focused on how television texts are meaningful to viewers, and how viewers are positioned by texts in order to gain pleasure and understanding from them. One of the assumptions behind this kind of analysis is that television does not usually reveal the construction and positioning activities of the text. However, television is an unusual medium in sometimes making its own production, and the failures in its production, a subject for television programmes. But this revealing of behind-the-scenes information and of mistakes in programme production is confined to particular kinds of text. In situation comedy, for instance, it became common in the 1990s for

**outtake** a shot or sequence which was omitted from a finished programme because of a mistake during production or an artistic decision.

**blooper** a mistake by a performer in a programme, or a technical error. The term often refers to humorous mistakes.

**postmodernism** the most recent phase of capitalist culture, the aesthetic forms and styles associated with it and the theoretical approaches developed to understand it.

**pastiche** the imitation of forms or conventions in another text. The term can convey a negative view that the imitation is less effective or valuable than the original.

**globalisation** the process whereby ownership of television institutions in different nations and regions is concentrated in the hands of international corporations, and whereby programmes and formats are traded between institutions around the world.

episodes to end with a compilation of **outtakes** and mistakes, or '**bloopers**', from that episode or from several episodes. The animated series *The Simpsons* adopted and made fun of this trend by showing a whole episode supposedly comprised of mistakes, even though obviously animation is made frame by frame and so cannot possibly involve these errors. Compilation programmes such as *It'll Be Alright on the Night* are entirely composed of outtakes and mistakes from all genres of programme. There is an interesting parallel between these programmes and the compilation programmes of viewers' ridiculous home videos (people falling down, pets doing amusing things, etc.). The widespread use of domestic video equipment, and viewers' increasing familiarity with the means by which programmes are made, has led to new kinds of viewer positioning.

The recognition that television programmes play on their own and each other's conventions is one of the components of **postmodernism**. This theoretical term rose to prominence in Television Studies in the 1980s, as a way of distinguishing how programmes since that time appear to be more self-conscious and sophisticated than before. Among the features of television which mark postmodernism are self-consciousness, irony and the **pastiche** or imitation of familiar conventions, formats and structures, like the pastiche of chat show conventions in *The Kumars at No. 42* and *I'm Alan Partridge*, or the pastiche of television and film conventions in *The Simpsons*.

So the term 'postmodern' can be used as a way of describing the textual and narrative characteristics of programmes. But it can also be used to signify a more general shift in television culture, and culture in general. In Chapter 3 it was explained that the **globalisation** of television could be described as postmodern in character. Here, the term is used to denote a shift from national broadcasting culture to an increasingly global one, where the ownership of television networks, the international sale of programmes and the worldwide broadcast of some television channels, such as CNN and MTV, seem to have changed the character of television, at least in Western nations. But in each use of the term 'postmodern' it signifies a changed situation. This change is not assumed to be progress from an earlier state of affairs, much less an improvement, but a development which calls into question notions of evolution and progress. Indeed, in some formulations of what postmodernism is, it is argued that the very idea of history as a process of progressive improvement has ceased to match up to what is happening in culture. The increased awareness on the part of audiences that what they watch are artefacts or textual products (rather than visions of reality) can be adduced as support for this argument.

---

**ACTIVITY 4.6**

Are television programmes with the most plural meanings the best programmes? How do standards of value draw on criteria of complexity, plural meaning and innovation?

---

While television programmes and advertisements offer positions from which pleasure and sense require acceptance of the position laid out by the text, contemporary viewers are increasingly able to recognise, sidestep and reject these positions.

Becoming part of the audience is perhaps much more of a conscious choice than some models of television text and narrative might admit. In particular, psycho-analytic models of unconscious positioning need to be supplemented with studies of audiences' conscious and negotiated relationships with television. For, just as much of what the audience sees on television is performance, becoming-audience is also a performed role which viewers partly unconsciously and partly consciously adopt. For these reasons, studies of television texts and narratives are not a self-sufficient set of approaches in Television Studies. They need to be supplemented by studies of real viewers' relationships with television, to explain how some positions for the viewer are taken up while others are not.

## Case study: the Guinness 'Surfer' commercial

This case study begins with a close textual analysis of a television advertisement first shown in 1999, aiming to demonstrate how a **semiotic** and **narrative** analysis works in practice. Because television commercials are short, but often take the form of a story told by com-binations of image, language and sound, they function well as demonstration pieces for textual analysis. But the later parts of this case study raise some questions about alternative ways of understanding this commercial. Information about the production of the advert, its historical and commercial context and the intentions of its makers both support and challenge the conclusions of a close textual analysis. So, as well as showing the power of textual analysis itself, this case study aims to draw attention to the exclusions and blind-spots which it involves.

The narrative of the commercial can be divided into four segments. First, the surfers wait on the beach; then they ride a huge wave; next they celebrate together; and finally an image of a pint of Guinness is connected with this narrative of expectation and fulfilment. The first three segments of the narrative unfold in chronological order, as a story, while the final segment reflects back over the narrative as a whole.

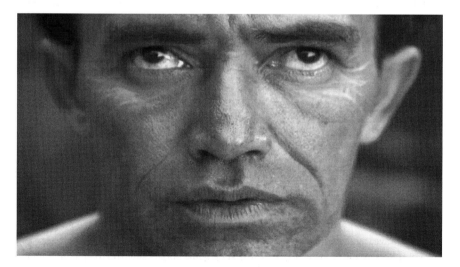

Figure 4.3 Close-up on the surfer's face. 'He waits. That's what he does.' Courtesy of Abbott Mead Vickers BBDO.

*continued*

Figure 4.7  The surfer raises his arms in exultation. [Music ceases.] Courtesy of Abbott Mead Vickers BBDO.

Figure 4.8  The surfers celebrate on the beach. 'Here's to waiting.' Courtesy of Abbott Mead Vickers BBDO.

collapse on to the sand celebrating and hugging each other. The narration reintroduces the toasting motif, connecting the surfers' celebration with the bar-room scene involving the sailors, Ahab and the drummer. The two narratives are parallel to each other.

The still, front-on shot of the pint of Guinness shares its static quality and positioning with the opening shot of the surfer's face, creating a cyclical resolution to the advertisement. The black beer and its white foaming head connect with the dark water, white surf and white horses of the earlier sequences. The drink of beer connects with the toasting motif and bar-room

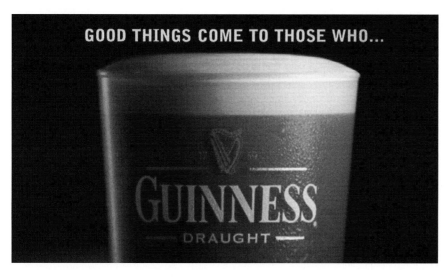

**GOOD THINGS COME TO THOSE WHO...**

GUINNESS

DRAUGHT

Figure 4.9   Close-up of a pint of Guiness with the foaming head settling. Courtesy of
Abbott Mead Vickers BBDO.

scene in the voice-over. The written signs 'good things' and 'wait' connect with the anticipation
of the 'dream' and the surfers' waiting at the start of the advertisement. The pint of Guinness
appears to be equivalent to, or to contain, the various meanings of the action and narration in
the commercial as a whole.

A close textual analysis of this commercial shows that its meanings are developed through
**metonymies** and **metaphors**. White rolling surf, white plunging horses and white-headed
Guinness share traits of whiteness which link them together, so they are metonymies for each
other. Waiting for an exciting surfing experience is parallel to waiting for a delicious drink, so,
although these are different experiences, they are metaphors for each other. The semiotic
structure of the commercial enables it to correlate seemingly different contents with each
other, so they apparently share similar meanings. The exotic, dangerous, masculine achieve-
ments of the surfers are correlated with the Guinness brand, giving this product meanings
which are attached to it by the quite poetic and self-consciously artistic construction of
the advertisement as a narrative. The analysis of the commercial above tried not to explain its
constituents except in the terms which it seems to offer unproblematically to its viewers, but
some of the ambiguities and puzzles can be explained by historical information, production
context and cultural associations. Close analysis of the advertisement remains unfinished
without introducing some of these factors, which seem to belong outside the commercial
itself.

Guinness advertisements appeared first in newspapers in 1929 with the original slogan
'Guinness is good for you'. Advertisements then drew either on variations of this slogan
('Guinless isn't good for you'), on characteristics of the beer ('Tall dark and have some', 'Not
everything in black and white makes sense'), or on the less specific slogan 'Pure Genius'.
(Incidentally, a Guinness commercial was one of the advertisements shown on the first night
of ITV in 1955.) The 'Surfer' advertisement draws on some of this history. While it does not
say that Guinness is good for you, since this would now be a dubious claim that would almost
certainly get the company into trouble, it does associate the product with the vigorous outdoor

**metonymy** the
substitution of one
thing for another,
either because one is
part of the other or
because one is
connected with the
other. For example,
'the Crown' can be a
metonym for the
British state.

**metaphor** the
carrying-over from
something of some of
its meanings on to
another thing of an
apparently different
kind. For example, a
television narrative
about life aboard ship
could be a metaphor
for British social life
(the ship as
metaphor for
society).

*continued*

activity of surfing. It is shot in black and white, picking up on the colours of the product itself, and some of its contents, like the Ahab references and bar-room toasting **syntagms**, seem at first glance not to make much sense. The viewer is asked to work on making connections between signs in the advertisement; and the more knowledge available to the viewer about the history of Guinness advertising and the story of Ahab, the more he or she will find this narrative satisfying. Interpreting the advertisement means treating it less as a 'realistic' narrative and more as a complex multi-levelled piece of creative work. Certainly, the white horses appearing in the wave are non-realistic, and can be explained as representations of the surfer's fantasies about his experience.

The production of the advertisement began with Tom Carty and Walter Campbell of the advertising agency Abbott Mead Vickers BBDO. They measured that it takes 120 seconds to pour a pint of Guinness and leave it to settle before serving, so the slogan 'Good things come to those who wait' arose from a combination of this long waiting time and the old 'good for you' slogan. They had created an earlier commercial about an elderly Italian swimmer who crosses a harbour in the time taken to pour a pint, and the sea connections and waiting time in 'Surfer' sought to connect that advertisement with its predecessor. But they were cautious about the connections between surfing and a vintage Old Spice aftershave advertisement (1977) featuring a surfer, widely regarded as outdated and naff. Carty and Campbell enriched the surfing motif with references to the climactic sea sequences in the film *Moby Dick*, where the whaler Captain Ahab obsessively pursues a gigantic white whale, and a painting by Walter Crane which shows white horses mingling with waves. The advertisement's aim was to position Guinness as a sophisticated drink for younger consumers. So the production context of the commercial reveals an awareness of the history of Guinness advertising, an attempt to draw on notions of obsession, risk and a history of sea adventure fiction, together with a target market of youthful drinkers who might be expected to respond to its complex narrative structure, and the aspirational theme of the 'dream' of excitement and physical prowess.

'Surfer' is in some ways representative of television narrative, especially in advertisements. It uses dramatic codes of narrative structure, music and visual effects which could be found in many other advertisements and television fiction programmes. But it is also unrepresentative, partly because it gained widespread public recognition, and partly because it is longer, more expensive to produce (it cost about a million pounds) and more self-consciously artistic than many commercials. It asks for, and rewards, viewers who can make imaginative connections between the surfing narrative and Herman Melville's novel *Moby Dick* (1851), or the 1956 film which was based on it, and who take the trouble to piece together these intertextual components.

By the age of thirty-five, the average person has seen 150,000 television commercials, amounting to about 75,000 minutes or two months. In this context, an advertisement which makes a public impact is both unusual and very valuable to the market presence of the product it advertises. 'Surfer' came top in Channel 4's poll of 2000 to select viewers' *100 Greatest TV Ads*. Ten thousand votes were cast in the poll, and the Bank Holiday Monday screening of *100 Greatest TV Ads* drew four million viewers.

The final point to make in the context of this case study, therefore, is to note that this advertisement and the production context and history behind it are unusually accessible compared to the great majority of unremarked and poorly remembered commercials alongside it. A close textual analysis of its narrative is a special form of attention to the making of meanings in television which sets the procedures of Television Studies apart from the more usual kinds of attention which television receives from its viewers.

**ACTIVITY 4.7**

Do all television advertisements address potential buyers of the products they advertise? If not, what function do these other commercials serve?

## SUMMARY OF KEY POINTS

- Methods of close analysis deriving from the study of film can show how meanings are constructed in television texts.
- This approach to close analysis relies on analysing the audio-visual 'language' of television.
- The meanings that can be made from television also depend on relationships between viewers and texts.
- Television programmes use conventions and codes to structure their meanings, and television viewers become expert in recognising conventions and decoding meanings.
- Television guides the viewer by using narrative and offering points of identification where viewers can become involved in programmes.
- A knowledge of the production context and history of a television text can affect the meanings which the television text itself may have.
- The meanings of television have ideological significance that shapes relationships between television texts, audiences and society.

## Further reading

Bignell, J., *Media Semiotics: An Introduction*, second edition (Manchester: Manchester University Press, 2002).

Corner, J., *Critical Ideas in Television Studies* (Oxford: Clarendon, 1999).

Creeber, G., *Serial Television: Big Drama on the Small Screen* (London: BFI, 2005).

Fiske, J., *Television Culture* (London: Routledge, 1992).

—— *Introduction to Communication Studies* (London: Routledge, 1990).

Fiske, J. and J. Hartley, *Reading Television* (London: Methuen, 1978).

Hall, S., 'Encoding/decoding', in S. Hall, D. Hobson, A. Lowe and P. Willis (eds), *Culture, Media, Language* (London: Hutchinson, 1980), pp. 128–38.

Hammond, M. and L. Mazdon (eds), *The Contemporary Television Series* (Edinburgh: Edinburgh University Press, 2005).

Kozloff, S., 'Narrative theory and television', in R. Allen (ed.), *Channels of Discourse,*

*Reassembled: Television and Contemporary Criticism* (London: Routledge, 1992), pp. 67–100.

Lacey, N., *Narrative and Genre: Key Concepts in Media Studies* (Basingstoke: Macmillan, 2000).

Lewis, J., 'Decoding television news', in P. Drummond and R. Paterson (eds), *Television in Transition* (London: BFI, 1985), pp. 205–34.

Masterman, L., *Television Mythologies: Stars, Shows and Signs* (London: Comedia, 1984).

Mullan, B., *Consuming Television* (Oxford: Blackwell, 1997).

Seiter, E., 'Semiotics, structuralism, and television', in R. Allen (ed.), *Channels of Discourse, Reassembled: Television and Contemporary Criticism* (London: Routledge, 1992), pp. 31–66.

Selby, K. and R. Cowdery, *How to Study Television* (Basingstoke: Macmillan, 1995).

Thornham, S. and T. Purvis, *Television Drama: Theories and Identities* (Basingstoke: Palgrave Macmillan, 2005).

Tolson, A., *Mediations: Text and Discourse in Media Studies* (London: Arnold, 1996).

# Television and Genre

# Television and Genre

## Introduction

**Genre** derives from the French word meaning 'type', and its study has been carried out in relation to television using approaches and terms deriving from the study of genre in film, literature and other cultural forms. This is appropriate since some of the most established television genres derive from types found in other media. For example, the genre of **soap opera** began in radio broadcasting, where continuing **serials** focusing on the emotional relationships of a group of characters were created to address the mainly female audience during the daytime. These radio programmes were called soap operas because they were sponsored by companies producing such domestic products as detergents and soaps. Drama is, of course, a form deriving from theatre, and in the early years of television broadcasting many fiction programmes were television adaptations of theatre plays. News and current affairs television share conceptions of **news value** and the institutional structures of reporters and editors with newspapers and news radio broadcasting. Entertainment genres, such as sketch shows and situation comedy, also have theatrical roots in music hall and variety, which were adapted for radio and later became established in television.

The study of genre is based on the identification of the conventions and key features which distinguish one kind of work from another, such as the characteristics of Westerns, musicals and thrillers in cinema. It allows theorists to link the conventions and norms found in a group of texts with the expectations and understandings of audiences. In this respect the study of genre aims to explain how audiences classify what they see and hear on television according to:

● features of the text itself
● generic cues which audiences identify in programme titles
● supporting information in listings and advertising publications
● the presence of performers associated with a particular genre (in the way that Bruce Forsyth is associated with television entertainment programmes, for example).

As Neale and Turner (2001: 1) note: 'Most theorists of genre argue that generic norms and conventions are recognised and shared not only by theorists themselves, but also by audiences, readers and viewers.' Theorists have disagreed about the origins of genre categories:

● Do genre forms arise naturally from the properties of texts?
● Are they categories used by the producers of programmes?
● Are they categories brought by audiences to the programmes they watch?

Furthermore, there is disagreement about whether the task of the theorist is to identify genres so that programmes can be evaluated, or to describe how actual audiences make use of genre in their understanding of programmes. From an evaluative point of view, both television theorists and television fans might regard some programmes as transgressing the rules of genre and therefore evaluate these programmes as inferior. For example, some fans of science fiction regard *Star Trek* as lacking the scientific basis of 'true' science fiction and so consider it an adventure series that is simply dressed up with an outer space setting. By contrast, some television theorists might argue that programmes which transgress the boundaries of a genre are more valuable because they potentially draw the audience's attention to the conventional rules of television genre and therefore have a critical dimension. This argument derives from the perception that genre applies most neatly to mass-market **popular culture** texts, so that programmes which are firmly within the boundaries of a genre are regarded as formulaic whereas texts that mix genres are more interesting. For example, *Life on Mars* is a police series set in the 1970s in which the main character seems to have time-travelled there from the present, and confronting him with the outmoded attitudes of the 1970s police force is a way of critiquing the conventions of the police series by using a science-fiction premise. Nevertheless, all texts participate in genre to some extent, and often participate in several genres simultaneously. The study of genre provides a means of pinning down programmes and a means of explaining how programmes become interesting and pleasurable by working against genre conventions as well as with them.

## Identifying programme genre

The **title sequences** of programmes are sequences of signs which signify the boundaries between one part of the **flow** of television and those parts of the flow which precede and follow them. In this respect, title sequences offer cues to viewers which enable them to identify the genre of a programme. There are many different kinds of **sign** that a title sequence might contain, which will enable a viewer to identify the pleasures offered by a programme, and many of these pleasures are connected to genre. For example, the title sequences of news programmes often contain:

- dramatic orchestral music
- images signifying the global coverage of news events
- the immediacy of news signified by a clock face
- signifiers of institutions such as Parliament that are the producers of newsworthy events.

But it is rare for the components of programmes to belong exclusively to a single genre. In news, for example, there are interviews between presenters and experts or officials that are coded in the same ways as interviews in sports programmes. The address to camera found in news programmes can also be seen in sports programmes, weather forecasts and even quiz programmes. News programmes contain sequences of **actuality footage** accompanied by a **voice-over**, but similar sequences can be found in **documentary** and current affairs programmes, wildlife programmes and

**popular culture** the texts created by ordinary people (as opposed to an elite group) or created for them, and the ways these are used.

**title sequence** the sequence at the opening of a television programme in which the programme title and performers' names may appear along with other information, accompanied by images, sound and music introducing the programme.

**flow** the ways that programmes, advertisements, etc. follow one another in an unbroken sequence across the day or part of the day, and the experience of watching the sequence of programmes, advertisements, trailers, etc.

**sign** in semiotics, something which communicates meaning, such as a word, an image or a sound.

**actuality footage** television pictures representing an event that was filmed live. The term usually refers to pictures of news events.

**voice-over** speech accompanying visual images but not presumed to derive from the same place or time as the images.

**documentary** a form aiming to record

actual events, often with an explanatory purpose or to analyse and debate an issue.

format the blueprint for a programme, including its setting, main characters, genre, form and main themes.

other factual genres. Although the content of news programmes is necessarily different in each programme because, by definition, the events in the news are new, the **format** of news programmes exhibits a strong degree of continuity. The separation of news programmes into separate items, the importance of the news presenter and reporters as a team which appears regularly in programmes, and the consistent use of settings such as the news studio, logos and graphics make today's news programme look very similar to yesterday's and tomorrow's news.

Television commercials also use consistent performers who become associated with a product brand, and graphics, logos and music which recur. Television police series personalise law and order in the personas of detectives and policemen, as do other genre programmes, such as hospital drama. One of the difficulties in the study of genre in television is identifying which features of programmes are unique to a particular genre, to the extent that these features could form a list enabling the critic to establish the boundaries of that genre.

---

## ACTIVITY 5.1

Examine the brief descriptions of terrestrial television programmes included in listings magazines and newspapers. How many programmes are described using a genre designation (such as 'soap opera', 'teen drama', 'thriller', 'sitcom')? Are there other kinds of designation which seem important (such as featured performers, or the mention of writers, directors or producers)? Why are programmes designated in these ways?

---

ideology the set of beliefs, attitudes and assumptions arising from the economic and class divisions in a culture, underlying the ways of life accepted as normal in that culture.

The **ideological** functions of television programmes cross the boundaries between genres. Television police series are structured around the opposition between legality and criminality. Narratives are organised by establishing the central character of the detective or policeman as a personal representative of legality, against whom the otherness of crime and its perpetrators are measured. The television audience is encouraged to identify with the central figure, whereas the criminal is established as an other responsible for disruption. In television news a similar opposition is established between the public, the news presenters and the institution of television news, on one hand, and the other nations, public institutions, perpetrators of crime and the impersonal forces of chance, the weather and natural processes which produce the disruptions and disorder reported in the news, on the other. Although audiences recognise television news and television police series as different genres, the ideological oppositions between order and disorder, continuity and disruption animate both genres at the level of structure and narrative. Within television news itself, internal boundaries separate news events into different genres. Separate news items and separate teams of reporters and presenters may be devoted to categories of news event such as party politics, economic affairs and sport. These categories are also arranged in a hierarchy, where party politics and economic affairs are generally considered more newsworthy and significant than sport, for instance. The representation of society in television news depends on the use of a principle of categorisation in order to make sense of events. News could potentially include any event, but it depends on a basic categorisation which divides those events considered to be of importance, newsworthy, from those which are not. There is an unspoken assumption that society is potentially unified, but further categorisations divide the society into groupings based on relative wealth, age, gender, race, institutional power and political outlook.

---

**ACTIVITY 5.2**

Nick Lacey (2000: 133) proposes that the elements within texts that need to be examined to identify their genre are: character types, setting, iconography, narrative and style. Try applying this list to two programmes within the same genre. Can you find a programme containing similar elements but which seems to belong to a different genre? If so, what do you need to add to your list of elements to maintain the boundaries of the genre you first considered? How stable are those boundaries?

---

Just as categorisation is used in television news to make sense of the potentially infinite events occurring each day, genre categories are used in Television Studies to make sense of the differences between broadcast material and arrange it into hierarchies and groupings. The study of genre in Television Studies has tended to begin from the assumption that what are being studied are complete, individual programmes. This is because genre study borrows its methodology from other disciplines, such as literary criticism, where discrete and complete works (like novels and plays) are the basic units. As discussed earlier in this book, however, television consists of a flow where programmes are interrupted by advertisements and **trailers**, and where **teasers** may precede the title sequences that declare the beginnings of programmes. For viewers accustomed to **zapping** between channels and fast-forwarding through videotapes, television is experienced in a much more fragmentary manner. On one hand, whole channels – such as the Sci-Fi Channel, CNN and the Cartoon Network – are devoted to one genre of programme. On the other, as discussed throughout this chapter, programmes borrow **intertextually** from a variety of genres and blur the boundaries between them. As Neale and Turner (2001: 2) argue, 'The degree of hybridity and overlap among and between genres and areas has all too often been underplayed.' But they go on to note that 'Underplayed, too, has been the degree to which texts of all kinds necessarily "participate" in genre . . . and the extent to which they are likely to participate in more than one genre at once.' To make sense of the complexity of the contemporary television landscape, viewers become expert in recognising genre, and also derive pleasure from the manipulation of genre and from the ways in which television plays with its boundaries.

**trailer** a short television sequence advertising a forthcoming programme, usually containing selected 'highlights' from that programme.

**teaser** a very short television sequence advertising a forthcoming programme, often puzzling or teasing to viewers because it contains little information and so encourages curiosity and interest.

**zapping** hopping rapidly from channel to channel while watching television, using a remote control (a 'zapper').

**intertextuality** how one text draws on the meanings of another by referring to it, by allusion, quotation or parody, for example.

---

**ACTIVITY 5.3**

Examine the schedules of the digital channels in listings magazines or newspapers. Many channels are named after or based on genres. Which genres are these, and which genres do not have channels based on them? What could be the reasons for this?

---

## The generic space of soap opera

adaptation
transferring a novel,
theatre play, poem,
etc. from its original
medium into another
medium, such as
television.

It has been customary in Television Studies to define genres by the content and setting in which programmes take place, but an alternative set of genres could be established by focusing on the representation of fictional space, geographic region or basis in another source text (there could be a genre of literary **adaptation**, for example). It would be possible to divide up television programmes in different ways from the categories customarily used to describe genres if attention were paid less to the content of the programmes and more to their form and ideology. For example, a genre could be constructed of television programmes focusing on community. This could include the communities of people inhabiting a shared space in television soap opera, the communities working together in television hospital drama and television police and detective fiction. Within this large generic category, distinctions could be made to establish sub-genres in which communities are bound together primarily by family and emotional relationships (as in British soap opera), by an institutional hierarchy (as in hospital and police drama) and by the pressure of an external threat (as in *Buffy the Vampire Slayer*).

The significance of space and setting to the definition of a recognised television genre can be seen in the importance of setting in British soap opera. The titles of *Coronation Street*, *Hollyoaks*, *Emmerdale* and *EastEnders* demonstrate how location functions as a force linking characters with each other, not only as a positive basis for community but as a boundary which characters find it difficult to transgress. Characters in soap opera are, in a sense, trapped by their location, and their proximity to each other within the space creates not only alliances but rivalries and friction. Several categorisations link characters together in soap opera:

- family relationship
- working relationship
- age group
- race
- gender.

These function in a similar way as either a positive ground for connection or a source of rivalry and tension. The overlapping of these categories also produces possible storylines in soap opera, since one character is likely to belong to several different categories, perhaps working in the local shop, belonging to a family and being friends with other characters of the same age group. Soap opera narrative manipulates these connections and distinctions, changing them over time, thus producing different permutations of connection and distinction which form the basis of storylines.

In the genre of soap opera the multiple storylines built around a large group of characters living in the same location produce an impression of rapidly occurring events, since the scenes and sequences in any one episode are likely to involve several different combinations of characters. Short scenes involving different combinations of characters follow each other rapidly, producing forward movement in the story-lines. But on the other hand, any one episode of a soap opera usually occurs in a very short space of represented time, such as one day or even just a few hours. The exchange of information between characters through gossip and conversation and the withholding of information which has been revealed to the audience also encourage the viewer to be aware of developments a long time in the past, to speculate about future events and to experience pleasurable uncertainty about which of the numerous occurrences in any one episode will have effects on the networks of relationships which connect the characters.

The ways in which soap opera works in terms of form have been used as the components to define this genre, but many of the features discussed here are also evident in other programmes which are not soap operas but share some of the same elements. For example, hospital drama series such as *Casualty* and *ER* focus on relationships between characters, exploit the audience's memory of the past and encourage speculation about future events, and they take place in a restricted location where a relatively large group of characters enables the tensions in relationships to be explored. The most significant difference between soap opera and television hospital drama is in the degree of narrative closure in each episode. Hospital drama and police drama are characterised by narratives in which transitional characters appear and produce a disruption to the social space represented in the programme, but at the end of an episode this storyline is completed.

Figure 5.1 *CSI: Crime Scene Investigation.* Courtesy of CBS-TV/The Kobal Collection.

## The police genre: seeing and knowing in *CSI*

**computer generated imaging (CGI)** the creation of images by programming computers with mathematical equations that can generate realistic two-dimensional pictures.

**diegesis** the telling of events as narrative. Diegetic sound emanates from the represented environment, while extra-diegetic sound comes from outside that environment.

**shot-reverse-shot** the convention of alternating a shot of one character and a shot of another character in a scene, producing a back-and-forth movement which represents their interaction visually.

**close-up** a camera shot where the frame is filled by the face of a person or a detail of a face. Close-ups may also show details of an object or place.

**pan** a shot where the camera is turned to the left or turned to the right. The term derives from the word 'panorama', suggesting the wide visual field that a pan can reveal.

**realism** the aim for representations to reproduce reality faithfully, and the ways this is done.

The American police drama *CSI: Crime Scene Investigation*, made for the CBS network from 2000, was so popular with viewers in the USA that by 2005 it had spawned the spin-off series *CSI: Miami* and *CSI: New York*. The original *CSI* continues to be shown in the USA and is also sold to overseas broadcasters, including Five in the UK. Shown in the evening as part of a group of imported US police series also including *Law and Order*, *CSI* helped Five to improve its reputation for quality by heavily marketing these expensively made and innovative US programmes. Five labelled these police series 'America's Finest', referring not only to the slang designation of the police force in the USA but to the claim that the programmes represent the highest-quality television imports.

*CSI* is primarily structured through following the work of police forensic scientists, and in common with *Homicide: Life on the Street*, it is much less about physical action than the process of solving crimes. The relationship between visual style and the human body is *CSI*'s greatest innovation (Bignell 2007). The use of rapid zooms towards and inside the body or items of evidence (often at extreme magnification and using **computer generated imaging**) develops the common theme that seeing in a special way is the key investigative activity in the genre (Lury 2005: 44–56). The most important thing that the forensic investigators and the camera do is to look carefully.

*CSI* is distinctive in its use of long sequences showing the processes of autopsy and the scientific analysis of fragments from bodies or crime scenes. Fluid but very slow camera movements track around the dimly lit spaces of the crime labs while the characters conduct procedures such as examining clothing fibres or skin cells through microscopes, or painstakingly arranging the fragments of an object so they can identify how it was broken. Pace is created in these long sequences by the addition of non-**diegetic** music, and the camera's elegant dancing motion. The emphasis is on the concentration of the investigators and their systematic absorption in their work, connoting their professionalism and efficiency. Long camera shots produce the impression of continuity through time, and allow the camera to follow characters as they reveal their thoughts and their relationships with each other and their environment. This generosity with time provides the viewer with the opportunity to consider what can be seen, thus providing the audience with relevant clues and encouraging identification with the main characters. Extended shots of the scientists working enforce the viewer's concentration on the detail of how the characters act and react across a sustained period of action. At the same time, these long sequences show the characters moving in space and allow for a physical and emotional distance from them, so that an analytical and critical understanding of them can be gained by revealing movements of the body, gesture or costume.

This is a distinctly different television code from the rapid alternations of **shot-reverse-shot** and **close-up** which are more common in police drama that focuses on physical action, in which scenes are performed several times with the camera positioned differently each time in order to capture the reactions of one character to another and to provide a coherent sense of fictional space. There is no need for the camera to **pan** quickly between speakers, since scenes move relatively slowly. The generates a sense of **realism** in following the investigators' work as it occurs and also requires the audience to observe them and interpret their actions without the camera providing the movements from wider shots to close-ups, and the dramatic contrasts which usually offer an interpretative point of view on the action. The segmentation of scenes using rapid cutting and extensive close-up can be analytical, presenting interpretations of character and action, but the long sequences in *CSI* allow the viewer to make sense of space and character in a different way, where he or she must work alongside the forensic investigators to interpret the images.

The camera in *CSI* seems to force objects to reveal their secrets, paralleling the work of the forensic investigators with the looking done by the camera. But the camera not only matches the investigators' look but adds to it, explains it and actively gathers knowledge for the viewer. So one of the functions of close-up, and especially zooms into an object or body, in *CSI* is to link the camera as narrator with the actions of the programme's characters. The relative lack of conventional physical action in the series is related to this. The stillness and reticence of the characters, especially the chief investigator Gil Grissom, are parallel but opposite to the fluid movement and freedom given to the camera. This also sets up a relationship between present and past. The present is characterised by its stillness, seen especially in the forensic scientists' absorption in their work and the literal stillness of dead bodies or pieces of evidence. But this stillness is made to reveal movement and passion that happened in the past. From the evidence they gather, the team reconstructs a crime that is then either restaged in the manner of a conventional television flashback, or an attack on the victim's body is analytically re-enacted by means of **CGI**, prosthetics and models so that the processes that gave rise to physical injuries become known. In doing justice to the evidence, the forensic reconstruction of the process of the crime gives back a story to a body or an object. The present is therefore known by restoring a past that led to it, and what is seen in the present is explained by another form of seeing that projects a past backwards from that present.

This emphasis on how seeing leads to knowing, and presents are given meaning by the restaging of pasts, has important effects on the significance of the lead actors' performances in *CSI* and again distances the series from the often action-driven drama of the police genre. Referring to critical reaction to the series' beginning, and the principal characters of its Las Vegas, Miami and New York versions, *CSI*'s executive producer, Carol Mendelsohn, explained that 'because CSI was very black and white – the evidence never lies – it was comforting in a grey world. There is comfort when Gil Grissom or Horatio Caine or Mac Taylor are on the case. There aren't many people you can trust in the world today' (quoted in McLean 2005). However, there is little character development in CSI, and only fragments of the characters' domestic lives or past experiences are revealed. This is also something of an exception to the way in which characters in long-running series are usually explored in ever-increasing depth, so that series are drawn towards the character-based narratives of soap opera. These people who can be trusted are almost unknown except in their roles as professional investigators who see scientifically and know because of how they see. However, the characters' reconstructions of events are hypotheses, and they are sometimes wrong. Events in the past are reconstructed fragmentarily, sometimes repeated with differences as more facts become clear, and attention is drawn to the processes of investigation. The investigative look is presented as a process of seeing that emphasises its linkage with knowing, and how that link might sometimes be broken.

The emphasis on seeing and the process of constructing knowledge about crime in *CSI* are by no means new to the police genre, though they take a distinctively new form in the series. *CSI*'s visual style has given the police genre a new twist, and the series works with audience expectations of the police genre but also plays with genre because of its emphasis on how evidence of a crime leads to knowledge and a solution to a mystery. *CSI* is exciting television because of its negotiation with genre and its audience's expectations. The conventions of the police genre with and against which CSI works are explored further in the case study at the end of this chapter.

---

### ACTIVITY 5.4

Series drama on television has tended to develop towards the serial form. Does this potentially mean that all drama tends towards the genre of soap opera? What features of soap opera make it a special form of continuing drama?

---

## Sitcom and the problem of humour

Theorists of television genre have found it very difficult to establish clearly how television comedy programmes, especially sitcoms, work. Obviously the primary characteristic of television sitcom is that it is funny, and this has to do with the relationship between the programme text and the audience. Some components of the programme text can be identified as consistent elements of sitcom, but even these are not exclusive to the genre. Audience laughter, for example, is clearly important to the genre. The moments when laughter breaks into the soundtrack provide cues for the audience about what is expected to be funny. At these points the audience is encouraged to join in with the studio audience laughter and recognise the jokes or comic actions. Within the programme text, jokes and comic actions can be identified to some extent as **signs** of comedy. For example, a surprising contrast can be established between what characters say and what they do. Or in a scene involving two or more characters, surprising contrasts between the **discourse** of one and the discourse of another can provide the misunderstanding or conflict of interpretation that becomes comic. Excessive action such as slapstick or pretend violence can also function in this way. Yet sitcom is not the only television genre where each of these textual elements can be found, since shows based on short comic sketches, shows featuring impressionists (such as Rory Bremner) and cartoons can also exhibit several of the same characteristics. The genre of sitcom is usually composed of a particular combination of elements, such as:

**discourse** a particular use of language for a certain purpose in a certain context (such as academic discourse or poetic discourse), and similarly, in television, a particular usage of television's audio-visual 'language' (news programme discourse or nature documentary discourse, for instance).

- fictional narrative
- self-conscious performance
- jokes and physical comedy
- the presence of a studio audience denoted by laughter on the soundtrack.

Rather than claiming that sitcom has unique characteristics which define the genre, it is necessary to take account of signs and forms that overlap with other television genres.

Television comedy depends more than most kinds of television on the self-consciousness of performance, and the willingness of the audience to engage with the excessive speech and behaviour of characters that are designed to cue the recognition of a social norm and to surpass it in a manner which becomes funny. Frasier and Niles Crane in *Frasier*, for example, are snobbish and self-involved to the extent that their breaking of norms of behaviour becomes funny. The taping of sitcoms in the television studio using three camera set-ups where the set is open at one side to the studio audience underlines the theatricality and performance aspects of sitcom. The fact that actors will allow pauses in their dialogue for audience laughter, even occasionally acknowledging the audience by building its presence into the format of the series (as in the 'Tool Time' sequences of the American sitcom *Home Improvement*, where a television show is supposedly being recorded), encourages the **identification** of the television audience with the studio audience present at the taping of an episode. Focusing on performance in this way discourages the audience from judging speech and behaviour according to cultural norms, and instead suspends these norms in order for them to be reacted against for comic purposes.

But these analytical ways of describing how sitcom works are not explanations of how television programmes become funny. What is funny to one viewer may be quite unamusing to another, since humour depends not only on social **codes** and cultural understanding that may be common across a broad age group, nation or region, or **gender** but on the numerous and largely indiscoverable variables that make up an individual **subject**'s personality. For this reason, the only major body of analytical work on comedy derives from **psychoanalytic** criticism, and even this is less a theory of comedy than a descriptive account of how conscious and unconscious factors may predispose individuals to find certain kinds of speech and action amusing.

---

## ACTIVITY 5.5

Repeated programmes are often those which fall into established genres, and are advertised as 'classics', such as (in sitcom) *Dad's Army*, *The Good Life* and *The Vicar of Dibley*. In what ways might audiences' pleasurable nostalgia for these programmes be the pleasure of their familiar generic form? Are 'classic' programmes always solidly generic?

---

## Talk shows and the performance of morality

The genre of the television talk show has undergone significant changes in the past decade. Talk shows can be regarded as television representations of a **public sphere**. The public sphere is a conceptual space in which issues of concern to society as a whole can be debated, using the shared discourses and assumptions which are necessary to rational debate. As discussed earlier in this book, television provides instances of such debate and constitutes a public sphere, at the same time as contemporary broadcasting atomises individuals within their homes and fragments society into

**identification** a term deriving from psychoanalytic theories of cinema, which describes the viewer's conscious or unconscious wish to take the place of someone or something in a television text.

**code** in semiotics, a system or set of rules that shapes how signs can be used, and therefore how meanings can be made and understood.

**gender** the social and cultural division of people into masculine or feminine individuals. This is different from sex, which refers to the biological difference between male and female bodies.

**subject** in psychoanalysis, the term for the individual self whose identity has both conscious and unconscious components.

**psychoanalysis** the study of human mental life, including not only conscious thoughts, wishes and fears but unconscious ones. Psychoanalysis is an analytical and theoretical set of ideas as well as a therapeutic treatment.

**public sphere** the world of politics, economic affairs and national and international events, as opposed to the 'private sphere' of domestic life.

niche audiences
particular groups of
viewers defined by
age group, gender or
economic status, for
example, who may be
the target audience
for a programme.

ever-smaller **niche audiences**. Television's public sphere simulates the kind of democratic debate for which the term was first invented, both keeping alive the sense of the public sphere and at the same time standing in for an absent public debate in highly developed societies.

American talk shows which rose to prominence in the 1970s, such as the *Oprah Winfrey* show and *Donahue*, conventionally focused on individual guests who represented a large minority constituency which sought a voice. For example, black single mothers, the disabled or people struggling with drug addictions were able to give voice to an under-represented and stigmatised group, by individualising the problems of that group through the confessional and personal discourse of the guests. This ventilation of personal concerns, connected with the concerns of groups, was itself a mechanism of empowerment and resistance to dominant social values. The contributions of experts on the talk show connected the experiences of the guests to institutional discourses, such as medicine, psychoanalysis and civil rights. The translation of personal experience into institutional discourses was also a mechanism of empowerment, though of course it also had the effect of incorporating resistance into society's dominant forms, and converting anger into some more socially acceptable force.

Beginning in the 1980s, however, the genre of the talk show modulated into a much less liberal form of television, with less focus on empowerment and the valuation of resistant and excluded voices. The reason for this change in the genre was that broadcasters' research into audience preferences led to the creation of new programmes, and the reshaping of old ones, to gain new and larger audiences. Neale and Turner (2001: 6) note that 'the cumulative effect of repeated tweaking of the format and content amounts to a change in genre [as] more finely grained, and more readily available, viewing figures have the effect of influencing content, format and, ultimately, genre'. American television talk shows such as *The Jerry Springer Show* and the *Morton Downey Junior* show by the 1990s were as internationally successful as *Oprah Winfrey*, but with a very different and much more aggressive attitude to their guests. The hosts of these programmes are much more inclined to make accusations about the opinions and behaviour of their guests than to support them in their resistance to a norm. The most widely discussed feature of the programmes is the prevalence of aggressive physical behaviour when guests confront each other in front of the cameras and the audience. For example, couples appear as guests and suddenly it is revealed that the secret lover of one of them is also present, without their knowledge. The confrontation between one of the partners and the lover has given rise to fistfights, the throwing of furniture across the set, and the intervention of burly security guards. The role of the host – who previously functioned both as a representative for social norms signified by the collective audience behind him or her and as a mediator between the guest, the audience and experts – has become instead that of an orchestrator of confrontation and a ringleader, encouraging the audience to vent its condemnation of one or more of the studio guests. The prominence of 'experts' has diminished in parallel with this, so that the conversion of social exclusion and violent emotion into the rational terms of institutional discourse is much less the project of the programmes. A remnant of the liberal discourse of empowerment remains at the end of each *Jerry Springer Show*, however, when Jerry delivers his three-minute address direct to camera, containing a more considered homily on the foibles of human nature. Nevertheless, the transformation of the talk show genre demonstrates the erosion of these programmes as a public space in which liberal and democratic ideologies of inclusion, empowerment and personal development are enacted in television form. Instead, their ideology has become increasingly focused on the reinforcement of social norms, where audiences (represented by the studio audience) close ranks against perceived deviance.

A further aspect of this development is the controversial centrality of performance to the talk show genre. There have been celebrated cases (for example, in 1999 on the *Vanessa* and *Trisha* shows in Britain) when popular newspapers have revealed that some of the guests have been 'fakes'. Rather than members of the public discovered 'naturally' by researchers, these fake guests have been consciously performing their roles in order either simply to fulfil a desire to appear on television or to make money from appearance fees and **spin-off** newspaper and magazine features. The appetite for new guests on programmes sometimes broadcast every day during the week has led to the scavenging of guests from one show by the researchers on another, and the creation of an informal pool of guests who can be relied on to give dramatic and emotional performances. In the context of this emphasis on performance and the importance to programme **ratings** of guests' extreme emotional responses or violent outbursts, it is not surprising that the line between a 'genuine' and a 'fake' guest has become blurred. The importance of the public display of guilt, shame and rage in the contemporary talk show further contributes to the blurring of the boundaries of the genre. These factors link the talk show to the dramatic fiction genre of soap opera, for example, where these emotions and their exaggerated display are the focus of the narrative.

Of course, it is no accident in this respect that both talk shows and soap opera are conventionally associated with, and scheduled to appeal to, a **feminine** sensibility and a female audience. For in Western societies it is a conventional attribute of femininity to display emotion openly, and to take an interest in the confessional revelations of others. Indeed, the movement of many genres of programme mentioned in this chapter, such as documentary and actuality programmes, as well as soap opera and talk shows, towards these conventional attributes of femininity is in itself an interesting development in contemporary television. Programme genres, and their assumed audiences, appear to be moving towards a more generalised social dissemination of femininity.

**spin-off** a product, television programme, book, etc. that is created to exploit the reputation, meaning or commercial success of a previous one, often in a different medium from the original.

**ratings** the number of viewers estimated to have watched certain programmes, as compared to the numbers watching other programmes.

**feminine** having characteristics associated with the cultural role of women and not men.

---

## ACTIVITY 5.6

The preceding section suggested that contemporary television has introduced attributes conventionally associated with femininity (such as emotional display, confession and gossip) into a wide range of programmes genres. Are there 'masculine' genres? Which programmes would you include in these genres, and what makes them masculine?

## Reality TV and social control

found footage
television or film
sequences 'found' in
previously made
programmes or films,
and which can be
incorporated
unchanged into the
programme being
made.

It has become commonplace for television not only to rely on **found footage** supplied by others, such as police camera and surveillance footage, but to install covert, hidden surveillance systems in order to generate **actuality** evidence of wrongdoing and criminality. Programmes such as Granada Television's *Rattrap*, *Nannies from Hell* and others in the . . . *from Hell* series, such as *Neighbours from Hell* and *Plumbers from Hell*, have adopted this technique. There is an assumption behind these programmes that they are engaged in a public service, so that, for example, the advertisements in *Yellow Pages* and newspapers showing the names of plumbing companies are shown on screen to inform viewers of exactly which businesses have been exposed as cowboys. Programme narrators provide tips and information on how to spot inferior and overpriced work, and give guide prices for what particular common jobs should cost. But several points should be raised about programmes such as these. If the cowboy workers exposed by the programme are already known to be operating in dangerous and exorbitant ways, the programme does nothing to change this situation, except add evidence. If large numbers of other workers have been found to do the same work well, this footage would be undramatic and so would not be used, though it may be the case that the vast majority of workers are both competent and reasonably priced. These programmes feature only the most disturbing and shocking incidents, and are necessarily unrepresentative.

The audience for the first programme in *Neighbours from Hell*, was 11.5 million in 1997. This is a much larger audience than is conventionally gained for documentary programmes in their more traditional forms. The . . . *from Hell* format has been copied by the BBC, and was sold by Carlton to America in 1999. By contrast, conventional documentary **strands** such as *World in Action* and *Panorama* have faced declining audiences and ever-later **schedule** positions. The generic markers of documentary in its conventional form include the journalistic structuring of stories, where not only are events denoted but a 'balanced' selection of expert opinion offers opposing views and different contextual frameworks in which to understand them. Conventional documentary narrative hierarchises these elements so that a **hegemonic** discourse is established in which an issue is enfolded by the reliable and responsible discourse of the mediator, represented both by the presenter and the television institution. The . . . *from Hell* series and other kinds of quasi-documentary factual programmes focus instead on the dramatic and on barely contextualised actuality. One of the interesting consequences of this is the reduced importance of expertise and the discourse of professionals in making sense of the issues denoted in programmes. A different ideological pattern is being established. The discourses of expert professionals tended to value middle-class virtues:

strand  a linked
series of
programmes, sharing
a common title.

schedule  the
arrangement of
programmes,
advertisements and
other material into a
sequential order
within a certain
period of time, such
as an evening, day or
week.

hegemony  a term
deriving from Marxist
theories of society,
meaning a situation
where different social
classes or groups are
persuaded to
consent to a political
order that may be
detrimental to them.

- specialist knowledge
- rational discourse
- reasoned debate and discussion
- the solution of problems by institutional means.

But new documentary and actuality television formats have dispensed with this. Risk, unpredictability and danger are represented as endemic to society, and institutions are represented as impossibly distant and too preoccupied with administrative and bureaucratic issues to deal with these problems. Instead, individuals are expected to monitor their own environments (often by using video technology to gather evidence and record deviance since the police and other authorities are too busy to undertake this) and work out their own balance between accepting crime and nuisance and taking independent action against it. In this ideological framework nothing is certain, individuals are largely on their own and the future is viewed pessimistically. The generic shifts in the television documentary mode both represent and encourage shifts in ideology and the perception and meaning of society.

The images from **closed-circuit television (CCTV)** which appear in reality segments of television programmes carry powerful political and social **connotations**. The places where closed-circuit television cameras are installed are often where their job is to police the poor and those who are suspected of being socially deviant. CCTV cameras have become a popular means of controlling public space, such as shopping malls and railway stations, in the absence of sufficient police to patrol them. The function of these cameras is to police the boundaries between normal and deviant or criminal behaviour, and sequences shot by the cameras appear in television programmes as evidence of deviance. The very visual style of the footage, grainy, in black and white, with still cameras, has come to be associated with the visible evidence of deviant behaviour and the identification of deviant people. Whereas documentary has a history of representing and arguing for those in society who are the least privileged, the most vulnerable to exploitation and the most marginalised, documentary footage from CCTV in reality television programmes is used to the opposite effect. It reinforces marginalisation, deprives deviant behaviour and deviant people of the opportunity to explain and provide context for their actions, and removes their actions from larger social and political contexts. In the case of *Nannies from Hell*, it also generates anxiety among the audience, and potentially exaggerates the divisions between the employers of underpaid care workers and those workers themselves. The television audience is placed in the position of the 'normal' parent and may be encouraged to stigmatise and fear the young and often exploited care workers who appear in the programmes only as the perpetrators of disturbing crimes. The mothers employing the nannies vowed to stay at home and care for their own children, thus also lending weight to conservative definitions of femininity and motherhood. The ideological action of the programme may have been to imply that mothers who work outside the home are both irresponsible and unnatural.

Reality TV is appropriate to a society which is increasingly under surveillance. One effect of this is to separate the scene of crime and deviant behaviour from the process of dealing with it by enforcing the law. Unfortunately, having camera footage of crimes does not guarantee that the criminals will be caught, or charges against them proved. The evidence that criminal behaviour has occurred is only a first stage in a long and complex process of investigation and prosecution. So the fact that television cameras can gather such apparently incontrovertible evidence has the effect of reassuring the audience that criminals can be identified, yet it does not automatically lead to the capture of criminals or the prevention of crime. A second effect of reality crime images like these is that they accustom the audience to the fact of being seen and potentially having images of oneself broadcast and judged. At any time, especially in a city, your movements can be captured by the many surveillance cameras in operation. The knowledge that you are being observed may well affect your behaviour. Not only in the sense that you might be persuaded not

**closed-circuit television (CCTV)** a small-scale television system where the images and sound are not intended for broadcast: for example, a network of security cameras.

**connotations** the term used in semiotic analysis for the meanings that are associated with a particular sign or combination of signs.

to commit a crime (perhaps this is a good thing), but that you might monitor yourself so that nothing you do could be misunderstood as a threatening or criminal activity. Loitering outside a shop, hanging around with a group of strangely dressed young people or approaching strangers to ask them questions might all be misunderstood either as criminal behaviour or at least as suspicious. Footage of such activities often appears on reality TV programmes as supporting evidence to show that a particular person had been behaving 'strangely', and it identifies him or her as deviant. Knowing this, often unconsciously, increasingly affects the ways in which people act in public space.

## Case study:  true crime and fictional crime

This case study compares the generic form of the police series with reality TV programmes that use actuality footage of criminality (such as *Police, Camera, Action* and *Car Wars*). Narratives in the police and detective genre begin with a disturbance in the social world depicted in the programme. A disruption, such as a murder, a robbery or an attack, has taken place, unsettling a family, community or business. It is the task of the detective to restore the equilibrium of the social world by:

- finding the explanation for the disturbance
- removing the destructive force (usually a person who has committed the crime)
- providing the conditions for the restoration of order and balance.

The ideological work that the police series does is therefore to provide a means of representing society as a fundamentally ordered and balanced network of relationships, introducing a challenge or threat to society, and dramatising the ways in which this threat is removed. In order to do this, the central character of the detective has to be established in the narrative as the representative of law and order. He or she embodies the values acceptable to the audience as the **consensus** view of right and wrong, and by his or her actions shows how ideological, commonsense justice works in practice to keep society on a more or less normal and comfortable track.

**consensus**
a shared and accepted opinion or attitude among a certain group of people.

But the ideology of society is not a single or stable structure. In the police series genre the conflicts within the central character, among the workers in the police institution, and conflicts between the upholders of the law and the criminals they pursue are often equally of interest. Inspector Morse, for example, sometimes overlooked the guilt of a murderer and let him or her go because of his respect or even admiration for the perpetrator of the crime. His sense of fair play, and moral justice, were occasionally at odds with the letter of the law and demonstrated that the character's ideological position could conflict with the normally unquestioned rightness of the law. The work of the narrative, establishing the central character in a complex and realistic way, can produce such a strong identification with the character that he or she appears superior to the system of law which he or she is engaged in supporting. It is commonplace in the police and detective genre for there to be conflicts between the central character and his or her superior. The requirement to play by the rules of police procedure can in itself be an obstacle to upholding the law and solving a crime. The characteristics and forms of action used by the perpetrators of crime can be very similar to those of the detective. Telling lies, casual violence, disrespect for authority and rules are all characteristics which can be found both in the central characters and in the criminals whom they pursue. What distinguishes the detective from the criminal is the effectiveness of the methods they use, and the aim which justifies their behaviour. John Fiske and John Hartley (1978: 29) have argued that this similarity between detective and criminal, and the value placed on efficiency, are symbolic means of presenting ideological conflicts:

> What the police versus criminal conflict may enact symbolically, then, is the everyday conflict of a competitive society in which efficiency is crucial . . . The common concern that television police are becoming more and more like the criminals in their methods and morals means that the few factors that distinguish them take on crucial significance. Of these distinctive features, efficiency is the most marked.

The aim of a criminal might be to solve an emotional problem, for example by murdering a man with whom his wife is having an affair; or to make money by dealing in illegal **commodities**, such as drugs or guns. In the first case the criminal has a misplaced sense of justice, and in the second they are misusing the **capitalist** system of business and exchange. Narratives in the police and detective genre establish some activities as criminal and excessive, as the misapplication of the principles which underlie a law-abiding society. The representation of crime on television is a means of defining the boundaries between the legal and the illegal in terms of the reasonable versus the excessive, though the desires and motivations behind legal and illegal behaviours may be identical.

The mechanism for identifying the criminal and bringing him or her to justice is the acquisition of information. The narrative usually comprises acquiring different kinds of information, such as:

- the testimony of witnesses
- scientific forensic evidence
- observing the behaviour of suspects.

The task of the detective is to assemble this information into a narrative of the crime. So the narrative of the programme is occupied with the construction of this other narrative, whose events usually occurred either before the beginning of the programme or in its opening few minutes. The closure of the narrative and the resolution of the programme are achieved when the detective has completed the assembly of the narrative of the crime. This is presented to the perpetrator, or perhaps to a court or the detective's superior. The programme can end when this narrative of the crime is confirmed as true, most often by the confession of the criminal. At this point the ideologically correct positions of the characters can be established: the criminal is captured, justice is done for the victims, the detective has done his or her job and the superior is satisfied. The stability of society and the security of the positions occupied by the various characters are confirmed.

The central characters of police and detective series often work in teams of two or more. One reason for this is that it provides opportunities for explaining plot points, evaluating the behaviour of witnesses and suspects and assessing evidence. Conversations between the central characters deal with the difficulty of following the internal cognitive processes by which the detectives go about solving the crime. In terms of the structure of characters, the differences between one and the other not only serve to create possible tension for the audience but enable each character to make up for the inadequacies of the other and supply his or her own special knowledge. Buddy teams in television police series include, for example,

**commodity** a raw material or product whose economic value is established by market price rather than the instrinsic qualities or usefulness of the material or product itself.

**capitalism** the organisation of an economy around the private ownership of accumulated wealth, involving the exploitation of labour to produce profit that creates such wealth.

*continued*

a younger and an older man, a man and a woman, a married woman and a single woman, a black man and a white man. The central characters of police series were most often unmarried men until the 1970s, and the work of restoring the ideological values of society, solving the problems represented by crime and embodying the values of justice were associated with heterosexual white masculinity. Buddy teams of detectives in more recent years have challenged this convention. Single central characters have been personally vulnerable in physical and emotional terms, and the individual members of buddy teams have been unable to function successfully as the vehicles of police genre narrative without the assistance of their partners to provide the knowledge and characteristics which they lack.

The majority of television police series are set in urban environments. The city is a place where people do not know each other, where they are mobile and can be difficult to trace. Plain-clothes detectives are characters who can merge with the locality in which they work, and work semi-independently of the hierarchy of the police institution. It is possible for them to go undercover, to simulate the behaviour of the criminals whom they are seeking and operate in the same world with the same rules. In the confusing, anonymous and mobile environment of the city, the detective needs to take on some of the ambiguity, anonymity and mobility which enable criminals to commit their crimes. In this environment appearances are deceptive. The narrative has to work hard to establish that, despite the apparent indistinguishability of the detectives from the criminals (in terms of their physical appearance, behaviour and attitudes), the police officers are fundamentally supporters of normality and justice, whereas the criminals are forces of violence, disorder and destruction. It is important that the central characters of the police genre are established as having an innate sense of justice. The detectives' success in catching criminals and doing the right thing is proof of their efficiency and the appropriateness of the ideologies which underlie their actions. The satisfying shape of the narrative – moving from an initial problem or disruption through investigation and the gathering of information, to a final resolution where balance and harmony are restored to the represented world – is itself part of the ideological work of the police genre. For the ordered structure of the narrative, its movement from beginning to middle to end, is a kind of proof that the assumptions and actions of its central characters are justified. The world of the police genre programme is set up so that the events in that world justify the behaviour of its central characters. The structure of the narrative supports the structure of ideology.

It is interesting to compare the ideological work of fictional police series drama with the ideological implications of programmes in the new genre of reality TV that deal with law and order. Reality TV accustoms the audience to perpetual surveillance and self-surveillance, and contributes to the installation of ideological norms within each subject. Knowing that we are potentially being observed by surveillance cameras, and therefore taking care to monitor our behaviour so that it conforms to the norms expected in our culture, amounts to the internalisation of surveillance. The observing camera has in effect become part of our own mental world. The self-monitoring and self-policing of behaviour are a powerful way of disciplining and controlling society, and eventually might lead to the redundancy of real policemen and real cameras. Each person would discipline and police himself or herself. This concept of internalising norms of behaviour is exactly how the concept of ideology has been explained in Media and Cultural Studies. As explained earlier in this book, an ideology is a taken-for-granted set of norms and assumptions which determines how the subject thinks of himself or herself, his or her relations to others and his or her place in society. It is not imposed by force, but is gradually learned and internalised through the institutions of the family, education, the media and culture in general.

Reality TV programmes customarily use hidden cameras whose images resemble those of the closed-circuit television systems used to gather evidence in police investigations and in public space to monitor and police deviant behaviour. Those people who are pictured in such images in reality TV programmes are therefore already categorised as potentially deviant. *Nannies from Hell*, for example, showed brief extracts from grainy black-and-white covert surveillance footage that 'proved' that particular nannies were physically abusing children. There is a danger of a rush to judgement in this television form, however, since it is very unusual for the people captured in this covert footage to have a right to defend themselves and reply to the accusations based on the footage. Explanation, justification, background and context are all factors which in a court of law might either excuse or at least explain such actions, but in reality TV the moment of seeing is simultaneously a moment of judging. The pleasure for the audience is in seeing something hidden, seeing the very moment when something shocking and disturbing is happening, and the provision of this pleasure takes much greater precedence than the investigation and exploration of the behaviour which is portrayed.

*Police, Camera, Action* is a factual programme which has connections with both news and police drama. It consists of a collection of extracts from police camera footage linked by the narration of Alastair Stewart. Stewart is a newsreader, and the programme gains some of its connotations of **public service** from his association with the values of objectivity, seriousness and reliability which derive from television news programmes. The footage in the programme comprises mainly shots from the cameras installed in police cars, as they follow or chase drivers who are either engaged in criminal activities (such as making a getaway from a robbery) or committing dangerous driving errors. Television police series fiction revolves around identifying illegal acts and their perpetrators. The detectives discriminate between the innocent and the guilty, creating justice by finding out how crimes have been committed and capturing the people responsible for them. Television is a visual medium, and television drama relies particularly on following the point of view of the protagonist and on providing information through dialogue. The central characters of police series gather evidence by watching and observing. Seeing the scene of the crime and watching the behaviour and body language of suspects enable the central characters to establish the evidence which points to the guilty. Discussions between detectives give order and structure to the unfolding narrative of the case, while interviews and confrontations with witnesses and victims provide clues by spoken language, and also opportunities to observe the physical signs which might point to the guilty person. These processes in the police and detective genre place the central characters in a similar position to that of the television viewer: both assemble fragments of information, and read clues and signs which promise to solve the case and bring the narrative to a close.

Programmes using police camera footage sometimes also include CCTV pictures from shops or other premises, and footage from police helicopter cameras used to track suspects who are being pursued. The car chase is, of course, a conventional element of the police drama series, especially American action police drama, where the chase normally occurs in the third quarter of the drama as a prelude to the capture of the criminal. Car-chase sequences in *Police, Camera, Action* do not have the several camera set-ups available to drama programmes, or the reverse shots showing the drivers of the police car, or shots showing the drivers who are being pursued inside their own cars. The visual quality of the police camera footage is less polished than professional television pictures and there is little alternation between points of view or manipulation of narrative time. But despite these important differences between police camera footage and television narrative fiction, the function of the chase is still as an action sequence as a prelude to the capture of an offender.

**public service** in television, the provision of a mix of programmes that inform, educate and entertain in ways that encourage the betterment of audiences and society in general.

*continued*

Dramatic music is used to underscore this excitement and anticipation, and the voice-over narration by Alastair Stewart adopts a point of view which mediates between the pursuing police's commentary and the anticipated reactions of a normative viewer. Stewart points out the stupidity of errors made by drivers, the recklessness of criminals attempting to escape and the danger posed to other road users by them. Since it is customary for police pursuit drivers to give a running commentary on their actions as they follow an offender, there is also a **diegetic** soundtrack running alongside the pictures which helps to explain the action and provides Stewart's narration with a means of access to the police understanding of events.

*Police, Camera, Action* draws connotations of public service and authority from news programmes; it draws music, the narrative functions of the car chase and pursuit from the police drama series; and it draws the visual conventions of the surveillance camera and found actuality footage from documentary. It is a hybrid composed of the codes of several different television genres. Neale and Turner (2001: 7) explain the conflicting forces at work in situations such as this by arguing that

> The 'liveness' of television, its investment in immediacy and provisionality, is in direct conflict with the regulated production imperatives implied by genre and format. Further, the cultural richness of the television message, its capacity to carry an excess of meaning for its viewing audience, means that the television message is always difficult to control.

While genre is a way of drawing boundaries between one kind of programme and another, the television industry's perpetual search for new combinations of generic elements and the audience's skill in 'reading' genre in complex ways mean that genre boundaries are always being redrawn by viewers and programme-makers.

## ACTIVITY 5.7

This case study has argued that 'true crime' reality footage combines the observational conventions of documentary with the narrative oppositions between 'us' and 'them' in police fiction drama. Do 'true crime' programmes also reassure the audience that order will triumph over deviance, or is this an alibi to protect programme-makers from accusations of exploitation?

## SUMMARY OF KEY POINTS

● Genre study is a way of dividing up and classifying groups of television programmes, and also understanding how viewers make use of genre in order to understand and enjoy programmes.
● Television theorists have debated whether genre is a property of television texts themselves or a way for viewers and critics to understand them.

- All television texts participate in genre to some extent, and often participate in several genres simultaneously.
- Different genres of television programme address their audiences in different ways, and reveal different assumptions about the interests, pleasures and social meanings of programmes in that genre.
- Comparing and contrasting programmes from different genres can illuminate the similarities and differences in how television deals with related ideas and themes.

## Further reading

Allen, R., *Speaking of Soap Operas* (Chapel Hill, S.C.: University of South Carolina Press, 1985).

Bignell, J., 'Seeing and knowing: reflexivity and quality', in J. McCabe and K. Akass (eds), *Contemporary American TV Drama: The Quality Debate* (London: I.B. Tauris, 2007).

—— *Big Brother: Reality TV in the Twenty-first Century* (Basingstoke: Palgrave Macmillan, 2005).

Brunsdon, C., *The Feminist, the Housewife, and the Soap Opera* (Oxford: Oxford University Press, 2000).

—— 'Structure of anxiety: recent British television crime fiction', *Screen*, 39:3 (1998), pp. 223–43.

Buckingham, D., *Public Secrets: EastEnders and its Audience* (London: BFI, 1987).

Clarke, A., '"You're nicked!": television police series and the fictional representation of law and order', in D. Strinati and S. Wagg (eds), *Come on Down?: Popular Media Culture in Post-war Britain* (London: Routledge, 1992), pp. 232–53.

Corner, J., *Critical Ideas in Television Studies* (Oxford: Clarendon, 1999).

—— *Television Form and Public Address* (London: Edward Arnold, 1995).

Creeber, G. (ed.), *The Television Genre Book* (London: BFI, 2001).

Dahlgren, P., *Television and the Public Sphere* (London: Sage, 1995).

Dovey, J., *Freakshow* (Cambridge: Polity, 2000).

Dyer, R., C. Geraghty, M. Jordan, T. Lovell, R. Paterson and J. Stewart, *Coronation Street* (London: BFI, 1981).

Feuer, J., 'Genre study and television', in R. Allen (ed.), *Channels of Discourse, Reassembled* (London: Routledge, 1992), pp. 138–60.

Geraghty, C., *Women and Soap Opera: A Study of Prime Time Soaps* (Cambridge: Polity Press, 1991).

Hammond, M. and L. Mazdon (eds), *The Contemporary Television Series* (Edinburgh: Edinburgh University Press, 2005).

Jacobs, J., *Body Trauma TV: The New Hospital Dramas* (London: BFI, 2003).

Kidd-Hewitt, D. and R. Osborne (eds), *Crime and the Media: The Postmodern Spectacle* (London: Pluto, 1995).

Lacey, N., *Narrative and Genre: Key Concepts in Media Studies* (Basingstoke: Macmillan, 2000).

Livingston, S. and P. Lunt, *Talk on Television: Audience Participation and Public Debate* (London: Routledge, 1994).

Lury, K., *Interpreting Television* (London: Hodder Arnold, 2005).

Neale, S. and F. Krutnik, *Popular Film and Television Comedy* (London: Routledge, 1990).

Neale, S. and G. Turner, 'Introduction: what is genre?', in G. Creeber (ed.), *The Television Genre Book* (London: BFI, 2001), pp. 1–7.

Shattuc, J., *The Talking Cure: TV Talk Shows and Women* (London: Routledge, 1997).

Sparks, R., *Television and the Drama of Crime* (Buckingham: Open University Press, 1992).

Wagg, S. (ed.), *Because I Tell a Joke or Two: Comedy, Politics and Social Difference* (London: Routledge, 1998).

# Television Production

# Television Production

**genre** a kind or type of programme. Programmes of the same genre have shared characteristics.

**slot** the position in a television schedule where a programme is shown.

**treatment** a short written outline for a programme, usually written for a commissioning producer to read, specifying how the programme will tell its story or address its subject.

**pitch** a very short written or spoken outline for a programme, perhaps only a few sentences, often used to persuade a commissioning producer to commission the programme.

**location** any place in which television images are shot, except inside a television studio.

**storyboard** a sequence of drawn images showing the shots to be used in a programme.

**director** the person responsible for the creative process of turning a script or idea into a finished programme, by working with a technical crew, performers and an editor.

**off-line editing** the first stage of editing a completed programme, where the sequence of shots, sounds and music is established.

**online editing** the final stage of editing a completed programme, where effects are added and a high-quality version of the programme is produced.

## Introduction

The stages in television programme production discussed in this chapter are:

- *development*, where programme ideas are being worked out, researched and planned in an audio-visual form appropriate to a certain television **genre**, **slot** and size of budget, and where the **treatment**, budgets and **pitch** are devised.
- *pre-production*, where after commissioning further research is conducted for **locations** and contributors or performers are selected, the script is written, **storyboards** and production schedules are drawn up, and the design, props, costumes and music are selected.
- *production*, when the shooting takes place, following the plan outlined in the budget and schedule, using the **director**, performers, presenters, contributors and the technical crew that have been selected and organised at the preproduction stage.
- *post-production*, when editing takes place, normally first **off-line** at below broadcast quality, then **online** editing is completed, when effects and sound mixing are achieved. At the end of this process final accounts are prepared.

The chapter discusses the many professional roles involved in making television, with emphasis on the creative and managerial roles of producer, director, screen-writer, editor and camera operator. It is not possible in the space available here to provide as much detailed descriptive information about these roles, or the competences needed to carry them out to professional standards, as can be found in the many 'how-to' books on the market about television production. (A few such books are listed in the Further Reading section at the end of the chapter.) Nevertheless, the chapter considers the different roles in television programme-making and gives an overview of the different stages of the production process, including some of its key terminology. The chapter includes practical exercises which individuals or groups can work on in order to explore these processes for themselves.

The aim of this chapter is to develop an analytical understanding of how television production communicates with audiences through the skills and techniques used by professional television-makers. The assumption behind it is that learning about television is not only a critical and theoretical enterprise: television is an industry, a technology and a set of working practices. So the student of television should understand the broad principles of audio-visual composition by learning about the production practices that bring programmes into being, watching a range of television programmes to consider their audio-visual strategies and gaining as much experience as possible of making his or her own short television films in creative and reflective ways.

Television has long been regarded as a producer's medium, meaning that the television producer has the predominant authority over and responsibility for television-making. While there are several other roles that could claim such creative and managerial authority, particularly those of director and scriptwriter, this chapter devotes the greatest space to the key elements of the producer's role. The producer contributes to the process of selecting and working with writers, controls the process of making a programme, and fulfils a responsibility to the television institution that has commissioned the programme by overseeing budgets, personnel, the production schedule and the delivery of the programme. The chapter explains how producers work with a script editor and production assistants in this process, as well as with creative personnel on the production such as the director, performers and designers. As far as possible, the chapter offers a discussion that can apply across the genres of factual and fictional television production, but there are specific discussions of genres that have particular patterns of organisation and production, such as the independent documentary in contrast to the big-budget drama. News is not discussed in this chapter (for news production, see Harrison 2000), and nor is the making of television commercials, because the emphasis is on the major contemporary modes of drama and documentary and the ways in which their production can be explored in simple practical exercises.

---

### ACTIVITY 6.1

Watch the opening and closing credits of several programmes chosen from different genres (e.g., documentary, news, drama, game show). Compare the total number and different job titles of people listed in the credits. What conclusions can you draw from your analysis about the relative significance of members of the production team (including performers and presenters) in the different genres?

---

## Development

Although the production of television programmes is a linear process from the initial idea to the final broadcast of the programme, making programmes demands anticipation of later stages at every point in the process. An initial idea will need to be shaped so that it will appeal to the audience imagined by the programme-maker. So right from the start the programme-maker will have an audience in mind for the subject, style, genre, aesthetic form and pace of the programme. As the production continues, this sense of the audience may be modified, but it will always be present as a check on the probable effectiveness of each individual decision. At the same time, programmes will have been pitched to producers or commissioning editors, so the idea and the intended process of its realisation will also need to appeal to those people. Although there is potential conflict, then, between the programme-maker's conception of the audience appeal of a programme and the commissioning producer's or editor's conception of the programme's appeal, this degree of difference or similarity may vary considerably. For example, a scriptwriter may be primarily motivated by a sense that his or her documentary or drama production will communicate important messages about gender, ambition, legislation, fear, love, courage or whatever other idea the programme-maker wishes to communicate. The scriptwriter's sense that the audience will be informed, educated or entertained by their project may not be shared by the producer or commissioning editor to whom the idea is pitched. In practice, there is always a process of negotiation between all of the parties involved in making a television programme, and it is the responsibility of all the parties involved to maintain the integrity of their ideas yet also to be persuaded by the ideas of the others. So tensions, power struggles and ulterior motives are endemic to television production, as well as the more positive factors of teamwork, creative co-operation and pride in one's expertise.

Whereas cinema has been a medium in which the director has creative control over the film, in television considerably more power is wielded by the producer. Television producers manage all the staff involved in the making of a production, including the director, and have traditionally enjoyed a more secure position in employment. Those working for large broadcasting institutions will have control over a series of programmes, and are likely to employ directors, writers, performers and technical staff on a more ad hoc basis for individual programmes in a series. Even though British broadcasting institutions have contracted-out increasing proportions of television production since the 1980s, independent producers as well as producers working for the large institutions remain the central figures in the planning, shooting and post-production of television programmes. Producers are primarily managers, but they also work closely with creative staff and require a broad range of knowledge. Their primary role is to lead the team making a programme, to deliver that programme to a deadline imposed by the institution which has commissioned it and to maintain a standard of quality that will ensure approval from industry colleagues and prospects of further work. The skills needed to achieve this include:

- management skills of wielding authority effectively while maintaining the coherence and harmony of the production team
- commitment to the project
- an ability to understand and evaluate the work of others.

**copyright** the legal right of ownership over written, visual or aural material, including the prohibition on copying this material without permission from its owner.

Since television programmes are subject to a range of legal considerations, such as **copyright**, health and safety, and libel and defamation, the producer also needs to know the basics of these legal frameworks as well as the guidelines provided by broadcasting organisations. As producers will be managing technical specialists, such as camera operators, lighting and sound technicians, graphic artists, designers and editors, they need to know enough about these experts' fields to recruit them and manage and evaluate their work.

In many television genres the producer will need writing skills in order to advise scriptwriters and to edit and sometimes rewrite their work, and an understanding of the visual and sound qualities of television that will be used to realise a programme idea or script. In drama programmes producers work closely with writers and may often have experience and skill in writing themselves. Pitching a programme for commissioning will be done on the basis of a storyline created by a writer, and the episodes of a series, serial or single television film will be planned, shot and post-produced starting from a script bought from a professional writer. The relationships built up between producers and writers are crucial to the success of television programmes. In factual genres such as **documentary**, even though a programme will not be scripted for performance in the same way as a drama, nevertheless producers are required to have some skill in writing. Documentaries also require scripts, often including written sequences of voice-over, and will be pitched and commissioned on the basis of written outlines. As discussed earlier in this book, documentary is a form of storytelling as well as a genre in which realities are represented, and documentary producers need to be aware of **narrative** structure, structures of argument and the production of dramatic effects, all of which are skills inherited from and connected with the written forms of journalism, drama and literature.

**documentary** a form aiming to record actual events, often with an explanatory purpose or to analyse and debate an issue.

**narrative** an ordered sequence of images and sound that tells a fictional or factual story.

### David Chase, writer–producer and creator of *The Sopranos*

David Chase, creator and producer of *The Sopranos*, went to film school and wanted to be an arthouse *auteur*. But he could not sell a film of his own so he wrote for television (for the 1970s detective series *The Rockford Files*, for instance). Nevertheless, he continued to develop his best film idea, about a tough mobster and his annoying mother. The mobster feels he has to care for her, but she is in some ways tougher than him and even contracts a killer to murder him. Insight into the mobster's dilemmas about family, violence and power are provided by the device of having him talk to a psychoanalyst. The drama works by the collision and tension between two behavioural codes: the mobster must be tough and secretive, whereas the psychoanalyst expects speech to reveal and unload worrying emotions and weaknesses. The psychological context allows for non-naturalistic forms, such as dream sequences, in contrast to the naturalistic portrayal of the details of organised crime.

Chase's idea became series one of *The Sopranos*. Fox Television commissioned the show, but Chase felt they were trying to smooth out and tame the ideas they had seen in the pilot scripts he showed them, so he took the idea to HBO Original Programming, which supported the tone and ideas of the scripts. *The Sopranos* contains a mix of genres – family story and mob gangster show – and has achieved the status of 'quality television': aesthetically interesting, psychologically and morally complex, yet sufficiently connected to existing genres and forms to draw large audiences.

### ACTIVITY 6.2

Use a few short sentences and simple drawings to create a character on which a short drama can be built. Specify as closely as possible the age, gender, race, history and occupation of the person. Think of a simple activity (cleaning shoes, hanging a picture, talking on the phone) that you could shoot using basic video equipment. Draw seven simple pictures in a sequence (a storyboard) to show how the activity could be shot to reveal the character, using only static wide shots, mid-shots and close-ups.

Figure 6.1 Example of a storyboard. Courtesy of Jeremy Orlebar.

series a television
form in which each
programme in the
series has a different
story or topic, though
settings, main
characters and
performers remain
the same.

serial a television
form in which a
developing narrative
unfolds across a
sequence of
separate episodes.

## Pre-production

Producers working in **series** or **serial** television depend heavily on the quality of
the scripts they can obtain for their programmes. Production planning will typically
begin more than a year before any shooting takes place, and at this stage storylines

and scripts need to be commissioned and approved. Maintaining connections with writers and finding new writers to contribute to the series are therefore important aspects of the producer's job. During the pre-production process producers will often spend considerable amounts of time outside their office in discussions with writers, seeking ideas and negotiating terms for scripts. For a run of thirteen programmes, for example, producers may need to commission several more scripts than will ultimately be used, to allow for late delivery or refusal of a script by the producer or their superior owing to cost implications, unsuitability for the agreed format or conflicts with production guidelines or ethical standards. Even when scripts have been delivered, the producer and the script editor will continue to work on them. Revisions may be required in order to make the script shootable within the agreed budget. Extensive rewriting or polishing of the script might be necessary in order to:

- maintain continuing characters
- adapt scripts to the strengths or weaknesses of performers
- add or remove special design elements or effects.

Because of the numerous other demands on producers, script editors often do much of the detailed work in revising scripts and consulting with writers, and this extensive experience enables them to build up expertise and contacts which later enable them to become producers themselves. It is conventionally agreed in the television industry that writers retain credit for the scripts they produce, although in practice the script used during the shooting itself may well have been extensively revised by a script editor and the producer. The authorship of television programmes is therefore difficult to assign to one person: in practice, authorship is a collective activity involving the whole production team.

In television, the rare single television drama and the increasingly common mini-series or low-frequency repeated drama (such as the police drama *Prime Suspect*) are marked by their prominent display of the author's name (Murdoch 1980). The theatrical inheritance in television production leads to the privilege granted within drama to the writer and the notion of creativity. In contrast, all soap operas and high-frequency repeated dramas use a team of writers, either invariant in number or supplemented and exchanged with other writers at intervals. Series are usually commissioned from a single author or an already constituted team of authors, for a contractually agreed number of scripts. Television is regarded by writers as an instrument in which their creative work is distributed to an audience, as well as an occupation that makes them a living. But the script may be altered or drastically changed. It is not simply a transcription of dialogue but also an interrelated set of instructions for all the professional workers involved in production. For the production team and performers, the script directs and restricts their activities. It is the authority to which interpretative and expressive questions are referred, through the figure of the director, who controls the process of realising the written word, such that the script is finally exhausted by being 'translated' into a television programme. In this sense the script is unlike a play text, which not only is performed more than once but can be transferred between theatre companies and is subject to entirely different interpretations when different directors are in charge of staging it.

Although a producer may have the initial idea for a programme in factual genres such as documentary, he or she relies on researchers to flesh out the details of the topic and find contributors. Researchers in factual television are normally young people with a background or interest in journalism, who are often aiming to move up the professional hierarchy into the role of producer or director. They work for producers, who in turn are employed by executive producers contracted to oversee the making of a series of programmes. The sources of programme research are varied, and include not only resources in the control of television institutions but numerous outside sources, most of which can be accessed free of charge. Researchers will commonly rely on a list of contacts established in earlier projects, such as experts based in academic institutions, government-funded policy units and charities, and a varied collection of people who have contributed to research for previous programmes or appeared in them. These sources do not normally require payment, though researchers can spend a lot of time on the telephone attempting to make contact with them and to shape their contribution into a form that is useful to a programme.

Sources available to researchers within broadcasting institutions are now more accessible with the advent of computer databases, which make access possible to the institution's archives, previous programmes and libraries of press clippings. However, since programme-making is increasingly contracted out to independent companies who must conduct research at their own expense and using their own facilities, the resources built up by large organisations such as the BBC are not accessible to the researchers working on many contemporary programmes. Research sources such as newspaper archives, libraries and the internet can be important to programme research, but the pressure of time and the requirement to travel make it more likely for today's researchers to telephone people directly and request instant information. Working in this way demands various skills from researchers, particularly persistence, diplomacy and persuasion, since information sources will normally see their contribution as an additional, unpaid responsibility outside their normal work. But organisations that have a vested interest in providing information to publicise or support their cause can be very helpful: for example, charities may be willing to supply packs of information, documents and spokespeople, and may be keen to contribute directly to programmes by providing experts. Clearly, the ulterior motives of research sources and contributors need to be assessed carefully by researchers, and potential problems referred to the producer for whom they are working.

## Storylines in *Coronation Street*

*Coronation Street* did not perform too well in 2001. Its stories were being driven largely by plot rather than character, despite a cast of more than fifty, so its recently appointed executive producer Carolyn Reynolds decided to concentrate more on the core characters. Reynolds had worked on the programme for over twenty years, as a production assistant, then producer, then executive producer in the mid-1990s. As executive producer she had a strategic remit to integrate *Coronation Street* with

Granada Television's other drama output, with producer Kieran Roberts (formerly working on *Emmerdale*) running the programme week to week. Granada's new director of programmes, John Whiston, explained:

> There are tensions between storyliners, who want a story that gets them logically and clearly to a particular point, and writers, who want to free up enough time for their characters to be what they want them to be. If the balance swings too far to the storyliners, you get a very plot-driven show that is a bit ploppy and for my money there has been too much emphasis on the storyliners.
>
> (quoted in Moss 2002: 2)

The background to this shift in power from storyline (plot) to characters (script) was audience ratings: *Coronation Street* was challenged strongly by *EastEnders* in 2001. Partly because *EastEnders* had an omnibus edition at the weekend, its ratings almost always exceeded those of *Coronation Street*. Granada TV executives, and the programme's producers, made strategic management decisions about the programme based on their perceptions of audience demands and the balance of power between the staff in their production team.

New programmes are commissioned on the basis of a treatment. This is a short one- or two-page document which organises the ideas on which the programme is based, and provides an indication of its structure, cost and target audience. A treatment normally begins with one or two sentences stating the idea of the programme, followed by an indication of the target audience. Then the style of the production will be outlined, including the creative approach to be taken (for example, documentary or drama, location or studio, on-screen narrator or presenter, cinematic or arthouse style, **observational** or narrated documentary). The structure and content section of the treatment is in effect a condensation of the script, where scenes and sequences are briefly described. A storyboard can be used to give a more precise indication of the key visual sequences in the programme. The treatment will specify the level of equipment used to shoot and edit the programme, and provide background information on the creative team and the skills of the technical staff to be used. The budget completes the treatment. Writing production budgets is a skilled and complex task, but the basic principles are to establish the number of days required to shoot the programme and the editing time required to complete it. These facts will determine the cost of employing the people in front of the camera and behind it, who are employed at daily or hourly rates. Shooting days on location are more difficult to estimate because of such factors as travel to and from locations and between locations, and variables such as weather. Editing time is also difficult to estimate, since sequences cut to music can be very complex to edit, whereas interview contributions to a documentary programme can be edited directly into a finished master tape. On average, a programme-maker could expect to edit about ten minutes of a finished programme in one day. Nevertheless, the basic elements of a budget can be listed on a spreadsheet such as the one shown below, based on an imaginary two-episode 180-minute medium-to-high-budget drama for the BBC, shot mainly

**observational documentary** a documentary form in which the programme-maker aims to observe neutrally what would have happened even if he or she had not been present.

on film on location. The categories in this budget should be mainly self-explanatory, and are divided into:

- 'above-the-line' costs relating to the pre-production staff and tasks, and
- 'below-the-line' costs relating to the period of production itself.

The budget would also be broken down into sub-categories under each of the headings, with each sub-category having an estimated cost attached to it. The 180-minute drama using this budget is a quite expensive production, but it usefully illustrates the approximate costs of all commonly used categories of staff and service in television production. A low-budget documentary using a small crew, no performers (also known as 'talent') and shooting on digital video cameras would, of course, be much cheaper.

| Budget category | Estimated cost (£) |
| --- | --- |
| Story and script | 100,000 |
| Producer's and director's fees | 150,000 |
| Main cast | 75,000 |
| **Sub total** | **325,000** |
| Production management | 90,000 |
| Assistant director | 40,000 |
| Camera crew | 50,000 |
| Sound crew | 20,000 |
| Editorial staff | 55,000 |
| Stills camera staff | 1,500 |
| Wardrobe staff | 35,000 |
| Make-up staff | 15,000 |
| Casting | 25,000 |
| Production accountants | 50,000 |
| Art department | 70,000 |
| Supporting cast | 130,000 |
| Stand-ins, doubles and stunts | 30,000 |
| Crowd | 55,000 |
| Music | 50,000 |
| Costumes and wigs | 15,000 |
| Productions stores | 7,500 |
| Film and laboratory charges | 75,000 |
| Studio rental | 90,000 |
| Equipment | 100,000 |
| Travel and transport | 100,000 |
| Studio and other transport | 15,000 |
| Hotels and living expenses | 60,000 |
| Studio hotels and living expenses | 3,000 |
| **Sub total** | **1,182,000** |

| | |
|---|---:|
| Insurances | 15,000 |
| Publicity | 5,000 |
| Miscellaneous expenses | 20,000 |
| Construction labour | 10,000 |
| Construction materials | 20,000 |
| Set dressing labour | 20,000 |
| Operating labour | 30,000 |
| Lighting and spotting labour | 40,000 |
| Properties | 65,000 |
| Special effects | 10,000 |
| Location facilities | 80,000 |
| **Sub total** | **315,000** |
| Finance and legal | 75,000 |
| **Total above the line** | **325,000** |
| **Total below the line** | **1,572,000** |
| **Grand total** | **1,897,000** |

Figure 6.2  Example of a programme budget.

Because of the very high costs of drama production, for instance, co-production deals with broadcasters or production companies in the United States or Europe are a frequent means of support for British programmes. Co-production is increasingly common in all genres of television production. This is not only the case with major broadcasters such as the BBC, which has a long-standing track record of co-production agreements with the United States (Arts and Entertainment Network, the Discovery Channel, the PBS non-commercial channel) and regional broadcasters in Germany and other European countries. Independent production companies in Britain also seek to finance drama by making agreements with programme financiers in a range of countries, such as Canal+ in France, the ABC network in Australia and a range of smaller institutions worldwide. In factual television certain genres, such as the nature documentary, are well-established formats in which co-production contributes significantly to the budget. In the case of nature programmes the key production expense is filming on location, spending large amounts of time and money seeking interesting footage despite difficulties in locating rare animals, coping with difficult weather conditions, working without adequate technical support and recruiting local staff on an ad hoc basis to support the production. But if good-quality footage can be obtained, the resulting film will be adaptable for translation of its commentary into innumerable languages, and can therefore be sold to a large number of international buyers. Genres in which this kind of translation and suitability to a wide range of markets is more difficult, such as documentaries on British social problems, may be much more difficult to finance by co-production. And even if a co-production deal is forthcoming, producers need considerable expertise in negotiating the legal contractual arrangements. Negotiating with co-production partners for rights to broadcast in particular territories, or for worldwide rights, and making agreements about such potentially lucrative income streams as **merchandising** and the distribution rights of programmes on DVD for retail sales require specialist legal advice.

Television directors are appointed by the producer. This usually occurs on the basis of the producer's previous contact with the director, or the producer's knowledge of the director's strengths and weaknesses as exhibited in earlier work. A director may be known for their work in a particular genre, or work which involves the use of particular television forms. For example, some directors specialise in working closely with actors, and may be best suited to television drama where there is the budget and time to develop performances and explore the possibilities of the script prior to shooting. Other directors may be particularly skilled in working quickly on productions with a limited budget and time, where their effectiveness in getting several pages of script shot in a few takes would be the primary reason for the producer to employ them. Television drama such as soap opera clearly needs directors with these skills, since performers and characters are already established and the main requirement is to complete the required number of scenes in only a few days' filming. Yet other directors may be schooled in integrating particular technical processes or services into a production. Integrating special-effects shots, model shots and post-produced digital effects for science-fiction television is a particular directorial skill, while directing in inhospitable locations far from base or working with unpredictable animals may be important for the director of a nature documentary programme.

Once appointed, the director will be provided with the script and will engage in extensive discussions with the producer about the choices of lesser performers, members of the technical team and the selection of music and costumes, for example. Because the director is responsible for the final look of the programme, and the aesthetic style achieved by the use of vision and sound, he or she has considerable input into the production process, though the responsibility and control of the production will ultimately remain with the producer.

**merchandising**
the sale of products associated with a television programme, such as toys, books or clothing.

## ACTIVITY 6.3

Using the storyboard and brief treatment you created in Activity 6.2, decide how you would cast a performer to play the character, and how you would choose a setting and any costume or props needed without spending any money. How would you use a short voice-over narration in the first person ('I') or third person ('he' or 'she') and some music to give tone and meaning to your seven shots? Write the narration and obtain your music.

Figure 6.3 David Attenborough with an iguana in *Living with Dinosaurs*, BBC1, 2000. Photograph by Simon Smith, courtesy of BBC Photograph Library.

## Production

The five most common types of camera and tape or film stock used in television broadcasting are:

● *DV*: digital cameras and tape producing higher-quality images than the now outmoded VHS tape format, using cameras and tape stock that can be bought from conventional retail outlets, and edited on inexpensive home computer equipment. DV is commonly used in educational institutions and the early stages of vocational training. It is good enough for broadcast in some genres of documentary programming.

● *Beta SP*: digital camera and tape formats available from professional sources, used for a lot of low-budget television production and corporate video-making, and requires editing facilities available from specialist providers of technical services.

● *Digital Betacam (DigiBeta)*: a higher-quality professional format that is more expensive in camera and tape costs, and more expensive to edit. Higher-budget television productions use this format.

● *16 mm or 35 mm* film: a format that has become increasingly rare in television production, although it is still used for high-budget drama productions. The cost of this equipment and associated hardware (such as camera **dollies**) as well as the film stock and professional editing of footage are rarely justified for television programme-making now that small, lightweight digital cameras have become more accessible and cheaper.

dolly a wheeled camera platform. A 'dolly shot' is a camera shot where the camera is moved forward or back using this platform.

● *HD (High Definition)*: electronic cameras that record images with greater quality than previous digital cameras, producing much more precise detail or 'resolution' that can be seen especially well on new television sets designed for HD programmes.

Human vision is binocular, meaning that having two eyes close to each other but in different positions provides two slightly different images of the world which the brain interprets as a three-dimensional image that has depth and perspective. While cameras are designed to mimic many features of human vision, television pictures are noticeably flatter, so techniques of lighting, sound and shot composition are used to produce the impression of depth and coherence in the space which is shot. Television pictures have also normally been much less visually sharp than cinema pictures. The quest for ever-greater sharpness of image and detail (the resolution of the television picture) has led to the recent introduction of High Definition (HD) cameras, which the BBC, for example, began using on the prestigious documentary series *Planet Earth* and the drama series *Bleak House* before gradually introducing it for all drama productions. Retail television sets are now being sold that have the screen resolution to display the greater detail visible in programmes shot in HD, and they have already become common in the USA and Japan. Television resolution depends on how many lines make up the picture, scanning back and forth horizontally across the screen. Television pictures in Britain are made up of 625 lines, but HD pictures can be made up of as many as 1080 lines, eliminating much of the fuzziness that can be seen if you look very closely at a conventional television screen. HD also eliminates the flickering effect of conventional 625-line television, and produces a very stable and clear picture, like that seen on a high-quality computer monitor.

Programme-makers have to have in mind the relationships of one shot to another. When they talk about shots which 'will cut' and shots which 'won't cut', they are describing shots which will or will not connect with the previous and subsequent sequences. Shots which will cut are those where the point of view of the camera and the relationships that comprise the shot composition fit the conventions of editing to be used in the programme. Shots which will not cut are those where conventions are not being followed, and for the viewer there will appear to be a leap from one represented space to another, from one camera point of view to another, in a way which does not respect the coherence of the narrative or the coherence of the space which has been shot. In drama, for example, the conventions of a shot-reverse-shot will allow alternations of point of view between speakers as long as the camera does not break the **180-degree rule**. The position of the camera in individual shots and the use of camera movement have to be planned in advance so that one shot will cut with another. In documentary and other factual genres, relationships between shots also have to respect audience expectations of how figures and spaces are represented. **Noddy shots** and **cutaways** are used to provide bridges between shots, and voice-over, music or other sound are also used to produce the impression of coherence and continuity.

The Steadicam allows smoother and more complex shots than can be achieved with a conventional hand-held camera, which will be affected by movements of the operator's hands and body whenever the operator takes a step or moves around. Shots where the camera is moving have conventionally been created by placing

**180-degree rule**
the convention that cameras are positioned only on one side of an imaginary line drawn to connect two performers in a scene. This produces a coherent sense of space for the viewer.

**noddy shot**
in television interviews, shots of the interviewer reacting silently (often by nodding) to the interviewee's responses to questions.

**cutaway** in fictional dialogue or interviews, shots that do not include people speaking. Cutaways often consist of details of the setting or of interviewees (such as their hands).

the camera on a dolly equipped with wheels, sometimes running on miniature railway tracks laid on location to facilitate smooth movement, whereas the Steadicam consists of a camera equipped with a complex system of counterweights that stabilise it when it is attached to an arm linking the camera mounting to a vest worn by the operator. The operator can alter the camera's position on the mounting almost without touching it, and can walk around and turn while the camera remains stable, without shaking or jerking. Although Steadicam operators have to be specially trained to use this cumbersome equipment, it is usually cheaper to employ a Steadicam operator when productions require a number of moving shots, so Steadicam has become common across all genres of television production. It was developed as a more effective way of creating moving shots in cinema than technology had hitherto allowed, with the aim of keeping the operation of the camera unobtrusive to the viewer and not disrupting the flow of shots within a sequence. This follows the long-established convention in film and television that the means for creating the visual image should not be apparent to the viewer, and that the technique of shooting should be as 'natural' as possible.

But in some programmes, the sheer versatility and smoothness of Steadicam shots has become a badge of quality and style in itself, drawing attention to the moving camera. The technique is especially evident as a prominent part of a programme's visual style in American drama series such as *ER*, *The West Wing* and *CSI*, where information about complex issues of medical procedure, the workings of American government, or forensic investigation are being conveyed by dialogue. By shooting such sequences with the Steadicam, the characters can continue their conversation while walking together along a corridor or between a series of offices, and the moving camera shots provide an ever-changing background of settings to the dialogue, adding visual interest. The Steadicam shot enables the narrative to move between spaces within the setting, and to penetrate different rooms, laboratories or treatment areas in a hospital to give an impression of rapid movement in the narrative of a programme at the same time as information is being conveyed by the dialogue. The giving and withholding of knowledge is always important to the unfolding of narrative in television, especially in fiction. Although much of the time the role of the camera is to deliver significant information to the viewer in order to understand character and plot, the restriction of a point of view and the withholding of knowledge from the viewer can be equally important. Relatively static camera positions, or editing between two or more static camera set-ups in a scene, are conventionally designed to provide the viewer with the best possible view of the activities of the characters in the setting, to deliver the information that the viewer is thought to need in order to understand the narrative. But to place the camera in a position where it can see only partially, or where the view of what is going on in the scene is partially obscured from the camera by objects in the frame, can also have powerful connotations, suggesting that there is something more for the viewer to discover, or that the viewer is set at one remove from the action and must wait for further revelations to occur. Moving shots accomplished by Steadicam can contribute to both of these processes.

The moving-camera Steadicam shot can be a way of following characters smoothly from one space to another, maintaining the audience's attachment to the character as he or she accomplishes a series of tasks or engages in several short conversations while walking from place to place. More information can therefore be given to the audience about the character and his or her activities, placing the character against a shifting background of different locations. But, on the other hand, using exactly the same technique, the moving Steadicam shot can provide an excess of information because there are too many things to see in the background of the frame, and too many actions or moments of dialogue occur in a sequence for the viewer to be able to absorb their meaning satisfactorily. So by delivering such a great deal of information to the viewer as the camera moves and the visible space in the frame changes rapidly, use of the Steadicam shot can paradoxically produce a sense of information overload, or a gap between the understanding of the viewer and the dramatic material being presented in a scene. Furthermore, when it moves with characters who progress through the space of the scene, or when it moves independently through the rooms and corridors of a location, giving a sense of the whole space, the camera itself functions as a participant in the scene, like another character. These sustained Steadicam shots present an extended experience of time and space that suggests privileged observation of a real world as it is lived, since the real viewer's experience of space and time is that they are seamlessly connected one moment to another and one space to another. But viewers are accustomed to the segmentation produced by editing, and the jumping from one moment to another and one space to another that it produces. So the Steadicam shot can also be experienced as relatively unusual, and thus not a means of observing a world that is much like the one we experience ourselves, but instead a special televisual experience of moving smoothly across an extended time and space that stands out as an exception within the 'language' of television.

The conventional forms of television shooting seem to centre on sets of three. The three most commonly used shot sizes are **long shot**, **close-up** and a range of medium-long and medium close-ups in between. To create a coherent sense of space, sequences often begin with a long shot to establish the environment, followed by alternations between mid-shot and close-up to follow the action. In studio production for both factual and fiction genres, three camera positions are the standard minimum for covering the studio space and offering the director choices of long shot, mid-shot and close-up from each camera. In location shooting for drama, scenes shot with one camera will normally be played three times, with the camera positioned in three different places: a general view for establishing shots and cutaways, with the remaining two positions used for shot-reverse-shot cutting between two points of view on the action. A similar three-position format is used for documentary subjects and interviews, so that mid-shots or close-ups of

**long shot** a camera shot taking in the whole body of a performer, or more generally a shot with a wide field of vision.

**close-up** a camera shot where the frame is filled by the face of a person or a detail of a face. Close-ups may also show details of an object or place.

Figure 6.4 Shot-reverse-shot. Photographs courtesy of Jeremy Orlebar.

contributors and presenters can be alternated either with close-ups or with wide shots to be used as cutaways. The reasons for this apparent rule of three are that:

- a single point of view is conventionally regarded as boring
- alternations between two points of view can appear unrelated if there is not a third shot to bridge them
- more than three shot sizes for cameras can be confusing to audiences.

Published guides to television production focus almost exclusively on the standard conventions for shooting and develop these in much more detail. But as the discussion of Steadicam above shows, interesting ways of adapting these rules of three, or even breaking them radically, can produce creative and involving programmes.

---

**ACTIVITY 6.4**

Going back to your treatment, storyboard and choices of narration and music from the previous exercises, revise your storyboard to make it conform to broadcast conventions of shot size, cutting for narrative coherence, and integration of image, speech and music. Then make changes to some of these aspects of the sequence to try out more radical strategies. You should end up with plans for two different short films.

---

Shot composition allows the relationships between people, and between people and things, to be expressed in spatial terms. There are basic conventions of shot composition which enable shots to cut together in the editing process. For example, when one character is looking at or speaking to another, the speaker is usually positioned to one side of the frame with a blank space in front of him or her, across which he or she can look towards the other person. Similarly, a person walking normally has space left in front of them in the shot, into which the person can walk. Static shots of people should always leave a small amount of space above the head so that the person is framed by the environment behind them. These conventions are easy to see and understand when watching broadcast television, and have become conventional norms used unthinkingly by programme-makers. More interesting uses of shot composition contribute to narrative progression and the tone and meaning of television sequences. The distance between speakers in two-shots, for example, and the relative closeness of each of them to the camera, can be manipulated to signify the quality of their relationship and to generate dramatic tension between them. Similarly, positioning characters in frames within the camera frame (such as doorways, windows or mirrors) can create relationships between spatial areas of the frame that **connote** entrapment, or produce a feeling of distance between the audience and the character. Shot composition is inseparable from the issue of point of view, where the camera's closeness to or separation from the action being shot is extremely influential on the audience's relationship with the action and the people carrying it out. For instance, the sense of being involved in the action or kept separate from it, the sense of being given information transparently by the camera or being denied it, is produced by the interactions between shot composition

connotations the term used in semiotic analysis for the meanings that are associated with a particular sign or combination of signs.

and point of view, and by the dynamics of the relationship between one shot and those before and after it.

The tone and meaning of television sequences can be further enhanced by the use of lighting, sound and music. As a matter of principle, no single element of a shot or sequence carries an intrinsic meaning, but attains its meaning by interaction with the other elements of the programme in the context of a broader interpretation. Lighting for drama works hand in hand with shot composition to direct the audience's attention to significant aspects of the shot or scene, and light gives texture to the image. Harsh lighting produces strong shadow when cast by a dominant key light, and can evoke fear or mystery. Soft or diffused light has a placid tone and can also connote romance. The addition of gels to light can produce warm colours, or cold and foreboding sensations. In factual and entertainment genres frontal lighting is likely to be used for clarity and coverage of the represented space, supported by **back lighting**. It is worth emphasising that the tone and meaning of a shot or sequence can never be designed by mechanically following a set of rules. Tone and meaning depend on all the elements that contribute to ***mise en scène***: the lighting, music, sound, shot composition, props and objects in frame, costume, and camera movement. The best book about *mise en scène* is actually about cinema (Gibbs 2002), but its discussions apply nearly as well to television; analysis of key aspects of television *mise-en-scène* is conducted by Karen Lury (2005). The effective direction of television requires the ability to understand and work creatively with all of the elements of *mise-en-scène*.

**back lighting**
lighting the subject of a shot from behind to provide depth by separating the subject from the background.

*mise en scène*
literally meaning 'putting on stage', all the elements of a shot or sequence that contribute to its meanings, such as lighting, camera position and setting.

---

### ACTIVITY 6.5

Shoot the two different seven-shot films you have planned, using a single static camera. In what ways do the shots 'work' on their own, and in what ways do they require the relationships between shots, and relationships with the speech and music that you have planned in your treatment and storyboard? Why is this?

---

During a shoot the details of day-to-day and hour-to-hour activities are the responsibility of a production manager, who is responsible to the producer, and works closely with the director. He or she is responsible for the smooth running of travel, accommodation, catering and the hiring of technicians, equipment and facilities, and may assist the producer by doing reconnaissance (recces) for locations and keeping an eye on the production budget. The production manager will also produce a daily progress report on the shoot which lists the starting (call) and finishing (wrap) times of the day's work, the locations used and the time in minutes of screen time shot during the day. Similar calculations will show the number of scenes scheduled to be shot, those actually completed and the number of pages of script completed. From these numbers an average screen time per day can be calculated, and the **shooting ratio** worked out. A shooting ratio of 10:1 is usual for television drama, though an effective and lucky production might manage 7:1. The purpose of all this detail is to record the hours worked, facilities used and supplies of film etc. consumed during the day, so that progress in keeping to the budget can be monitored.

**shooting ratio** the number of minutes of film used to film a scene or complete programme as compared to the screen time of the finished scene or programme.

The role of a production assistant (PA) is to log and update changes to the script, to monitor continuity and to ensure that shots match and will cut. The PA logs takes and matches them with the script. The technical crew is headed by the lighting director, who assists the director to achieve his or her desired aesthetic effect by liaising with the camera operator and lighting electricians. The camera operator works the camera and may be the same person as the lighting director. The sound recordist operates sound equipment, sometimes assisted by a sound assistant, who will operate microphones and check equipment. Electricians position and adjust lights, and are known as sparks. If there is more than one electrician, the chief is called the gaffer and his or her assistant is the best boy. A grip is a cover-all term for someone who carries cameras and positions them, and lays the track along which cameras can be moved on location. Shoots conducted in television studios will also involve a vision mixer, who selects from among the outputs of the different cameras, and a vision controller, who is responsible for the picture quality of cameras. The studio sound supervisor operates a mixing desk; the floor manager controls activity on the floor of the studio and is the key link person between the director, performers and contributors, and technical staff. Runners are low-paid staff who support the work of others by running errands, making coffee and generally helping out. Being a runner is often the recent graduate's first job in television.

## Post-production

The processes of editing, sound dubbing and adding music are the final and crucial steps of television production and are known by the collective term post-production; they often take place when money is running out and deadlines are approaching. The post-production period is liable to create an overspend on the budget, often due to the interference of the broadcaster or financier attempting to assert control over the programme to improve it or even 'rescue' it. Another reason why post-production can be a long, complex and expensive business is that modern digital editing technology allows for an extraordinary range of interventions to be made during the process. The addition of digital effects for cleaning up footage or importing animated elements and complex graphics, for example, is all done after the production shoot at the editing stage. While, on one hand, the availability of inexpensive high-quality desktop computer editing systems can enable students and tiny independent producers with equally tiny budgets to make effective television programmes, on the other hand the expectations of audiences and commissioning broadcasters have increased as the capability of post-production technology has expanded.

Editing is crucial to television programme-making. Again, the producer will be heavily involved in the editing process, working alongside a professional editor who is expert in the use of contemporary digital editing software and hardware. Although directors have a contractual right to the **final cut** of a programme, in the same way as directors in cinema, the fact that the director is normally employed by the producer for a specific programme, rather than having responsibility for the overall look of any serial or series, means that they are likely to defer to the producer's authority in the editing suite. Editing can be done in analogue ('linear')

**final cut** the final edited version of a programme that is delivered to the television institution for broadcast.

form or in digital ('non-linear') form. Linear editing involves rerecording selected shots from the original camera tape, choosing them from the camera tape in the order that they are needed in the finished programme. Picture quality is lost in the rerecording process, and it is time-consuming to change the editing decisions made during the process. Digital tape formats became commonly available in the 1990s, and involve the storage of sound and image information as numerical code on the tape, in the same way as data is stored on computer disks. Digital editing involves no loss of picture or sound quality when data is moved from the tape to the editing system and downloaded on to an editing master tape. It is also much easier to revise and rework the programme during editing using digital technology. However, the principles of linear editing are useful for thinking through creative decisions, and for this reason students of television production will often be taught to edit using linear equipment before progressing to digital techniques. The production team will have ensured their familiarity with all the footage prior to editing, logged it and noted ideas to be used in the edit. The factors in the minds of the director, producer and editor will be:

- possibilities for creating progression through the programme
- the revelation of dramatic or interesting turning-points
- possibilities for intriguing and holding the audience.

The rhythm and flow of the programme will be dependent on the careful structuring of these elements, referring back to the script and storyboard (in drama) to check that the aims of the programme idea are being effectively achieved.

The editing process begins with viewing rushes from the shoot with burned-in timecode in vision. The rushes are logged so that particular shots or sequences can be identified later and chosen for editing, and this process also enables the director to remind himself or herself of the various takes and their possible usefulness. Particular shots and sequences are logged along with a label that identifies them descriptively, since this is much easier to remember than numbers or timecode. The next stage is a paper edit, where a provisional order is established for the programme. It is called a paper edit because it is a written list of shots and sequences that will form the material at the first assembly edit stage off-line. The ingredients of the paper edit are always longer than the finished programme, and the editing process in general works by gradually paring down and simplifying. It is likely that chosen shots or sequences will be part of a somewhat longer shot or sequence, so the beginning and end points desired for the next stage are identified by marking the script of the documentary or drama with the words 'In' and 'Out', to specify where the selection from the shot will be made. Next the off-line assembly edit is produced by transferring the sequences identified in the paper edit to the editing software. It is followed by the rough-cut stage, where the material from the paper edit is trimmed and ordered more precisely so that it is close to the planned length of the finished programme. The rough cut enables the director to determine the pace and rhythm of the programme, often by cutting on action (where the sequence begins just at the important action rather than including the lead-up to it) and generating interest and suspense by cross-cutting between one scene and another. In documentary, voice-over commentary is written at the rough-cut stage, when the interaction between image and voice can be tested.

Sound as well as music will contribute to the world evoked on screen, either emphasising what is already present in the image or contradicting it. Sound adds dramatic perspective to images by providing a 'sound point of view' on the action: action in long shot can be accompanied by sound appearing to bring the action much closer to the audience by its volume and clarity; or, on the other hand, close-up action can be distanced from the audience by muting or blurring sound. Recorded sound from various locations (seaside, city street, in rooms with different kinds of acoustic tone) or sounds available on CD specifically for use in television productions (sound effects) can be assembled to form a 'library' for use in various projects. In documentary, background sound will be captured by the sound recordist, as well as the speech or other sync sound, for use to cover edits and provide a background soundscape for the programme. In drama, sound can subtly suggest off-screen intrigue, or provide a rhythmical foundation to the programme, as in the ticking of a clock or approaching footsteps. Contrasting sound and image provoke moods and tones that shape the predominant interpretations of action for the audience, while sound montage opens up a range of meanings when running parallel with montages of images. These considerations apply not only to sound in general but to speech. The factors offering connotations in recorded speech include:

- the apparent acoustic source of speech (within the represented world, or from outside it)
- the gender of the voice
- the accent of the voice
- the relative volume of the voice
- the speed of the speech
- the timbre or tone of the voice.

Broadcast television soundtracks are complex layers of sound edited on to the images in the online edit.

## ACTIVITY 6.6

Using desktop editing software or whatever non-linear editing you have access to, digitise and log the seven shots you have filmed for each of your two mini-dramas. Record the narration and music, and input them into the editing system. Produce a rough cut of each film, leaving blank spaces and gaps if your image and sound and music tracks do not line up perfectly. How would you fill these gaps, if any? How would you change your films to make the shots 'cut' better?

Digital off-line editing systems, such as Avid, are based on the difference between the digital rushes from the shoot that are stored on the hard disk (known as the 'media') and the control information that the computer uses to determine the order of shots (timeline, timecode and editing instructions, known collectively as the 'project'). While the media require large amounts of hard disk storage space, the project is a small document that can be downloaded on to a floppy disk or memory stick and used in another computer. As the off-line edit procedure is carried out, the amount of media stored digitally declines as selections are made from the whole, based on the instructions contained in the project. Eventually the off-line edit will produce a finished tape containing all the right shots and sequences in the right order. The online edit is where this material is fine-tuned, minor repairs can be carried out to unsatisfactory frames, graphics and visual effects are added, and sound and music tracks are attached to images (unless complex sound is being added, in which case it would be added separately in a dubbing theatre). Online editing effects include transitions between shots such as when one shot is blended seamlessly ('mixed') into another, and three-dimensional effects where moving images can be pasted on to shots and parts of the shot can be shifted around within the frame. All of these online effects can be viewed as soon as they are created, but the computer system needs to render them (process and record them) before the programme can be played back. The resulting programme after online editing is called the fine cut, and at this point the director will review the programme to make minor final changes before the master copy is at last produced.

Making television programmes is extremely gruelling, and it is often hard to tell whether the programme has 'worked' until after it has been completed. The success of a television production is evaluated in several different ways. Newspaper comment on programmes and the previews of programmes published in listings magazines are available to the public and have important effects in establishing perceptions of the quality of programmes and the attraction of audiences. For the production team, creating good publicity in advance of a programme may be crucial to attracting an audience and establishing a reputation. Gathering a dossier of clippings and reviews can be useful to the scriptwriter, producer or director seeking future employment. But the television industry is an enclosed world, with powerful internal hierarchies and codes of shared knowledge, status, competition and gossip. So indicators of success deriving from the industry itself are relatively more significant than indicators deriving from more public sources. The key indicator within the television industry is the response of the audience. This is determined in terms of both total size and **audience share**. The raw numbers denoting audience size and share are crude, though, so programme-makers are keen to discover more detailed information, such as the distribution of age groups in the audience of their programme, and its social class distribution. These numbers are also of most concern to the hierarchy within television institutions, such as channel controllers, commissioning editors, heads of network programming, department heads, etc. – that is, the people who employ (or choose not to employ) the programme-makers. Professional reputation among fellow workers within a programme-maker's own specialism and recognition from more powerful television executives are at least as important as recognition by the press and public, since these are the fellow professionals and television executives with whom programme-makers compete and from whom they may gain further employment.

**audience share**
the percentage of viewers estimated to have watched one channel as opposed to another channel broadcasting at the same time.

Figure 6.5  The Avid Media Composer Adrenaline editing suite. Courtesy of Avid.

## ACTIVITY 6.7

How would you evaluate the two simple practical projects you have completed in this chapter using the following criteria: as training for making conventional genre television programmes; as ways of opening up creative ideas in video production; as mini-dramas that might appeal to viewers (which viewers?); as team-building exercises for the people you worked with? How are these criteria connected or opposed to each other?

## Case study:   the Avid editing system

The basic principles of the Avid and other digital editing systems include:

- the transfer of rushes or 'media' to the computer and the logging of their timecode so that they can be identified by the software
- the selection of the desired shots and sequences from the media and their ordering into an edit decision list (EDL)
- the manipulation of the chosen shots and sequences using the capabilities of the editing software
- the final assembly of the programme from the shots chosen in the EDL.

Cameras automatically record invisible timecode on to the tapes or memory chips used during shooting. But since the same timecode numbers could appear on more than one roll of tape, the editing system will remember each shot for a particular production so that each has a unique number that the system can recognise. It is possible to do an off-line edit on a simpler and cheaper system such as a home computer in order to produce an EDL. This can then be loaded into the Avid or other professional system, and the Avid will automatically select the

*continued*

sequences on the EDL for a high-quality online edit. This enables the programme-maker to save expensive editing time by doing preliminary work using an off-line system that may not be much more complex or expensive than a good domestic computer system such as the Apple iMac.

Editing systems treat camera pictures as objects. The picture is treated as though it were a flat, two-dimensional surface, such as a piece of paper. This enables the system to appear to move images by flipping them over so that they look back to front, lifting the corners or edges of the picture as though it were the page of a book, enlarging or reducing the size of the image so it appears to move towards or away from the viewer, and distorting the image as though it were being turned at an angle to the viewer, folded, squeezed or torn. These effects are different from the importation into television editing of techniques that are already possible with celluloid film, such as cutting, fading, tinting and slow motion. They are possible because the image is stored as a sequence of bits of digital information. Because the image has been decomposed into numbers, and these numbers can be manipulated mathematically by the computer and then turned back into an image, the image is 'plastic', meaning that it can be worked on and transformed. Similar processes are used to record and process sound in digital equipment such as the Avid, so that it can also be manipulated and transformed by the mathematical operations performed by the computer software. It is possible to smooth out jumps between sound sequences, to adjust pitch and acoustic quality, and to layer different soundtracks in relation to each other. However, very complex sound is likely to be completed in a sound studio or dubbing theatre, where specialist audio equipment is available that surpasses the capabilities of online editing equipment that has been designed to work primarily with images.

The first point to note about the Avid system is the different conception of how editing is done, in comparison to the editing of film that preceded both analogue and digital tape editing systems. A piece of film is a material object that can be handled, cut with scissors and chemically processed to bring out different features of the images recorded on it, and bits of film can be pasted together in any order using sticky tape. The experience of editing film is of a closeness to the material and an ability to perceive it through the senses of sight, touch and smell that is akin to the skills of carpentry or oil painting. Editing images and sound captured on tape is a quite different experience. There is nothing to see on the camera tape, and no moving parts inside the memory chips that hold the media used to edit. Instead of physically cutting pieces of tape and sticking them together (although this was done in the early days of magnetic tape for television programme-making), the process is to rerecord selected portions of tape on to another tape. Digital non-linear editing is still based on these principles of rerecording, though it is batches of numerical data that are being moved around and reassembled inside the computer rather than sequences being physically copied from one tape to the next. But since sequences can be pasted together into any order on the Avid, rather than assembled one after another as on videotape, Avid editing is similar to the cutting and pasting done with cinema film. Non-linear editing is a hybrid of the different approaches to editing in film and analogue video.

One consequence of the Avid's capability to treat images as objects that can be manipulated and transformed in digital form is that the possibilities for transforming images and sounds are multifarious, and it would be rare for any individual television programme to use more than a few of the great variety of processes that the Avid can perform. Whereas in principle the editing of a piece of film could be done with such simple equipment as reel-to-reel Steenbeck editing tables, a sharp knife and some special sticky tape, the Avid cannot be operated without specialist training to understand the architecture of the software that controls it. While the system is logical in its operation, the accompanying technical manual takes about 1,500 pages to explain all of its functions. Editing systems such as Avid are, however, similar to personal computers in that a few training sessions will enable the user to complete basic processes competently, while professional users will be able to accomplish subtle and individual results by adjusting the numerous parameters that are open to modification. The capability of the Avid extends the features of professionalisation and hierarchy in the different employment categories in television production. The technical knowledge required to operate it well consists both of systems thinking and organisation that are common in computer technician work, and also of the lateral and creative thinking that characterises direction, lighting camera work and design in television. The non-linear editor is highly professional and competent across different kinds of expertise. He or she is also a specialised worker who operates at a particular level in the hierarchy of a trade group. In general, the computerisation and complexity of digital editing produce extended vertical hierarchies of status in the editing profession, and work specialisation that increasingly separates the experience of editors from others in the television industry. This is ironic given that digital technology potentially connects the hardware used to shoot, edit, record sound and display audio-visual media, since it all works on the same principle of translating information into numerical form (digits).

Interestingly, some of the commands on the Avid system refer to one or the other of the cinematic or video editing conventions that preceded digital non-linear systems. The basic command Splice, for example, inserts material selected from the Source Monitor and marked with an In and an Out point. The term Splice derives from the film editing procedure of physically cutting a strip of frames and splicing or joining it to another. The second most basic and useful command on the Avid interface is Overwrite, which lays a selected sequence on top of another, replacing what was previously there at that point on the timeline. Overwrite derives from the video editing process by which an audio-visual sequence from a source tape player is recorded on to the edit master at a point where an existing sequence had previously been recorded. The recording head of the videotape player would write the new material over

Figure 6.6   An example of Avid Xpress Pro with Avid Mojo on a Macintosh laptop.
Courtesy of Avid.

*continued*

the top of the previous material, leaving no trace of what was there before. The principles of basic editing on the Avid are a combination of the cutting and joining processes involved in film editing, and the transfer and rerecording processes involved in analogue video editing. In a similar way, the timeline displayed at the bottom of the Avid screen represents the project as a linear strip, like a piece of film or videotape. Representing the project in this way provides a useful graphic representation of the programme as it is edited. Jogging and shuttling using the Avid's keyboard or mouse mimic the freeze-frame (jog) and cue and review (shuttle) functions of a videotape recorder, where the play head moves rapidly across the tape and provides a speeded-up version of the pictures. The Avid's Trim mode allows individual shots to be shortened or lengthened by any number of frames, and is particularly useful to refine cuts on action so that the pace of a sequence can be adjusted. As its name suggests, the effect is what would happen if frames of film were snipped from a sequence using scissors, and joined back on to the preceding or following sequence, slightly shortening or lengthening the complete programme. But again, nothing physical happens to the audio-visual information in the Avid, and frames which have been trimmed out using the control remain invisibly present so that they can be restored at any time.

The centre of an Avid system is the software program loaded on to the computer. Attached to this are the special keyboard which operates the system via a connecting device called a dongle, a storage device in which the digitised rushes or 'media' are stored on a computer hard disk, two television monitors which display media and the cut which is being worked on, sound input devices such as DAT (digital audio tape) players, speakers for sound output and devices for audio-visual input, such as videotape players. The Avid is therefore a concrete example of media **convergence**: it can access a wide variety of analogue and digital information sources operating in different formats and standards, and integrate and store these various kinds of input information. By integrating all of these input sources encoded in digital form, it is able to treat them in the same way, manipulate them and produce a new output that can be perceived via the electronic and mechanical devices of the television monitor and loudspeakers. The ways in which the Avid separates one project from another in its memory, sets up Bins (like folders on a word processor) containing the digitised rushes or media, and orders the sequences (Clips) manipulated during the edit all bear no relation to the physical position or arrangement of information in the computer. While the human user requires an interface that separates and categorises these different kinds of information, arranges them in a hierarchy and represents them in understandable ways, the information represented by the interface is virtual. The ability to display representations of media in virtual forms allows the user of the Avid to try out effects, revise and modify the elements of a programme without ever affecting the original form of the media digitised and held in the hard disk drive. It is only at the stage when captions and effects have been added that the Avid editor will declare that he or she has reached the point of Picture Lock. This is when the visual sequences of the programme have been fixed and finalised, and after this is done sound and music will be added until the programme is complete.

convergence
the process whereby previously separate media technologies merge together. For example, computers can now send faxes, show DVD films and play music.

## SUMMARY OF KEY POINTS

- Studying the professional processes of making television gives a deeper understanding of television institutions, programmes and how meanings are made.
- Development is the stage when programme ideas are being worked out, researched and planned.
- Pre-production is when locations, contributors and performers are selected, scripts are written, storyboards and production schedules are drawn up, and the design, props, costumes and music are selected.
- Production is the shooting stage, when the creative and technical personnel produce the audio-visual raw material for programmes.
- Post-production includes the editing of the material that has been shot, and the inclusion of effects and a sound mix.
- The hierarchy of roles in television production and the ways in which technology is designed to be used reveal assumptions about the relative status of television professional staff, and how images and sound should be put together.

## Further reading

Bayes, S., *The Avid Handbook*, second edition (Woburn, Mass.: Butterworth-Heinemann, 2000).

Dominick, J., B. Sherman and G. Copeland, *Broadcasting/Cable and beyond: An Introduction to Modern Electronic Media*, third edition (New York: McGraw-Hill, 1996).

Gibbs, J., *Mise-en-Scène: Film Style and Interpretation* (London: Wallflower, 2002).

Harrison, J., *Terrestrial Television News in Britain: The Culture of Production* (Manchester: Manchester University Press, 2000).

Hart, C., *Television Program Making* (Oxford: Focal Press, 1999).

Hood, S. (ed.), *Behind the Screens: The Structure of British Television in the Nineties* (London: Lawrence & Wishart, 1994).

Kauffmann, S., *Avid Editing* (Woburn, Mass.: Butterworth-Heinemann, 2000).

Lury, K., *Interpreting Television* (London: Hodder Arnold, 2005).

Messenger Davies, M., 'Production studies', *Critical Studies in Television*, 1:1 (2006), pp. 21–30.

Millerson, G., *Video Production Handbook*, third edition (Oxford: Focal Press, 2001).

Moss, S., 'New kids on the block', *Guardian* Media section, 28 January 2002, pp. 2–3.

Murdoch, G., 'Authorship and organization', *Screen Education*, 35 (1980), pp. 19–34.

Orlebar, J., *Digital Television Production* (London: Arnold, 2002).

Rolinson, D., *Alan Clarke* (Manchester: Manchester University Press, 2005).

Tunstall, J. *Media Occupations and Professions: A Reader* (Oxford: Oxford University Press, 2001).

—— (ed.), *Television Producers* (London: Routledge, 1993).

Wayne, M., *Dissident Voices: The Politics of Television and Cultural Change* (London: Pluto, 1998).

# Postmodern Television

# Postmodern Television

## Introduction

The term 'postmodern' (or 'postmodernist') is used in relation to television with several related meanings, but taking apart the two component words which make up the term shows that it involves distinguishing between one state of affairs and another. 'Post' means after, while 'modern' means contemporary. Therefore, 'postmodern' signifies newness, whether this newness is regarded positively (postmodern television might be experimental, innovative and exciting) or negatively (postmodern television might be shallow, mindless and trivial). Discussing television in relation to postmodernism is a way of analysing how television, and culture in general, has changed.

## Postmodernism as a style

When the term is used to describe the form or style of television, 'postmodern' denotes self-conscious playing with the conventions of television in programmes such as the animated series *The Simpsons* or in the many advertisements which refer, often humorously, to other advertisements or advertising conventions. The pleasure of viewing programmes and advertisements such as these derives from the viewer's recognition of this playing or '**reflexivity**'. One episode of the sitcom *Father Ted*, for instance, involved the main characters encountering the actor Richard Wilson (Victor Meldrew in the sitcom *One Foot in the Grave*) and pestering him by repeating Meldrew's catchphrase, 'I don't believe it!' Much of the comedy in *The Simpsons* comes from the reflexive parody of the conventions of, among others:

**reflexivity** a text's reflection on its own status as a text: for example, drawing attention to generic conventions, or revealing the technologies used to make a programme.

● other animated series
● horror films
● television news
● children's television.

Rather than using these parodic reworkings to criticise the television and other forms which are being referred to, postmodern television involves the celebration and enjoyment of mixing up the conventions of the source texts. It is this lack of critical edge which leads some theorists to attack postmodernism. The richness of meaning which results for the viewer from this postmodern parody might be highly pleasurable, but it has little to offer in terms of the ideological critiques of television forms and conventions which underlie Television Studies' tradition of looking for 'committed', critical and politically progressive programmes.

An example of postmodern television which Umberto Eco (1984) gives is when programmes seem to be made in order to celebrate the 'television-ness' of something. So televised awards ceremonies or celebrity chat shows are called 'neo-TV' by Eco. Programmes such as these represent celebrities whose personas have been created on television, for television, and the programmes appear simply to be a vehicle for extending the artificial existence of these figures who seem to exist in the bubble of a television universe. Neo-TV programmes refer to each other and cannibalise each other's formats, celebrities and presenters. They are 'intra-textual', meaning that they are parasitic on themselves. Eco is describing an epoch of **simulation** where television becomes divorced from reality, no longer a medium of representation but instead an independently existing virtual world which is simultaneously exciting and banal.

The interpretation of texts such as these and the decision to call them postmodern because of the many **intertextual** references which they contain depend on the theorist's and the viewer's ability to identify those references. Postmodern playing with allusions to other texts needs to be subtle and to some extent hidden in order for viewers to enjoy the references and congratulate themselves on their skill at decoding them. As Robin Nelson (1997: 246) suggests: 'Postmodern texts might be summarily characterized by a formal openness, a strategic refusal to close down meaning. They create space for play between discourses allegedly empowering the reader to negotiate or construct her own meanings.' But allusions do not enrich a text if only a very small number of viewers notice them. In 2005 the film director Quentin Tarantino wrote the storyline and directed a two-part episode of the crime drama *CSI* entitled 'Grave Danger'. The **voice-over** introduction to the programme by Five's continuity announcer informed viewers of Tarantino's involvement, newspapers, internet sites and television listings magazines mentioned the fact and Tarantino's name appeared in the opening credits of the programme. Having been prompted to regard his involvement as significant, many viewers would have noticed the intertextual reference in the episode to Tarantino's preoccupations in the films he has directed, such as *Reservoir Dogs*, *Pulp Fiction* and *Kill Bill*. These films demonstrate Tarantino's interest in film history, film stars and the extreme violence of 'exploitation movies', such as the sequence in *Reservoir Dogs* in which a captured policeman is tortured by having his ear cut off. The 'Grave Danger' episode of *CSI* included a brief appearance by film star Tony Curtis, the discovery on a Las Vagas street of a pile of entrails, and the imprisonment of one main character in a transparent coffin, where he is attacked by flesh-eating ants. But for viewers to make sense of the episode it was not essential that they recognised these references to Tarantino's films, and in fact there was no overt reference to Tarantino in the script; nor were individual camera shots direct imitations of those in his films. Instead, the allusions were an enriching aspect of the meaning of the episodes for some viewers, a subtle joke which added a self-conscious postmodern playfulness.

The consequence of identifying postmodern features of style and form in television is that it leads to the argument that television is changing the ways in which people's **subjectivity** is formed. If television programmes and advertisements are made up of fragmentary moments which often gain their meanings by referring intertextually to other television programmes, advertisements and other media texts, this might mean that the viewer's subjective identity is also fragmented. There is a question, however, about whether it is television which causes a change in sub-jectivity, or whether television reflects ways of being which are caused by other factors. Nevertheless, emphasising how one television programme is constructed by

**simulation** a representation that mirrors an aspect of reality so perfectly that it takes the place of the reality it aims to reproduce.

**intertextuality** how one text draws on the meanings of another by referring to it, by allusion, quotation or parody, for example.

**voice-over** speech accompanying visual images but not presumed to derive from the same place or time as the images.

**subject** in psychoanalysis, the term for the individual self whose identity has both conscious and unconscious components.

sign in semiotics, something which communicates meaning, such as a word, an image or a sound.

combining and repeating **signs** and **codes** from other programmes and other media discourses has an effect on the methods of study which are needed to understand and critique it. It would no longer be appropriate to draw on the theories of viewer positioning which have been adapted from theories of classical Hollywood cinema, for example, because the logical unfolding of involving narratives with beginnings, middles and ends, and psychologically realistic characters which are assumed to lay out a secure spectator position, seem inappropriate for the reflexive, intertextual and ironic processes of meaning in much contemporary television.

code in semiotics, a system or set of rules that shapes how signs can be used, and therefore how meanings can be made and understood.

TV viewers construct sense from the diverse fragments of narrative, character, visual pleasure and intertextual reference which postmodern television offers. Indeed, one of the more publicly controversial aspects of irony in postmodern television is that some programmes may be taken at face value by some audiences, but read ironically by others. Contrasting reactions to Channel 4's light entertainment programme *Bo' Selecta!* are a recent example of this. The main character Avid Merrion's apparent racism and sexism in celebrity interviews, impressions and caricatures can be claimed either to critique these ideologies or to perpetuate them. While there are moments of stability and involvement in television, the role of fragmentary signification, the withholding of resolution and the sense of being suspended in a perpetual middle is what makes the term postmodern useful for describing what watching television is like now. Features of television programmes seem to match descriptions of contemporary culture which focus on how people's identity is mobile and fluid, and composed of partial fragments.

## ACTIVITY 7.1

Intertextual references are common in television advertisements. Make a note of advertisements you have seen which refer to television programmes, films or other media texts. How might intertextual references serve the needs of advertisers in positioning products and brands, and engaging viewers' interest?

Intertextuality is essential to television. Programmes and advertisements find their place in the schedules and address their audiences by establishing their similarity to and difference from other programmes and advertisements, and from other media texts. Because of its associations with liveness and with the provision of news and other information to its audience, television is associated with the now. This suggests that television is inherently postmodern in that:

● it forgets the past and history
● it is obsessed with what is new and different.

But, on the other hand, there is a strong presence of the past in television since

genre a type of programme. Programmes of the same genre have shared characteristics.

● past programmes are always being repeated.
● contemporary programmes communicate about their **genre** and how they should be watched by referring to programmes which viewers already know.

Television classics such as the sitcoms *Dad's Army* and *Porridge* return every few years and attract large audiences. On **digital television**, cable and satellite, channels such as UK Gold, ITV4 and Granada Plus have schedules composed entirely of repeated programmes. Channels also repackage television from the past in order to sell it to a new audience. For example, *Star Trek* was packaged by BBC2 in the early 2000s as a cult classic, with trailers featuring the more outrageous examples of sexist behaviour, **melodramatic** overacting and laughably low-budget special effects. This ironic repackaging sought to bring a new, younger audience to a programme which was first shown almost forty years before. Old television becomes new when watched by a different audience from a different subject position. A BBC internet project in 2007, 'My Science Fiction Life', requested recollections of science-fiction television and collected numerous messages from viewers of different age groups recounting their respectful, irreverent, devoted or dismissive attitudes to *Star Trek*.

The immersion of subjects in television culture and media culture more generally means that media choices and identities marked out by patterns of television consumption become the co-ordinates which define a person's social role. This is clearly connected with advertising since advertising associates consumable products with liveable identities. This is not only a positive process of taking on an identity, for example by characterising oneself as a *Newsnight* viewer or a *Neighbours* viewer, but a negative process of stigmatising those groups of viewers whose difference from oneself enables each person's identity to be constituted. Identities constructed in this way are necessarily temporary as cultural fashions change, and the sense of the individual subject having a continuity of identity across decades and a life becomes more difficult to sustain. Instead, identity is fragmentary, temporary and contingent. In this situation nostalgia is a powerful force which allows viewers to remember a sense of themselves in the past, to connect the present with the past by using memories of television as a way of engaging with who they once were. The popularity of such programmes as *100 Best Kids TV Shows*, *I Love the Seventies*, etc. is a result of this. It is reassuring to share memories of television programmes with others of a similar generation, and because television has until recently been relatively 'scarce' because of the small number of channels and relatively few mass audience programmes, as John Ellis (2000) has argued, it is likely that adults will have similar television memories.

Indeed, it is not only the programmes which are the focus of nostalgia but the experience of collective family viewing around a single television set in the home. The BBC sitcom *The Royle Family* was based on nostalgia for such family viewing, and gently ridicules the notion of the television as the focus of family interaction. The irony of this programme also reminds us that nostalgia is a double-edged emotion, which includes a distance from the experience being remembered in order for sentimentality and regret to be kept at bay. Mastering the past of television by keeping an ironic distance from it allows people to maintain their confidence in the security of their present identity and their control of their uses of television. Television is important to the creation of the past and the creation of the self, and part of this importance can be shown in the ways in which television is denied and repudiated by its viewers at the same time as it is celebrated.

digital television
television pictures and sound encoded into the ones and zeros of electronic data. Digital signals can also be sent back down cables by viewers, making possible interaction with television programmes.

melodrama
a form of drama characterised by exaggerated performance, a focus on reversals of fortune and extreme emotional reactions to events.

**ACTIVITY 7.2**

How might the repackaging of old television programmes as 'cult' programmes, 'classics' or subjects of irony serve the interests of broadcasters with extensive libraries of programmes, seeking to mobilise valuable sections of the audience?

## Postmodern times

Both of the component words in the term postmodern have to do with time. Since 'post' means after, postmodernism has to be thought of as a stage or moment in time which follows another stage or moment previous to it. For television, using the term postmodern means having to establish what 'modern' television is, the kind of television which precedes the postmodern, and this means constructing a history of television which can be divided up into periods. This problem of identifying what modern television would be is a conceptual issue which affects the term postmodern in general. Modern means what is characteristic of the present period, in distinction to what things were like before, in a pre-modern period. The modern age might refer, for example, to the times after mass communication and industrial society had transformed the nations of the Western world in the late nineteenth century. But as culture moves on, the distinction between what was modern and what is happening in the present tends to break down. New experiences lead commentators to describe their own time as modern, assigning what had previously been called modern to part of the pre-modern epoch. Because modern means what is new, the sense of what is modern keeps changing to keep up with new developments, and the pre-modern period keeps expanding, always ending just before the new times that are described as modern.

In a similar way the postmodern period must refer to a time when changes occur that react against what is modern or transform it. One of the interesting consequences of this is that the postmodern could be characterised by a *return* to features which are thought of as pre-modern. Umberto Eco is a scholar of medieval culture, a **semiotician** and media critic also contributing to media culture by writing novels and journalism and appearing on television. In the medieval period the group with the most access to knowledge was the Catholic Church, which disseminated the religious ideology through which culture was understood. The cathedral's architectural form, frescos, statues and sculpture were the equivalents of advertisements, television screens and comic strips, and were the media which aimed to explain everything. In postmodernism the elite communicating explanations of culture is not so much the leaders of the Church but rather those who run media culture: television, advertising and popular culture. So Eco is interested in the similarities between the postmodern epoch and the medieval period.

As well as the multinational control of information and culture by a privileged elite, a further similarity is the dominance of visual communication. Today this is the dominance of visual media such as television, the internet, print and poster advertising and cinema over written media of communication. In the medieval period Eco notes the importance of physical visual representations such as stained-glass windows, statues and frescos.

semiotics the study of signs and their meanings, initially developed for the study of spoken language, and now used also to study the visual and aural 'languages' of other media, such as television.

The parallel between the postmodern and the medieval periods suggests both positive and negative characteristics of contemporary media culture. Like the dominance of the Catholic Church over the Western world during the medieval period, the domination of multinational capitalism in the international media scene could be thought of as oppressive and stifling. Yet also, because of their shared experience of culture, the audiences of postmodern media have a ready-made 'language' in which to speak to each other and to understand each other's realities, giving them the potential to become a powerful political and cultural force, just as in the Middle Ages the massed peoples of the West could be moulded into a powerful crusading army with shared aims and beliefs.

If postmodernism reacts against the modern, one way of establishing a difference from the modern would be to go back to pre-modern features of culture and recycle them in new ways. So a further implication of labelling television postmodern is to suggest that the elements of past culture which it recycles from either modern or pre-modern epochs are plundered equally. If so, these past elements lose their historical place and significance, and the past is deprived of its 'pastness'. Because of this erasure of pastness, some theorists of the postmodern claim that post-modernism erases history, and produces the sense of a perpetual present. The French philosopher of culture Jean-François Lyotard, in his book *The Postmodern Condition* (1979), argued that postmodernism entails a loss of confidence in theories which map out historical progress. Such theories as Marx's, which consider that history moves by **dialectical** struggles between the world-views of different social classes and that it is inevitable that the working class will eventually triumph over the **bourgeoisie**, or the liberal theory that humankind evolves towards ever-greater understanding between peoples and the betterment of most people's lives by the spread of technology and democracy, are challenged by Lyotard. He regards these and other large-scale historical theories as 'grand narratives' of emancipation and progress that have lost their legitimacy and purchase in postmodern times.

**dialectic** a term associated especially with Marxist theories, meaning a struggle between two opposing ideas.

**bourgeoisie** the middle class, who are owners of property and businesses.

## Postmodern and avant-garde

Lyotard (1993: 44) argued that something is 'modern only if it is first postmodern'. He proposes that postmodernism describes something which we cannot get a handle on, something for which we cannot set criteria for

- judging whether it is good or bad
- deciding what category it should fit into
- deciding what kind of approach we should take in order to make sense of it.

What we think of as modern, as appropriate to our current state of culture, has to pass through this postmodern state of ambiguity and confusion. So Lyotard thinks of the postmodern as a state which we can recognise only after the event, once our categories and criteria have been applied and our example has become modern and comprehensible. Once this has happened, and the example is part of the modern, we can look back to that state of confusion in which it first appeared and describe that moment as postmodern. His notion of the postmodern therefore includes these important features:

- The term postmodern is retrospectively attributed to things.
- Being postmodern is a momentary condition which lasts for a short time.
- The postmodern is not an epoch or period but is a characteristic of how cultural products appear and are perceived.

Lyotard approves of the postmodern, because he values things which are hard to categorise and difficult to judge. Once something can be explained, judged and categorised Lyotard believes that its creative challenge and artistic interest are lost. Once it is possible to create a narrative or a **discourse** about something which will contain it and make sense of it, the potential for new ideas and experimentation is gone. History is a narrative about the past, which takes control of events by putting them in order and telling stories about them (see Chapter 2), and the fact that the postmodern is something which cannot be controlled and narrated in this way is part of why Lyotard regards it positively. The postmodern, in Lyotard's definition, cannot be part of a historical narrative because it cannot be controlled and ordered by criteria for judgement and the application of rules and standards which we already know.

**discourse**
a particular use of language for a certain purpose in a certain context (like academic discourse or poetic discourse), and similarly, in television, a particular usage of television's audiovisual 'language' (news programme discourse or nature documentary discourse, for instance).

### ACTIVITY 7.3

If postmodernist theorists such as Lyotard claim that 'grand narratives' have lost their legitimacy, does this claim make postmodernism a 'grand narrative' itself?

**aesthetic** a specific artistic form. Aesthetics means the study of art and beauty.

Lyotard's argument shows little interest in the groups which have been backed in the past by theorists of society and culture. His interest is in **aesthetics** rather than in the working class, women or people in the Third World. *The Postmodern Condition* discusses the state of highly developed Western societies. Other theorists have protested that people in the Third World are still struggling for development and wealth against the former colonial powers, that women are still struggling for economic and social equality in a society dominated by men, that there are still millions of people in the West who are low paid and socially excluded and therefore unable to experience the luxury of the artistic and cultural experimentation which Lyotard values. His conception of the postmodern does not allow any agency, any possibility of conscious political action for these underprivileged groups.

Lyotard's definition of the postmodern applies particularly well to non-referential images such as abstract paintings. In work such as this, it is not clear how to decide whether the painting is good or bad, beautiful or ugly, let alone what its message might be. Lyotard (1993: 43) argues that work like this, rather than representing something, tries to present what is unpresentable: 'to present the fact that the unpresentable exists. To make visible that there is something which can be conceived and which can neither be seen nor made visible.' It is hard to identify material on television which would fit into Lyotard's category of the postmodern, but one possible candidate is experimental **art video**. The American theorist Fredric Jameson (1987) uses the term 'video-text' to refer to commercial television and video art. He argues that video is postmodern,

**art video** the use of video technology in artistic work intended for gallery exhibition.

closely related to the dominant computer and information technology of the late or third stage of capitalism . . . is a sign-flow which resists meaning, whose fundamental inner logic is the exclusion of the emergence of themes as such in that sense, and which therefore systematically sets out to shortcircuit traditional interpretive temptations.

(Jameson 1987: 219)

Because video makes possible the manipulation of time, cutting it up, slowing it down, by using the capabilities of electronic technology, it can contrast with the ordered control of time, pacing and narrative which television and film have customarily used. However, Jameson's conception of video and television is much closer to art video than to network television programmes and the aesthetic conventions and scheduling practices which they involve.

In the early twentieth century artists such as Picasso and writers such as Virginia Woolf were developing ways of representing in images and language that reacted against traditions inherited from the nineteenth century, but they found it hard to gain an audience for their experimental and unconventional works. They were part of an **avant-garde**, seemingly ahead of their time (avant-garde can be translated as 'ahead of the pack'). But by the Second World War these various artists, writers, architects and film-makers had been accepted by the highly educated elites of the Western world as a loose grouping of modernists whose work represented important engagements with the ethos of the time. Their paintings appeared in galleries, their books were being taught in universities and their buildings were commissioned by powerful patrons. Modernism became part of the sanctioned official culture, and was considered valuable partly because it was very different from the mass **popular culture** of Hollywood, paperback fiction and popular music. Postmodernism involves mixing the hitherto experimental and innovative methods of the modernists with commercially distributed mass commercial culture, and the theorist Andreas Huyssen (1986: 57) wrote, 'it is by the distance we have travelled from this "great divide" between mass culture and modernism that we can measure our own cultural postmodernity'. In other words postmodernism breaks down the division between culture for a small elite group and culture for a mass audience. Television, especially the **public service** television of European nations, has been a crucial contributor to this process. For example, television arts programmes have introduced mass audiences to the modern tradition of painting, often using a recognised television personality or presenter to front the programmes. In 2001 the examples with the largest audiences were *Rolf on Art: Monet* (BBC1, 6.4 million viewers) and *Rolf on Art: Gauguin* (BBC1, 5.4 million viewers), presented by entertainer, painter and television personality Rolf Harris.

avant-garde work aiming to challenge the norms and conventions of its medium, and the group of people making such work.

popular culture the texts created by ordinary people (as opposed to an elite group) or created for them, and the ways these are used.

public service in television, the provision of a mix of programmes that inform, educate and entertain in ways that encourage the betterment of audiences and society in general.

**ACTIVITY 7.4**

How would you use the ability of video recorders or computer editing systems to make 'scratch' videotapes that might qualify as postmodern in Lyotard's and Jameson's sense of the term? In what ways might such texts 'shortcircuit traditional interpretive temptations'?

Figure 7.1 Video still from *November*, by Anthony Discenza, 2003. An example of video artwork. Courtesy of Anthony Discenza.

## Postmodernism and value

An important question which arises from this mixing of 'elite' and 'popular' culture, though, is how to ascribe significance and value to postmodern television. Thinking of an example from earlier in this chapter, it seems quite legitimate to claim that *The Simpsons* is a very important piece of cultural work, at least as important as any contemporary novel, play or painting, because of

- its intertextual complexity
- its self-awareness
- its relevance to the fragmented media landscapes and audiences of the present.

The values of complexity, self-consciousness and engagement with cultural issues in *The Simpsons* make it fit the criteria for 'art', yet it is obviously part of popular culture, not least because it is a widely distributed television programme.

There are three kinds of answer to this question of value in postmodern theory. First, theorists such as Fredric Jameson (1992) argue that postmodernism is the result of the dominance of powerful global forces of economics and political power centred in the USA and its allies, and, while *The Simpsons* might be interesting and important, it testifies to the success of the Fox television network in producing and distributing a programme which fits the new cultural order of multinational **capitalism**. For Jameson, postmodernism is the cultural form which is produced alongside the dominance of global capitalism, a world economic system which is unjust and ripe for criticism. In a second approach to this question the French theorist Jean Baudrillard (1983a) would argue that the whole issue of value has been

**capitalism**
the organisation of an economy around the private ownership of accumulated wealth, involving the exploitation of labour to produce profit that creates such wealth.

made redundant by the postmodern mixing of elite and popular cultural forms. Art has become a commodity (think of the innumerable merchandising opportunities associated with art in today's galleries), while commodities (such as *The Simpsons* or Madonna's videos) are discussed as if they were art. For Baudrillard, the question of value is an amusing and irrelevant hangover from an earlier age. In a third manner of answering this question, theorists from the Cultural Studies tradition such as Lawrence Grossberg (1987) have argued that value resides in the different ways that audiences use *The Simpsons*. It is enjoyed by children as a cartoon comedy series, by students and young people as a sophisticated sitcom and by cultural theorists as a fascinating instance of postmodern theories. For Grossberg, value is not absolute, but is a product of the audience's relationship to the programme and the ways in which this audience draws the programme into its own discourses. What is perhaps most interesting about these three answers is that each of them defers the question of value by linking *The Simpsons* with another theoretical issue (multinational capitalism, the commodity form, audience cultures). As I have argued elsewhere (Bignell 2000b), this very strategy of skidding away from addressing examples on their own terms is part of postmodern theory, and one reason why some critics find postmodernism so frustrating.

---

### ACTIVITY 7.5

In what ways does the discipline of Television Studies attribute value to some kinds of television and not others? To what extent does studying television require you to justify your work by comparing it to work in more traditional disciplines, such as sociology and literary criticism?

---

An example which has been commonly used to define what postmodern television is like is the American 'cult' drama serial *Twin Peaks*, which began in the United States in April 1990. The advertising for the first episode of the serial in newspapers and magazines promoted the programme as a highly unusual piece of work master-minded by David Lynch, a 'maverick' film-maker responsible for *Eraserhead* and *Blue Velvet*. The television serial was granted the artistic status of being an experimental work that challenged the norms of television, and was attached to the name of an acknowledged cinema director whose work carried prestige among audiences of art cinema. But once *Twin Peaks* had attracted a sizeable audience it began to be promoted as a soap opera that viewers would find addictive, and was advertised in the American magazine *Soap Opera Weekly*. *Twin Peaks* addressed two different audiences, one defined in relation to cinema, art and experimentation and focused on the authorial input of one man, and the other in relation to a mass-audience genre regarded as downmarket and **feminine**. This characteristic is called **multi-accentuality**. *Twin Peaks*' producer Mark Frost designed the serial to appeal to audiences of American '**quality** drama', especially the wealthy and discerning viewers of most interest to US television networks. Following the arrival of cable television as a significant force in the United States in the 1980s, network television viewing in evening **prime time** had fallen from 91 per cent of the audience

**feminine** having characteristics associated with the cultural role of women and not men.

**multi-accentuality** the situation where meanings are able to be read in different ways by different groups of viewers because a text offers multiple meanings at the same time.

**quality** in television, kinds of programme that are perceived as more expensively produced and, especially, more culturally worthwhile than other programmes.

**prime time** the part of a day's television schedule when the greatest number of viewers may be watching, normally the mid-evening period.

in 1979 to 67 per cent by 1989. *Twin Peaks* was an effort to attract cable viewers back to network television by offering them what appeared to be a prestige 'art' television programme. But the mass audiences associated with network soap opera were also targeted, confusing the boundaries between elite and popular audiences, and blurring the distinctions between 'art television' and popular culture.

Something similar could be seen in the promotional material for the American Second World War serial *Band of Brothers*, screened in Britain in early 2002. This was shown in the prime-time mid-evening slot, and was heavily promoted by television trailers and newspaper and magazine advertising. The promotion focused partly on the fact that the producers were Tom Hanks and Steven Spielberg, known in particular for the war film *Saving Private Ryan* and more generally for such mass-market popular cinema as *Jurassic Park*. Spectacular action sequences, and a focus on the emotional impact of war on the newly trained recruits plunged into combat were the two focal points of the advertising. However, aspects of the advertising and the programme itself also addressed a different, more **media-literate** audience. Very detailed reconstructions of battles were featured in the programme, whose title sequence began with faded black-and-white images suggesting historical truth and documentary accuracy. Each programme opened with elderly veterans speaking to camera about their experiences and their knowledge of the real-life characters who were to be fictionally recreated in the episode. These techniques of using reminiscence and documentary conventions had been used in the film *Reds*, about the Russian Revolution, and in Spielberg's *Schindler's List*, focusing on the Nazi persecution of the Jews. The visual conventions of the serial, some of its subject matter and characteristics of its production, such as the use of a large cast of previously little-known actors, connected it to epic cinema and 'serious' historical film as well as to popular entertainment.

**media literacy**
the skills and competence that viewers learn in order to understand easily the audio-visual 'languages' of media texts.

## Audiences and postmodernism

As we have seen, the term postmodernism can be used to discuss the stylistic and formal properties of television programmes, and the distribution of television programmes as part of a global consumer culture, but it is also a way of thinking about how audiences interact with television. Since the 1970s academics working on television have drawn on the theory of **ideology** (deriving from Marxist analysis of society) and the theory of how texts position viewing subjects in order to communicate meanings (originally from the theory of film), and united these approaches to show how television programmes and advertisements perpetuate dominant ideologies in which consumption is the basis of identity, and class and economic relations between people are obscured. Television programmes become the agents of communicating these ideas, with only minimal opportunities for the viewer to resist their meanings or interpret them in alternative ways. The more recent recognition that different audiences interpret television in different ways, and integrate their use of television into the whole diverse field of their cultural lives, challenges the assumptions of these critical approaches to television, and contributes to postmodern thinking about the medium.

**ideology** the set of beliefs, attitudes and assumptions arising from the economic and class divisions in a culture, underlying the ways of life accepted as normal in that culture.

Work on postmodernism has been part of a shift in discussing television from *structure* to *agency*. Structure refers to the institutions, networks of relationships and professional practices which condition the ways in which television is produced and broadcast. It includes theories of ideology and **globalisation**, for example, which seek to explain audience responses and preferences, and the features of television programme texts, as the result of these structural conditions. Agency refers to a new value attributed to viewer choice, and the ways in which audiences engage in negotiations with television texts and media structures in order to define themselves and empower themselves as individuals. The contest and tension between these two approaches are important, however, since neither approach can be correct on its own. Indeed, part of postmodern theory is the realisation that explaining television culture requires more than one model, set of critical terms and group of examples.

The arguments about postmodernism are a way of addressing the political impact of the mass media. For some theorists, the increased significance of the mass media is part of postmodernism and includes the liberating effects of the widespread distribution of information and ideas around the globe. On one hand, this can provide people with an unprecedented access to information, ideas and creative possibilities. On the other hand, the global spread of the mass media reduces the uniqueness of each individual and the specific cultures to which individuals belong, so that places and people become virtually the same and are all infected with the same assumptions, desires and fears presented by multinational commercial broadcasters. For much of our knowledge of the world comes through television, especially television news and other factual programmes. At the time of the Gulf War in the early 1990s, Baudrillard (1997) claimed that the almost non-stop coverage of the war smothered the reality of the event, so that the war itself was in effect replaced by the television pictures which claimed to represent it. Only a very small number of people in the West took part in the war, and for almost everyone the war was a media event. The characteristics which allowed this to happen were:

- the simultaneous broadcast of events as they happened
- the global distribution of news pictures
- the use of very simple narrative frameworks (good versus evil, spectacular technology achieving bloodless victories, masculine heroism) to represent it
- the importance of **iconic** images representing complex events
- a global network of interconnected television broadcasting.

In 2001 a similar example happened when terrorists attacked targets in the United States. Complex issues surrounding resistance to the power of the United States in various regions, the several terrorist attacks on 11 September, and questions about what the terrorists intended to achieve and what the proper response should be were overwhelmed by a small number of brief and dramatic sequences of television pictures. A few seconds of footage of airliners crashing into the World Trade Center, a few seconds of the huge towers collapsing to the ground and a few seconds of reaction to the event from shocked pedestrians in New York became the iconic images which represented this complex of issues and events, and which were repeated innumerable times in television programmes around the world. As in the debates about the Gulf War, television provided the images which encapsulated a complex reality in a few seconds of coverage and enabled this complex reality to be experienced vicariously worldwide. While no one would deny that the events of

**globalisation**
the process whereby ownership of television institutions in different nations and regions is concentrated in the hands of international corporations, and whereby programmes and formats are traded between institutions around the world.

**iconic sign**
in semiotics, a sign which resembles its referent. Photographs, for example, contain iconic signs resembling the objects they represent.

11 September happened, their reality was superseded by television representations of their reality.

---

**ACTIVITY 7.6**

Baudrillard's arguments about the 1991 Gulf War and their extension to the events of 11 September 2001 are deliberately provocative. How would you defend these ideas against the criticism that they underestimate the emotional impact of television coverage?

---

Baudrillard is critical of media culture but also celebrates the triumph of the media over society. He does not argue for a political resistance to media culture because political activity would need to stand up for a reality, society or community which he thinks are already absorbed and nullified by the media. He argues (1983a: 108) for conformity and passivity, to make the system collapse on itself: 'the strategic resistance is that of a refusal of meaning'. Baudrillard regards the passive mass audience of television positively, because it absorbs and nullifies the messages of the medium. The process by which he arrives at this conclusion depends on the theory of the sign which was discussed in Chapter 4. It is customary to assume that signs gain their meaning by referring to the conception of real things which we hold in our minds. Television images are signs which are meaningful because they are grounded on the concepts of reality which we understand. Baudrillard undermines and reverses this relationship between signs and realities. He argues that the conventions of media representation are so powerful and widespread that it is no longer necessary for conceptions of reality to act as the grounds on which signs rest. The codes and conventions of television stand in the place of conceptions of reality, and render those conceptions of reality either unnecessary or redundant. Our conceptions of reality are shaped by the television conventions and other media forms with which we are so familiar. Baudrillard argues that in fact we do not experience reality at all, except in terms of the conventions and codes of television and other media. For example,

- our family relationships are perceived in terms of the melodramatic narrative structures of soap opera and romance.
- our experiences of law and order and crime are perceived in terms of the codes of television police series.

He calls this state of affairs 'the hyperreal', in which the experience of reality has become indistinguishable from the television and media conventions which shape the ways in which we perceive it. He calls the process by which this occurs **simulation**, which means the staging of events, feelings and relationships by means of the codes and conventions of television and media culture.

These ideas had already been hinted at in the 1960s by Marshall McLuhan, a charismatic theorist of communication and information who frequently appeared on television programmes about the rapid changes occurring in youth culture and the media during that decade. McLuhan was interested less in what the media communicate than in how the form of media communication shapes what the content can be. He coined the term 'global village' to describe how international flows of information were bringing different cultures together and creating a new global society, and the phrase 'the medium is the message' to describe how media such as television have their greatest effect by:

- establishing an expectation that media information is addressed to us: that each of us belongs to its audience
- establishing familiarity with conventional narrative forms used in the media, so that certain kinds of story pattern can be used repeatedly
- establishing the media as our way of experiencing the world remotely and at second hand.

These features of media communication by the likes of television are more important, he argued, than the information content which any specific programme might impart. For McLuhan, media extend the capacities of the human mind and body. He regarded television as an extension of the human senses of sight and hearing, by which people could experience exciting, exotic and innovative ways of being. And he viewed television viewing as an active experience, in which the viewer fits together the different visual sequences, sounds and music of programmes like a child making a collage or a mosaic. This active television viewer could be a creative and artistic figure, more like a poet or painter than a **couch potato**: 'the viewer of the TV mosaic, with technical control of the image, unconsciously reconfigures the dots into an abstract work of art' (McLuhan 1987: 313).

> **couch potatoes** a derogatory term for television viewers supposedly sitting motionless at home watching television passively and indiscriminately.

## Postmodernism and globalisation

The Western model of media culture and media use has recently begun to penetrate China, which has increasingly adopted aspects of the consumer economy with which European and American people are already familiar. This makes China one of the newer members of a global media culture and offers support for the postmodern concept of media globalisation. In 2004, a new annual television singing competition titled *Super Voice Girl* (like Britain's *Pop Idol* and the USA's *American Idol*) began there, sponsored by the Mengniu ('Mongolian Cow') corporation, a dairy products company based in the Chinese province of Inner Mongolia. The show declared its winner in August 2005, and in the final months of broadcast it secured the largest audiences in Chinese television. Like its European and American counterparts, *Super Voice Girl* offered the chance for any woman to audition and move through stages of elimination and voting by the public with the chance to become a media celebrity. The talent competition was marketed with the slogan 'Super Girls, sing as you want!', and over 150,000 women took part in the auditions held in cities all over the nation, including a large proportion of young schoolgirls. The final episode of *Super Voice Girl* attracted 400 million viewers, equivalent to almost one-third of China's population, and the three finalists collected more than eight million votes. The winner was a twenty-one-year-old music student from the city of Chengdu called Li Yuchun. Her performance of a mixture of traditional Chinese folk songs and American pop songs gained her 3.52 million votes. Li's choice of songs was calculated to include some which connected her to traditional folk culture and a conception of China that is different from the global pop music culture epitomised by MTV. But the phenomenon of mass television audiences following a talent competition that promises to transform an ordinary person into a media celebrity, and does this by including the audience in the selection of the winner by means of the interactivity of telephone voting, shows how this example of Chinese television followed Western models.

*Super Voice Girl* was screened on Fridays on Hunan Satellite TV, broadcast from studios in Changsha. This southern industrial city was where the Chinese revolutionary Mao Zedong went to college before becoming the leader of the Communist Party and the ruler who set the tone in the second half of the twentieth century for China's anti-Western, anti-consumerist political and economic stance. The coincidence of the Western-style pop contest's production in Changsha and its association with Mao was often remarked on in the massive press coverage that accompanied *Super Voice Girl*. The major newspapers representing the views of the Chinese Communist Party, such as the *People's Daily*, described the programme as a positive example of a contemporary people's movement in which all social classes could participate, a demonstration of 'grassroots' activity along the lines of the enthusiastic mass support for Mao's Communist policies decades earlier. On the other hand, other Chinese media discussed *Super Voice Girl* as part of China's gradual Westernisation, since it is based on commercial pop music and its procedure of voting for a winner resembles the political voting characteristic of Western democratic nations. Many members of the programme's audience were active and far from being couch potatoes, but the Chinese media disputed what the significance of *Super Voice Girl* was, and what its **preferred reading** might be. Chinese media coverage described the programme's fan culture as either evidence of spontaneous organisation led by ordinary people themselves or as 'mad girl disease' (using an analogy with BSE or 'mad cow disease') infecting the entire population with Western attitudes. Certainly, the *Super Voice Girl* contestants exhibited Western fashions, with miniskirts, dyed hair or casual 'street style' clothes. The active fans of the programme included people of all ages, social positions and geographical locations in China, and the fans rallied in the streets, holding up posters and shouting slogans supporting their favourite contestant, waving the mobile phones on which they voted, and occasionally scuffling with fans who were supporting rival contestants. Internet chatrooms and online bulletin boards were used by fans to exchange gossip, and finalists had websites run by fans. Fan clubs were formed, each with a name and its own T-shirts showing a picture of the club's preferred Super Girl, and the largest of these organised propaganda and finance to support their contestant.

Voting for the finalists of *Super Voice Girl* was by mobile-phone text message, after earlier stages in which a panel of professional judges had decided on which singers would go forward to the later rounds. The fans of the eventual winner set up meetings in cities across China to rally supporters and voters. The rules of the contest stipulated that any individual mobile-phone number could be used to send 'only' fifteen text message votes, but the more phone numbers in the possession of voters, obviously the more votes they could send. Temporary phone cards can be bought in China, each providing a different phone number, so the organisers of Li Yuchun's fan club gathered money to buy these cards, and campaigned in shop-

**preferred reading**
an interpretation of a text that seems to be the one most encouraged by the text; the 'correct' interpretation.

ping areas and outside mobile-phone shops, begging people to lend them their phones to send in votes. The voting for *Super Voice Girl* thus became very lucrative for the channel broadcasting the series, and in addition Hunan Satellite TV charged 20,000 yuan (£1,330) for each fifteen-second advertisement in the commercial breaks during the programme. The channel also released an album of songs sung by the ten finalists in the week following the final episode, and organised live Super Girl concerts in ten Chinese cities. Hunan Satellite TV began negotiations with Li Yuchun to put her under contract with the channel for further television programmes, and deals were made to market dolls and a book about her. Reporting on the *Super Voice Girl* phenomenon, the Chinese business newspaper the *Standard* estimated in September 2005 that Hunan Satellite TV would profit from the text message voting alone by at least 30 million yuan (almost £2 million). Further beneficiaries were China's four telecommunications companies, which also received income from the text message votes. Overall, the example of *Super Voice Girl* shows how Western forms of television, media culture and technology were integrated into the culture of China, and in many ways matches arguments discussed in this chapter and earlier in this book about the spread of postmodern television:

- It promotes consumer culture.
- It integrates global and local cultural meanings.
- Its mix of traditional music and modern pop blurs the boundaries between past and present.
- It draws on the audience's familiarity with media technologies (phones, the internet, print media, etc.) and integrates them.

Earlier in this chapter, it was assumed that postmodern television is something which happens in the Western world, and in theoretical books on postmodern television and postmodernism in general it is usually examples from Western, and more specifically American, television which are used to explain it. Among the reasons for this is postmodernism's relationship to modernity. If modernity consists of the period of industrialism and mass culture, surpassed by postmodernism's post-industrial cultural landscape and the fragmentation of mass audiences into **niche audiences**, it is much easier to find evidence for these shifts in the European nations and the USA, where industrial and mass culture first took root. It is harder to explain postmodernism in terms of these shifts in parts of the world (such as Africa and South America) where industrial and cultural development has not taken place in this staged way. It is no accident that these areas are where European nations established colonies and empires, for these now postcolonial societies have very mixed cultures in which there are highly developed media cultures but also deeply traditional and rural cultures. The theories of fragmented subjectivity and changed senses of space, time and identity, which can work quite well as explanations of how Western culture has changed, fit much less comfortably on to societies where inequalities in access to media, culture and wealth are more marked. Theories of postmodernism tend to assume that it is a global phenomenon, though it is easy to find examples of nations that are still struggling to become even modern industrial mass societies.

**niche audiences** particular groups of viewers defined by age group, gender or economic status, for example, who may be the target audience for a programme.

## Whose postmodernism?

The use of the term postmodern, though it derives from Western intellectual culture, has made possible an alternative to the discourse of hierarchy and supervision of a 'common' culture which is associated with modernity, and facilitated the entry into the debate of feminist and non-Western critics. Debates in media theory about postmodernism, although they have been conducted mainly from a Western point of view, have provided alternative ways of thinking about culture. The result of this is to produce a discourse in which the certainties of the grand narratives of imperialist Western modernity can be challenged by a focus on difference in media consumption practices. But these practices need also to be placed by their interrelation with larger-scale determinants, demonstrating that the specific and the local are articulated in reference to them. Postmodernist theories are alternatives to the notion of culture as a hierarchy of taste with an elite at the top and a mass popular audience at the bottom. They have shown that there is no such thing as a common culture, a national culture or an international culture. Instead, there are numerous overlapping and competing cultures at local and regional levels, which coexist with a multinational and global culture. These ways of recognising differences in terms of place, gender, race, age group and other ways of conceptualising identity have enabled voices representing diverse audiences and identity groups to question the dominant imperial model of media dissemination and consumption that is associated with modernity.

While the other theorists mentioned in this chapter often favour the irrational, the momentary and the ambiguous, the cultural theorist Jürgen Habermas aims to support the power of rationality and communication to make society better. Improved communication between people, and rational debate about politics and society, would enable people to liberate themselves from the apparently stifling bureaucracy of contemporary societies. In order to achieve such liberation and debate, access to the media and the free exchange of ideas in the media are key priorities for Habermas. The centralisation of ownership and control of the media, and ordinary people's lack of interaction with them, are the main problems which he diagnoses: 'Insofar as mass media one-sidedly channel communication flows in a centralized network – from the center to the periphery or from above to below – they considerably strengthen the efficacy of social controls' (Habermas 1987: 390). In contrast to this, Habermas calls for individual subjects to speak up and take practical action to gain access to media and to use them for reasoned political debate.

Feminist theorists have adopted a similar approach to the postmodern. **Feminism** has always valued the connections between the everyday lives of people and political theories of how to address inequalities in society. It also places a value on active subjectivity – especially, of course, the subjective experience of being a woman. Feminist postmodernists accept that contemporary experience is bound up with fragmentary identities such as sometimes being:

**feminism** the political and theoretical thinking which in different ways considers the roles of women and femininity in society and culture, often with the aim of critiquing current roles and changing them for the better.

- a worker
- a mother
- a daughter
- a television viewer
- a fan
- a consumer.

Indeed, one woman could have all of these identities at different times in a single day. What is important for feminist postmodernists is to claim the agency that Habermas recommends, and the activity which allows people to create change. Jennifer Wicke and Margaret Ferguson (1994: 1) argue for agency, based on a feminist understanding of the postmodern: 'postmodernism is, indeed, a name for the way we live now, and it needs to be taken account of, put into practice, and even contested within feminist discourses as a way of coming to terms with our lived situations'. Wicke and Ferguson regard postmodern theory and feminism as sharing concerns to multiply discourses and identities.

The fact that television is so closely connected to consumer culture, to the desire for commodities and shopping, to virtual tourism and the representation of exotic and foreign places, connects television with the history of consumerism. Whereas in the past, shopping and gazing at exotic sights were experiences which took place outside the home, on tours or cruises and in shopping malls, now these experiences can be indulged in at home, by watching television and interacting via a remote control. Leisure and consumption have always historically been associated with women, with femininity. Television, too – since the medium belongs in the home, in domestic space – has also been regarded as feminine. For Andreas Huyssen (1986), postmodernism's celebration of mass culture is a celebration of feminisation. Postmodernism entails feminisation, and means both the distraction and disempowerment which are associated with the feminine, but also the importance of the feminine as the new dominant force in contemporary culture. But feminist theorists of postmodernism, such as Meaghan Morris (1993), have argued that the result of the mass of academic articles and books published on postmodernism is a set of ideas which are worryingly similar to those that the most fashionable postmodern theorists claim to have rejected. All of the leading postmodern theorists are white European or American men (this chapter has mentioned Baudrillard, Lyotard, Eco and Jameson, the four most well known). Despite the argument that postmodernism overthrows the hierarchies of the past, celebrates difference and rejects the dead hand of cultural authority, a select band of male theorists have therefore become the new authorities, at the head of a hierarchy of thinkers, who argue among themselves about the complexities of postmodern theory. Despite the fact that postmodernism and feminism share many emphases, postmodernism can appear to be a taking over of feminists' theoretical and political efforts, a diversionary sidetrack from feminism, or a strategy to deprive feminists of their hard-won academic distinction.

## Case study:   MTV as postmodern television

MTV seems to be a perfect example of postmodernism: the material it broadcasts appears to be shallow, based around commodity images with no 'message' except the injunction to buy; and it broadcasts a flow of short videos producing an endless present or perpetual flow in which the division between daytime and prime time and the fixed points of conventional terrestrial television schedules are largely absent. These characteristics encouraged the American theorist E. Ann Kaplan to analyse MTV as a postmodern form in one of the first substantial studies of the channel in the 1980s. Kaplan (1987: 41) compared MTV to cinema:

*continued*

'The main differences between MTV and the classical Hollywood film arise from the structuring of the station as a 24-hour continuous flow with its three- to four-minute texts . . . and from the song-image format.' One definition of postmodernism is that it describes a society in which images have precedence over reality: where the mediated experiences presented by television and other media are more constitutive of our everyday experience and have a greater role in shaping our assumptions and conceptions of our reality than those experiences which we actually undergo ourselves. MTV provides a twenty-four-hour soundtrack to the lives of its viewers, in which the repeated infusion of music works in combination with a restricted repertoire of imagery presenting celebrities. The Spice Girls, for example, were represented through the adjectives which supposedly described the personalities of each member of the group: Posh, Scary, Ginger, Sporty and Baby. Such imagery can be easily manipulated, however, showing that the celebrity pop performer on television is a cluster of signs which can mutate, rather than the representation of a real personality which precedes the images seen on MTV. Kaplan (1987: 44) argued that this is a development that matches postmodern versions of identity:

> Perhaps most relevant to our discussion of the postmodernist devices in MTV videos generally is the blurring of distinctions between a 'subject' and an 'image'. What seems to be happening in the play with the image of the various kinds discussed is the reduction of the 'self' to an 'image' merely. Television in this way seems to be at the end of a whole series of changes begun at the turn of the [twentieth] century with the development of modern forms of advertising and the department store window.

Madonna's manipulation of her persona is the most famous example of this, and more recently performers such as Kylie Minogue and Britney Spears have transformed their images from girlish innocence to more sexual maturity. MTV is a key part of a much wider culture of celebrity which involves the music industry, the internet, newspapers, magazines and radio.

Celebrity is the commodification of personality, and MTV not only furthers this process but advertises itself as a **commodity** which is purchased along with the other channels received by multi-channel audiences. In order to achieve this, MTV needs to present its own personality attractively so that it can be bought by its viewers. This is achieved by simultaneously marketing MTV's worldwide engagement with the global music and entertainment industry, and by addressing local and regional audiences in discourses and languages familiar to them. MTV is a global brand, and therefore exemplifies the global capitalism characteristic of post-modernism, yet it has a local dimension. It is programmed differently in each territory to which it is broadcast, though the formats remain largely the same and many of the products that it advertises are also global brands appearing in different languages and different territories.

The academic literature on MTV rose to prominence in the late 1980s and early 1990s, but MTV has changed considerably since then. Rather than one channel, it is a portfolio of channels (including MTV itself, which is a general pop music channel, MTV2, which plays more rock and alternatives to dance music, MTVHits, which is a pop chart channel, and MTVBase, which focuses on rap, rhythm-and-blues and soul), and in Britain there are several widely accessible music channels which compete with it. MTV originated in the United States, and is owned by an American media corporation. It can be argued that it is a vehicle for the global spread of American capitalist values, expressed through the international pop music market, which sells products with no intrinsic value that remain fashionable for a very short time and are part of a wider attempt to extract money from the youth market by selling

**commodity** a raw material or product whose economic value is established by market price rather than the intrinsic qualities or usefulness of the material or product itself.

representations of celebrity identities. In its early years MTV advertising seemed to proclaim this in the slogan 'One world, one image, one channel: MTV', which celebrated the erosion of local differences and diversity by the global spread of the channel. Connections between MTV and wider global consumer culture could be seen in the deals made between pop stars and the soft drinks industry, such as the association of Madonna and Michael Jackson with Pepsi. Commercials featuring the performers and the soft drinks appeared on MTV, making a vicious circle of advertising which encompassed American performers, American television, American soft drinks and American record companies.

More recently, MTV has diversified into making programmes as well as screening music videos. Its **reality TV** series *The Osbournes* has been the biggest earning success for the channel in its history, gaining 8 million viewers in the USA and 500,000 in the UK, for example (Bignell 2005: 34–5). The programme's producer, Greg Johnson, initially intended to shoot the episodes on location at the Osbourne family's Beverly Hills home for three weeks, but the appeal of the programme led to over three years of production. Despite the fact that *The Osbournes* is produced and structured as a factual series adopting the conventions of many other docusoaps, it retains both historical and textual connections with the international pop music culture that MTV promotes. Ozzy Osbourne had been the subject of MTV's house tour series *Cribs*, in which cameras are shown around the usually luxurious homes of pop stars, and this led to the commissioning of *The Osbournes* by the channel's US controllers. As the singer and frontman of the heavy rock band Black Sabbath, Ozzy had an established reputation in the UK, USA and elsewhere as a music performer, though the high-point of his career had occurred in the mid-1970s, so he could be presented in the series as to some extent an ordinary person rather than a star.

*The Osbournes* gained MTV wide press coverage, public profile and large audiences when shown originally on the channel in the USA, demonstrating that **docusoap** had a continuing potential to draw the predominantly young audiences that MTV already targeted with its music video programming. But the show also became an internationally traded programme, already established on MTV and saleable to Channel 4 in Britain as a relatively predictable hit which would attract young viewers to the channel.

**reality TV** programmes where the unscripted behaviour of 'ordinary people' is the focus of interest.

**docusoap** a television form combining documentary's depiction of non-actors in ordinary situations with soap opera's continuing narratives about selected characters.

Figure 7.2 MTV logo used with permission by MTV: MUSIC TELEVISION. © 2007 MTV Networks. All Rights Reserved. MTV: Music Television, all related titles, characters and logos are trademarks owned by MTV Networks, a division of Viacom International Inc.

*continued*

ACTIVITY 7.7

To what extent is the inclusion of 'world music' in MTV a recognition of non-Western local cultures, and to what extent is it an example of the commodification of these cultures for the benefit of the music industry?

On one hand, *The Osbournes* documents the everyday lives of a family and suggests that celebrities might be a lot like the programme's ordinary viewers, but it also gives an apparent insight into people who are famous, wealthy and unconventional in their behaviour. This suggests that *The Osbournes* engages with the social conventions of family life and simultaneously shows how these conventions are distorted in the rarefied atmosphere of rock celebrity. Viewers' expectations about 'normal' family life or the desirability of stardom might be questioned as a result. At the same time, watching MTV serves the interests of pop culture consumerism. The same can be said of MTV in relation to some of its music video output, where performers and performances both celebrate commercial pop stardom and may use it to challenge powerful ideologies in Western society.

The arguments about MTV in postmodern theory in the 1980s were also carried through in relation to the performances, especially the music video performances, of Madonna. She can be regarded as a performer who offers radical challenges to conventional norms, especially in the representation of femininity by the repeated changes to her celebrity persona, suggesting a freedom of self-expression and pleasure for women. She has also been critical of the Catholic Church, especially in its condemnation of sexual pleasure and homosexuality, and has confronted the limits of mass media representation, especially of sexuality, by producing pop videos and other commodities which have generated controversy and occasionally censorship because of their explicit sexual imagery and promotion of sexual pleasure for its own sake. From this point of view, Madonna's economic success as a pop performer frequently appearing on MTV, and the financial assistance for her career provided by her associations with major corporations such as Pepsi, can be seen as ways of using the capitalist media system against itself.

For Kaplan (1987: 47), MTV videos have the positive effect of blurring the boundaries between art and commerce, between critique of culture and complicity with consumerism: 'In the case of MTV, video artists are often playing with standard high art and popular culture images in a self-conscious manner, creating a liberating sense by the very defiance of traditional boundaries.' Perhaps by drawing on the global media presence of MTV to get her messages across, and by drawing on connections with other globally recognised brands which keep her own celebrity image to the forefront, Madonna is able to disturb the very structures and ideologies which underlie contemporary television. The most interesting characteristic of postmodern theory, and of postmodern media culture, is the way in which contrasting ideas can be shown to be two sides of the same coin. The complexity and confusion which this produces in theories of television mirror the complexity and confusion that postmodern theorists see in television itself.

## SUMMARY OF KEY POINTS

● Postmodernism is a critical term that addresses the style and form of television, its place in contemporary culture, and the notion that a new phase of culture has been reached.
● Postmodernist television style includes self-conscious playing with the conventions of other television programmes and the pastiche of earlier television forms.
● As a way of describing the contemporary moment, postmodernism means both a break with the past and a new way of engaging in a dialogue with the past.
● The way in which television and other media are deeply embedded in culture and society, at least in developed countries, is evidence of a new postmodern epoch of history.
● Postmodernism can also refer to the sense that our customary ways of judging the value of television, and understanding its significance, may no longer apply.
● Theorists have debated whether postmodern thinking makes possible progressive criticism of television and media culture, or whether it is too accepting of the state of affairs it tries to describe.

## Further reading

Alleyne, M., *News Revolution: Political and Economic Decisions about Global Information* (Basingstoke: Macmillan, 1997).

Barker, C., *Global Television: An Introduction* (Oxford: Blackwell, 1997).

Bertens, H., *The Idea of the Postmodern: A History* (London: Routledge, 1995).

Bignell, J., *Postmodern Media Culture* (Edinburgh: Edinburgh University Press, 2000).

—— *Big Brother: Reality TV in the Twenty-first Century* (Basingstoke: Macmillan, 2005).

Brooker, P. and W. Brooker (eds), *Postmodern After-Images: A Reader in Film, Television and Video* (London: Arnold, 1997).

Dahlgren, P., *Television and the Public Sphere* (London: Sage, 1995).

Goodwin, A., 'MTV', in J. Corner and S. Harvey (eds), *Television Times: A Reader* (London: Arnold, 1996), pp. 75–87.

—— *Dancing in the Distraction Factory: Music, Television and Popular Culture* (London: Routledge, 1993).

Herman, E. and R. McChesney, *The Global Media: The New Missionaries of Global Capitalism* (London: Cassell, 1997).

Holmes, S. and S. Redmond, *Framing Celebrity: New Directions in Celebrity Culture* (London: Routledge, 2006).

Juluri, V., 'Music television and the invention of youth culture in India', *Television and New Media*, 3:4 (2002), pp. 367–86.

Kaplan, E. A., *Rocking around the Clock: Music Television, Postmodernism and Consumer Culture* (London: Methuen, 1987).

Kellner, D., *Media Culture: Cultural Studies, Identity and Politics between the Modern and the Postmodern* (London: Routledge, 1995).

Lewis, L., *Gender Politics and MTV: Voicing the Difference* (Philadelphia, Pa.: Temple University Press, 1990).

McLuhan, M., *Understanding Media: The Extensions of Man* (London: Ark, 1987).

Mundy, J., *Popular Music on Screen: From Hollywood Musical to Music Video* (Manchester: Manchester University Press, 1999).

Nelson, R., *TV Drama in Transition: Forms, Values and Cultural Change* (Basingstoke: Macmillan, 1997).

Wicke, J. and M. Ferguson, 'Introduction: feminism and postmodernism; or, The way we live now', in M. Ferguson and J. Wicke (eds), *Feminism and Postmodernism* (London: Duke University Press, 1994), pp. 1–9.

Woods, T., *Beginning Postmodernism* (Manchester: Manchester University Press, 1999).

# Television Realities

# Television Realities

## Introduction

**realism** the aim for representations to reproduce reality faithfully, and the ways in which this is done.

**Realism** is a particularly ambiguous term in the analysis of television. One meaning focuses on the referent of what is represented: that actual scenes, places and people are represented rather than imagined or fictional ones. A second meaning refers to television's representation of recognisable and often contemporary experience, such as in the representation of characters in whom the audience can believe, or apparently likely chains of events. This meaning of realism relies on the familiarity of the forms and conventions, the **codes** which represent a reality. But, finally, another meaning of realism would reject the conventions of established realistic forms, and look for new and different forms to give access to the real. In each of these meanings, however, realism posits the separation of the text from a reality which pre-exists it.

**code** in semiotics, a system or set of rules that shapes how signs can be used, and therefore how meanings can be made and understood.

## Factual television

**documentary** a form aiming to record actual events, often with an explanatory purpose or to analyse and debate an issue.

For workers in the television industry, many programmes discussed in this chapter fall into the category of 'factual' television. This category includes programmes which feature non-actors on location, in the modes of:

**docusoap** a television form combining documentary's depiction of non-actors in ordinary situations with soap opera's continuing narratives about selected characters.

- **documentary**
- drama-documentary
- **docusoap**
- **reality TV**.

**denotation** in semiotics, the function of signs to portray or refer to something in the real world.

Programmes such as these aim to represent reality, to dramatise events which occurred in the past, or **denote** people living or working in a continuing factual serial. It might seem that television technology and the conventions of television programme-making are used in these examples as neutral media for representing personalities and situations which already existed or would have existed even if the programme were not being made. However, although the representatives of the holiday firm Club 18–30 in Spain might have behaved in similar ways whether or not the docusoap *Club Reps* had been made for ITV, other programmes which appear to be factual cross into the territory of fictional entertainment because they are based in situations designed specifically for television. *Big Brother* is the most well-known example of this type of television, a '**reality TV**' programme where the members of the public are chosen to appear, in a house specifically built for the programme, and are aware that they are being recorded twenty-four hours a day. Similarly, some programmes aim to reconstruct events which actually happened, such as the crimes

**reality TV** programmes where the unscripted behaviour of 'ordinary people' is the focus of interest.

reconstructed in *Crimewatch UK*, but use actors performing scripted dialogue and action to do this. Some apparently real events in television programmes become performances, and some performances are designed to be equivalent to real events. Television realism is a flexible category, containing at one end of the spectrum news footage which claims to document events occurring independently of the fact that they are being recorded, and at the other end drama entertainment programmes which claim to be realistic but are constructed for television. Television realism is a matter both of content and of the conventions or codes which structure the representation seen on the screen. It is the interaction between what is on television and the ways in which an audience understands a programme that is at the heart of television realism. Television has a 'language of realism' which programme-makers and audiences share.

In Television Studies, theorists have tried to establish what makes television different from other media, such as cinema or radio.

- Like radio, television is broadcast across a wide area and its viewers receive the same signals simultaneously.
- Like radio, television can broadcast live, and both media have a history of addressing nations and regions with public service information as well as entertainment.
- But television is like cinema in its combination of image and sound.
- Like cinema, television addresses its viewers as consumers of entertainment and fiction.

Figure 8.1   The cast of *I'm a Celebrity . . . Get Me out of Here!* © Nigel Wright/ITV

In relation to forms of realism, however, television factual programmes aim to present information about the diverse ways in which people live and to broaden the horizons of understanding for the audience. Television audiences are invited to experience the lives of others through the mediation of television documentary forms, for example, so that television realism carries an assumption of social responsibility.

- Television realism aims both to hold up a mirror to society itself and to show the diversity that exists within a society which is assumed to have an overall unity.
- Television realism constructs a sense of an organic and unified culture, partly by exhibiting the complexity and diversity of culture.
- Television realism consists of a negotiation between ideas of unity and difference, familiar and unfamiliar, and thus performs an **ideological** role in shaping the norms of society.

## Realism and television technologies

Television programmes are coded as transcriptions of the real world, but they are assembled from the different discourses of image and sound which are available in the 'language' of television. Television cameras admit rays of light through a lens on to an electronic grid which registers them as quantities of red, green and blue. These signals are encoded for transmission, and the corresponding colour tubes of the television set resynthesise the signal as a beam scanning across 312.5 lines, twice for each image, producing the effect of a 625-line image. In sound recording, the recording mechanism isolates and intensifies some sounds and not others. It produces an implied perspective on the sound source, representing sound through the hidden electronic processes of recording, transmission and reproduction. Television realism is reinforced by the combination of sound and image, each providing references to and 'evidence' of the smooth unity of the television text as a transcription of reality. There is a separation between the objects or people which are recorded and the recording itself. Since television uses technologies of recording images that seem to transcribe realities 'objectively', or in **semiotic** terminology 'denotatively', television images acquire the status of evidence. But because of this separation, because they are representations of realities rather than realities themselves, television representations are ideological: they encode social points of view which condense, displace or forget social relationships.

Programmes often conceal the work of their production, just as other kinds of product made for our mass society (such as tins of soup, cars, newspapers and clothes) are abstracted from the work processes and institutional arrangements which created them. Products like this are called **commodities**, and in the early twentieth century the German theorist Walter Benjamin (1969: 212) argued that mechanical reproduction processes which give rise to the media of photography, cinema and now television substitute 'a plurality of copies for a unique existence'. Television images are 'copies' of reality not in the sense that they are fakes but in that they are the result of a mechanical process and circulate remotely from the physical body of their producer. Television's 'copies' of reality can be distributed widely, and are seen at the same time by mass audiences either on their own or in groups. Media images

**ideology** the set of beliefs, attitudes and assumptions arising from the economic and class divisions in a culture, underlying the ways of life accepted as normal in that culture.

**semiotics** the study of signs and their meanings, initially developed for the study of spoken language, and now used also to study the visual and aural 'languages' of other media, such as television.

**commodity** a raw material or product whose economic value is established by market price rather than the intrinsic qualities or usefulness of the material or product itself.

produced by mechanical reproduction free what has been recorded from its social and historical environment, and (to some extent) from control by the state or elite groups. The interpretation of television images is not controlled by these contexts and social relationships, either. Three of the effects of this are that:

- television images seem to float free of the frameworks which determine them
- television images circulate in culture as commodities
- television images are separated from the people, places and events which were recorded.

These effects occur despite the **iconic** relationship between those people, places and events and the images themselves.

---

**ACTIVITY 8.1**

Consider the limits on the ways the term 'realistic' can be used about television: are there ways in which science-fiction and fantasy programmes – such as *Doctor Who* and *Xena Warrior Princess* – can be realistic? What criteria for realism are you using to formulate your answers to this question?

---

**iconic sign** in semiotics, a sign which resembles its referent. Photographs, for example, contain iconic signs resembling the objects they represent.

Contemporary **digital** technologies for recording and editing television, and for transmitting it over networks, pose a potential challenge to the iconic realism of the medium. These digital processes extend the process of unfixing the image from its referent, its maker and its social and historical determinants. Digitisation:

- increases the ease of manipulating images
- allows the transmission of images as electronic units of data along phone cables in the global communications system at high speed and across national boundaries
- permits the digitisation of existing footage into electronic data which can be stored and accessed remotely
- allows the **convergence** of television with interactive systems.

New technologies have modified the realist claims of television, so that digital images or the grain of video (which is recorded digitally onto the analogue medium of magnetic tape) can connote immediacy, in surveillance video footage, for example, in the same way as the visibility of photographic grain produced by chemical record-ing in film, and apparently proving the simultaneity in time and space of the person who made the recording and the event which has been recorded. The photographic grain of film, which is inseparable from the celluloid on which it is carried, is an iconic sign and physical trace of the object photographed. This separation of the production of the registering material from the activity of making the image by exposing the chemical surface to light underlies film's claim to show reality as it occurred. But we know that post-production effects are used in film to alter images. In digital recording, images and sound are converted into numerical values which

**digital television** television pictures and sound encoded into the ones and zeros of electronic data. Digital signals can also be sent back down cables by viewers, making possible interaction with television programmes.

**convergence** the process whereby previously separate media technologies merge. For example, computers can now send faxes, show DVD films and play music.

can be easily manipulated with a computer. Although they seem like different media, with film seeming to show what was really before the camera more reliably, both technologies' claims to realism are mythical.

---

## ACTIVITY 8.2

Research how 'fake' television pictures have been used in the past. Do contemporary technologies of digital manipulation amount to a significant challenge to the reliability of 'realistic' television images?

---

**discourse**
a particular use of language for a certain purpose in a certain context (such as academic discourse or poetic discourse), and similarly, in television, a particular usage of television's audio-visual 'language' (news programme discourse or nature documentary discourse, for instance)

**subject**
in psychoanalysis, the term for the individual self whose identity has both conscious and unconscious components.

**identification**  a term deriving from psychoanalytic theories of cinema, which describes the viewer's conscious or unconscious wish to take the place of someone or something in a television text.

**narrative**  an ordered sequence of images and sound that tells a fictional or factual story.

There is a correspondence between thinking of realism as a set of codes which document recognisable realities and thinking of society as constituted by the exchanges of speech and expression between individuals. For realist television forms assume the transparency of the television medium, just as society assumes transparent communication between individuals. In the same way that different kinds of people use different **discourses** deriving from their social class, gender, religion or political outlook, so television realisms represent realities in ways which are recognisable to some viewers and not others. If television realism can never match its codes and conventions to the different versions of reality which actual viewers experience, we need to ask how the notion of realism has become such a widely understood and widely used criterion for discussing and evaluating television. The answer to this problem is to understand how some forms of realism have become dominant codes, and why.

The dominant form of realism in television, labelled by theorists 'classic realism', roughly coincides with the epoch of modern industrial society. It can be seen in the majority of television fiction programmes, and also affects the representation of people in television factual programmes and documentary. Individuals' characters determine their choices and actions, and human nature is seen as a pattern of character differences. These differences permit the viewer to share the hopes and fears of a wide range of characters. The comparisons and judgements about identifiable human figures represented on television are reliant on a common code of judgement, a notion of 'normality', which is the terrain on which the viewer's relationships with characters can occur. Classic realism represents a world of psychologically consistent individual **subjects**, and addresses its viewers as the same kind of rational and psychologically consistent individual. The action of the television text is to establish communication and offer involving **identification** with the images it shows. Individual television texts need to be constructed as wholes which promise intelligibility and significance. The realist assumption of the match between the television text and a pre-existing reality underlies this process, by posing the image as equivalent to a real perception of recognisable social space. This depends on the equivalence between what and how the viewing subject might see and be seen, and what and how the television point of view might see and be seen. So the category of the rational perceiving subject is the connecting assumption shared by the viewer and television, and by his or her world and the world represented on television. The viewer's varied and ordered pattern of identifications makes **narrative** crucial to classic realism, for the different kinds of look, point of view, sound and speech in narrative are the forms through which this communication between text and audience is produced.

## British soap opera and realism

The television form of British soap opera exhibits several kinds of realism, for it is a continuing form, flowing onward like our conventional experience of time in reality. British soap opera's social realism derives from the historical circumstances in 1960 when the first regular British television soap, *Coronation Street*, was created. The portrayal of Northern working-class life contains the same nostalgia for community which was being dramatised in the cinema films and television and theatre plays of the late 1950s, at a time when this culture was no longer representative of how most British people lived. Community is always already lost, and persists as the impossible dream of binding separated families and groups together.

Soaps are multi-character dramas, and their stories, settings and concerns are embedded in the mythologies of community in national popular culture. They appear to 'reflect' reality, with their fictional worlds functioning as a microcosm of 'ordinary life', but the condensation and narrative progress which are necessary to television fiction mean that they do more than 'reflect'. There are frequent breaking-points in soap opera families and communities (such as divorce, birth, death, gossip and antagonism between characters), which enable new stories to begin. So while the foundations of soap opera reflect ideological norms in being centred on the family, community and regional identity, it is the lack and disturbance of these structures which drives the narrative. Plots are often based on 'common-sense' wisdom about human nature, such as 'pride comes before a fall' and 'a little knowledge is a dangerous thing'. These axioms are the ideological assumptions which underlie dramatic dilemmas. Charlotte Brunsdon (1981: 35–6) has explained that

> The coherence of the serial does not come from the subordination of space and time to linear narrativity, as it does in classical narrative cinema, but from the continuities of moral and ideological frameworks which inform the dialogue . . . [A]lthough soap opera narrative may seem to ask 'What will happen next?' as its dominant question, the terrain on which this question is posed is determined by a prior question – 'What kind of person is this?' And in the ineluctable posing of this question, of all characters, whatever their social position, soap opera poses a potential moral equality of all individuals.

The action in soaps takes place within a set of values that provide the norms for characters' lives, and, even though characters continually violate these norms, they remain bound by them and have to learn to adjust to them or suffer the consequences. While the narrative of the serial poses these moral questions of its characters, the leakage of the questions out of and back into the realities of the viewer's life, and out of and into other media discourses, such as newspaper stories, spreads them across society as a whole. It is soap opera realism which allows this transfer between fiction and reality, and enables soaps to claim social responsibility and **public service** functions. Phil Redmond (quoted in Nelson 1997: 114–15), the

public service in television, the provision of a mix of programmes that inform, educate and entertain in ways that encourage the betterment of audiences and society in general.

creator and producer of Channel 4's soap opera *Brookside*, set in Liverpool, explained that, when the programme began in the early 1980s, 'I wanted to use the twice-weekly form to explore social issues, and, hopefully, contribute to any social debate . . . From the outset one of my main aims was to try and reflect Britain in the 1980s.' Soaps are an arena for the mediated 'debate' about morality and social behaviour in modern societies, and pose television institutions as socially responsible. The proof of this concern is measured by the responses of viewers (in phone-ins, viewers' letters and audience **ratings**) to programmes. But there are no issues without the media to represent them and direct them back to their source in society, so the important question for Television Studies becomes how particular forms of address and representational form are used to 'reflect' and respond 'responsibly' to social life.

The realism of soaps depends not only on their construction and form within their television **genre** but on the discourse generated around them. The stories about soap operas in newspapers and television listings magazines offer information and advertise soaps in ways which support the kinds of realism established by the forms of the programmes themselves. The soaps are represented as entirely familiar: the articles profiling the actors presuppose familiarity with the names, identities and major events in the lives of the characters; and the fascination with what will happen, and with the continuing production of the series, particularly in relation to the changes in personnel among the actors, helps to support the creation of a continuous present in the soaps. The television industry is able to publicise its soaps extensively, while maintaining secrecy about forthcoming events in the narrative and its technical mode of production. But the popular press is also involved in the comparison and testing of the soap narratives against reality, running articles on the 'real' people of the East End of London alongside others on the lives of the actors in *EastEnders*. The exaggerated **melodramatic** forms of soap opera narrative (its use of comic, grotesque or stereotypical characters, for instance) play against its realism, and the viewer's pleasure must therefore partly depend on his or her recognition of the mediation of realism by television forms and institutions. The back-and-forth movement between fiction and fact in these discourses both maintains their separation from each other and shows how interdependent they are, testifying to the unstable border between what is considered 'real' and what is a performance or representation of reality.

The television theorist Robert Allen (1985: 85) has argued that 'soap opera trades narrative closure for paradigmatic complexity', meaning that although soap opera storylines flow on daily and weekly at a pace close to the viewer's experience of time and do not offer a satisfying conclusion, the result of this is that very large numbers of narrative strands can be kept going in parallel. For any one character, change and unpredictability are the norm, but in the long run this has no effect on the community as a whole. Yet, at any one moment, a change in any character will affect all the other characters with whom he or she comes into contact. The realism of soap opera refers not only to this apparent unpredictability and change but to the programme's consistently represented world and fidelity to its own fictional identity.

The shifting relations of characters in soap opera are paralleled by the shifting of the camera's points of view, which give access to the widely differing people and locations that appear in each episode. *EastEnders*, like all soaps, represents a community with a regional identity. It has a residential setting in an urban area. Flows of characters and interaction between them occur in Albert Square, around and

**ratings** the number of viewers estimated to have watched certain programmes, as compared to the numbers watching other programmes.

**genre** a type of programme. Programmes of the same genre have shared characteristics.

**melodrama** a form of drama characterised by exaggerated performance, a focus on reversals of fortune and extreme emotional reactions to events.

through which characters walk, and the various shops, pubs, houses and the market where characters meet. There is a sense that there is no escape from Albert Square, but the roads into it also lead outwards, to Walford and the rest of London, allowing the diffusion of the action towards the edge of the represented space and the invasion of that space from the outside. Sandy Flitterman-Lewis (1992: 224) has argued that within the rooms and other smaller spaces where scenes are set, the camera does not create a consistent space by alternating establishing shots and **shot-reverse-shots** in order to situate the drama securely for the viewer, 'for what the reverse shot accomplishes in the soap opera is something altogether different. The quality of viewer involvement, instead, is one of continual, momentary, and constant visual repositioning, in keeping with television's characteristic "glance".' The movement of the narrative point of view allows the sense of incompletion and future necessary to the soap opera form. This maintenance of 'the now' is supported by the emphasis in journalistic discourses on each soap's identity and unity as it unfolds in this week or this year.

> **shot-reverse-shot**
> the convention of alternating a shot of one character and a shot of another character in a scene, producing a back-and-forth movement which represents their interaction visually.

---

**ACTIVITY 8.3**

In what ways do the realisms of British soap operas depend on the mythologies and stereotypes that represent the regions of Britain in which the soaps are set? Does this make them more or less realistic?

---

## Realism and ideology

Television realism places the viewer in the position of a unified subject 'interpellated' with, or folded into, the discourses of a dominant ideology (Althusser 1971), subjected (made into a subject, and subject to the ideology) to a version of reality in which he or she misrecognises that reality and misrecognises himself or herself. This theory of how ideology in television separates the subject from his or her 'real' self shares its structure with the French psychoanalyst Jacques Lacan's theory of subjectivity. For Lacan, the subject is the result of a division between his or her 'real' self and the means (such as words, photographs or other representations) through which the subject comes to know himself or herself. Theorists of television have therefore turned to **psychoanalytic** theory in order to explain how individuals are hailed into ideology and subjectivity by the experience of watching television. One of the consequences of the ideologies of television realism is a contradiction between the viewer's working activity, where he or she is producer, and his or her leisure activity, in which he or she is positioned as a consumer. Althusser makes the very important point in his essay that ideology is not just a question of ideas circulating in people's heads but is inscribed in certain material practices. The reactionary practice of television realism involves the entrapment of the viewer in a position of apparent dominance and control over the represented reality offered by television's discourses about reality. Realist television discourse resolves contradictions by representing a unified and rational world of causes and effects, actions

> **psychoanalysis**
> the study of human mental life, including not only conscious thoughts, wishes and fears but unconscious ones. Psychoanalysis is an analytical and theoretical set of ideas as well as a therapeutic treatment.

and consequences, moral choices and rewards or punishments. It distances the viewer from the contradictory and ambiguous dynamics of reality and suggests that political action to intervene in the ways in which reality is produced from day to day is unnecessary.

If television, particularly realist television, is performing ideological work in concealing a more correct vision of social and political realities, the makers of television might be under an obligation to draw the attention of the viewer to the non-equivalence of television and reality. According to this view, television cannot be a 'true' representation, but it may be a medium in which the beginnings of a recognition of the true state of affairs could occur. In this context realism is no longer a reflection of an exterior reality but one of the forms in which representations and audiences connect with each other. The makers of television must draw the viewer's attention to their relationship with the medium in order to make them recognise the social relations that this relationship involves. So perhaps the strangeness or unrealistic nature of television versions of reality might draw the viewer's attention to the fact that they are watching a representation, not a reality. When familiar recognitions and identifications break down, viewers might grasp what it is that the relations between television and audience, and between real and representation, involve. This strategy is known as 'critical realism', and involves recognising a relationship between the television text and material social realities, yet resisting the television text's transcription of reality as if television were a neutral medium, so that the work of the forms through which representation takes place is recognised as not natural but cultural and constructed.

## News and liveness

One of the uses of photography has been for military surveillance, first by placing cameras in balloons to observe enemy troops and positions, and now with modern uses of satellite surveillance and computer enhancement of images, which continue this aim to provide a superior and powerful vision of space and detail beyond the capacity of the human eye. The broadcasting of such images, however, is controlled by military institutions:

- by allowing or withholding access to the action
- by exercising powers to censor information, or
- by encouraging television crews to self-censor the images they acquire.

In the Gulf War of 1991, for example, television journalists were organised into 'pools' or collective groups called Media Response Teams, where, in exchange for accepting military discipline and following rules on reporting, they were provided with transmission facilities that enabled them to send information to London less than an hour after acquiring it. **CNN** was able to broadcast television pictures live, and its reporter Peter Arnett in Iraq's capital Baghdad was able to observe American cruise missiles destroying buildings a few blocks from his location and transmit pictures of the action using a portable satellite dish. Television pictures of air attacks on Baghdad became available worldwide, beamed by the communications satellites which now reach 85 per cent of the world's surface. As further conflicts have

**CNN** Cable News Network, the first international satellite news channel, operating from the United States.

occurred in Afghanistan and Iraq in more recent times, viewers have become increasingly accustomed to seeing television images of events almost at the same time as they occur.

The attraction of television as a medium relies in part on its ability to broadcast events live. The excitement of live television derives not only from the sense of participation and presence at an event which live broadcasting provides, but from the assumption that what we see and hear in live broadcasting is unmediated, uncontaminated and accurate. When sports events such as the Olympics or the FA Cup final are broadcast live, or when a national event such as a royal wedding or the occurrence and aftermath of a disaster are televised, it is the accidental detail and unpredictable unfolding of events which are fascinating. And now, because live broadcasting is relatively rare, anything broadcast live gains a particular importance. Live events are those which it is assumed have a universal importance for society. Live television gives the audience access to an 'other' space and also to an alternative time: the viewer's present and the present experience of others in a distant place are equivalent but different. The caption 'live' is significant in itself, for it means 'alive', connoting that a living reality for other people is being shown, and is open to the audience's involvement.

Contemporary networks of electronic mediation allow digital images denoting realities to be circulated around the world from television news crews back to their producers at home, and also to the news agencies which sell packages of news pictures to broadcasters. Television technologies are not neutral, and the capacity to circulate images denoting realities has political effects. One example of this is the perception of the Third World by Western television audiences, where some categories of event are the most frequent versions of reality denoted in news and current affairs television. Large-scale political violence and natural disasters are the predominant form of news image broadcast of Third World countries and developing countries such as China. Media theorists have studied the patterns of regional and global news coverage, and discovered that, although the greater part of news imagery relates to the country in which news is made or to the neighbouring countries, it is the United States and other Western nations which appear in news coverage as the *active* makers of news, while countries in the developing world are portrayed as the *passive* suffering objects of news events. These divisions between active makers and passive sufferers are parallel to the division between the rich Western nations which intervene in world affairs and control world institutions such as the World Bank and United Nations, and the relatively impoverished and politically disempowered nations in the rest of the world.

## ACTIVITY 8.4

Collect samples of television news stories relating to nations in Africa. What patterns do you find in these stories and in how they are represented in image and sound? What conclusions can you draw from this exercise?

## The documentary mode

Factual programmes denote society, and inform and educate the audience about aspects of life with which they are familiar, or aspects signified as unfamiliar. Factual programmes make the 'other' into the familiar, and make the familiar seem 'other' by denoting it in unfamiliar ways, and they are a key part of the contemporary television landscape. For example, Channel 4's top-ten-rated programmes in 2003 were dominated by factual series. *Big Brother* headed the list at 7.2 million viewers, followed by *Wife Swap* (5.9 million) and *How Clean Is Your House* (5 million). While the sitcom *Friends* was the fourth-highest-rated programme for the channel at 5 million viewers, the property-themed factual programmes *Property Ladder* and *Grand Designs* were eighth and ninth, each with 4.6 million viewers.

As head of Channel 4, Mark Thompson's aim, subsequently realised, was to retain *Big Brother* as a core programme aimed at sixteen to thirty-four-year-old viewers, but to diversify the factual television offering into programmes that would use the form in different ways for different audiences. Thus *Operatunity*, in which members of the public competed to become opera singers, was aimed at more upmarket audiences, while a series about hairdressers, *The Salon*, and *Wife Swap*, in which households swap partners, attempted to develop factual subjects in different ways for viewers seeking entertainment. This is in part because the denotation of different aspects of society in factual programmes is part of television's public service function.

John Corner (2006: 90) draws attention to what he calls an 'economy of intensity' in documentary:

> The regularity of such material is often a key requirement and it may vary in its nature from scenes of violence through angry interaction and verbal abuse to scenes of celebration and joy (for example, the moment of arrival of good news; the reunion). It may close down entirely around personal testimony, the intensity of a 'speech event', perhaps a personal revelation or other form of disclosure or difficult recollection, signalled not only in its content but by changed forms of speech and facial demeanour.

Clearly moments like these in documentaries are dramatic, but Corner notes that this mixes two meanings of the word 'drama': first, something that is sensational or surprising; and, second, something that is scripted or fabricated by the programme-maker. Surprising or intense moments can be introduced in documentary by, for example, the use of surveillance footage that shows something shocking happening, like a crime being committed, an accident taking place, or police action. However, surprising moments can also take place when people do surprising things in a situation that has been set up in advance, but where the actions or speech of the participants could not in themselves be pre-planned (in *Big Brother*, for example).

In order to produce the impression of realism in television documentary, several very unnatural procedures have to be carried out. The documentary subject will almost always be aware that he or she is being recorded, witnessed or even pursued by the camera operator (and often also by a sound recordist). Once the footage has been gathered, the documentary-maker will edit the footage in order to produce a coherent argument or a narrative. While the finished programme may acknowledge the presence of the documentary-maker, it is often the case that documentaries imply that the subject is behaving 'naturally' or at least representatively. So there

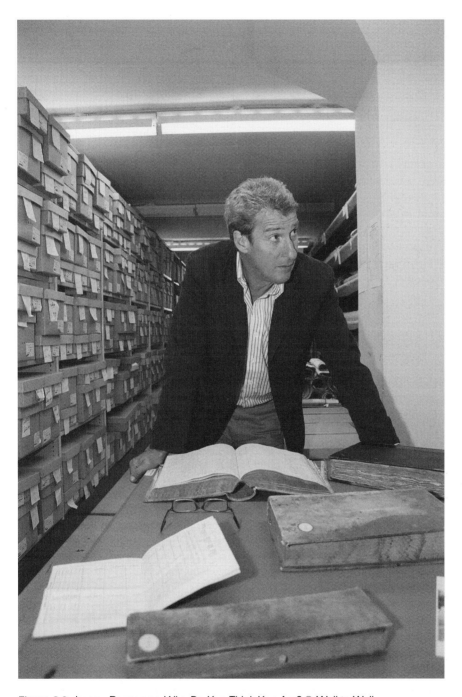

Figure 8.2 Jeremy Paxman on *Who Do You Think You Are?* © Wall to Wall

is a tension between producing a documentary which is representative and 'accurate' and providing the audience with a programme which conforms to the conventions of argument or storytelling. It is this tension which gives rise to complaints, and occasionally legal cases, raised by documentary subjects against documentary-makers, where the subject claims that he or she has been misrepresented or made to look foolish. The assumption of accuracy which always accompanies the documentary mode brings with it the danger of claims of misrepresentation. Techniques such as covert filming, or showing the documentary-maker on screen developing a relationship with the subject, are two ways of coping with these problems.

To attract viewers and guide their understanding, story has always been important to documentary. It can be created in a range of ways (Corner 2006: 92–4). Re-enactment can show the unfolding of events that occurred in reality in the past and were not observed by the camera. A **voice-over** commentary can describe, explain or make an argument that has a sequence and a story-like flow. The presenter can seem to find things out, leading the viewer through a story of discovery and understanding. It is not only the observation of the documentary subject which provides an impression of reality in documentary television but the inclusion of supporting **narration**, testimony or expert commentary. These devices make links with other factual genres, where:

- the authority of a narrator provides coherence and continuity
- testimony of members of the public supports the authenticity of the programme
- expert commentary provides backing for the assertions and arguments of the programme-maker or the figures appearing in the programme.

Devices such as these are found in, for example, sports, science, nature and current affairs programmes. It is always the case that television programmes gain their meanings by their similarity to and difference from each other, and the overlap of codes and conventions among them. Some documentary conventions connote unmediated reality, such as hand-held camera, 'natural' rather than expressive lighting and imperfect sound, while other conventions connote drama, argument and interpretation, such as voice-over, narrative structure and dramatic music.

The device of **metonymy** in documentary enables part of reality to stand for the larger real world which it represents. One day in the life of a hotel metonymically stands for any other day. The work of an inner-city social worker stands metonymically for that of all inner-city social workers. Specific images or sequences, or specific documentary subjects, have metonymic relationships with the reality of which they are a part. This device is one of the unstated assumptions which enables television programmes to claim implicitly that they represent society to itself, and connect the specific subjects of programmes to larger social contexts. But the impression of realism in television depends on the relationship between the codes of the programme and the codes available to the audience for interpreting it. Kilborn and Izod (1997: 39) use the term 'accommodation' to describe the shaping of documentary programmes to accord with the assumed knowledge of the audience. Documentaries about hotels or social work accommodate themselves, to some extent, with ideological assumptions about hotels and social workers that circulate in society. Television's claim to present the real rests on the ideologies which shape that reality for the audience.

**voice-over** speech accompanying visual images but not presumed to derive from the same place or time as the images.

**narration** the process of telling a story through image and sound. Narration can also refer to the spoken text accompanying television images.

**metonymy** the substitution of one thing for another, either because one is part of the other or because one is connected with the other. For example, 'the Crown' can be a metonym for the British state.

Television drama-documentary retells events, often recent events, in order to review or celebrate them. Recent examples of this form have included *9/11 The Twin Towers*, about the attacks on the World Trade Center in 2001, and *Hiroshima*, about the nuclear bombs dropped on Japan in 1945. The key figures and turning-points of the story are often familiar to the audience, though opening statements and captions make clear the factual basis of docudramas, while disclaimers may state that some events and characters have been changed, amalgamated or invented. Derek Paget's (1998: 82) definition of drama-documentary is that it 'uses the sequence of events from a real historical occurrence or situation and the identities of the protagonists to underpin a film script intended to provoke debate . . . The resultant film usually follows a cinematic narrative structure and employs the standard naturalist/realist performance techniques of screen drama.' Drama-documentary offers a single and personalised view of a dramatic situation, in which identification with central figures allows access for the audience but where the documentation of a historical situation 'objectively' sets these identifications into a social and political context. Narrative provides the linkage between the forms of documentary and of drama, as John Caughie (1980: 30) describes: 'If the rhetoric of the drama inscribes the document within narrative and experience, the rhetoric of the documentary establishes the experience as an experience of the real, and places it within a system of guarantees and confirmations.' British docudrama is based in carefully researched journalistic investigation, and follows the conventions of journalistic discourse, such as the sequential unfolding of events and the use of captions to identify key figures. It has become more common than ever in recent years as a way of speculating in a fictional drama about how real threats to society might impact on Britain: for example, *Gas Attack* and *Smallpox 2002*, each of which explored the consequences of terror attacks by small groups of extremists.

## Realism and public service: *Crimewatch UK*

*Crimewatch UK* both represents recent crimes in realistic ways and, as John Sears (1995: 51) has argued, performs 'a social function by helping to solve crime, and drawing on the collective responsibilities, experiences and knowledge of the viewing audience in order to do so'. This monthly BBC1 mid-evening programme has been running since 1984, and performs a 'public service' function by informing the audience, involving them in solving crime and constituting a community whose boundaries are defined by the criminals outside it. *Crimewatch* often features crimes which have been reported already in television news and newspapers, and it borrows **intertextual** meanings from other media, such as the brassy and military music used in news and police drama. The fictionalised reconstruction of crimes aims to achieve change by dramatising events, emphasising particular details, sometimes shocking the audience and drawing them into the dramatic narrative of investigation.

*Crimewatch* reduces its codes and conventions, and the problems it addresses, to a few highly coded images and devices which engage viewer knowledge derived from other genres of television, particularly crime drama. E-fits (images of suspects derived from witnesses' reports), photographs of stolen property, security camera footage and physical clues also appear in television police fiction. These coded images are metonyms, parts of the narrative of the crime which are connected with

**intertextuality** how one text draws on the meanings of another by referring to it, by allusion, quotation or parody, for example.

each other and stand in for the crime. Conversely, reconstructions on *Crimewatch* are **metaphors**: they parallel the facts of the crime but are fiction. Metaphoric reconstructions stand in for the actual crime, and represent it. *Crimewatch* title images in the 1990s signified 'information'. Visual signifiers represented:

**metaphor** the carrying-over from something of some of its meanings on to another thing of an apparently different kind. For example, a television narrative about life aboard ship could be a metaphor for British social life (the ship as metaphor for society).

- police using computers
- police photographing evidence
- police knocking on doors, and
- members of the public telephoning the police.

The sequence of information-gathering draws attention to audience participation and in the rest of the programme banks of phone operators in the studio metonymically represent police information-gathering. Specific callers' information metonymically signifies all the callers ringing in, and all the information collected. Crucial detailed clues lead to the solving of the crime, and this technique is shared with television detective fiction. This factual programme borrows intertextually from television fiction, and its realism sometimes derives from the mixing of factual and fictional conventions. Victims or witnesses sometimes appear in reconstructions playing themselves. It uses codes from several television genres, including current affairs, crime drama, documentary and phone-ins. *Crimewatch* has been successful in assisting the police to change the reality denoted in it by helping to catch criminals, thereby fulfilling a role as part of television's public service function.

But although the programme constructs a sense of community, and works on behalf of society in general, it individualises its address to the viewer and the crimes which it features. Despite the fact that television is a mass broadcast medium, viewers are addressed as individuals who might personally be able to assist in the solving of crime. The individualised notion of address is also evident in such public service formats as telethons and the BBC's annual charity fundraiser *Children in Need*. The presenters of *Crimewatch* address viewers directly with questions such as 'Were you there that morning? Did you see him? Can you help?' The individual action requested from viewers is represented as a response to crimes perpetrated by individuals against individuals.

Abstract and structural problems such as the complex of factors which cause crime, and crimes perpetrated by corporate bodies or government agencies, are never represented in *Crimewatch*. This also leads to the under-representation of what are known as 'white-collar' crimes, such as fraud, since these rarely have direct impacts on individuals who could feature in *Crimewatch* as the victims. White-collar crimes are a generally committed within large institutions, against other institutions, and their complexity makes it unlikely that they could be featured in the few minutes available for a *Crimewatch* item. The 'reality' of crime for *Crimewatch* is that it is committed by a small group of deviant outsiders, against certain unfortunate individuals. The practices of gathering information and solving crimes undertaken by institutions, especially the police force, are also not represented, since these are carried out by collective structures rather than individuals. The consequence of this emphasis on individuation in *Crimewatch*, in common with many other programmes concerned with social problems, is a blindness to the large-scale forces which animate individual action and give it its social meaning. This form of television representation cannot accommodate the ways in which individual action is determined by factors of

- social class
- economic position, and
- ideologies of gender or race.

So the realism of *Crimewatch* uses metonymy to connect the individual viewer into the larger collective television audience, to connect particular individual experiences to a social experience of crime that remains vague, and to connect representatives of the law to the unseen institutions of law enforcement. The particular is linked to the general in *Crimewatch* by the form of the programme, through the metonymy which it uses.

---

### ACTIVITY 8.5

How are reconstructions used in programmes other than *Crimewatch*, such as history programmes? Are these reconstructions always included for 'public service' informational and educational purposes?

---

## Docusoap: actuality and drama

Docusoap combines the observation and interpretation of reality found in documentary with the continuing narrative centring on a group of characters in soap opera. It observes real people and structures this observation into dramatic narrative, both denoting everyday experiences of ordinary people and focusing on performance and narrative. But docusoaps have been criticised for lacking the depth of insight into character or situation for which television documentary has conventionally striven. Formally, docusoaps use rapid cutting between scenes and characters to maintain audience interest, and do not adopt the sustained focus on the subject which has signified television documentary's quest for understanding. They adopt some of the conventions of drama, and their own conventions have migrated into those of drama as a way of invigorating scripted, fictional programmes.

The conventions of docusoap were used in the BBC situation comedy *The Office*, where the camera seemed to be witnessing action and interview material with the characters, who reflected on events and analysis of their own and others' behaviour. Docusoap is already a hybrid genre, and its extension into sitcom meant that *The Office* could blur distinctions between observed reality and scripted performance. The characters normally behave as if they are not being filmed, but sometimes they acknowledge the presence of a camera and perform to it. The series focused on the character of David Brent, who would like both to be a comedy performer for his audience of workmates and an ordinary person who might become a star through his appearance in this docusoap. *The Office* therefore demonstrates awareness of the problems inherent in docusoap as a genre, and its history of turning ordinary people into celebrities, such as Jane McDonald in *The Cruise* and Maureen Rees in *Driving School*. As Brett Mills (2004: 74) states:

By illustrating how docusoap 'characters' are capable of using the camera to their own ends, *The Office* articulates concerns around documentary fakery. And by using the conventions of documentary for humour, *The Office* undermines the distinctions between sitcom and documentary, between seriousness and humour, demonstrating that the outcomes of one can be achieved through the conventions of the other.

The 1990s and 2000s witnessed other comic variations on the uses and effects of documentary convention, especially the docusoap and video diary format, such as *Marion and Geoff* and *People Like Us*. The imitation of documentary conventions for dramatic and comic purposes gave new vitality to television at the turn of the twenty-first century.

Docusoap is a middle genre between documentary and drama. Its subjects are drawn from the 'middle' of society: neither members of a powerful elite nor power-less and socially excluded. They are typically in service-sector jobs – hotel workers, holiday reps, driving instructors or shop assistants – and deal with the public. They are 'like us', as ordinary as their audience, but being on television makes them not 'like us', so they occupy a middle position between ordinariness and celebrity. Docusoaps focus on another kind of middle by documenting their subjects' public working lives as well as their private lives, crossing a boundary between two kinds of experience. For Graeme Burton (2000: 159), docusoap 'stands for a growing use of viewers to entertain the viewers – an approach familiar from the game-show genre and the use of studio audiences. It creates the illusion that television recognises its audience and works for its audience.' In docusoap the divisions between television and ordinary reality, programme and audience, public and private, stardom and anonymity, are crossed.

---

### ACTIVITY 8.6

Find examples of 'spoof' or 'parody' documentaries, such as *The Office*. How do these programmes draw attention to the problems of documentary-making and the codes of documentary? What impact might they have on audiences' attitudes to 'real' documentaries?

---

## Changing people

Programmes featuring ordinary people have become commonplace on British television. This movement began in the BBC series *Video Nation*, made between 1995 and 2000. Its producers were keen to bring to television the heritage of amassing the comments and personal accounts collected in the 1930s and 1940s by the Mass Observation project, in which a large number of people kept diaries of their everyday lives and commented on the social and political events of the time. *Video Diaries* continued this interest in ordinary people, and the concept of collecting reports from a wide range of social classes and regions of Britain. But instead

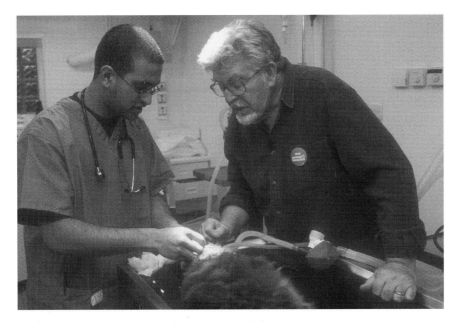

Figure 8.3 Rolf Harris and a vet on *Animal Hospital*. Courtesy of BBC Photograph Library.

of providing a picture of social and political attitudes, it focused on the detail of people's everyday lives, their work and leisure, worries and attitudes. In the last twenty years, in *Video Diaries* and many other programmes featuring ordinary people, the video diary format has been introduced into reality TV and documentary. Participants speak privately to camera about themselves, knowing that this private speech will become public when the programme is broadcast. In contemporary television the boundaries between private and public are blurred by the video confessional.

The 'makeover' genre is factual, and programmes such as *Changing Rooms*, *Ten Years Younger* and *Ground Force* denote the transformation of homes, gardens, meals, clothing, hair, etc. by 'experts'. But these programmes' climax is a dramatic moment of revelation when the transformed house, garden or person is presented to an internal audience in the programme (such as members of a family) and the television audience. The reaction to the transformation highlights the public nature of a normally private process, and the programme presenter manages the turning of the 'ordinary' person he or she has befriended towards the public audience of the programme. In *Stars in Their Eyes* members of the public turn themselves into imitation celebrities, and are thus seemingly transformed into public figures. Television combines dramatic and documentary modes, and narrows the gap between private and public experience, between ordinariness and celebrity.

*Pop Idol* and *Celebrity Fit Club* are in effect versions of the makeover show where what is made over is the person. The BBC has adopted the same format of the makeover for its programme *Would Like to Meet* (2002). In each of these programmes members of the public are advised, but importantly they are also abused, by a team of experts who guide their transformation. In some cases the objective of the trans-formation is explicitly public fame and recognition, as in *Pop Idol*, and the narrative progress of the serial is from ordinariness to extraordinariness, from alignment with the television audience to separation from that audience as the central figure becomes a star. But even in programmes where the objective is simply to become more attractive by losing weight, or to begin a satisfying relationship with a member of the opposite sex, in all cases the focus is on the often aggressive moulding of the subject. The assumption behind these programmes is that the self is a malleable and transformable object, which can be worked upon with the assistance of experts and through personal self-discipline. There is a persistent injunction for the subject to take control of himself or herself and to embark on a potentially infinite programme of self-improvement. In many of these programmes, though not all, the proof of success in the programme of self-improvement has a sexual dimension. Since sexuality is considered to be the prime location for the expression of personal identity, and sexual activity is a test of the subject's integration into the social norms of (hetero)sexual interaction, this aspect of subjective identity is a readily available demonstration of the integration of the subject.

## Reality TV: *Big Brother*

The first series of *Big Brother* was shown in the Netherlands in the spring of 1999, produced by Jon deMol's television production company Endemol. The format has been successfully sold around the world, and its value to television companies in attracting audiences is shown by the willingness of CBS in the United States to pay twenty million dollars to Endemol for the rights to the format.

The programme combines material from several different television genres:

- It is a competition in which there is a prize.
- It is a real-life soap opera with that genre's emphasis on the expression of emotion and the formation of sub-groups in the community and the exclusion of outsiders from those groups; and the use of bounded physical space as a symbolic representation of a wider society.
- It is a documentary featuring a social experiment that aims to explore the patterns of interaction between people under various kinds of 'natural' and 'artificial' pressures.

This final form of realism was emphasised in the first British version by the prominence of inserted sequences featuring the programme's two resident psychologists analysing and discussing the behaviour of the participants. This psychological discourse appeared both in the 'serious' form of the commentaries by Professor Beattie and Professor Collett and on the *Big Brother* website, which alluded to psychometric data in its flirting index, its kissing index and its statistics on who had hugged whom. Psychologists and other professionals still offer opinions now, on *Big Brother's Little Brother*, for example.

A significant focus of interest in *Big Brother* for its participants, its commentators and the audience is the question of whether any of the participants would begin sexual relationships with each other. Sexuality is, of course, a common means of attracting audiences to television programmes by promising voyeuristic coverage of sexual behaviour. The nudity of participants early in the first series of *Big Brother* was a prominent part of its visibility as a programme (demonstrated in the popular press), and in the second series the producers installed a hot-tub in the house, thus providing further opportunities for the display of the participants' bodies. Partly because there is little else for them to do, participants spend a lot of time exercising and developing their bodies, at the same time presenting and developing their physicality for the cameras. Sexuality is a particularly intimate aspect of social behaviour; it also corresponds to the programme's emphasis on the construction of identity, and the potential conflicts both within individuals and between them over matters of desire and the formation of relationships which include some and exclude others. These questions of internal conflict and conflict between participants over sexual relationships also conform to the pseudo-scientific discourse justifying the programme, where the enforced hothouse situation could be argued to correspond to a laboratory experiment in which sexual behaviour could be observed. The inclusion of gay and lesbian participants in *Big Brother* in Britain places further strains on these individuals and their fellow participants, because of the still prevalent homophobia of British society. The potential for the formation of alliances and the stigmatisation of individuals around their sexuality becomes another possible focus of interest for the audience, which is also invited to support participants on the basis of their sexuality or their potential for sexual activity, and to exclude others from the programme by voting them out.

In the first series of *Big Brother* ten volunteers were observed by permanently installed cameras in a specially built house in London for nine weeks. Seventy thousand pounds was on offer to the contestant who survived weekly nominations for ejection by his or her housemates and the public vote. The private space of the house became public (even more so on the internet, where real-time footage was screened), promising access to private space and the opportunity for interaction by phone-in voting. As Vivian Sobchack (1996: 82) has noted, 'While our personal access to the space of others has been appreciably amplified through television and computers, our privacy has been simultaneously reduced.' *Big Brother* gossip is a key pleasure for viewers since the programme's realism encourages them to feel they know the contestants. The programme consists largely of sequences of the participants interacting and conversing, with frequent close-ups reinforcing an apparent intimacy between the audience and the contestants. For Graeme Burton (2000: 146): 'The dominance of this way of using and experiencing television gives the illusion of physical closeness, invokes those rules of social interaction which demand attention and which create some sense of social proximity.' Press coverage of *Big Brother* builds up a selection of character types (most famously the manipulative and deceptive 'Nasty Nick' Bateman – the 'villain' of the first series; and later the rude and combative Jade Goody), and the producers' selection of outgoing and dominant contestants provokes dramatic conflict and performance comparable to soap opera fiction. The participants attempt to play roles that will stop other participants voting them off, and which would enlist audience support. Just as in docusoap, the realism of 'reality TV' is partly performance, and it is telling that several *Big Brother* contestants have subsequently become television presenters.

The genre of the television talk show and 'reality TV' like *Big Brother* exemplify an uneasy shift in the contemporary ideologies of television from a liberal emphasis on personal empowerment and public service concern with social issues to an aggressive surveillance of the individual subject and the engagement of the audience in a process of stigmatisation, competition and risk. It is appropriate that, early in its history, the participants in *Big Brother* were all aged between twenty-two and thirty-eight, and that its audience mainly comprised viewers in the sixteen to thirty-four age group, of whom 75 per cent watched the programme during its first run. This is the age group most sought by television advertisers because of its high spending power, so any programme that attracts it in large numbers, such as *Big Brother*, will be a commercial success. For this younger generation, the dynamic shift to a liberal, free market, individualist ideology is appropriate to their lived experience: student grants have been abolished, low-paid work is common, conspicuous consumption and excessive behaviour are conventional, some illegal activity (such as drug use) is accepted and threats such as sexually transmitted diseases and violence against the person are more likely than for other age groups.

*Big Brother*'s title alludes to George Orwell's novel *Nineteen Eighty-four*, where the citizens of a future totalitarian society were monitored by video surveillance: 'Big Brother is watching you.' Including surveillance systems operated by local authorities, government agencies and private organisations or individuals, there were approximately 1.5 million security cameras in operation in the UK in 2002 (Addley 2002: 14). The city of Newcastle had over 300 in locations such as shopping centres, housing estates and industrial zones, while Manchester opened a £1.3-million digital surveillance system using 400 cameras in the same year. The Home Office spent £170 million on surveillance cameras between 1999 and 2003, and local authorities spent the same amount.

The programme's title connotes entrapment, restriction and control, and it was marketed at first as an experiment about how human society works, with the contestants like rats trapped in a laboratory maze. As if in a psychological test, the selfishness of desiring the prize of £70,000 conflicted with the contestants' need to gain loyalty from their housemates. Rules are imposed by the production team, and tasks are set through which contestants are rewarded with necessities and rewards, in the way that laboratory animals are trained to undertake tasks to gain food. *Big Brother* sets up the tensions between freedom and control, individual and community, work and pleasure, which model social reality. So its realism also consists of its representation of the real conditions of existence in society in a coded form. *Big Brother* shows society to itself, largely unconsciously, by putting key aspects of contemporary ideology into real physical forms.

---

### ACTIVITY 8.7

Perhaps the oddest feature of the *Big Brother* house is its lack of a television set. How is the realism of the programme either increased or reduced by depriving its inhabitants of the chance to watch television?

## Case study: actuality in television news

Television has overtaken newspapers as the dominant source of news in Britain and other developed nations. This is partly because broadcasting regulations demanding '**balance**' and 'objectivity' govern television news but not newspaper publishing. But another key consideration, which is the focus of this section, is the value of immediacy in television news deriving from its incorporation of **actuality** pictures and live reporting. Television news programmes can, on rare occasions, incorporate live footage during programmes, although the technological complexity of doing this can make producers wary of links with crews in distant locations. News programmes are planned to the second, so the immediacy of live **ENG** footage potentially conflicts with the desire to connote orderliness and authority in news broadcasting. A more common use of ENG footage is therefore to create packages where sequences of actuality pictures have been edited together with a voice-over by the news reporter. The package will be of a known length and can be combined with live studio discussion and other commentary. But since television news attracts its audience with the promise of seeing and hearing news events happen, especially when they are happening live, there is both a professional pride for broadcasters and a hook for potential audiences in using actuality footage. Therefore, on-screen captions denoting a live report and the frequent mention of the word 'live' in the pieces to camera by presenters are notable features of television news programmes.

There is a hierarchy of **news value**, in which live actuality pictures are the most attractive to the producers of television news programmes, followed by actuality pictures which have been pre-recorded, and finally those stories which cannot be illustrated by actuality footage or other visual forms such as interviews. These are the stories which are least likely to appear in the producer's running order for a programme. News programmes depend on a mythology in which the television audience can apparently witness directly any significant events occurring anywhere in the world. Television news claims to denote events objectively and immediately, offering a neutral and transparent channel of communication. The iconic quality of television images, which appear simply to record what is unfolding in front of the camera, are key signifiers of this mythology of transparency in television news and in other television factual genres. The word 'television' means seeing at a distance, and television news is a central example of the mythology underlying the medium. For almost everyone in the television audience, the public world of politics, war, business and natural catastrophe is distant, but television news advertises its ability to connect the relatively isolated and dis-engaged viewer with this more dramatic and apparently important reality. Television news bridges the gap between public space and private space, which has ambivalent ideological effects:

- On one hand, the audience is linked by the medium of television with the wider public world.
- On the other hand, this wider world is shaped according to the codes and conventions of television news, and necessarily remains at a distance from the audience.

The institutional and representational structures of television news simultaneously involve the audience and disempower it.

When two Boeing 767 airliners were flown into the side of the twin towers of the World Trade Center in New York on 11 September 2001, television channels cleared their schedules

**balance** the requirement in television news and current affairs to present both sides of an argument or issue.

**actuality footage** television pictures representing an event that was filmed live. The term usually refers to pictures of news events.

**electronic news-gathering (ENG)** the use of lightweight cameras and digital technology such as portable satellite transmission dishes to record and transmit news pictures and sound.

**news value** the degree of significance attributed to a news story, where items with high news value are deemed most significant to the audience.

*continued*

in order to present live actuality footage and studio discussion. In the jargon of television production, this is when programmes become 'open ended', meaning that they continue as long as new information is available, rather than finishing at the scheduled fixed point planned by the schedulers. Television news, because of its liveness or potential liveness, is usually the medium that viewers turn to when major news stories are breaking in order to see pictures of the events and discover the most recent developments. On the 11th the maximum audiences for news on terrestrial British channels were:

- BBC1            9.4 million
- BBC2            2.6 million
- ITV             7.7 million
- Channel 4       1.8 million
- Channel 5       0.6 million
- Sky News        0.99 million
- BBC News 24     0.37 million
- ITN News Channel  0.17 million.

Although channels began to cease open-ended coverage of the event on the evening of the first day, news audiences remained high until the end of the week. The BBC adopted the strategy of simultaneous broadcast on its terrestrial BBC1 network and its digital channel BBC News 24. This simplified the management of news broadcasting in a potentially chaotic and highly complex situation, and also functioned as an advertisement for the recently launched BBC rolling news channel. ITN, by contrast, broadcast live news across five different networks: ITV, Channel 4, Channel 5, ITN News and Euronews. This enabled each network to maintain the well-known presenters associated with its programmes and provided different programming to viewers on each of the channels.

There was some difference in approach between the BBC and ITN coverage. Although both news organisations often repeated video sequences showing the airliners crashing into the twin towers, the BBC quickly introduced analysis and discussion into its coverage as well as live updates from reporters in the United States. ITN, on the other hand, persisted with live footage (usually of presenters in New York and **vox pop** interviews) rather than analysis. All commercial breaks were dropped from the schedule during ITN news programmes.

Four airliners were hijacked at the same time, one crashing into the Pentagon, a second coming down in Pennsylvania en route to another target, and two flown into the World Trade Center. The television coverage focused primarily on the World Trade Center events, partly because of the larger scale of casualties but also because of the availability of several different points of view on the attack itself filmed by amateur camera users and the comparative ease of access to eyewitnesses, officials, government spokespeople and experts in the New York metropolitan area. News coverage quickly reduced to extracts of a few seconds' duration showing the impact of each airliner as it hit its target, brief soundbites from witnesses close to the scene and a grainy still photograph of Osama bin Laden. Ironically for a news event for which such dramatic pictures were available, and where numerous correspondents were present in New York to provide live coverage of the developing crisis, many of the microwave dishes used to transmit television pictures back to the UK had been located on the top of the World Trade Center and were therefore destroyed. Communications between live news studios in London and presenters in New York were therefore fragile during the first day of coverage.

**vox pop** literally meaning 'the voice of the people', short television interviews conducted with members of the public, usually in the street.

Figure 8.4   The second hijacked plane moments before crashing into the second tower of the World Trade Center, New York, on 11 September 2001. Photograph by Masatomo Kuriya/Corbis Sygma.

Television networks also had to rely on those journalists and presenters who were already present in America at the time, since within hours the United States and Canada closed their airspace to foreign flights. While British television networks wanted their main presenter, their 'anchor', in New York, and hastily chartered aeroplanes and sent their reporters to airports around London in order to fly there immediately, the most well-known anchors never made it to the city. Programmes remained anchored in London, with live satellite pictures presented by less famous correspondents in New York. Whereas live broadcast coverage had been developed into a recognised form which could be managed by the networks, after their experience in covering the Gulf War of 1991 and the Balkan conflicts of the late 1990s, all news broadcasters were dismayed and frustrated that they were unable to broadcast pictures from 'ground zero', the wreckage of the World Trade Center itself, which had been closed to all but emergency personnel. Nevertheless, the days following the attacks were saturated with television coverage. CNN broadcast live to a worldwide audience of almost one billion, in ten languages, including English, to nine hundred affiliated television stations.

But the images broadcast by all Western television sources had a Western, and particularly American, point of view. Although there were difficulties in gaining access to satellite **uplink** facilities to transmit pictures from the United States to Britain and Europe, these were the result of overloaded facilities and of preference being given to American news crews. The satellite uplinks were the only way of relaying pictures quickly, and had to be booked in advance, with intense competition between broadcasters for access to the available slots. It was very difficult for news broadcasters to provide actuality footage representing the point of view of anti-American individuals or institutions, particularly in Afghanistan, because of the complex restrictions on Western television personnel there. On 11 September 2001 there

**uplink** the electronic system which beams television signals from the ground to a satellite for onward transmission to a television institution elsewhere.

*continued*

were very few Western journalists in Afghanistan, there are very few uplink points there, and access to these is strictly controlled. But in any case, Afghan government restrictions on Western journalists prevented them from filming in the country in the first place, so, for myriad reasons, explanation for or justification of the attacks on the United States could not be presented. The result was that poor-quality pictures of Osama bin Laden and a few seconds of controversial footage apparently showing Palestinians jubilantly celebrating the attacks were the primary images representing alternatives to the vengeful and racist discourses emerging from the United States in their aftermath. CNN was exceptional in having a reporter – Nic Robertson – in Kabul (the capital of Afghanistan) equipped with a satellite videophone. This technology allowed Robertson to report live from the city. However, the videophone had been smuggled across the Afghan border and had to be used illegally only for short periods in different locations. The efforts made by television news teams to gather images such as these demonstrate the significance of realist television footage to the news genre in particular, but more generally to the whole television medium and its audiences.

## SUMMARY OF KEY POINTS

- Realism in television can refer to an adequate relationship between what television represents and how it is represented.
- The technologies for recording images and sound in television predispose the television medium to realism, but reality can never be captured unproblematically.
- Realism also refers to the conventions used in particular forms of programme to convey the impression that something real is being represented.
- Television audiences are accustomed to realist conventions, and expect realism from some kinds of programme, such as news and documentary, more than others.
- The factual genres of television have a special relationship with realism because they seem to represent something that would have happened anyway.
- Fictional programmes also make use of realist conventions, in their representations of place, character and narrative.

## Further reading

Allen, R., 'Audience-oriented criticism and television', in R. Allen (ed.), *Channels of Discourse, Reassembled: Television and Contemporary Criticism* (London: Routledge, 1992), pp. 101–37.

Bignell, J., *Big Brother: Reality TV in the Twenty-first Century* (Basingstoke: Palgrave Macmillan, 2005).

Boyd-Barrett, O. and T. Rantanen, *The Globalization of News* (London: Sage, 1998).

Bruhn Jensen, K. (ed.), *News of the World: World Cultures Look at Television News* (London: Routledge, 1998).

Brunsdon, C., '*Crossroads* – notes on soap opera', *Screen*, 22:4 (1981), pp. 32–7.

Bruzzi, S., *The New Documentary: A Critical Introduction* (London: Routledge, 2000).

Buckingham, D., *Public Secrets: EastEnders and Its Audience* (London: BFI, 1987).

Caughie, J., 'Progressive television and documentary drama', *Screen*, 21:3 (1980) pp. 9–35.

Corner, J., '"A fiction (un)like any other"?', *Critical Studies in Television*, 1:1 (2006), pp. 89–96.

—— *The Art of Record: A Critical Introduction to Documentary* (Manchester: Manchester University Press, 1996).

Dovey, J., *Freakshow* (Cambridge: Polity, 2000).

Flitterman-Lewis, S., 'Psychoanalysis, film, and television', in R. Allen (ed.), *Channels of Discourse, Reassembled* (London: Routledge, 1992), pp. 203–46.

Geraghty, C., *Women and Soap Opera: A Study of Prime Time Soaps* (Cambridge: Polity Press, 1991).

Holmes, S. and D. Jermyn (eds), *Understanding Reality Television* (London: Routledge, 2004).

Kilborn, R. and J. Izod, *An Introduction to Television Documentary: Confronting Reality* (Manchester: Manchester University Press, 1997).

MacGregor, B., *Live, Direct and Biased? Making Television News in the Satellite Age* (London: HodderHeadline, 1997).

Mills, B., 'Comedy verité: contemporary sitcom form', *Screen*, 45:1 (2004), pp. 63–78.

Nelson, R., *TV Drama in Transition: Forms, Values and Cultural Change* (Basingstoke: Macmillan, 1997).

Nichols, B., *Introduction to Documentary* (Bloomington, Ind.: Indiana University Press, 2001).

—— *Blurred Boundaries: Questions of Meaning in Contemporary Culture* (Bloomington, Ind.: Indiana University Press, 1994).

—— *Representing Reality: Issues and Concepts in Documentary* (Bloomington, Ind.: Indiana University Press, 1991).

Paget, D., *No Other Way to Tell It: Dramadoc/Docudrama on Television* (Manchester: Manchester University Press, 1998).

Sreberny-Mohammadi, A. with K. Nordenstreng, R. Stevenson and F. Ugboajah (eds), *Foreign News in the Media: International Reporting in 29 Countries* (Paris: UNESCO, 1985).

Winston, B., *Claiming the Real: The Documentary Film Revisited* (London: BFI, 1995).

# Television Representation

# Television Representation

## Introduction

This chapter discusses television representations of particular groups, especially those defined by gender or race, with attention to their differences in different television forms and **genres**. This involves considering the different methodologies that can be used in Television Studies to approach these issues, and the strengths and weaknesses of different means of answering related questions. The chapter includes a case study on the representation of women in factual television, noting the significance of the long-running factual series *Wife Swap*, and exploring the critical arguments advanced about this programme. Activities in this chapter include suggestions for applying a range of methodologies to the issues of television representation and the underlying assumptions about television's role in society on which this depends.

genre a type of programme. Programmes of the same genre have shared characteristics.

There are three central questions that have informed work in Television Studies on the issue of representation. Each of them stems from an initial assumption that television has connections with the real world of culture and society in which it exists. Earlier chapters have noted that the television medium has a continuing interest in the present moment, in documenting what is happening now, and engaging with the lives lived by its viewers. Connected with this is the historical relationship between television and the present that comes from the fact that television began as a medium of live broadcasting, and still broadcasts both live programmes and programmes that are not live but masquerade as if they are. So the question of representation in television is connected to the issue of realism discussed in Chapter 8. The three concerns that Television Studies has addressed about representation are:

- Who is doing the representing? – a question about production.
- What is represented and how is this done? – a question about textuality.
- How are representations understood by audiences? – a question about reception.

Each of these questions draws attention not only to content but to the forms and processes of representation. In Television Studies television is approached as something that is actively made by someone, using particular textual forms to communicate some meanings and not others, with meanings that are not simply delivered to the audience but are appropriated and used by them in complex ways.

## Quantitative research: content analysis

In contrast to many of the theoretical methodologies discussed in this book, there is a long tradition in the social sciences, including the study of television, that seeks to find empirical data to answer research questions. As John Fiske (1990: 135) explains, the aims of empiricism are to:

- collect and categorise objective facts
- form hypotheses and explain them
- eliminate human bias from the process of investigation
- devise experimental methods to prove or disprove the validity of the data.

Content analysis works by gathering a sample of material to be studied, such as a group of television programmes broadcast on the same day, or programmes that feature representations of a particular gender, economic or ethnic group, and devising a method for subdividing the sample into relevant units that can be counted. While content analysis is sometimes used as a method of television analysis on its own, it is more common for it to be deployed as one of several different method-ologies, including, for example, **textual analysis** or audience research. Content analysis is quantitative in that, rather than making an interpretation of the meanings of selected components of television programmes, it attempts to offer precise information on the relative quantities of one kind of representation or another, so that these can be compared with each other. The method is effective when there is a sufficient quantity of recorded material available to be analysed. Since it is now quite easy to record television and amass a considerable volume of potential research data, content analysis is not difficult to carry out on the medium, though the design of a study and the specific methodology used to answer any particular research question can be difficult to establish.

> **textual analysis**
> a critical approach which seeks to understand a television text's meanings by undertaking detailed analysis of its image and sound components, and the relationships between those components.

There are five steps in conducting a content analysis:

- selecting the sample
- defining the categories to analyse
- reviewing and coding the data
- analysing the data
- drawing conclusions based on the results.

Using a term from statistical analysis, the sample of material to be analysed is called a 'population'. The population might be, for example, all of the programmes, advertisements, trailers and other linking material broadcast on Five between 6.00 a.m. and midnight on a particular day. Or it might be all of the situation come-dies broadcast on **terrestrial** channels in the month of October 2007. The sample will be chosen to answer a research question. This might be, for example: how many acts of violence involving the use of firearms appeared in programmes, advertise-ments and other kinds of broadcast during the hours of Five's programming that have been recorded? Clearly, the most productive answers to a research question will depend on having a suitably large sample population to study. The aim of content analysis is often to provide a snapshot that gives a reliable sense of the frequency of representation of a particular chosen type of content. When television

> **terrestrial**
> broadcasting from a ground-based transmission system, as opposed to broadcasting via satellite.

analysts have sought to conduct studies of the representation of particular groups of people on television, they have often adopted content analysis in order to produce representative quantitative figures that may be interesting in themselves or useful to compare and contrast with other samples that have been analysed in the same way.

Once the research question has been decided, and the sample population recorded, the analysis of data usually requires the definition of categories of content. For example, in a content analysis of the representation of disability in television programmes, it might be useful to separate the categories of physical and mental disability, perhaps introducing further sub-categories representing various types of disability. It can be a long and frustrating activity to apply all of the categories and sub-categories to the sample population and to record the data. The application of categories to the sample is called coding, since each instance of relevant content will be represented in a numerical form. As the analysis goes on, it may also be necessary to refine the categories or even to reassess the usefulness of the research question. Categories of content may be too vague, and too difficult for the researcher to assign to cases which seem to belong to more than one category. Nevertheless, the end result of the coding and recording process will be a numerical count of the instances in each category, so that these can be displayed in a useful way, in a graph, table or pie chart, for example. The next step will be to analyse the data; computer packages for analysing statistics are now often used for this purpose. Some knowledge of the significance of statistical analysis is necessary at this stage, in order to understand how to use procedures involving standard deviation, means, medians and modal distributions, for instance. Once the data have been analysed by these methods, it will then be possible to draw inferences and make interpretations about the results, and also to relate them to other kinds of research method (such as textual analysis or audience research) that may have been used to address the research question.

---

**ACTIVITY 9.1**

If you were conducting a content analysis to find out how often black characters have leading roles in television detective fiction series, what kind of sample 'population' of programmes would be representative of television programming? What decisions would you take about how much material to study, and what 'leading role' means?

---

An example of how content analysis was supplemented by audience research can show how important criticisms can be made of television conventions in representing conflicts between ethnic groups. A long-established group of media researchers, the Glasgow Media Group, studied the representation of Israeli and Palestinian Arab conflict currently continuing in the Middle East (Philo 2002). This conflict arose from a series of historical events. When the state of Israel was established in 1948, Palestinians living there were displaced from their land and became refugees. In May 1948, a war between Israel and its Arab neighbours produced more refugees, many of whom moved to the Gaza Strip (then controlled by Egypt) and to the West

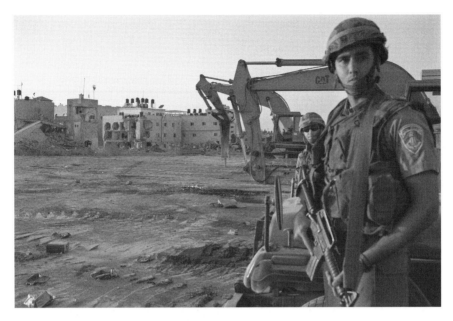

Figure 9.1 Israeli soldiers at Ramallah on the West Bank, 2002. Photograph by
Ricki Rosen/Corbis SABA.

Bank (controlled by Jordan). In 1967 Israel was at war with its Arab neighbours again
and occupied Gaza and the West Bank, bringing the Palestinian refugees in those
areas under its control. Eastern Jerusalem (formerly controlled by Jordan) was also
occupied by Israel. To cement its control, Israel built settlements in the areas it had
occupied. These caused anger among the refugees because of the presence of Israeli
citizens in former Arab territories, and also because their farming activities deprived
Palestinian farmers of water. The subsequent violence in the Middle East consists
of attempts by Israel to maintain its control over the occupied territory, and attempts
by Palestinians to resist the occupation and regain their land.

The Glasgow Media Group sought to explore the degree of understanding among
television viewers of this conflict by undertaking a content analysis of television news
stories on BBC and ITN and interviewing sample viewers. The researchers interviewed twelve groups of viewers, totalling eighty-five people, from a cross-section
of ages and social backgrounds. They also interviewed 300 young people aged
between seventeen and twenty-two. All of those surveyed were asked what they
had understood about the conflict from television news. Of the whole sample,
82 per cent named television news as their main source of information, and regarded
the main message of the coverage as being that conflict and violence were occurring.
The news stories analysed related to the uprising by Palestinians from September
2000 until the middle of the following month. Eighty-nine bulletins were broadcast,
comprising 3,536 lines of transcribed text. Of these only seventeen lines explained
the history of the conflict. The majority of the people surveyed did not understand
who was occupying the occupied territories, or why. Among the sample of 300 young
people, 71 per cent did not know that the Israelis were occupying the territory, and
11 per cent believed (incorrectly) that the Palestinians were occupying it and that
the settlers were Palestinian. Although many more Palestinians have been killed

in the conflict to date than Israelis, only 30 per cent of the sample of young people recognised this. Discussing the research in the *Guardian*, Greg Philo (2002) of the Glasgow Media Group suggested the following reasons for this situation:

- Television journalists did not provide any explanation of the history of the conflict, or referred to it only by brief shorthand phrases that the viewers did not understand.
- Television news programmes focused more on actuality coverage of violence occurring than explanations for that violence.
- The content analysis revealed that Israelis spoke twice as much on television news as Palestinians, thus favouring the Israeli perception of events.
- The close relationships between British politicians and the United States government tend to favour the pro-Israeli position adopted by the United States, and this official position was reflected in television coverage.

---

### ACTIVITY 9.2

Why do you think the Glasgow Media Group wanted to interview viewers as well as conduct their content analysis of Middle East coverage? How did audience research support content analysis in this case?

---

## Feminist work on popular television

**melodrama**
a form of drama characterised by exaggerated performance, a focus on reversals of fortune and extreme emotional reactions to events.

Television **melodrama** is marked by its focus on women characters, on the emotional and the psychological and on moments of dramatic intensity. The melodramatic mode supplies the means to interpret dramatic turning-points and crises through a repertoire of stock character types and familiar **codes** of gesture and expression. As Ien Ang's (1997: 157) research on *Dallas* showed (see Chapter 12), the appeal of **prime-time** soap melodrama in the 1980s rested primarily on the central women characters, especially Sue Ellen Ewing: the viewers who communicated with Ang 'assert that the appeal of Sue Ellen is related to a form of realism (in the sense of psychological believability and recognizability); more importantly, this realism is connected with a somewhat tragic reading of Sue Ellen's life, emphasizing her problems and troubles'. Sue Ellen hated her husband but lacked the strength to leave him. She was a successful businesswoman in a masculine world, but her business (Valentine Lingerie) was set up as a tactic to separate her husband J. R. from her rival, his mistress. While activity in the masculine world of business intrigue was present, its significance lay in its relationship to Sue Ellen's personal dilemmas. In prime-time melodrama, conflict between characters produces emotional drama, and characters also experience conflicts within themselves which are expressed by rapidly alternating and conflicting emotions, often expressed through physical, bodily behaviour. The restricted repertoire of characteristics which defines melodrama characters comprises facial expressions, tones of voice and gestures.

**code** in semiotics, a system or set of rules that shapes how signs can be used, and therefore how meanings can be made and understood.

**prime time** the part of a day's television schedule when the greatest number of viewers may be watching, normally the mid-evening period.

In the other major prime-time melodrama of the 1980s, *Dynasty*, the central woman character was Alexis Colby, whom the audience was invited both to admire and despise. Jostein Gripsrud (1995) has commented on Alexis's ability to transform traditional feminine weaknesses into the sources of her strength, through her uninhibited use of her (and men's) sexuality in her struggle for power, combined with her own skills at business manoeuvring, previously deemed masculine. Alexis was regarded as the ultimate bitch, aggressive and sexually manipulative, but all because of her untimely separation from her beloved children. In other words, her masculine behaviour was the result of a thwarted and distorted femininity. Alexis in *Dynasty* was fascinating because of the contrast between masculinity as a role and the femininity expected of women. She was determined to control the Colbyco corporation, and manipulated the men around her.

The expression of emotion, as David Lusted (1998) notes, is a marker both of femininity and of working-class culture. While masculine values entail the suppression of emotion in favour of efficiency, achievement and stoicism, feminine values encourage the display of emotion as a way of responding to problems. Similarly, elite class sectors value rational talk and writing as means of expression, versus emotional release. These distinctions, which are of course culturally produced rather than biological or natural, have been important to work in Television Studies on the relationship between **gender** and the different genres of television, where news and current affairs are regarded as masculine, and melodrama as feminine. On the basis of these gender, class and genre distinctions, the role of emotional display takes on increased significance. The US prime-time soaps of the 1980s were set in a world controlled predominantly by men, but offered pleasures to the woman viewer by showing that male power can be challenged by moral questioning, and by women's refusal to be controlled. **Patriarchy** was critiqued by women using feminine *and* masculine gender traits as weapons against male competitors. Melodrama presents characters as simplified types: for example, as good mother or bad mother, faithful spouse or unfaithful spouse, conformist or rebel, princess or bitch. Christine Geraghty (1991) and other feminist critics have argued that the world depicted in melodrama is potentially **utopian**, since the suggestion is always there that it could be reorganised in terms sympathetic to women's desires for community, and for openness and honesty of feeling.

> **gender** the social and cultural division of people into masculine or feminine individuals. This is different from sex, which refers to the biological difference between male and female bodies.

> **patriarchy** a social system in which power is held by men rather than women, and masculine values dominate.

> **utopia** an ideal society.

---

## ACTIVITY 9.3

What examples can you find of melodramatic codes in contemporary television? Are these in programmes containing strong women characters, and/or in programmes that appeal to women viewers more than men? Is social class important to the programmes you have listed; if so, how?

---

## Gender representations: *Sex and the City* and *Desperate Housewives*

The American series *Sex and the City*, made by the US production company Home Box Office (HBO) and shown in Britain on Channel 4, gained a high profile in the press and among audiences as an example of the representation of women and feminine sexuality in popular television (Bignell, 2004). It combines the ongoing storylines of the television serial form with the new narratives in each episode that are found in the television series form. It is a comedy where each week the characters face problems that put them into comic situations, and where witty lines and jokes are important to the scripts, as in the situation comedy form. But it also has moments of social comment and psychological insight, which are conventional aspects of serious drama on television. This mixture of elements from different television forms and genres has led to *Sex and the City* being referred to by journalists and critics as a 'dramedy', a hybrid of drama and comedy.

It focuses on the collective and individual day-to-day activities of four women friends in New York. The four characters are very rarely seen at work, but they are wealthy enough to spend much of the on-screen time shopping, going to parties, lunching with each other and dating wealthy professional men. The programme derives from the journalistic writing published originally in a column by Candace Bushnell. Her book *Sex and the City* was a popular bestseller, and derived from the newspaper columns she has published since 1994 in the *New York Observer*. It was in this print context that Bushnell's apparently autobiographical alter ego, the central character of the programme, Carrie, was developed. Bushnell had earlier written about the New York party-going elite for the magazine *Beat* before writing freelance for *Self*, *Mademoiselle* and other magazines.

The three aspects of the series that this section considers in relation to women's magazine **discourse** are:

- *confession*: episodes always contain voice-over narration in which Carrie presents her self-doubt about her attractiveness, the state of her relationships with friends and lovers, her future and the morality of her behaviour, for example.
- *sexuality as the key to identity*: happiness in sexual relationships, the prospect of sexual pleasure or worry over the unavailability of sex, and a sense that characters' identities are expressed through their sexuality are all fundamental to the four women's sense of themselves.
- *commodity fetishism*: this term (deriving from **Marx**'s analysis of capitalist societies) describes a fascination with consumer objects whose value lies in their power to signify as signs of luxury, social power, sexual attractiveness or some other valued meaning in the context of the ideology of Western societies. Examples of fetishised commodities in *Sex and the City* include designer shoes and clothes.

The television series draws on concerns with the components of feminine gender identity that are found in the discourse of women's magazines, and feminist media critics writing about women's magazines have argued that magazines such as *Cosmopolitan* and *Marie Claire* define the concerns of what Janice Winship (1987) calls a 'women's world'. This world is composed of representations that present a set of interests, problems and desires that may sometimes be incoherent and contradictory but nevertheless construct an identity for the feminine. In **semiotic** terms this world is a set of **signs** that define the signified meaning 'feminine' in distinction to the masculine: it is not a representation of the 'natural' reality of being a woman, but instead a structure of meanings that provide significance and social

---

**discourse** a particular use of language for a certain purpose in a certain context (such as academic discourse or poetic discourse), and similarly, in television, a particular usage of television's audio-visual 'language' (news programme discourse or nature documentary discourse, for instance).

**commodity** a raw material or product whose economic value is established by market price rather than the intrinsic qualities or usefulness of the material or product itself.

**Marxism** the political and economic theories associated with the German nineteenth-century theorist Karl Marx, who described and critiqued capitalist societies and proposed communism as a revolutionary alternative.

**semiotics** the study of signs and their meanings, initially developed for the study of spoken language, and now used also to study the visual and aural 'languages' of other media, such as television.

**sign** in semiotics, something which communicates meaning, such as a word, an image or a sound.

identity to women who buy into it. Magazines are themselves commodity products, whose costs of production are covered not simply by their purchase price but by the advertisements for products presented to their readers. For Winship and other feminist critics, magazines sell to women a representation of femininity that shapes the social place of women. Ellen McCracken (1993: 3) argues that 'women's magazines exert a cultural leadership to shape consensus in which highly pleasurable codes work to naturalise social relations of power'. The pleasure of reading glossy women's magazines, like the pleasure of watching *Sex and the City*, is the medium through which these ideological meanings of femininity are passed on.

Magazines provide a location in which a sense of community and shared interest among women can be established, and where certain pleasures are attributed to feminine identity. These pleasures include:

- self-adornment (using cosmetics, adopting a personal style, being fashionable)
- self-improvement (how to have better sex, better hair, healthier food)
- sharing a collective identity (sharing in the same concerns and problems as other women).

But as McCracken (1993: 136) argues, 'within this discursive structure, to be beautiful, one must fear being non-beautiful; to be in fashion, one must fear being out of fashion; to be self-confident, one must first feel insecure'. Feminists have argued that the pleasures offered by women's magazines rest on the assumption that women's lives offer relatively few pleasures, and that the aspirations addressed in them (to be beautiful, fashionable and confident, for example) show that women's real lives deserve to be changed, rather than made temporarily more tolerable by the short-term enjoyment of reading magazines.

From this point of view, the emphases of *Sex and the City* episodes are on the wrong things, and perpetuate the agendas set by the women's magazines that Winship, McCracken and others criticised. Carrie and her friends' ability to live lives of consumption, seeking happiness through relationships and exchanging gossip and insecurities, must depend on a relatively high level of income. Even the fact that they live in comfortable apartments in Manhattan shows that they belong to a small and privileged group of young professionals who can live single, independent lives.

From this perspective, *Sex and the City* can be argued to render invisible the questions of economic status, work and social power for women. Furthermore, the central characters' fascination with clothes, shoes, hair and personal style is a focus on relatively trivial aspects of women's lives, in contrast to questions of gender equality and the difficulty that real women face in employment and opportunity. But perhaps most significantly for a feminist critique of gender representations in *Sex and the City*, the discourses of confession and self-doubt that occupy so much of Carrie's voice-over and the conversations among the group of friends perpetuate the assumption that feminine identity is a perpetual struggle with dissatisfaction about oneself. Feminine identity is represented in *Sex and the City* as something centred on lack and potential disappointment. The fact that the programme is a comedy is significant here, because, if it were not, the anxieties and struggles of the characters might have a more critical function. Comedy enables *Sex and the City* to engage with questions of feminine identity but also to dissipate them into physical comedy and verbal wit. Indeed, the sophisticated character comedy, the witty phrases, moments of insight and minor revelations that Carrie's voice-over presents distance the viewer from the issues that are the subject of the **narrative** and instead focus attention on the television form in which they are communicated. Jokes, clever turns of phrase and comic reversals of fortune in *Sex and the City* focus the audience's attention on Carrie and her friends' ability to cope with emotional and social problems rather than their inability to analyse them critically and politically, or to change them.

The *Sex and the City* television series draws on modes of confession that are also found in talk shows, in which individuals represent themselves by airing their problems and by bearing witness to the tribulations of other people. The programme establishes a '**structure of feeling**' that is not unique to *Sex and the City* – television audiences are already familiar with it and are invited to participate in it. What marks out *Sex and the City* from this context is its focus on a social elite, rather than the lower-middle-class participants in the majority of television confessional programmes. The series features millionaires, wealthy men who date models and the fine art scene, and is peopled by characters who are rich, attractive and well connected. So while *Sex and the City* uses television forms that are already significant in programmes such as *The Oprah Winfrey Show*, where the audience is invited to identify with 'problems' and share in discussions of how to improve the lot of participants and themselves, the series transfers these worries about the self and how to live into an elite social group, and places them in the context of comic fictional narrative. The significance of the transfer of the confessional discourse from women's magazines and talk shows into this class and status group is that it enables the programme to address a valuable television audience sector.

The fact that *Sex and the City* was nominated for nine Emmy awards (the American television 'Oscars') in 2001 is not simply a recognition that it is promoted and watched as '**quality**' television in the US broadcasting context and in the international markets where it is sold. It is also a recognition of the programme's success at attracting relatively affluent, mainly female audiences, and the consequent profitability of the programme for HBO. That channel is not funded by advertising but by subscription payments made by its viewers, but *Sex and the City* was sold by HBO to advertising-funded channels in the USA and other countries, such as Channel 4 in the UK. For broadcasters funded by advertising revenue, a programme that attracts a large and relatively affluent audience group, such as women between eighteen and thirty-five, is attractive because it offers a place where advertisements for aspirational products (branded clothes, cars and perfumes, for example) as well as products aimed at women in general can be placed. So there is a connection between the commodification represented narratively in the programme and the commodity status of the programme itself. Carrie and her friends' concern that they are seen in public to best advantage when wearing Manolo Blahnik shoes and carrying Gucci handbags provides a very supportive environment for the commercials that are screened between segments of the programme.

Taking a critical Television Studies position in relation to this programme, *Sex and the City* can be regarded as a commodity in which a gendered discourse of confession and witness becomes commodified itself, as a means of addressing a particular class and gender group in the television audience. Its creator, Candace Bushnell, has been quoted in magazine interviews saying that she regards the programme as concerned less with gender than with the dynamics of wealth and power. She means

---

**narrative** an ordered sequence of images and sound that tells a fictional or factual story.

**structure of feeling** the assumptions, attitudes and ideas prevalent in a society, arising from the ideologies underpinning that society.

**quality** in television, kinds of programme that are perceived as more expensively produced and, especially, more culturally worthwhile than other programmes.

that, in her view, *Sex and the City* is about people's relationships that have more to do with their social position and status in relation to each other than with whether an individual is male or female. In one sense this is accurate, since, for the production company and its parent company, *Sex and the City* is primarily important as a vehicle to address a specific audience and thus to generate revenue and profit, whether that audience is male or female, and irrespective of whether the representations of characters in the programme are socially and politically progressive. But an analytical approach to the show would be concerned not only with this economic context but with the detail of how representations of gender and sexuality are constructed in it, and how audiences might understand them. From a point of view interested in the representation of femininity and the political impact of those representations, *Sex and the City* can be argued to perpetuate discourses about women's self-absorption, the focus on heterosexual sex as the barometer of personal and social success, and the normalisation of commodity fetishism as the environment in which women exist 'by nature'.

For more than thirty years, feminist critics have been reacting against these kinds of representation, and aiming to liberate women from their oppressive restrictions on what being female and feminine mean. But comedy-drama continues to focus on many of these representations of femininity, for example in the US series *Desperate Housewives*, which at first glance seems to be a show that focuses much more on women than men, and seems to focus on those women's independence and activity. However, it could be argued that the four central women in *Desperate Housewives* are for various reasons disempowered and severely restricted in their scope for independent action. In its first episode Mary Alice Young commits suicide despite apparently having a perfect house and family in a wealthy suburb. In subsequent episodes her narration introduces her family, friends and neighbours as they gradually delve under this perfect surface to reveal her involvement in murder and conspiracy. Two of these female neighbours are Susan Mayer, a divorced single parent with her own career who is nevertheless driven by her need to complete herself by finding a satisfying relationship with a man, and Lynette Scavo, who is frustrated by juggling the roles of wife, mother and successful office worker. In addition, Bree Van De Kamp's alcoholism and poor relationships with her children belie her surface appearance as the ideal housewife, while Gabrielle Solis's material possessions and glamorous appearance contrast with her ongoing competitiveness and jealousy towards her husband, and Edie Britt schemes to undermine her supposed friend Susan, especially by using her overt sexuality as a weapon.

Far from being a community of women friends (as the characters of *Sex and the City* are), the women of *Desperate Housewives* are indeed 'desperate'. On one level the series offers resources for a devastating critique of the ideals that real women might have, and the distance between the images of success that representations such as women's magazines display and the complexities of actual experience. But within the codes of television comedy-drama, these problems are quickly raised as obstacles to generate storylines and dramatic moments and then passed over as the next twist in the story appears. As in *Sex and the City*, the comic aspects of *Desperate Housewives* work to deflect the action from the ideological issues. Instead, the show focuses on characterisation and skilled performances by the actors, and on the creation of cliffhangers that ask the audience to speculate about what resolution or further disaster will happen next.

Figure 9.2 The cast of *Desperate Housewives*. Courtesy of ABC-TV/The Kobal
Collection/Brakha, Moshe.

## ACTIVITY 9.4

Watch at least one episode of *Sex and the City* or *Desperate Housewives*. What
pleasures are represented as important to the main women characters? How do they
conform to, or diverge from, conventional feminine roles?

## Race, ethnicity and disability

Factual programmes have attempted to deal with issues of race and disability by using **observational documentary** and **reality TV** conventions, rather than conventional current affairs documentary conventions, in order to make the issues more accessible to viewers. In *Skin Deep*, British celebrity businesswoman Anita Roddick (founder of the Body Shop) was transformed by make-up and a body suit so that she could experience what it would be like to be grossly overweight, elderly and homeless. The programme, made for the Discovery Channel in 2002, was a three-part series that sought to encourage viewers to follow Roddick's learning experience and thus to consider social barriers, discrimination and injustice for themselves. It is interesting that the programme-makers chose a central figure with an existing public reputation, and in programmes of this kind that have been broadcast since then celebrities have often been used as the hook to draw viewers into the programme's agenda. Channel 4's *Celebrities Disfigured* (2004) was clearly given its surprising title as a way of attracting viewers to a difficult subject, and made use of the actor and comedian Craig Charles and the model Caprice to lead viewers through the problems experienced by people with facial disfigurements. More recently, Five adopted a similar strategy for *Jordan Gets Even* (2005), in which the glamour model Jordan was transformed into a homeless woman of about forty-five years of age for part of the programme.

While these attempts to link such issues of concern to recognisable faces and celebrity personas are an innovative way to short-circuit audiences' potential resistance to sober documentary treatments, their use of celebrities can have less positive consequences. Much of the programme's focus can be on the reaction of the celebrity to their transformation (sequences looking into the mirror and detailing the processes of make-up and changing body-shapes take up much of each episode) and thus the significance of ordinary people's reactions to disability or race have less impact. Since discrimination can also be very subtle (visibly evident in what people do not say as much as in what they do say, and in bodily posture or gesture, for example), finding telling footage to include in a programme can be a challenge for editors and directors. The most successful programme in these respects was perhaps the BBC's two-part series *Trading Races* (2002), which did not feature celebrities and which was not especially dramatic in its revelations. In the first episode Daniel (a black hairdresser) swapped places with Simon (white) thanks to elaborate make-up. In the second episode Sofina (an Asian student) changed lives with Carolynn (an older white nurse). Each participant was surprised at how little overt racism they encountered, which provided a promising starting-point for considering racism less as a 'problem' that could be shockingly revealed and more as a question of assumptions and attitudes about race and identity.

One of the ways in which channels try to improve their record in catering for minority audiences is to employ more people from minority groups in programme-making, on the assumption that this will eventually change the programmes that appear on the screen. In June 2006 the BBC secured Mary Fitzgerald, formerly head of diversity at Channel 4, to work for the corporation as editorial manager of cultural diversity. The role involves working with the controllers of BBC channels, programme commissioners and programme-makers to encourage them to employ a wider range of people behind the camera and in front of it. Although the BBC has

**ethnicity**
membership of a group with a specific identity based on a sense of belonging, such as British-Asian or Italian-American.

**observational documentary**
a documentary form in which the programme-maker aims to observe neutrally what would have happened even if he or she had not been present.

**reality TV**
programmes where the unscripted behaviour of 'ordinary people' is the focus of interest.

targets for employing minority staff, these are not easily enforceable, and the only changes that have been notable recently have been in the use of women newsreaders from ethnic minority backgrounds and the introduction of non-white characters in some **prime-time** programmes (such as soap operas and drama series). However, the latter have tended to be marginal and appear only for a handful of episodes. Furthermore, it is very difficult for the BBC to demand that its targets are met in the many programmes it now commissions from **independent production companies**. In news programmes the production staff at all the larger channels remain overwhelmingly white (and often male). However, given the recent political focus on Muslim people in Britain and abroad, because of the war in Iraq and Islamic terrorism, television executives are particularly keen on diluting this dominant presence of white journalists, reporters, news editors and other programme production staff, in the hope that this will lead to programmes that connect more effectively with Muslim and non-white people in Britain.

> independent
> production
> companies
> businesses making
> television
> programmes which
> can be sold to
> television networks
> that transmit and
> distribute them.

The major problems that television faces in increasing diversity are:

- Policy initiatives in large television institutions are laid down by senior management but have little impact on the day-to-day work of busy programme-makers.
- Diversity can seem like an add-on extra in programmes and in the way television institutions work, and potentially threatens existing staff and ways of working.
- High-profile individuals from minority groups conceal under-representation of minorities in the broad mass of producers and performers in television.
- There is little impetus from the majority of the audience for greater diversity in television, and audiences matter to television programme-makers.
- Minorities (black, disabled, gay and Chinese people, for example) do not all have the same concerns or the same kinds of cultural identity, but they are treated as if they did.
- People from minorities are perceived as having 'problems' that define them as victims, threats to society and outsiders, and they are stereotyped.
- Thinking about minorities assumes the presence of a unified majority, though the majority white British population is very diverse.

After a preview screening of *Shoot the Messenger* (BBC2) in 2006 the BBC and writer Sharon Foster were attacked by audience members and black community leaders who called the drama the most racist programme in the corporation's history (Amadiegwu 2006). One said the BBC would never have commissioned the programme if it had been about white or Asian people. But this is just the latest of several BBC programmes that have upset the African-Caribbean community, such as *The Trouble with Black Men* and the drama series *Babyfather*, both of which were accused of negatively stereotyping black men.

*Shoot the Messenger*'s protagonist is Joe (played by David Oyelowo, a main actor in the spy thriller series *Spooks*), a black IT worker who leaves his job to become an idealistic teacher. He tries to save his black students from gangs, crime and under-achievement by offering himself as a role model. But when a seemingly minor incident spirals out of control after his student Germal accuses Joe of assault, Joe turns against his own community, which he holds responsible for everything bad that has ever happened to him. The drama focuses on social issues including mental health, parenting, teacher–pupil relations, homelessness and the Church, and explores the issues of identity, educational underachievement, unemployment, and internal conflicts in the black community, between Africans and Caribbeans, and those with light and dark complexions. In one scene, for example, Joe's girlfriend (Nikki Amuka Bird) says to him: 'You don't make me feel good about myself.' Foster had originally titled the drama *Fuck Black People*, matching the graffiti slogan that Joe scrawls on a wall as he walks out of his teaching job.

The structural motif of a journey, in fact a descent into an ever-bleaker underworld of British society, is used in *Shoot the Messenger* to present Joe with multiple facets of life for black Britons. Unlike some representations of black people written and directed by white men, such as the sitcom *The Crouches*, however, the drama's black writer and director attempt to criticise constructively British black culture. The respect for authorship in British television drama protected *Shoot the Messenger* from some kinds of criticism: its writer Sharon Foster is of Jamaican parentage and grew up with seven brothers and sisters in the black community of Hackney in London. So her authorship lends the drama the stamp of authenticity, making it difficult for its detractors to claim that it is an ignorant representation. Attacks on the drama therefore tended to focus on the assumed ignorance of its audience, who might perhaps be misled into believing that black people simply represent a problem and a threat to the cohesion of British life, and who might be prompted to side with racist organisations such as the British National Party as a result.

In 2006 *Big Brother*'s housemates included Pete Bennett, who has Tourette's syndrome. His inclusion could be seen as a move towards greater visibility on television for disabled people. The syndrome causes people to lose control of the conventional censorship mechanisms that prevent them from using inappropriate language, such as swear-words and sexual slang. However, as Pauline Eyre (2006) argues, the problems caused by Tourette's syndrome contrast with the fact that some of its behavioural patterns are indistinguishable from 'normal' behaviour, such as shouting at another driver in a road-rage incident. If *Big Brother* introduced a more visible disability this might draw attention to the obstacles to such 'normal' activities as eating, cooking and having a shower. Some people's physical or mental disability affect them constantly, but their sense of identity is not necessarily centred on the disability. If a disability makes someone continually ill, this militates against television's preference for youth, health and physical activity. This connects with disabled activists' debates about whether able-bodied actors should represent disabled people, since the activity of playing a disabled character may be more effective as a representation (and more empowering to disabled viewers) than featuring a disabled person on screen. For example, the actor and comedian Peter Kay in *Phoenix Nights* played a wheelchair user as the comic protagonist of the series, and the recurring characters of the dark comedy series *Nighty Night* included a man with cancer, a woman with multiple sclerosis, and an obese woman with asthma. For some disabled viewers and commentators, these are challenges to social conventions for the representation of illness and disability.

After two weeks of the seventh series of *Big Brother* in 2006, charities and mental health groups, including the Samaritans, Sane, Rethink and the Mental Health Foundation, made public criticisms of the programme over its casting of participants with mental health problems. The charity Mind submitted an official complaint to the regulator **Ofcom** about the manipulative and irresponsible treatment of several

Ofcom the Office of Communications, a government body responsible for regulating television and other communications media in Britain.

people in the house. Clearly, one of the issues in this situation was the problem of identifying and labelling *Big Brother* contestants as mentally ill, whether as a result of their experiences on the programme or because of a previously diagnosed condition. The *Sun* newspaper, for example, identified *five* housemates as having mental health problems after the thirty-seven-year-old Shahbaz Choudhary from Glasgow had a breakdown on camera when his relationships with other housemates became increasingly problematic. His apparently irrational actions may have been one of the reasons for his voluntary departure from the house.

The two television professionals overseeing the series – Phil Edgar-Jones, the executive producer at Brighter Pictures (the company making *Big Brother*), and Danny Cohen, Channel 4's head of factual entertainment – were both interviewed about the furore (Gibson 2006), and Edgar-Jones responded: 'Lots of interest groups over the years have had something to say about *Big Brother*. That's one of the powerful things about this show, it raises issues and people talk about it.'

The shocked tone of media commentary on *Big Brother* is of course an advantage to the programme since the notion that each year's series is more controversial than the last is a reason for viewers to become attached to it. Edgar-Jones's defence of the problems experienced by Shahbaz was that the vetting of contestants and the support offered during and after the programme are designed to identify and deal with the personal pressures experienced by the housemates. Confidential discussions between housemates and the programme's psychologist and producers in the diary room are not shown in the broadcast version, and nor is the follow-up support after the series ends. Interestingly, however, this invisible aspect of *Big Brother* contrasts with the perpetual visibility undergone by the housemates during the series, which is one of its primary attractions for its audience.

Danny Cohen also defended the inclusion of Pete Bennett, on equal opportunities grounds: 'Why should he be excluded from expressing his personality and fulfilling his dreams?' The dream is for fame, but the desire of contestants to become celebrities increasingly fails for *Big Brother* participants, and some of them may be unable to cope either with the achievement of fame or its non-attainment. This creates further demands on the counsellors who support contestants for up to a year after the end of the series.

**audience share** the percentage of viewers estimated to have watched one channel as opposed to another channel broadcasting at the same time.

The competing forces at work around *Big Brother* are its importance for Channel 4's profile and **audience share**, its uncertain role as entertainment or factual programme, and the ambivalence of media commentators to it, despite its popularity with audiences. Edgar-Jones found it hard to pin down the programme's genre: 'It's a gameshow . . . It's a soap opera after all; it's a TV show'. And its inclusion of diverse and unusual housemates can be argued to be a challenge to the norms of both television representation and the expectations of its predominantly youthful viewers, despite criticism from 'serious' media commentators and academics. Edgar-Jones claimed that 'There's almost a sense that young people like this shouldn't be allowed on TV,' referring to Jade Goody, whose supposed vulgarity did not prevent her from launching a successful celebrity career. On the other hand, Edgar-Jones argued for the value of the series in terms of its morally educative qualities: 'There's a tremendous redemptive quality to *Big Brother*. The good person always wins' (Gibson 2006). Danny Cohen defended the programme as entertainment: 'The idea that an entertainment programme is in some way not worthy is just nonsense' (ibid.) but the worth of the series is also in its contribution to Channel 4's programme commissioning budget. The large audiences for *Big Brother* (increasing by about 9 per cent each year) and the consequent income for the channel enable it to fund the production of documentary series such as *Dispatches* and high-profile political drama like *The Road to Guantánamo*.

---

### ACTIVITY 9.5

Who are the black or Asian characters in soap operas you have seen? Are there ways in which their ethnicity is important to continuing stories? Why is this?

---

### ACTIVITY 9.6

Do you think it is acceptable for black and Asian performers on television to make jokes about racism and about the stereotypical representations of people of the same ethnic group? What are the main arguments for and against this kind of comedy?

---

## Audiences and race

The reasons why the representation of different races and cultures on television matters are:

- Social cohesion is enhanced by seeing and knowing about people who are different to yourself.
- Broadcasting in Britain should address all of the audience, not just some of it.
- All viewers pay for programmes (through the licence fee, or by buying products advertised on television) so they are all entitled to be represented.
- People from minority groups are keen to see representations of people like themselves.

These reasons all assume the principles of public service broadcasting, which involves the idea that television will contribute positively to British society, offer something to all viewers, and represent the nation to itself.

In 2006 the audience data-collection agency BARB released figures for the ten programmes most popular with black viewers in the year from May 2005 to May 2006. They averaged out the audience size when dealing with series, where audiences can fluctuate from week to week, and included imported programmes shown on British channels. The results were:

1 *EastEnders* (BBC1, soap opera): 250,000 black viewers
2 *Everybody Hates Chris* (Five, imported US sitcom): 186,000
3 *Champions League: Barcelona v. Chelsea* (ITV1, sport): 174,000

4 *Champions League, Real Madrid v. Arsenal* (ITV1, sport): 170,000
5 *Charlie's Angels: Full Throttle* (Five, film): 156,000
6 *Con Air* (BBC1, film): 154,000
7 *Waterloo Road* (BBC1, drama): 151,000
8 *Bodyshock: Half Ton Man* (Channel 4, factual): 147,000
9 *Holby City* (BBC1, drama): 147,000
10 *My Family* (BBC1, sitcom): 144,000

Although *EastEnders* comes top, the list contains surprisingly few of the drama and factual programmes for which British television producers and academic critics make claims for quality or importance. There are two Hollywood films, two programmes consisting almost entirely of sporting coverage, and one imported US sitcom. This seems to support the argument that the main terrestrial channels and the evening schedules do not cater appropriately for black viewers. The question remains as to whether some programmes might appeal to black viewers more than to non-black viewers; or, in other words, which programmes' audiences contain the greatest share of black viewers?

The list changes considerably when considering which programmes include the largest proportion of black viewers in their audiences, in comparison to the number of non-black viewers watching those programmes. The programmes in 2005–6 attracting the most black viewers as a proportion of their audience were:

1 *Everybody Hates Chris* (Five, imported US sitcom)
2 *Animal Attraction: Cheaters* (Five, factual)
3 *Cold Turkey* (Channel 4, factual)
4 *Charmed* (Five, imported drama)
5 *The Real Flying Saucers: Stranger than Fiction* (Five, factual)
6 *Two and a Half Men* (Five, imported US sitcom)
7 *The Child Who's Older than her Grandmother* (Five, factual)
8 *Gay Vicars* (Channel 4, factual)
9 *Capturing the Friedmans* (Channel 4, film)
10 *The Seven Year Old Surgeon* (Five, factual)

There has been an assumption that black viewers prefer to watch programmes featuring black characters, and the popularity of *Everybody Hates Chris*, featuring a mainly black cast (including the stand-up comedian Chris Rock as narrator) supports this. Following the same logic, BBC1 screened the 'black' sitcom *The Crouches* (although it was written by two white male authors) and BBC2 broadcast the series *Babyfather* in recent years, but both had short runs, were not well received by critics and did not gain significant audiences. According to the director of programmes at Five, Dan Chambers, who was interviewed when these figures were published in the press (Armstrong, 2006), it is the broadly appealing genre of the sitcom that has most potential to offer black audiences representations of themselves, and it is sitcom where British television is failing black audiences most: 'Where do ethnic minority audiences go to find their role models on TV when it comes to sitcoms?' Even *Everybody Hates Chris*, though clearly important to black audiences, did not draw a very large total audience, with just one million viewers on average.

The terrestrial channel whose programmes routinely gain the smallest audience sizes, Five, seems surprisingly popular with black viewers in comparison to its majority white audience. Channel 4, by contrast, whose remit has included the provision of programmes for minority audiences, has fewer programmes than Five in the top ten by share of black viewers. Mary Fitzgerald, when she was editorial manager for cultural diversity at Channel 4 (quoted in Armstrong 2006), summed up the black audience as 'a very selective audience looking for strong content and a strong storyline and very keen on good factual shows. I don't think there's a huge difference between the demands of black viewers and white viewers.' Nevertheless, the BBC has responded to a perception that British television does not serve black viewers by commissioning comedy sketch shows featuring black and Asian performers, such as *The Kumars at No. 42*, *3 Non-Blondes* and *Little Miss Jocelyn*.

---

### ACTIVITY 9.7

Which racial and ethnic group do you belong to? Do you consider that your group is represented correctly on British television, and what might 'correctly' mean? How might television representations of your group affect your sense of who you are?

---

## Case study: *Wife Swap*

As the previous chapter explained, the first phase of reality TV used footage provided by the emergency services or by camera operators following policemen, ambulance drivers or firemen. But more recent programmes have shifted their focus from the observation of action in public space towards the interior and private world of the home. This corresponds to the increased significance of programmes about home decor, property and gardening, and makeovers of individuals' dress, make-up or personal fitness (Piper 2004). The combination of a focus on the family, and especially central women within it, with questions of social **class** and lifestyle was the foundation for comparisons of the participants in *Wife Swap*, first shown in Britain in 2003 (Bignell 2005: 28–31). Viewers were invited to find the women and their companions in a household both fascinating and repellent, and the programme added an interesting twist to contemporary representations of women (and men). In contrast to earlier observational documentary programmes, such as *The Family* and *Sylvania Waters*, *Wife Swap* added a competition structure, where one wife was transplanted from her own family to one with very different cultural and class expectations, to see whether she would be able to change her new family or would be remodelled by it herself. The wives exchanged places for two weeks, and attempted to lay down rules for their new family in the second week, after living according to the expectations of the new family in the first. Editing was crucial to the format, since each one-hour programme had to condense the results of observation of two families for two weeks, as well as providing brief introductory information about the participants and a concluding segment in which each family (but primarily the wives) could confront and comment on each other.

Across the episodes, it was obvious that the women carried out the vast majority of domestic work, but that different families lived according to strongly contrasting gender roles,

> **class** a section of society defined by their relationship to economic activity, whether as workers (the working class) or possessors of economic power (the bourgoisie), for example.

*continued*

and rules of household schedule and hygiene. While a conventional documentary treatment might use this material as the basis for arguments about gender roles in contemporary Britain, and about the effects of differences of income, class status and educational expectations on private life, *Wife Swap* focused its interest on individuals, and the power struggles between the transplanted wives and their unfamiliar family environments. In this way, the strength of character of the wives and the families, and the competitiveness involved in attempts to change other people by persuasion, negotiation or tantrums took the place of analysis of the gender politics of either public or private environments. While the programme had value in exposing the surprisingly great differences between ways of living in contemporary British family life, it withdrew from evaluating or commenting on these differences, appearing simply to present them as personal challenges.

*Wife Swap* was made by the independent production company RDF. Its director of programmes, Stephen Lambert, was trained as a documentary producer at the BBC and made the critically acclaimed documentary series *Modern Times* for BBC2. RDF is the second-largest independent production company in the UK, with an annual turnover of fifty-three million pounds in 2003. The genesis of the series came at a creative meeting at RDF's headquarters, as Lambert explained: 'We were looking at an article in the *Daily Mail* about how a nurse on £15,000 lived, compared with a barrister on £200,000. What about them swapping lives, then what about a wife swap?' Lambert rejected the criticisms from within and outside the television industry that contemporary factual television 'dumbs down' society, and also the view expressed by the acclaimed documentary film-maker Paul Watson that his closely observed documentaries presented actuality whereas contemporary reality TV is artificial. Lambert argued that there were good and bad examples of all genres, including reality TV: 'As a genre, reality television is one way of telling us stories about human nature and in many ways it is more honest than observational documentary.' His rationale for this view was that reality TV does not pretend that it is observational, and thus comes clean about its manipulation, whereas observational documentary does not: 'look at how people's nature is revealed because of the situation we've put them in'. He drew attention to the pleasures of factual television **formats** for audiences because of their basis in a narrative structure that makes satisfying viewing, in contrast to the less obviously narrative-based observational documentary form. Referring to RDF's other factual series *Faking It*, as well as *Wife Swap*, he argued that these 'are formats that give you those narrative structures, but there's still an enormous variety and unpredictability about what will happen in them' (Lambert quoted in Brown 2004a: 10).

**format** the blueprint for a programme, including its setting, main characters, genre, form and main themes.

Episodes of *Wife Swap* usually set up the conventional domestic routine of each household, then follow the difficulties encountered as each woman deals with the differences between her expected routines and those of the new family. As tensions and crises build over the period of filming, an established pattern of parallel segments shot in each house develops towards the return of the women to their original homes and discussions among the members of each household about what they have loved and hated, learned or repudiated from their experience. As Helen Piper (2004) has shown, much emphasis is placed on the details of the decor and furniture in each house, as revealing evidence of the class and cultural expectations of the participants. The kinds of furnishing, level of cleanliness and tidiness, and the repertoire of items kept in the fridge and kitchen cupboards become key signs of definition for the two households and shorthand ways for the producers to indicate potential contrasts and differences between them. Having established this visual evidence of what each household is like, the dialogue between the new entrant into the household and its existing inhabitants focuses on what the household norms might be, according to the explanations that each person gives. There are many opportunities for statements to the camera, or statements made by one participant to another, to be confirmed or undercut by the evidence that the visual representation of the house provides.

The narrative pace of *Wife Swap* can vary markedly, notably from the very short montage of shots introducing the participants and their houses at the beginning to the often lengthy conversations, usually in the kitchen, between the newly arrived woman and her new family. Occasionally music cues are used to sharpen a dramatic incident, but both sound and voice-over more usually allow the action to speak for itself or simply frame an incident. This places the opportunity to identify with the participants and to judge them squarely with the audience. Since the programme has identified the houses and the people both through what they say and how they look, social codes of behaviour and class and cultural codes of homemaking are made readily available for the audience to use as its criteria. As Piper (2004: 281) points out: 'The text incorporates a tacit invitation for the audience to judge, not what is necessarily best for the participants, but the degree to which their relationship measures up to a societal ideal, and *ergo* it presumes society's right to know.' Nevertheless, the degree of detail presented in a single episode about the attitudes and lives of the different families makes it difficult to establish preferred **ideological** standards for individuals or families. Although *Wife Swap* assumes the possibility and even the desirability of television's intervention into the home and the family, Piper (ibid.) shows that 'the text collapses together ethical choices (the division of roles, childcare) with matters of taste and consumer preference', so that an easy identification of a norm becomes impossible. So *Wife Swap* is an example of a format which combines an observational style with highly controlled and structured episode form. It does not make an argument about the subject of women's gender role, though it does invite its audience to evaluate its participants and might offer resources for comparing the viewer's gendered and familial roles with those on the screen. It draws on video diary form, a kind of competition and an emphasis on lifestyle and consumer choices about food and decor, for example.

Each episode of *Wife Swap* lasts one hour, and begins with a voice-over asking: 'What's it like to try out a different spouse for a fortnight? Will the experience alter their views on their own family life?' As well as documenting what happens in this artificially created but actual situation, *Wife Swap* draws attention to three kinds of performance that Piper (2004) has discussed. First, the participants play a social role inasmuch as they do things that may be expected of wives, husbands or children. Each of these roles is inflected by issues of class and taste, which establish the playing of the role in terms of distinctions between different social classes or subcultural groups. Second, the playing out of the role is made concrete by the performance of particular tasks, such as cooking and cleaning, or contributing to the raising of children by undertaking particular responsibilities. Like the first kind of role, this performance can succeed or fail, and it is open to evaluation. Finally, these performances are supplemented by the performance of being in a television programme, potentially inflecting each choice, speech or action with the consciousness of its transmission to the television viewers and its evaluation by them, as well as by the fellow members of the household. Being a woman and a wife in *Wife Swap* involves putting oneself on stage in that role (and also as a husband or child for other people in the house) and being judged as a successful or unsuccessful woman and wife by the other participants and the viewing audience.

Dorothy Hobson (2006) has done recent work on audience reactions to television, involving talking to young girls about their understandings of soap opera and reality TV. The Birmingham

**ideology** the set of beliefs, attitudes and assumptions arising from the economic and class divisions in a culture, underlying the ways of life accepted as normal in that culture.

*continued*

schoolchildren whom she interviewed, aged from thirteen to eighteen, identified with younger characters and were appreciative of programmes that included information they thought was relevant to them. Hobson talked about *Wife Swap* with older children, and discovered that they understood it as a programme about mothers, rather than wives. For them, *Wife Swap* was about the power of the family and the mother within the family. In a discussion of her work, Hobson (2006: 127) quotes one girl saying, 'It makes me appreciate my own Mom. Yes, because I realized that if anybody else had come into my house and they started changing the rules, I realize how much I would have missed her.' This work reinforces the findings of earlier studies of television audiences by revealing that the girls brought their own life experiences to their understanding of the programme and interpreted it in ways that were meaningful to them. The impact of television programmes in shaping the understanding of social roles – and gender roles in particular, in relation to this case study – is important to the circulation of a repertoire of images of how life is lived and could potentially be lived.

## SUMMARY OF KEY POINTS

- The study of television representation includes the questions of who (such as which television institutions) are representing certain groups and for what reasons?
- It also includes the questions of who and what is represented, and in what ways?
- Studying representations involves considering how audiences understand and respond to the representations of people they see.
- Content analysis is a statistically based method for finding out about representation in samples of television.
- Textual analysis has been used by television theorists (such as feminist television theorists) to discuss the meanings of the representations of selected groups on television.
- Representations in television do not exist in isolation but in relation to other television representations and representations in other media.
- The meanings of representations in one context may differ from their meanings in another, such as a different region or country.

## Further reading

Ang, I., 'Melodramatic identifications: television fiction and women's fantasy', in C. Brunsdon, J. D'Acci and L. Spigel (eds), *Feminist Television Criticism: A Reader* (Oxford: Oxford University Press, 1997), pp. 155–66.

Bignell, J., 'Sex, confession and witness', in K. Akass and J. McCabe (eds), *Reading 'Sex and the City'* (London and New York: I. B. Tauris, 2004), pp. 161–76

—— *Big Brother: Reality TV in the Twenty-first Century* (Basingstoke: Macmillan, 2005).

Campion, M. J., *Look Who's Talking: Cultural Diversity, Public Service Broadcasting and the National Conversation* (Oxford: Nuffield, 2005).

Cottle, S. (ed.), *Ethnic Minorities and the Media* (Oxford: Oxford University Press, 2000).

Cumberbatch, G., S. Gauntlett and V. Lyne, *Minority Group Representation on British Terrestrial Television: Key Findings, 1993–2003* (London: BBC/Ofcom, 2004).

Dahlgren, P., *Television and the Public Sphere* (London: Sage, 1995).

Fiske, J., *Introduction to Communication Studies* (London: Routledge, 1990).

Geraghty, C., *Women and Soap Opera: A Study of Prime Time Soaps* (Cambridge: Polity Press, 1991).

Gray, H., *Watching Race: Television and the Struggle for 'Blackness'* (Minneapolis, Minn.: University of Minnesota Press, 1995).

Gripsrud, J., *The Dynasty Years: Hollywood Television and Critical Media Studies* (London: Routledge, 1995).

Hall, S. (ed.), *Representation: Cultural Representations and Signifying Practices* (London: Sage, 1997).

—— 'Black and white television', in D. Morley and K. Chen (eds), *Remote Control: Dilemmas of Black Intervention in British Film and TV* (London: BFI, 1996), pp. 13–28.

Hobson, D., 'From *Crossroads* to *Wife Swap*: learning from audiences', *Critical Studies in Television*, 1:1 (2006), pp. 121–8.

Livingston, S. and P. Lunt, *Talk on Television: Audience Participation and Public Debate* (London: Routledge, 1994).

Lusted, D., 'The popular culture debate and light entertainment on television', in C. Geraghty and D. Lusted (eds), *The Television Studies Book* (London: Arnold, 1998), pp. 175–90.

Macdonald, M., *Representing Women: Myths of Femininity in the Popular Media* (London: Arnold, 1995).

Modleski, T., *Loving with a Vengeance* (Hamden, Conn.: Shoe String Press, 1982).

Piper, H., 'Reality TV, *Wife Swap* and the drama of banality', *Screen* 54:4 (2004), pp. 273–86.

Thornham, S. and T. Purvis, *Television Drama: Theories and Identities* (Basingstoke: Palgrave Macmillan, 2005).

# Television You Can't See

# Television You Can't See

## Introduction

An analysis of the kinds of image not allowed to appear in television programmes can tell us a great deal about the television medium. For cutting images involves assumptions about how audiences watch television, and how television images can be meaningful to us. The decision to cut an image must be based on the ability to identify and determine what that image represents. So the act of seeing and making sense of the television image is the first precondition for censorship. Furthermore, the significance of what the image might mean for a viewer (for the person cutting it, and for another hypothetical television viewer) draws on assumptions about the image's **effects**. Cutting an image is motivated by a concern about how that image might provoke a response in the viewer who sees it. Television censorship, then, is a topic where questions of **ideology** (the political assumptions about right and wrong, good and bad), the **semiotics** of the television image (how images and sounds are meaningful as signs representing something) and pleasure and repulsion (what we enjoy seeing and what we would prefer not to see) are fundamental. Paradoxically, looking at what we cannot see can tell us much about what seeing and understanding mean.

**effects** measurable outcomes produced by watching television, such as becoming more violent or adopting a certain opinion.

**ideology** the set of beliefs, attitudes and assumptions arising from the economic and class divisions in a culture, underlying the ways of life accepted as normal in that culture.

**semiotics** the study of signs and their meanings, initially developed for the study of spoken language, and now used also to study the visual and aural 'languages' of other media, such as television.

## Free speech and regulation

The American Constitution, largely because of the global power and influence of the United States, has been an influential statement on the right to free speech. The First Amendment (added in 1787) to the Constitution declares that 'Congress shall make no law . . . abridging the freedom of speech or of the press'. A similar statement was included in 1948 in the United Nations Universal Declaration of Human Rights, in the Nineteenth Article: 'Everyone has the right to freedom of opinions without interference and to seek, receive and impart information and ideas through any media regardless of frontiers.' The European Convention on Human Rights seeks to protect freedom of speech in Article 10: 'Everyone has the right to freedom of expression. This right shall include freedom to hold opinions and to receive and impart information without interference by public authority and regardless of frontiers.' But this grand statement is soon subject to qualifications:

> The exercise of these freedoms, since it carries with it duties and responsibilities, may be subject to such formalities, conditions, restrictions or penalties as are prescribed by law and are necessary in a democratic society, in the interests of national security, territorial integrity or public safety, for the prevention of disorder or crime, for the protection of health and morals, for the protection

of the reputation or rights of others, for preventing the disclosure of information received in confidence, or for maintaining the authority and impartiality of the judiciary.

The claim that restrictions will be necessary for the proper functioning of a democratic society is misleading. The obstacles to free speech are in fact normally determined not by a democratic process but in the interests of the elite groups, especially governments, that have the power to determine standards of conduct. These are the people who determine what 'the public interest' may be, for example. In media theory, members of the elite group that has the power to determine what information can be circulated are referred to as '**gatekeepers**'. These include, among others, the executives of television companies, the editors of television news programmes and the producers of television programmes in all genres. The gatekeepers make use both of published **regulations** and guidelines about programme content, and of their own internalised sense of what it is right and wrong to broadcast. Broadcasting organisations are ultimately dependent on government, since it controls the level of the BBC **licence fee** and the renewal of the ITV **franchise** and other commercial channels' licences to broadcast. So while direct censorship is uncommon in Britain, television companies are reluctant to bring themselves into confrontation with the government.

Broadcasting in Britain is largely self-regulated, on the basis of codes and guidelines drawn up and interpreted by **Ofcom**, a body set up by the government in its 2003 Communications Act to supersede two previous regulators, the Independent Television Commission and the Broadcasting Standards Commission. Ofcom oversees the activities of all broadcasters to 'further the interests of citizens in communication matters'. It was created to reduce the confusion that broadcasters and the public felt in dealing with different television regulators, so it regulates both **terrestrial** and satellite commercial television, television advertising and telecommunications, including mobile-phone wavelengths and landlines. It also establishes rules on the mergers of media companies, such as that between the Carlton and Granada companies and the creation of a single ITV network; monitors bad language, violence and sexual scenes on television channels, including BBC programmes that were previously regulated by the corporation itself; and responds to complaints by viewers. In 2004, for example, Ofcom criticised the BBC for a sexually suggestive dance routine on *Top of the Pops*, although fewer than ten people had complained. Its guidelines require broadcasters to treat controversial subjects accurately and impartially both in news and in other kinds of programme, and to refrain from expressing an editorial view of their own. Broadcasters must also not make programmes which include anything that could offend against good **taste and decency**, or that could encourage crime or lead to disorder. Severe penalties, such as fines or, in the case of commercial companies, the withdrawal of their licence to broadcast, can be applied if broadcasters commit serious offences. This has introduced a culture of self-censorship among programme-makers, who know that regulators will review potentially controversial programmes and are required to investigate serious complaints made by viewers. Terrestrial broadcasters have long agreed on a 9.00 p.m. '**watershed**', before which time programmes that could be offensive or disturbing to children will not be broadcast. So, for example, uncut films with a '15' rating cannot be shown before 8.00 p.m., even on a dedicated satellite film

**gatekeepers** the critical term used for the people and institutions (such as commissioning producers and regulatory bodies) who control access to television broadcasting.

**regulation** the control of television institutions by laws, codes of practice or guidelines.

**licence fee** an annual payment by all owners of television sets, which is the main source of income for the BBC.

**franchise** the right to broadcast on the terrestrial ITV channel for a set number of years, secured by paying a fee to government.

**Ofcom** the Office of Communications, a government body responsible for regulating television and other communications media in Britain.

**terrestrial** broadcasting from a ground-based transmission system, as opposed to broadcasting via satellite.

**taste and decency** conformity to the standards of good taste and acceptable language and behaviour represented on television, as required by regulations.

**watershed** the time in the day (conventionally 9.00 p.m.) after which programmes with content that may disturb children can be shown.

channel, and films with an '18' rating cannot be shown before 9.00 p.m. on any channel.

Among the new demands made of Ofcom was the requirement to investigate in 2006 whether advertising 'junk food' during children's television programming might have health implications. This was because the health effects of obesity among children had become a matter of major concern. The proposed restrictions, supported by organisations like the National Heart Forum, were that all junk food advertisements should be banned in programmes aimed at children aged under nine years old, or at least such advertisements should be limited to thirty seconds per hour in the times when those children are most likely to be watching, and one minute per hour between six o'clock and eight o'clock in the evening. Consumer and health groups would like an even more stringent ban, preventing all junk food advertising before the 9.00 p.m. watershed. Ofcom commissioned research on the likely impact of this advertising ban on children's health, and calculated that it would significantly reduce childhood obesity and therefore save about one billion pounds currently spent on medical treatment for overweight children.

However, the producers of television programmes for children were concerned that these proposals would make children's television economically unviable, since the revenues deriving from advertisements would no longer be enough to cover the costs of making the programmes. The independent producers and makers of animated programmes who create the great majority of children's television, represented by their trade organisation Pact, estimated that the financial turnover in their sector of the industry could fall by between 12 and 50 per cent. Since the profit margins on children's programmes are already relatively small, this impact could mean that almost no new children's programmes would be made. The only major producer of children's programmes left would be the BBC, which is already the biggest producer of this genre of television, and spends about fourteen million pounds each year paying independent production companies to make children's programmes for its channels. The organisations representing independent producers, and organisations lobbying for the important role of children's television in child development and creating young people's sense of cultural identity, have argued that a government subsidy is necessary to guarantee the survival of television for children.

The decision about banning junk food advertising to children is closely related to other considerations affecting ITV's future planning and how it is regulated by Ofcom. ITV currently spends about twenty million pounds per year on new children's programmes, commissioned from independent producers, amounting to half of the total money spent on children's programmes by the biggest commercial broadcasters – ITV, Channel 4 and Five – put together. But since children's programmes are not as profitable as programmes aimed at a family audience or an adult audience, ITV has been seeking to reduce its commitment to providing them, even though this commitment forms part of its responsibility as a **public service** broadcaster. The public service commitment also requires ITV to provide religious programmes and regional programmes. When these were added to the costs of children's programmes, ITV claimed in 2006 that it spent 30 per cent of its £850 million budget for the ITV1 channel on these genres that generate very little income in return. Factual entertainment and comedy are much more lucrative for ITV and its competing channels. Children's ITV (CiTV), beginning at three o'clock

**public service** in television, the provision of a mix of programmes that inform, educate and entertain in ways that encourage the betterment of audiences and society in general.

on weekday afternoons, is regularly beaten in the ratings by *Countdown* and *Deal or No Deal* on Channel 4, thus reducing the amount that ITV can charge advertisers to place ads in its afternoon schedule because its programmes have smaller audiences. ITV would like to reduce the number of hours of children's programming on ITV1 from eight hours per week to two hours. Pact reported in 2006 that the number of hours of new children's programming on the main public service channels had already fallen from nearly twenty-five hours each week in 2000 to fewer than twenty hours in 2004.

So, although programmes for children have been part of the British television landscape since the beginning of the medium, commercial pressures, competition between the large numbers of channels now available, and wider political concerns about public health have come together to threaten the genre. Ofcom therefore has to find a compromise between the widely supported idea that children's programmes are a good thing, beneficial to society, and the realities of the new age of multi-channel television.

The terrestrial commercial television channels are all required to provide some public service programming and to conform to the guidelines and codes set up by Ofcom. (BBC programming on all its terrestrial and satellite channels also has a public service remit regulated by its own trust.) In 2004 Ofcom began a review of public service broadcasting on BBC, ITV1, Channel 4, Five, S4C and also television-related services such as the BBC's websites. Broadcasters provided details of their schedules, types of content and the cost of most of the public service programmes they had broadcast since 1998. There was also a public consultation in which members of the public were asked about what they want from public service broad-casting. The outcome of this review fed into the government's review of the BBC's role, and ensured the continuation of the licence fee as well as the requirement for all main channels to show some proportion of programmes regarded as a public service, such as arts, religious programmes and current affairs.

---

## ACTIVITY 10.1

Look up the current BBC Producers' Guidelines or the guidelines for a commercial channel on that channel's website. What do these say about the reasons for not broadcasting some kinds of programme content, and in what ways might these restrictions be necessary 'in a democratic society'?

---

While Ofcom has a largely negative role in that it determines what may *not* be shown, it also positively requires broadcasters to include in their schedules diverse programmes, programmes of 'quality', regional and educational programmes, and to maintain standards of political neutrality. Programme-makers retain close links with the regulator, and will often approach Ofcom at an early stage in the planning of a potentially sensitive programme to gain an opinion on whether it is likely to give rise to concerns over content or tone. These contacts form part of the day-to-day business of television executives and producers, who are aware that sustaining a good relationship with Ofcom enables problems and challenges to be anticipated and avoided. The internal culture of television production is also involved in this process since programme-makers use their experience and knowledge of industry histories, controversies and legal challenges to find rules-of-thumb that guide them as they plan and produce programmes. It can seem that high-profile cases of intervention by regulators are lamentable examples of programme-makers' creative freedom being attacked by distant, often ill-informed outsiders to the television production process. However, while this might occasionally be the case, it is more usual that problems with programmes should have been foreseen, either by the programme production team itself or by the institutional culture within production organisations, which always provides a sense of the limits and sphere of freedom of action that programme-makers can expect.

An issue which regularly receives a lot of coverage in the media itself, and which appears to be of concern to a substantial minority of television viewers, is the representation of sex and sexuality on British television. This has always been problematic because of the location of viewing. The fact that the television is physically located in the domestic environment leads to the fear that unsuitable material may be watched by children, and cause embarrassment to adults watching with them. The informal codes of behaviour governing family life that are imagined by the producers and regulators of television mean that bad language, sexual scenes and violence are considered to be outside the norms of behaviour expected in the family, and outside the norms of behaviour deemed acceptable for the family audience. However, attitudes to sex on television have liberalised significantly over the decades of television's existence, and indeed the issue itself has been discussed on television. The Channel 4 documentary series *Sex on TV* (2002), for example, did not simply celebrate this liberalisation but noted the changing forces that have affected its history, and this chapter draws some of its material from this source.

## A brief history of sex on British television

*1931: The statue of Ariel, a spirit representing broadcasting, situated on the front of the BBC Broadcasting House headquarters, had its penis shortened on the orders of Lord Reith, the first director-general.*

BBC programme guidelines on radio broadcasting were very strict, and extended not only to programmes but to their presenters. For instance, newsreaders could be sacked if they were involved in a divorce. The BBC *Policy Guide* on **variety programmes** for 1948 contained strict rules on the subject of jokes that could be broadcast in BBC Radio comedies. Prohibited subjects included:

- lavatories
- effeminacy in men, and
- honeymoon couples.

These subjects are understandable to us today as possibly offensive because of their connections with bodily functions, homosexuality and heterosexual sex. But we can see how what is offensive changes over time by noting the other subjects that were of concern to the BBC in the 1940s. Two other groups who were not allowed to be mentioned were chambermaids (stereotyped characters who were portrayed

**variety programmes** entertainment programmes containing a mix of material, such as songs and comedy sketches.

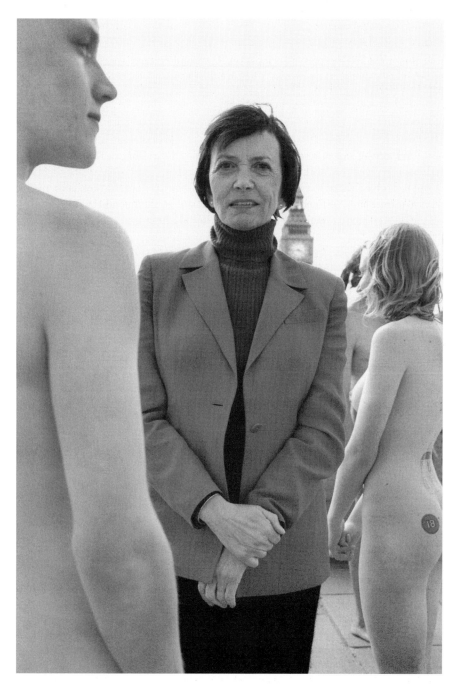

Figure 10.1  An example of nudity on television. Joan Bakewell presenting *Taboo: 40 Years of Censorship*, 2001. Courtesy of BBC Photograph Library.

as sexually available in lewd jokes about hotels and aristocratic country houses) and travelling salesmen (who were supposedly free to engage in temporary sexual relationships while they moved around the country on business). Evidently, what is offensive to standards of taste and decency depends on the norms of a culture at a particular time and in a particular location. Taste and decency are cultural concepts, not standards that arise by nature. They are the products of ideology, the system of beliefs and assumptions that shapes people's beliefs and attitudes, and which changes according to the social and political character of a given group or national population.

As we have seen in earlier chapters in this book, ideologies are always in conflict with each other, and in a state of flux. Even though the BBC in the early days of television decreed that nothing could be broadcast that was in bad taste, or offensive to public feeling, there were challenges to this by television performers looking for ways to attract large audiences. Successful comedians used innuendo to replace some of the more explicit material that they used in their music-hall and theatre performances. The competition with ITV was important for the BBC, and the attraction of audiences by the use not only of big-name performers but downmarket material was significant. Different forces were and are still involved in an often unconscious negotiation and conflict over what the standards of taste and decency should be, such as:

- television executives
- television performers
- audiences
- regulators
- the press.

*1958: Sexuality was significant to teenage viewers, and was evident, for example, in the pop music programmes on which openly sexualised performers appeared.*

As the category of the teenager became significant in Britain in the 1950s, television fulfilled its obligation to show society to itself partly by producing programmes for this audience. For television, the key issue was that it was a mass medium, increasingly available to all **classes**, and a majority of British households began to own or rent television sets. It was in this context that the BBC satire programme *That Was the Week That Was* began in 1962. The programme was regarded as a primary offender in the loosening of national morals, and the Clean-up TV Campaign was initiated to combat it. Mary Whitehouse (author of the book *Cleaning up TV*) was the leading figure in this movement. She objected, for example, to the BBC comedy sketch show *Between the Lines*, produced by BBC Scotland in 1964. It was broadcast at 6.35 p.m. on Thursday evenings, a time regarded as family viewing, and starred the actor Tom Conti in a sketch where his voice-over reveals his sexual curiosity in a young woman he meets at a dance. Whitehouse's chief opponent was the director-general of the BBC at the time, Hugh Carleton Greene, portrayed by Whitehouse as a purveyor of pornography and a corrupter of society.

Nevertheless, in television, programmes claiming highbrow qualities were able to deal with sexual matters. They could depict sexuality, although no nudity or explicit sexual behaviour was shown on screen, as in the BBC adaptation of the play *In Camera* (*Huit Clos*) by Jean-Paul Sartre in 1964, and the following year's *Bloomsday*,

**class** a section of society defined by their relationship to economic activity, whether as workers (the working class) or possessors of economic power (the bourgoisie), for example.

a version of James Joyce's 1922 novel *Ulysses*. This drama featured the sexual arousal of the character Gerty McDowell on the beach, depicted by cutting between the character's orgasmic expressions and shots of exploding fireworks. Documentary series such as *Man Alive* were also able to undertake serious investigations of contemporary sexual behaviour, recognising the effects of liberalisation of the laws on homosexuality, contraception, abortion and divorce, for instance.

*1965: The BBC* Wednesday Play: Up the Junction *attempted to represent realistically the lives of young working-class women in London, including sexuality and a shocking scene depicting a back-street illegal abortion.*

The aim for **realism**, coupled with a desire to compete with ITV for high ratings, led to unheard-of frankness about sex and its consequences. Perhaps the most significant aspect of this was its focus on young women. Female desire seemed to have been newly discovered by television. It was particularly significant that working-class women were depicted in active sexual relationships, rather than a particular liberated sector of the middle class in programmes aimed at the middle class themselves. The BBC's high-profile drama slot *The Wednesday Play* attracted audiences of fifteen to eighteen million, so its depictions of sexuality were socially significant since they triggered public discussion and press coverage.

Similarly, the immensely successful drama serial *The Forsyte Saga* on BBC in 1967 depicted rape within marriage for a mass audience, and brought this issue into public consciousness in a new way. After the episode which dealt with the rape of Irene Forsyte by her husband Soames – as an assertion of his power over her when she appeared to be unfaithful to him – the television review and commentary programme *Late Night Line-up* conducted a poll of viewers, asking whether the husband or the wife was in the right:

- 54 per cent of viewers supported Soames
- 39 per cent supported Irene
- 7 per cent were indifferent.

The issue was not whether the BBC should have screened the scene of marital rape but about the morality which might enable Soames to feel justified in punishing his wife in this way for her waywardness.

A play by Nigel Kneale from 1968, *The Year of the Sex Olympics*, depicted a society in which television was used to pacify its mass audiences by broadcasting a diet of explicit sex. By combining the **format** of the game show with the expert evaluation and competitive qualities of television sports programmes, the play debated the future of television as a mass entertainment medium and the possibility of its manipulation as a form of social control.

The representation of sexual behaviour involving scantily clad young people has certainly been a feature of television history over the past forty years. Pan's People, the dancers on the BBC chart show *Top of the Pops* in the 1970s, were renowned at the time for their sexualised choreography, and invited the viewer both to gaze **voyeuristically** and to share an ethic of liberation and promiscuity that their dancing appeared to represent. Under the banner of art, Ken Russell's film for the BBC arts programme *Omnibus*, *The Dance of the Seven Veils*, was a **drama-documentary** on the life of the composer Richard Strauss and included numerous scenes of simulated

**realism** the aim for representations to reproduce reality faithfully, and the ways this is done.

**format** the blueprint for a programme, including its setting, main characters, genre, form and main themes.

**voyeurism** gaining sexual pleasure from looking at someone or something surreptitiously.

**drama-documentary** a television form combining dramatised storytelling with the 'objective' informational techniques of documentary. Abbreviated as 'drama-doc' or 'docudrama'.

sex. The BBC drama *The Operation*, in 1973, was the first programme to depict oral sex performed on a man, while the ITV drama *A Point in Time* depicted group sex using naked actors in an exterior location in the same year. The latter play also featured the first penis to be shown on television. Although the representation of homosexuality was most often in the form of the camp humour of such television comedy personalities as Dick Emery and Larry Grayson, occasionally drama and documentary programmes represented it.

*1974: The BBC drama* Girl *depicted the first lesbian kiss on British television, nearly twenty years before the soap opera* Brookside *shocked audiences by breaking this boundary in a prime-time drama.*

Alastair Milne, later BBC director-general, objected personally to Dennis Potter's drama *Brimstone and Treacle*, due to be transmitted in the *Play for Today* slot in 1976. It not only suggested that good consequences could derive from evil actions, and thus challenged conventional morality, but dealt with the rape of a severely disabled young woman in a suburban living room by a man who was clearly an incarnation of the devil. The play was never banned under broadcasting regulatory law, but was instead withdrawn from transmission by the internal self-censorship of BBC programme executives. However, also in 1976, the BBC depicted numerous scenes of nudity and sexual activity in *I, Claudius*, a costume adaptation in which such scenes could be plausibly justified, and in the same year Andrea Newman's serial *Bouquet of Barbed Wire* was broadcast on ITV. This drama featured a suburban family and the numerous sexual relationships within it and beyond it, including the husband and his secretary, the wife and her son-in-law, the daughter and her many lovers, and the father's unrealised incestuous desire for his daughter. Clive James, a television critic at the time, described the drama as a 'The House of Atreus transferred to Peyton Place', in a reference to both the extraordinary violence and sexual complication in the Greek tragedies of Oedipus and his family, and the popular 1960s American television **melodrama** serial *Peyton Place*.

**melodrama**
a form of drama characterised by exaggerated performance, a focus on reversals of fortune and extreme emotional reactions to events.

The election of Margaret Thatcher as Prime Minister and the beginning of Conservative government in 1979 appeared to provide a political platform for conservative morality and censorship in broadcasting. Thatcher's espousal of 'Victorian values' seemed likely to lead to much tougher regulations on what could be depicted, and a return to repressive and infantile representations of sexuality such as the comedy programmes fronted by Dick Emery and Benny Hill. Both of these comedians had programmes in the top twenty highest-rated shows of 1980, drawing on the working-class vulgarity of music hall and seaside postcards. In costume drama two major BBC productions, *The Borgias* of 1981 and *The Cleopatras* of 1983, failed to gain audiences despite their combination of apparent historical seriousness and nudity. The arrival of Channel 4 into the British television landscape in 1982 changed the representation of sexuality, however. Since its remit was in part to cater for minority audiences, some of these audiences would necessarily be those with interests in alternative depictions of sexuality.

*1982: The youth audience was one of the first audiences targeted by Channel 4, both in programmes conventionally displaying erotic imagery, such as the pop videos on* The Tube, *and in programmes specifically targeting audiences defined by their sexuality, such as the gay community in* One in Five *(1983).*

Paradoxically, Thatcher's free market policies and the value given to social groups with economic power led to the increased public visibility and visibility on television of groups such as gay people and British Asians, who were economically significant and whose interests and identity could in part depend on the representation of their sexual identities. Indeed, the BBC drama *Oranges Are Not the Only Fruit* in 1990 dealt explicitly with the linkage between ideological repression expressed through religion and the liberation of its apparent opposite, lesbian sexuality. Channel 4's policy of screening 'art films' also increased the level of physical sexual activity on television under the rubric of culture. The screening in 1984 of Derek Jarman's film *Sebastiane*, for example, was problematic because Channel 4 was prohibited from including a scene depicting an erect penis. **Pan-and-scan** technology was ultimately used to shift the penis below the level of the frame. In 1986 a Channel 4 film season included the use of red triangles at the top corner of the screen in order to alert viewers to potentially offensive content.

**pan-and-scan** capturing a section of an image and enlarging it to fill the television frame; a technique used to fit wide film images into the square television screen.

The realisation in the mid-1980s that Aids was likely to be a significant threat to the UK population led to a dramatic reversal in policy on the discussion and representation of sexual activity on television. In 1987 especially, the year in which a massive government information campaign was launched, television discussion of the varieties of sexual behaviour and the mechanics of sex was unprecedented. Ironically, the severity of British broadcasting regulations in earlier decades led to a worry that the television audience was severely under-informed and at risk from sexually transmitted diseases. Channel 4's programme *Sex with Paula* in 1987, which involved Paula Yates chatting to pop stars about their attitudes to sex, was withdrawn by Channel 4 and never broadcast because it appeared to promote promiscuity. Writers, producers and programme controllers in all British broadcasting organisations were very careful always to depict 'safe sex' in their programmes.

The BBC transmitted Dennis Potter's serial drama *The Singing Detective* in 1986, at a time when the government had begun to give significant attention to Aids. The play's most controversial scene involved cross-cutting between the central character's mother having sex in the woods with her lover while her son observed them unseen from the undergrowth, and an elderly man dying of a coronary in a hospital ward while a large hypodermic was pushed into his heart in an attempt to save him. Penetration, life and death were therefore forcefully linked. Controversy followed in the tabloid newspapers, but the furore was deliberately provoked by the production team in order to boost the **ratings** of the third episode, in which the scene occurred, after the viewing figures for the first two episodes had been lower than expected. When Potter's drama *Blackeyes* (BBC 1989) represented female nudity but in addition used deliberately voyeuristic camerawork combined with agonised discussion of its eroticism in the voice-over spoken by the author himself, Potter as a writer, director and voice-over actor far exceeded the norms of representation of sexuality on British television in the 1980s. For, although it had become common to discuss sexual activity in current affairs, documentary and other public service discussion genres, the dramatic representation of sexual activity had become increasingly self-censored by broadcasters as a result of the Aids crisis.

**ratings** the number of viewers estimated to have watched certain programmes, as compared to the numbers watching other programmes.

Changes to broadcasting regulations opened the way to satellite broadcasting and cable television in Britain during the 1980s, and during the 1990s the **audience shares** acquired by broadcasters such as Sky became a significant concern for terrestrial channels. Satellite and cable broadcasters had already been able to offer

**audience share** the percentage of viewers estimated to have watched one channel as opposed to another channel broadcasting at the same time.

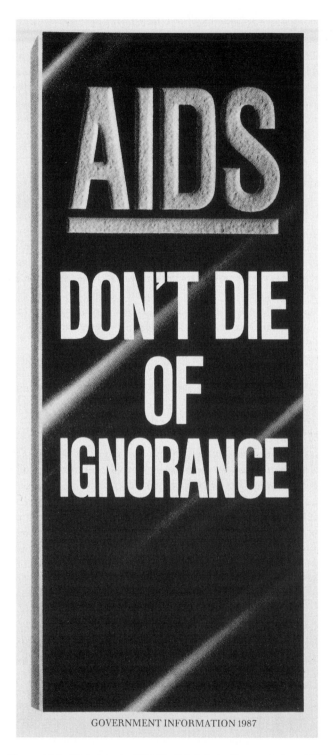

GOVERNMENT INFORMATION 1987

Figure 10.2 Department of Health Aids information campaign, 1987. Courtesy of HMSO/The Medical Photographic Library, Wellcome Trust.

greater sexual content in programmes than their terrestrial competitors, by offering dedicated channels such as the Playboy Channel, and terrestrial broadcasters began to compete on the same terrain by increasing the degree of sexual content in their own programmes. Since the Conservative government of the 1980s had relaxed broadcasting regulations, the primary concern for broadcasters was market share, in other words the acquisition of valuable audience segments. This was significant not only in terms of total audiences, in which mainstream terrestrial channels succeeded in maintaining their dominance, but more importantly in terms of the acquisition of audience groups of especially high value to advertisers. The most valuable group was the young, whose high disposable income and willingness to spend on inessential and impulse purchases were especially attractive. Furthermore, while audiences in their thirties and over can be expected to watch television the most, audiences in the eighteen to twenty-five age range watch relatively little television. The youth audience is therefore simultaneously economically attractive and elusive.

*1990: Channel 4's* The Word, *in which hedonistic sexuality and the eroticisation of the talk-show and chart-show genres became highly controversial, was part of efforts on the part of television broadcasters to capture the youth audience.*

Yet, in 1994, a television commercial for Neutralia shower gel in which a model briefly revealed a nipple was hastily shifted to after the 9.00 p.m. watershed. The depiction of sex was still controlled by powerful regulation and self-censorship, although discussion of sex, especially in documentary or in ironic comedies on youth television, had become common. In 1997 the youth audience was offered, for example, *Ibiza Uncovered* by Sky, in which the relatively uninhibited desire of a group of young British holidaymakers to have as much sex as possible in their fortnight away was documented in some detail.

The eroticised, youthful body has become a commodity for the attraction of youth audiences, and also a source of titillation for the older viewer. The launch of Five depended on the depiction of sexuality since the channel had very small amounts of working capital to spend on programmes and not all of the UK population could even receive its signal. In order to gain the 5 per cent audience share required for the channel to satisfy its backers, it therefore concentrated on what its first chief executive, Dawn Airey, called 'films, fucking and football'.

## ACTIVITY 10.2

On what days and at what times does Five schedule films and programmes that could be described (in listings publications, for example) as 'erotic'? Who might the audience for these programmes be, and why are they scheduled on these days and at these times?

## Taste and decency today

The force dominating the representation of sexuality on contemporary television is no longer the issue of what can or cannot be shown, or what can or cannot be discussed. Only two significant prohibitions remain in the television depiction of human sexuality:

- the representation of erect penises
- the representation of sexual behaviour involving children.

**prime time** the part of a day's television schedule when the greatest number of viewers may be watching, normally the mid-evening period.

In a *Big Brother* highlights programme on Channel 4, beginning after **prime time** at 10.00 p.m. on 2 August 2005, the contestant Kinga Karolczak engaged in various sexual acts that were highly publicised and attracted negative publicity and complaints to Channel 4 and Ofcom. The producers edited the sequence so that some of this could be gauged only by the horrified expressions on her housemates' faces. Ratings for the episode were 5.4 million, a 38 per cent audience share of the audience watching television that evening. Kinga had arrived in the house in June with two other contestants but was evicted after just three days. On 31 July she was brought back, and on 2 August she simulated sex with an inflatable dog and initiated a game of truth or dare in the jacuzzi that led to her kissing two of her male housemates, baring her breasts and asking the other female contestant whether she fancied her. After bursting into tears briefly, she then put a wine bottle up her skirt and appeared to be masturbating in front of her housemates, before going into the garden where she lay with the bottle between her legs. She denied doing anything sexual, claiming that neither her housemates nor the cameras could really see what she was doing. But during the next day's episode she apologised while talking to *Big Brother* producers in the diary room.

In the same episode, another contestant, Makosi, told Big Brother in the diary room that she could speak only with her eyes closed but could not say why because 'It's not safe', and fellow housemate Craig burst into tears and shouted, referring to the other housemates, 'They're evil! They all are!' It may be that the success of former housemates such as Jade Goody (whose prominence derived in part from her nudity on *Big Brother* when she lost a game of strip poker) has encouraged housemates to aim for a celebrity media career on the basis of extreme or outrageous behaviour in the **reality TV** series. The campaign group **MediaWatch** made critical remarks in comments to newspapers, and Channel 4 received phone complaints from viewers. A spokesperson for the channel explained that: 'Kinga's antics on Monday night went out post-watershed and as always with *Big Brother* there was a voice over before the programme alerting viewers to the nature of some scenes' (Kirkham 2005). Ofcom received about eighty complaints about the episode but as a post-transmission regulator it is not empowered to ban programmes in advance. It judges programmes case-by-case, on the basis of the way they are advertised and viewers' expectations are set up, so audiences watching *Big Brother* are assumed to be prepared for bad language and sexual content. This assumption applies not only to live programmes (where producer control over events can be incomplete) but to recorded programmes like the *Big Brother* highlights programme.

**reality TV** programmes where the unscripted behaviour of 'ordinary people' is the focus of interest.

**MediaWatch** previously the National Viewers' and Listeners' Association, an organisation devoted to monitoring the activities of British broadcasters, with a special interest in upholding standards of taste and decency.

Children's sexuality and the possibility that children may be objects of sexual desire for adults remain taboo subjects on British television. In July 2001 the current affairs comedy spoof *Brass Eye* screened a programme satirising hysteria over paedophiles which was much criticised in the press. Government ministers including Tessa Jowell (head of the Department of Culture, Media and Sport), attacked the programme but refused to view it. The regulator at the time, the Independent Television Commission, ruled that Channel 4 gave inadequate warnings to viewers but said it was not in breach of regulatory codes governing programme content.

Much of the regulation of television is based on the perceived need to protect children from programme content that may be disturbing to them. Although this may seem to be a straightforward notion, it is worth considering how the idea of childhood is constituted. From a semiotic point of view, 'childhood' makes sense only in distinction to 'adulthood'. Of course, adults are responsible for broadcasting regulations, and they make decisions about what children should or should not see on television. For adults, childhood is a time in their own lives and in the lives of other adults that is inaccessible to them except in memory or by imagining what it must be like to be a child.

In the developed nations of the Western world childhood is seen in two contrasting ways. Our current conceptions of childhood began to develop around the beginning of the nineteenth century. On one hand, children have been regarded as:

- irrational
- immoral
- in need of adult guidance.

There have been high-profile incidents (such as the abduction and murder of the toddler James Bulger by two older boys) that seem to show that children can be dangerously violent, uncivilised and threatening. But, on the other hand, children are also regarded as:

- innocent
- naturally predisposed to be good
- uncontaminated by adult problems.

It is very common to see representations, including many on television, of children as cute, endearing and able to teach adults lessons about how to see the world more clearly. There is a continuing conflict between these two quite different meanings of childhood, and, when considering how television regulations protect children, it is important to remember that the meanings of childhood are both contradictory and the product of adult thinking.

## ACTIVITY 10.3

List the ways in which children are represented on television as cute and innocent, and as uncivilised and threatening (remember to include advertisements). How are representations of childhood tied into the bigger issue of humankind as 'naturally' predisposed to goodness or to evil?

**Frankfurt School**
a group of theorists in the mid-twentieth century who worked on theories of contemporary culture from a Marxist perspective. Key members, notably Theodor Adorno and Max Horkheimer, left Nazi Germany in the 1930s to work abroad.

**dumbing-down**
the notion that television has declined in quality when compared to an earlier period, showing programmes that are more 'dumb' or stupid and addressing its audience as if they were stupid.

**commodity** a raw material or product whose economic value is established by market price rather than the intrinsic qualities or usefulness of the material or product itself.

**Marxism**
the political and economic theories associated with the German nineteenth-century theorist Karl Marx, who described and critiqued capitalist societies and proposed communism as a revolutionary alternative.

**capitalism**
the organisation of an economy around the private ownership of accumulated wealth, involving the exploitation of labour to produce profit that creates such wealth.

Protecting children from television content that could be disturbing or in some way bad for them is connected to assumptions about how other vulnerable groups in society can be adversely affected by the medium. Since television programmes and regulations have been largely made by well-educated and socially powerful elite groups in society, the underlying ideology of television regulation has considered the less socially powerful and less well-educated mass audiences that watch as vulnerable and prone to bad influences in the same way that children might be. Theodor Adorno and the **Frankfurt School** considered that the mass media perpetrated what we now call '**dumbing-down**' and encouraged the mass audience's fascination with trivia, immorality and indiscriminate consumption. There is a long tradition among commentators on television to consider mass audiences as 'them' in contrast to the more sophisticated 'us', represented by those commentators themselves. The mass audiences of television have been regarded as childlike and in need of protection. One of the ideological assumptions behind television regulation is that viewers (or at least some of them, who are not as sophisticated as the people who make the programmes or frame television regulations) are not able to discriminate for themselves between those programmes that have socially positive meanings and those that could encourage antisocial or dangerous behaviour. The way that broadcasting regulations refer to children or to vulnerable adults can be regarded as a means of justifying the ability of a small group in society to legislate for what the majority is able to understand.

Attitudes to the television viewer as a vulnerable person who needs to be protected tend to regard the viewer as an object, as separate and different from the elite who frame broadcasting regulations. The gradual liberalisation during the twentieth century of regulations on television programme content is partly the result of a recognition of this problem, and the granting to television viewers of greater agency and discrimination. Rather than thinking of the viewer as a passive object that programmes can directly affect – perhaps causing the viewer to imitate antisocial behaviour that they see on the screen, such as violence, sexual promiscuity or illegality – more recently television viewers have been thought of as people whose relationships with television are more complex. They do not simply copy what they see on the screen but are aware of how television operates as a medium, and how the images and sounds on television are not identical to those in real life but representations. This issue of how the audience is considered increasingly as a subject rather than an object, and how television viewers understand what they see in diverse and complex ways, is the subject of Chapters 11 and 12, which consider television audiences and how they can be studied and understood.

## Theories of regulation

Television programmes are **commodities**, offering pleasure to their viewers through the payment of money, whether via advertisements, subscription or a licence fee. When considered from a perspective informed by Karl **Marx**'s studies of economics, the real meaning of nudity, violence or sexual activity in television programmes is how programmes work within the exchange system of the **capitalist** economy. Viewers will pay money to see images of nudity or violence, for example by subscribing to 'adult' television satellite or cable channels. Television regulators largely support the position of television within the capitalist system, and are prepared to accept the exploitation of images of sexuality or violence as long as this is cloaked by an acceptable justification. This justification is the result of the discourses of **narration**, **genre** and form which contain images of sexual behaviour, violence or some other challenging content. Television representations mobilise the viewer's desire to see and hear these exciting or arousing images, and fix them in narratives. The question for regulators is how excessive the meanings and effects (such as sexual arousal or disposition to commit violent acts, for example) of programmes might be. But, as earlier chapters of this book have argued, the audio-visual representations on television never have only one meaning, but many. Since television texts are '**polysemic**', it is hard for regulators or campaigners (and for academics and students) to find a secure set of rules to describe the images and sounds which should be cut out. The meaning of television representations can appear to be immediately readable because many of them are 'realistic' (in semiotic terminology, television signs are **iconic** and **indexical**). Television regulators, just like academics writing analyses of television programmes or students writing essays about them, try to decode the meanings of television programmes. Regulating television involves processes of 'translation' which aim to determine the meanings of programmes, and so this always leaves room for debate about whether a programme really means what a regulator thinks it does.

Meaning in a television programme, the way that different images are linked together systematically, depends on how each moment is contained and limited by the moments around it. In most television programmes all the various components of the programme are ordered by narrative (whether a fictional story, a non-fictional documentary treatment or a news story, for instance), with the aim that the programme will make sense for the viewer. Meanings are coded and systematised. Programme-makers aim for each moment to fit well with the next, and they avoid excessive stillness, too much movement, meaningless images or images which are shocking and seem to leap right out of the programme's narrative flow. By setting up the regime in which programme-makers self-censor their programmes, regulators are taking further what programme-makers already do. They aim to cut what is excessive, while preserving the coherence, smoothness and comprehensibility which television culture accepts as the norm. The operation of television self-censorship at the programme planning stage or later in the editing suite depends on isolating particular images or sequences from the flow of the programme's narrative, identifying them as problematic and removing them in a way which does not challenge the coherence of the programme as a whole. What is at stake in this is therefore the **denotation** of something which might be worthy of being cut, and its relationship with the meanings of the programme.

Some of the laws which govern television regulation, in Britain and elsewhere, require that a television image must be cut if it denotes something which is prohibited. Regulators make use of a list of acts and words that television programmes are not allowed to represent, and programme-makers know these rules and make changes during post-production. Only occasionally are regulators required to intervene. For example, obscene words are 'bleeped out' from *Big Brother* when it is shown in mid-evening, and in one programme from the salacious talk show *So Graham Norton* a webcam image of a woman playing the penny-whistle with her vagina was technically processed to blur the details of the whistle's relationship to

**narration**
the process of telling a story through image and sound. Narration can also refer to the spoken text accompanying television images.

**genre** a type of programme. Programmes of the same genre have shared characteristics.

**polysemia** the quality of having multiple meanings at the same time. Texts such as this are called 'polysemic'.

**iconic sign** in semiotics, a sign which resembles its referent. Photographs, for example, contain iconic signs resembling the objects they represent.

**indexical sign** in semiotics, a sign which is the result of what it signifies, in the way that smoke is the result of fire.

**denotation** in semiotics, the function of signs to portray or refer to something in the real world.

her body. In these two examples programme-makers were following guidelines on taste and decency that do not in themselves have legal status. But some of the laws of the land in Britain can apply to television programmes. For example, the Protection of Children Act states that no image of a child in a sexual situation can be shown (on television, as well as in other media, such as magazines or newspapers). So in programmes in the documentary series *The Hunt for Britain's Paedophiles*, videotapes and photographs that the police had seized as evidence had to be obscured by black bars or blurred patches so that television viewers could not see them in detail. It is important to recognise that the regulation of television depends on the ideological assumptions about what is acceptable and what is unacceptable in a given culture. In other words, television regulation and censorship are political matters that are potentially open to debate, and not self-evident or natural. At present television images of naked women's bodies have become more acceptable than images of naked men: television programmes cannot denote an erect penis, although they can denote female genitals in some non-sexual programme contexts (such as medical documentaries). Television regulation is also affected by the genre that a programme occupies.

Some laws, such as the Obscene Publications Act (1959), can be contested by arguing for the good intention of a programme: for example, that it is in 'the public interest' or that it is artistically excellent. In other words, questions of **authorship** and **aesthetic** value are also significant. The Obscene Publications Act defines obscenity as something whose effect as a whole is to 'tend to deprave and corrupt persons who are likely, having regard to all relevant circumstances, to read, see or hear the matter contained or embodied therein'. For the Act, a programme might be considered obscene because of what is represented, but it can be legal because the intention and effect of the whole work is artistically excellent or morally improving. It is for this reason that programmes claiming to be '**quality** television' can contain more graphic violence, more explicit sexual behaviour or more obscene language than programmes that cannot easily make a claim to 'quality'. The Channel 4 drama serial *Queer as Folk* did not show explicit images of homosexual sex (it was, after all, performed by actors, and the sex was simulated rather than real), but there were numerous scenes in which penetrative sex and other kinds of homosexual activity were represented. Because *Queer as Folk* was an authored drama, with high production values and a recognised 'artistic intention', its representation of homosexual sex was able to be much more graphic than in any previous British television drama.

Television regulation of taste and decency tells us a lot about how television is organised in society, and how our assumptions about the meanings of programmes and the interpretative activity of audiences work. Regulation attempts to control the meanings the viewer can consume, and thus it is about the regulation of the viewer as much as the regulation of what the television set shows. Since television is a business and an industry, regulation predominantly follows the pattern of how society controls the channels of consumer culture more generally (in film, book publishing or advertising, for example). Regulation intervenes by naming, describing and prescribing ways of seeing and hearing. This rests on presumptions about how viewers perceive what they see and hear on television, how they identify with or are repulsed by the meanings of television programmes and how they might imitate what they see and hear or be prompted to adopt modes of behaviour that are

**authorship** the question of who an author is, the role of the author as creator, and the significance of the author's input into the material being studied.

**aesthetic** a specific artistic form. Aesthetics means the study of art and beauty.

**quality** in television, kinds of programme that are perceived as more expensively produced and, especially, more culturally worthwhile than other programmes.

represented. Inasmuch as television viewers' understandings and desires are not straightforwardly the product of television images and sounds, but are instead negotiated by viewers in complex ways involving images, sounds and the ideologies of culture in and around them, television regulation needs to be understood in this wider framework of social and political life.

---

## ACTIVITY 10.4

Is it acceptable for adults subscribing to cable or satellite channels to see greater violence or sexual content in programmes than is currently seen in free-to-air terrestrial broadcasting? Is it possible to compile a list of images, actions or words that would be acceptable in subscription television but not in terrestrial television, and how would issues such as programme genre and format affect this?

---

## Case study:   reporting war

The coverage of war and conflict in recent years has been dramatically affected by the ability of television news to convey very recently recorded moving images and sound both from battlefield sites themselves and from locations behind the lines from where journalists can relay information. This case study focuses on the control of television reporting during the war in Iraq that began in 2003, referring to previous conflicts which also raised these issues. Television coverage had a dramatic effect on the perception of the conflict not only in Britain but internationally. The topic of this case study is how television has shaped the representation of war, and how the coverage of conflict illuminates the technological, institutional and political organisation of television in such situations. As well as discussing the television images which were broadcast in the Iraq War, this section also considers the kinds of images that were not broadcast, and how the relationship between the visible and the invisible affects the meaning of world events of this type.

According to the New York media monitoring group Fairness and Accuracy in Reporting (FAIR), in the months before the beginning of the first Gulf War in 1991 the three major US television networks devoted less than 1 per cent of their airtime to organised popular opposition to President Bush's policy in the Gulf. In Britain BBC guidelines issued to producers stated: 'Programmes should make it known in general terms that some information will be held back for [Western allied] military reasons and that reports out of Iraq are censored.' The guidelines also required producers to state that Iraq restricted Western reporters in the country to approved areas. However, the guidelines did not state that the **pool system** operated by the allied forces imposed exactly the same restrictions. Research analysing coverage of the 2003 Iraq War found that more than 80 per cent of all stories supported the government's moral case, and these were often based closely on the media briefings provided by the leaders of the Western military coalition. Furthermore, government accusations of BBC anti-war bias were contradicted by evidence that Channel 4 News was least likely to report 'good' news for the Western military coalition, with Sky News and ITV most likely to do so and the BBC between these extremes. The academic researcher leading the study, Piers Robinson, was

**pool system**
in journalism, grouping journalists together to share information so that all of them need not be present at a news event.

*continued*

quoted as saying that 'in the end most media outlets tended to fall into line once things got under way' (Frost 2006). News broadcasters based in Britain tended to support British troops and thus, although coverage of the anti-war movement was largely positive at first, once the war began, anti-war and humanitarian views were marginal to the coverage. Robinson's team found that coalition officials featured in over 80 per cent of television reports during the conflict, and coalition spokespeople supplied more than 50 per cent of the direct quotations used in television programmes featuring reports on the war. The Iraqi government, against whom the Western forces were at first fighting, was mentioned frequently in television reports, but its spokespeople were quoted in just 6 per cent of the news stories.

Because of television news's emphasis on immediacy and dramatic visual footage of conflict, reporting focused on current military action, thus supporting the government position that British people should back their troops' brave contribution to the invasion of Iraq. Debate over the rationale for war, civilian and military casualties, and the breakdown of law and order in Iraq became increasingly rare. The few reports detailing the coalition's humanitarian operations were often critical of this effort (48 per cent of stories were critical versus 20 per cent supportive). The government argument that the reason for invading Iraq was to find and destroy Iraq's weapons of mass destruction was accepted in 54 per cent of television news reports, though the US government's parallel argument that the invasion was part of a larger 'war on terror' was directly challenged in 15 per cent of television reports and discussed ambivalently in many others. Large numbers of Iraqi civilians were killed and wounded in the invasion, and their plight received a substantial degree of media attention. However, Iraqi civilians were directly quoted very rarely: in just 5 per cent of reports on Channel 4 (the lowest percentage of any British broadcaster) and 11 per cent of reports on Sky News (the highest percentage).

## ACTIVITY 10.5

What arguments can be made for and against the view that television war reporting by British television should support the strategy of the British army, the British government and their allies?

Media theorists have often noted that there were very few images in the 1991 Gulf War coverage either of soldiers in action on the ground or of the dead who were killed in the conflict. It is also significant to the analysis of coverage of the wars of 1991 and 2003 that the dominant sources of television images were those provided by Western journalists, which were often provided to them by the commanders of the alliance of nations fighting against Saddam Hussein's supporters, the Western allies' opponents. The predominant military forces in the conflict were those of the United States, assisted by British troops and allies closer to the scene of the conflict, such as Saudi Arabia. In 1991 the stated reason for the conflict was the invasion of Kuwait by the Iraqi armed forces commanded by the Iraqi leader Saddam Hussein. The Western allies aimed to eject Iraqi troops from Kuwait, and to safeguard the relationships between Western nations and countries in the Gulf area, such as Kuwait and Saudi Arabia, which supply oil to the developed world. Although the conflict was portrayed largely as a way of protecting Kuwait and other neighbouring nations from the aggression of Iraq, commentators both at the time and since have argued that the war was rather about the maintenance of Western (and especially American) influence over oil supplies, and the international authority of the United States. Similar arguments were made about the 2003 invasion of Iraq, despite claims that its purpose was to prevent terrorism and introduce democracy to the country.

The ways in which television coverage concentrated on particular aspects of this complex situation and excluded others became the focus of widespread debate about the power and influence of television in the contemporary global media landscape. For critics of the television coverage of the 1991 Gulf War, such as Douglas Kellner (1995), the function of television was not primarily to provide knowledge or information about the day-to-day events of the war or the experience of those who fought in it. Instead, Kellner and others have argued that television was manipulated as a largely passive instrument to reinforce the **hegemony** of the United States and to promote the effectiveness of its military technology.

The 1991 and 2003 wars can be described as 'television wars' because television coverage in national broadcasting and in the international television sources such as **CNN** was so significant to the public's understanding of them. The reporter Rageh Omaar, who has regularly reported for the BBC and more recently for Al Jazeera (which broadcast only in Arabic until 2006, when a new English-language channel was launched), accused other television journalists of staying in the protected areas of Baghdad occupied by Western troops rather than going out into the conflict zone to witness events at first hand. His comments in the spring of 2006 suggested that the impartiality claimed by Western reporters was thereby compromised, to the extent that television coverage of Iraq should carry an on-screen 'health warning' that it is based on second-hand information. Omaar's concerns were that the BBC and other major international channels were being fed news stories by representatives of the Western armed forces in Iraq, and by freelance camera operators who might be trading in 'faked' or misleading footage, which would have the effect of distorting coverage since it would no longer be underwritten by the BBC's much-prized objectivity, balance and accuracy. The BBC's world affairs editor John Simpson, a veteran war reporter, responded strongly to these accusations (Simpson 2006), saying that there were almost no reporters based solely in Baghdad. Even the US channel Fox News, Simpson said, sent its reporters out around Iraq, even though that channel has traditionally linked its news teams closely with US troops for their own safety and convenience. In fact, the pooling of news footage was used in the early period of the Iraq conflict, but ceased to be a regular feature of television coverage in 2003.

The larger Western news organisations maintain bases in Iraq staffed by a combination of Western and Iraqi staff, and send news teams around the country to collect pictures and information. The BBC's base in Iraq, for example, consisted in 2006 of Western staff including their main correspondent Andrew North, a second correspondent from one of the BBC's news bases outside the UK who stayed for about six weeks before being replaced by another journalist, a news editor who also worked for a six-week period and co-ordinated the operation and worked on the material gathered by the correspondents, two camera operators, an engineer responsible for maintaining the BBC's satellite uplink to the home base in Britain, and three security staff who were former members of the British armed forces. This team was occasionally supplemented by a senior BBC news editor, flown into Iraq to do a series of special reports. All television channels currently make use of local Iraqi employees to assist them, such as translators, additional camera operators and engineers, and support staff like drivers and cooks. In the BBC case there are also journalists working in the Iraqi office who are attached to the corporation's Arabic Service (since the BBC broadcasts programmes made specially for international audiences in their own languages). In addition to the news footage and

**hegemony** a term deriving from Marxist theories of society, meaning a situation where different social classes or groups are persuaded to consent to a political order that may be detrimental to them.

CNN Cable News Network, the first international satellite news channel, operating from the United States.

*continued*

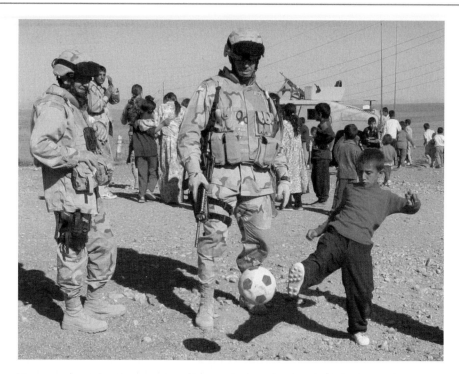

Figure 10.3  A US soldier plays soccer with an Iraqi boy in Mosul, Iraq, Wednesday,
26 October 2005. Photo by Mohammed Ibrahim. © EMPICS

journalistic information gathered by its own team of reporters and camera operators, the BBC's Iraq team can draw on the images supplied by the international news agencies Reuters and APTN (Associated Press Television News). The news agencies, like the BBC itself, have established news bases in most countries of the world, and similar standards of accuracy. Since they tend to employ camera operators with local knowledge and a family background in the region where they work, the agencies find it less difficult and dangerous to drive around a conflict zone like Iraq than is the case for the obviously foreign and Western BBC staff.

## ACTIVITY 10.6

In the 2003 Iraq War, reporters from Western nations were 'embedded' among Allied troops, and it was claimed that this made possible greater access to the action and greater understanding of the reality of the conflict. What are the gains and losses in arranging for television reports to be beamed live from the front lines, versus the reports mediated by military and political spokespeople?

**postmodernism**
the most recent
phase of capitalist
culture, the aesthetic
forms and styles
associated with it
and the theoretical
approaches
developed to
understand it.

The French theorist Jean Baudrillard (1991), encountered earlier in this book in relation to theories of **postmodernism**, regarded the television representations of the 1991 war as much more accessible and important than the fighting itself. Because television imagery in the coverage of the war, and of the military technology used in it, was so dominant over the reality of the fighting and death which it involved, he wrote that, in essence, the Gulf War did not take place. While the build-up to the war was escalating militarily and diplomatically, he argued that the non-declaration of war and the non-engagement of troops threatened Iraq with the possibility of invasion and prepared media audiences for the prospect of war, thus initiating conflict without actually fighting, so that the escalation of media coverage of the conflict between the West and Iraq was in effect a substitute for military action. When the war had begun, he argued in a similar way that the media representation of the conflict had taken the place of the reality of the fighting, and that the media commentators arguing about the significance of what was occurring were experienced as more real disputes than the conflict on the ground. In opposition to Baudrillard's view, critics including Christopher Norris (1997) were shocked by his apparent disregard for the death and destruction that actually occurred, and responded by detailing the statistics of the casualties. However, this misses Baudrillard's point that the extraordinary proliferation of television representations of the war so overwhelmed the distant reality of conflict that the war came to seem a media event rather than a real one for the millions of viewers whose only access to it was through television pictures.

During both the 1991 and 2003 conflicts television coverage made much use of the medium's ability to broadcast either live or almost live, and key parts of the coverage included:

- reports from the press rooms of the Allied generals
- live discussions among experts about how the war was progressing
- live reports from the Iraqi capital Baghdad.

As Chapter 7 on postmodernism argued, the saturation coverage of both Gulf wars has been most striking in the developed Western nations of Europe and the United States. The international reach of news organisations such as the BBC and CNN was one precondition for that to happen. Another was the advanced satellite news-gathering technology available to journalists representing these organisations.

The unreality of the Gulf War that Baudrillard described is part of the media **globalisation** that has been discussed as part of postmodernism. In highly developed Western societies where most people gain their information from television, and where only a tiny number of people have direct experience of warfare and the horror of death and destruction, it makes some sense to argue that war is more of a battle between representations than a reality directly engaging with the viewers' lives. The distance between the television audience and war is increased by the careful control over the media that is exercised by the military authorities. The military strategy for handling the media in the 1991 war was not to allow journalists and television camera operators access to images that could undermine public support for the military action. Allied military authorities therefore prevented television reporters from gaining access to the battlefield itself, and instead released to them footage of battles shot by military personnel under the control of their leaders. Aware of this, Iraqi authorities invited Western television reporters to the scene of missile attacks by the United States in which civilians had been killed. Both sides, then, were attempting to influence public opinion by manipulating television coverage.

The news images broadcast by Western television, and the contrasting images broadcast by Al Jazeera with a frequently anti-Western interpretation, produce a confused mix of information to audiences who can access the many different channels now available. This makes it much more difficult to understand the Gulf War in terms of simple oppositions between, for instance:

*globalisation*
the process whereby ownership of television institutions in different nations and regions is concentrated in the hands of international corporations, and whereby programmes and formats are traded between institutions around the world.

*continued*

- the United States versus Iraq
- Christians versus Muslims
- West versus East
- Allies versus Arabs
- white versus black.

**preferred reading**
an interpretation of
a text that seems to
be the one most
encouraged by the
text; the 'correct'
interpretation.

Furthermore, it is important not to presuppose just one interpretation of television images, to assume that the **preferred reading** of the coverage will be assimilated by everyone in the television audience. Some groups in the audience will have backgrounds and allegiances that predispose them to understand the coverage quite differently from the preferred reading, such as:

- gender
- race
- cultural environment
- family history.

Television viewers negotiate their relationship with television coverage both consciously and unconsciously, as a result of numerous factors. Furthermore, television viewers, like everyone else in society, are perpetually negotiating their identity and identifying themselves either in conformity or in contrast with the meanings of television at different times and in different places. Television viewers also use their understanding of the forms and genres of television in order to interpret the meanings of programmes. These issues of how different audiences respond to television in different ways, and how the meanings of television programmes can be interpreted differently, are the subjects of the following chapters on television audiences.

## ACTIVITY 10.7

If different groups within Britain could interpret news about the Iraq War in different ways, does this mean that researching the 'preferred reading' of war coverage by doing close analysis is unimportant? How do responses to this question depend on an assumption that media representations of war are the 'reality' of the war?

## SUMMARY OF KEY POINTS

- Preventing audiences from seeing something on television relies on an often unacknowledged theory of how audiences might be affected by what they see.
- It has been impossible for researchers to prove that what television viewers see has a definite effect on their behaviour.

- The ways in which the censorship and regulation of television happen in any society depend on the ideologies of that society, and change as the norms of society change over time.
- Conflicting ideas about freedom of speech versus the protection of vulnerable viewers have marked the ways in which censorship and regulation happen in Western societies.
- Institutions such as Ofcom lay down guidelines and rules about what can be shown on television.
- In times of war and other political crises, television regulation and self-regulation are much more evident than at other times in Western societies, and reveal the significance that television is thought to have on its audiences' understanding of events.
- But research in Television Studies on how audiences respond to television shows that different audiences respond to what they see in different ways.

## Further reading

Badsey, S., 'The influence of the media on recent British military operations', in I. Stewart and S. Carruthers (eds), *War, Culture and the Media: Representations of the Military in Twentieth-century Britain* (Trowbridge: Flicks Books, 1993), pp. 5–21.

Baudrillard, J., 'The reality gulf', *Guardian*, 11 January 1991, reprinted in P. Brooker and W. Brooker (eds), *Postmodern After-images: A Reader in Film, Television and Video* (London: Arnold, 1997), pp. 165–7.

BBC, *Producers' Guidelines* (London: BBC, 1993).

Bignell, J., 'Writing the child in media theory', *Yearbook of English Studies*, 32 (2002), pp. 127–39.

Buckingham, D., *Moving Images: Understanding Children's Emotional Responses to Television* (Manchester: Manchester University Press, 1996).

Freedman, L. and E. Karsh, *The Gulf Conflict 1990–1991: Diplomacy and War in the New World Order* (London: Faber, 1993).

Gillespie, M., 'Ambivalent positionings: the Gulf War', in P. Brooker and W. Brooker (eds), *Postmodern After-images: A Reader in Film, Television and Video* (London: Arnold, 1997), pp. 172–81.

Goodwin, P., 'The role of the state', in J. Stokes and A. Reading (eds), *The Media in Britain: Current Debates and Developments* (Basingstoke: Macmillan 1999), pp. 130–42.

Independent Television Commission, *The ITC Programme Code* (London: ITC, 1998).

Kellner, D., *Media Culture: Cultural Studies, Identity and Politics between the Modern and the Postmodern* (London: Routledge, 1995).

Lury, K., *British Youth Television: Cynicism and Enchantment* (Oxford: Oxford University Press, 2001).

Norris, C., '"Postscript": Baudrillard's second Gulf War article', in P. Brooker and

W. Brooker (eds), *Postmodern After-images: A Reader in Film, Television and Video* (London: Arnold, 1997), pp. 168–71.

Petley, J., 'The regulation of media content', in J. Stokes and A. Reading (eds), *The Media in Britain: Current Debates and Developments* (Basingstoke: Macmillan, 1999), pp. 143–57.

Poster, M., *The Second Media Age* (Cambridge: Polity, 1995).

Walker, I., 'Desert stories or faith in facts?', in M. Lister (ed.), *The Photographic Image in Digital Culture* (London: Routledge, 1995), pp. 236–52.

Whitehouse, M., *Cleaning up TV: From Protest to Participation* (London: Blandford, 1967).

# Shaping Audiences

# Shaping Audiences

## Introduction

In the decades when television was a new medium, viewing it was an event and an experience in itself. But now viewers are very familiar with the medium, and television is available twenty-four hours a day and is provided on numerous channels delivered by conventional **terrestrial** broadcasting, through **cable** and **satellite** transmission and increasingly through **interactive** digital services. These increases in the quantity of television and the choices of what to view have made it increasingly difficult for broadcasters to gain reliable information about what audiences watch. This chapter discusses the largely numerical means by which broadcasters gain information about audience sizes, and why this information is important to them.

A significant matter to bear in mind when reading this chapter is that numerical, quantitative information does not reveal answers to the questions of why and how people watch. But since the measurement of audiences in terms of numbers of viewers is crucial to the economics and organisation of television, this chapter is devoted to ways of studying this. The Dutch television theorist Ien Ang (1991) has analysed the practices of audience measurement, and shown that broadcasters have an insistent desire to find ways of measuring the number of viewers. But audience measurement techniques set limits on the conclusions that can be drawn from them. Audience measurement:

- is statistical
- is based on samples of viewers, and
- results in generalisations about what viewers find pleasurable.

Also significant are questions of why audiences watch television programmes, whether they enjoy them and what role in their lives programmes play. These are qualitative questions that require information about the value people attribute to television, rather than statistical information, and are addressed in the next chapter.

The competition between television channels and methods of delivering television by terrestrial or non-terrestrial means have made competition for audiences increasingly significant. The total television audience has become ever-more fragmented, although the number of hours per week that the average viewer watches has remained at about twenty-one. Broadcasters aim to capture a significant share of the available audience for their own programmes, especially if their source of funding is advertising. Clearly, they can charge advertisers substantial amounts of money to put commercials on their channel only if a large or valuable audience group is watching that channel when the advertisement is shown. Similar concerns are also important to broadcasters that are not funded by advertising. The BBC gains its income not through advertising but via the payment of the **licence fee**. But the

---

**terrestrial** broadcasting from a ground-based transmission system, as opposed to broadcasting via satellite.

**cable television** originally called Community Antenna Television (CATV). Transmission of television signals along cables in the ground.

**satellite television** television signals beamed from a ground transmitter to a stationary satellite that broadcasts the signal to a specific area (called the 'footprint') below it.

**interactive** offering the opportunity for viewers to respond to what is broadcast, by sending signals back to the broadcaster (along a cable or phone line, for example)

**licence fee** an annual payment by all owners of television sets, which is the main source of income for the BBC..

government is unlikely to keep increasing the cost of the licence fee, and might even abolish it, if the BBC does not gain audiences comparable to those of the commercial channels. All broadcasters therefore compete against each other to achieve large audience sizes for their programmes (**ratings**) and to encourage viewing of their own programmes rather than the competing programmes on other channels that are shown at the same time (**audience share**).

> ## ACTIVITY 11.1
>
> Which activities might compete for the time of the valuable eighteen to thirty-five age group and persuade them to watch less television? What connections might there be between time spent watching television and economic prosperity, rates of employment, other media in the household and leisure provisions?

## The economics of watching television

Television programme-making has to be paid for. While cinema audiences pay for films by buying tickets to see them (and buying products associated with films), television viewers pay indirectly either by buying the television licence or by buying products that are shown in advertisements. Commercial broadcasters sell audiences to advertisers by estimating the size of audience expected to view a particular programme and the composition of that audience (in terms of its age, gender and economic power). According to the size and composition of the audience, the broadcaster charges advertisers a particular sum of money per thousand viewers that it expects to view a certain programme. At the end of 2000 ITV charged advertisers £7.65 per thousand adults expected to be watching a programme in which the advertiser's commercial would be shown. The assumption behind this is that viewers are economically active in making purchases during the time that they are not watching television. The possibility that they will buy something advertised on television is assumed by both the broadcasters and the advertisers. So, although it may seem that watching television is a respite from the activities of earning money and spending it, the viewer's economic activity is the precondition that enables television programmes on commercial channels to be made.

Jhally and Livant (1986) establish parallels between Karl **Marx**'s theory of labour and watching television. When people are at work, for some of the time they are engaged in socially necessary labour. This is when they generate the money that pays for people's wages. For the remaining hours spent at work, people are engaged in 'surplus labour', which makes the money that generates profit for the **capitalist** (the owner of the business). In the hours people are not at work they are engaged in the reproduction of labour: sleeping, eating and recuperating in order to be ready to go to work the next day and do the same things all over again. The same model can be applied to commercial television broadcasting. Television networks make their money by selling advertising time. The commodity which is sold by the network is audience time. In a parallel with Marx's concept of labour power, 'watching

ratings the number of viewers estimated to have watched certain programmes, as compared to the numbers watching other programmes.

audience share the percentage of viewers estimated to have watched one channel as opposed to another channel broadcasting at the same time.

Marxism the political and economic theories associated with the German nineteenth-century theorist Karl Marx, who described and critiqued capitalist societies and proposed communism as a revolutionary alternative.

capitalism the organisation of an economy around the private ownership of accumulated wealth, involving the exploitation of labour to produce profit that creates such wealth.

power' is the cost of reproduction, in other words the cost of the programme. During socially necessary viewing time, audiences watch the advertisements equivalent to the amount of money the programmes have cost the network to produce. In surplus viewing time audiences are watching advertisements solely for the profit of the networks, since the production of programmes has already been covered during the socially necessary viewing time. For example, a programme might cost £400,000, which is the amount paid by the network to the producers who made it. This programme might last twenty-four minutes, with another six minutes filled with advertisements. One thirty-second advertisement might bring in £100,000 in payments to the network by advertisers. Six minutes would allow twelve of these thirty-second advertisements, bringing in £1,200,000. So, for this thirty-minute slot:

- the network income is £1,200,000
- the costs of broadcasting are £400,000
- so the surplus for the network is £800,000.

Once the operating costs of the network have been deducted from this final figure the rest is profit, for which Marx used the term 'surplus value'. From the audience point of view, four of the advertisements during the six-minute break are socially necessary viewing time, generating the £400,000 needed to cover the cost of the programme. The other eight advertisements are required to generate profit for the network.

The maximisation of profit by television networks depends on decreasing socially necessary viewing time and increasing surplus viewing time. This can be done by:

- selling shorter commercials which have proportionately higher cost per second
- reducing the cost of programmes
- reducing the amount of non-income-generating time by making programmes shorter and including more commercials.

**people meter**
a device resembling a television remote control, used in sample households to monitor what viewers watch. Viewers record which channels they watch and for how long.

Since advertisers pay for audiences' viewing time, they need to know that those audiences are watching the commercials. The '**people meter**' is a mechanism for monitoring this, in which people in a household punch in their personal identification number when they begin to watch television, and punch out when they stop. This is very similar to punching in to work in a factory, and punching out at the end of the day. While it might seem strange to equate watching television with doing paid work, the analogy is actually very close. It is just that we are accustomed to thinking of television viewing as leisure (the opposite of work), and separating it from the harsh calculations of profit and loss that govern life in such highly developed societies as Britain. But television is a business and an industry in which television viewers are increasingly regarded as a market and might also be understood as participants.

## ACTIVITY 11.2

If people watching television are generating income for television broadcasters by allowing them to charge advertisers to place commercials, why are viewers not paid by broadcasters to watch (viewers are, in a sense, 'working' for the broadcaster)? How does your answer illuminate the role of television as a 'leisure activity'?

## Ratings: measuring audiences

**BARB**, the television audience research body, introduced a new audience panel on 1 January 2002, covering 5,100 households. The results are crucially important to programme **schedulers** and channel controllers, who make decisions each week based on the overnight viewing figures provided by BARB. About three billion pounds a year in advertising revenue is traded on the basis of BARB figures, and, as Bob Mullan (1997: 16) notes, 'Counting the numbers of viewers allegedly watching television at certain times of day or night is essential to the requirements of advertisers as they attempt to target "audiences" and maximise their promotional messages.' Difficulties in making the early figures available from the new household sample are thought to have added to problems in early 2002 for ITV attracting advertising revenue (exacerbated by an economic downturn).

The 2002 sample was the first entirely new panel to be recruited in more than thirty years. BARB selected its group of households so that it was as representative as possible of the whole British television audience. It chose households from various regions of the country, comprising different combinations of household types, some with children, some without, across a range of ages and economic backgrounds. Complex statistical methods are used to ensure that the whole sample is representative, and that the results of the audience research information can be reliably multiplied to give national figures.

Opportunities to commission, continue or cancel a television programme are significantly determined by BARB's research. Although new forms of programme such as non-fictional **docusoaps** have been very popular with British audiences in recent years, fiction programmes have always attracted the largest audiences, and programmes in the long-established **genres** of the sitcom, the soap opera and the police drama, for example, as well as sports coverage, are still the most popular according to BARB ratings. In 2006 the football World Cup took place, and this distorted the ratings for the year, displacing the soap operas and drama series that usually occupy the top-rated positions. This demonstrates that television's role in broadcasting live events perceived to be of national importance continues to be key for the medium, and a very important programme type for the main terrestrial channels of BBC1 and ITV1, which have both battled to retain the right to show major sporting events.

Across the whole of 2006 the five highest-rated programmes on each of the terrestrial channels were as follows:

**BARB** (Broadcasters Audience Research Bureau) the independent body that gathers and reports viewing statistics on behalf of UK television institutions.

**schedule** the arrangement of programmes, advertisements and other material into a sequential order within a certain period of time, such as an evening, day or week.

**docusoap** a television form combining documentary's depiction of non-actors in ordinary situations with soap opera's continuing narratives about selected characters.

**genre** a type of programme. Programmes of the same genre have shared characteristics.

## BBC1

- *England v. Ecuador* (World Cup football), 25 June, 16.3 million viewers
- *England v. Portugal* (World Cup football), 1 July, 16.2 million
- *Italy v. France* (World Cup football), 9 July, 13.9 million
- *EastEnders* (soap opera), 2 January, 12.3 million
- *Portugal v. France* (World Cup football), 5 July, 10.2 million

## BBC2

- *The Apprentice: The Final* (game show/documentary), 10 May, 5.9 million
- *Top Gear* (motoring review/entertainment), 30 July, 5.2 million
- *Catherine Tate Show* (comedy sketches), 9 November, 4.9 million
- *Springwatch with Bill Oddie* (factual/nature), 29 May, 4.2 million
- *Coast* (factual/nature, history), 11 November, 4.1 million

## ITV1

- *England v. Sweden* (World Cup football), 20 June, 18.4 million
- *England v. Trinidad and Tobago* (World Cup football), 15 June, 13.6 million
- *Coronation Street* (soap opera), 13 March, 12.5 million
- *Dancing on Ice: The Skate-off* (entertainment contest), 21 November, 11.6 million
- *Lewis* (police drama), 29 January, 11.3 million

## Channel 4

- *Big Brother* (reality TV), 18 August, 8.1 million
- *Celebrity Big Brother* (reality TV), 27 January, 7.3 million
- *8 out of 10 Cats* (entertainment quiz), 18 August, 5.2 million
- *Lost* (imported US drama), 11 January, 5.2 million
- *Bodyshock: Half Ton Man* (documentary), 6 February, 5.1 million

## Five

- *CSI: Crime Scene Investigation* (imported US police drama), 21 February, 4.4 million
- *CSI: New York* (imported US police drama), 29 August, 3.8 million
- *CSI: Miami* (imported US police drama), 10 October, 3.4 million
- *House* (imported US hospital drama), 21 February, 2.9 million
- *The Seven Year Old Surgeon* (documentary), 20 March, 2.8 million

---

**ACTIVITY 11.3**

Why do you think international football on television is so popular with audiences? What could the channels without access to World Cup football do to compete against it, by offering different genres of programme or targeting different audiences?

---

The greater number of channels in homes equipped with Freeview digital television, cable or satellite increases the pressure on the five terrestrial channels to maintain audience sizes. Figures released by BARB in February 2002 revealed that 50 per cent of the UK television audience had access to multi-channel television. In May 2002 British Sky Broadcasting (BSkyB) reported an annual increase in profits of 33 per cent, to £129 million. The channel had six million subscribers, paying an average of £341 per year, and the collapse of the ITV Digital channel enabled it to gain about another 300,000 households (of the 800,000 that were left without programmes when the company collapsed).

Sky is a '**vertically integrated**' company, owning the digital satellite platform on which its channels are broadcast. It also controls the technology used in **set-top boxes** to receive satellite programmes and sets the prices paid by rival channels to gain access to the digital platform through its subsidiary Sky Subscriber Services (SSS). The electronic programme guide that allows viewers to navigate between the channels broadcast by the Astra satellite system is also controlled by Sky, which in 2002 charged £28,000 a year for a listing on the guide. Sky is one of numerous television businesses controlled by the media entrepreneur Rupert Murdoch, whose media interests also include film, newspapers, book publishing and magazines, as well as financial stakes in major sports teams whose games are covered in these media.

So there is powerful competition for audiences, and the struggle by established British broadcasters such as the BBC to develop strategies to survive in the contemporary environment must be seen in this context. If the BBC gains large audiences, critics accuse it of being low quality, yet higher ratings are required by the Corporation to justify its licence fee. In February 2002 the BBC launched its two new digital channels for children: CBBC and CBeebies, respectively for six to thirteen-year-olds and for pre-school children. BBC4, an arts and culture channel, was launched later in the same year. Ninety per cent of CBeebies' programmes and 75 per cent of CBBC programmes are either British- or European-made (a considerably higher proportion than their competitors, such as the Cartoon Network and the Disney Channel). Schedules are arranged into four-hour blocks, rotating three times a day. In 2002 there were fourteen other channels competing for the child audience.

John Ellis (2000: 28), considering the changing significance of ratings and targeted **niche audiences**, explains:

> Numbers still matter in that they provide the bench-mark for the performance of the channel as a whole. But overall audience numbers can only be increased by a subtle strategy of targeting particular sections of the audience on competing

**vertical integration** the control by media institutions of all levels of a business, from the production of products to their distribution and means of reception.

**set-top box** the electronic decoding equipment connected to home television sets that allows access to digital television signals.

**niche audiences** particular groups of viewers defined by age group, gender or economic status, for example, who may be the target audience for a programme.

channels and providing something that will appeal to or satisfy them more
... audiences can be specified according to age, class, gender, region, pattern
of viewing and even by their degree of appreciation of the programme.

The BBC has built on its well-known brand, with its values of 'quality' and
trustworthiness, to introduce channels that address niche audiences and particular
**demographic** groups and rival the companies currently dominating the new multi-
channel landscape.

**demography**
the study of
population, and the
groupings of people
(demographic
groups) within the
whole population.

**reality TV**
programmes where
the unscripted
behaviour of 'ordinary
people' is the focus
of interest.

## Competing for valuable audiences

Like *Big Brother* for Channel 4, **reality TV** game-show formats have been crucial
to gaining large audiences for terrestrial channels seeking to attract younger viewers.
The audience for ITV1's first series of *Pop Idol* peaked at 13.1 million viewers, with
a 56 per cent share of the audience, and 8.7 million viewers voted on the final night
when Will Young beat Gareth Gates. The first series of an earlier show *Popstars*
(which began in January 2001), produced the pop bands Hear'Say and Liberty X,
and had an initial audience of seven million and a peak audience of twelve million.
Its second series, *Popstars: The Rivals*, involved a boy band and a girl band competing
to get a Christmas number-one single, each releasing one record. It began with ten
thousand hopeful contestants who were reduced to ten male and ten female singers,
and then by viewer voting to a girl band and a boy band of five members each. The
series was produced by Granada, whose income derived partly from a share of the
phone call charges, the record sales, music tours and merchandising. In *Big Brother*'s
third series, six million people voted for the evictions, generating 25 per cent of
the twenty-million-pound total that Channel 4 gained from the programme. These
reality TV programmes have been spectacularly successful at gaining large
audiences, and audiences whose strong involvement with what they watch leads them
to buy associated products or pay for telephone voting. They also tend to target
younger audiences, the most attractive group to channels funded by advertising. But
the sophistication and social class of the audience are also significant to television
broadcasters, so they continue to produce programmes that claim to be stylish and
aspirational.

Programmes featuring gay characters and gay lifestyle identity have been
important to defining the brand identities of some American and British television
channels. In the late 1990s, the American ABC network broadcast the sitcom *Ellen*,
while NBC competed with *Will and Grace*. The cable channels Bravo and Showtime
have made claims to being quality providers, aiming their programmes at relatively
well-educated and upmarket audiences by developing gay-themed programmes, too.
Originality and innovation are signified by adopting gay-themed programmes, in
which unconventional visual style and the mixing of conventions from a range of
fictional and factual genres are offered to audiences as signs of sophistication. *The
L Word*, *Queer as Folk* and *Queer Eye for a Straight Guy* are examples of this strategy,
where settings and costumes immediately signal a cosmopolitan and sophisticated
look, and distinctive editing and polished visual style distinguish the programmes
and therefore the channels that broadcast them. Inasmuch as the characters live in
a world of contemporary, fashionable urban lifestyles, and the series are populated

by young adults concerned with their cool and trendy self-presentation and the complex rules of dating and relationships, these programmes brand the channels which show them and the audiences which consume them with signs of quality and distinctiveness.

---

### ACTIVITY 11.4

How has the history of the BBC enabled it to claim the status of a 'quality brand'? Look for evidence of this branding (on the BBC's website or in print advertisements for programmes, for instance) and analyse the 'brand values' that the BBC claims for itself.

---

As channels compete by attempting to challenge a competitor's superiority in one programme genre or **format**, the values associated with each channel's brand can gradually shift. When certain genres of programme are recognised as attracting large or valuable audiences, broadcasting executives are quick to imitate these popular formats for their own channel. The aforementioned *Popstars'* success led to a string of 'copy-cat' programmes, including *Pop Idol* and the BBC's *Fame Academy*. The *Pop Idol* format is owned by the production company Fremantle, which had sold it to twenty countries by 2003. In the context of the economic success of products and services linked to programmes, Fremantle predicted in 2003 that up to half of the company's total revenue would derive from income from licences and merchandising by 2006. (The entry of merchandising and licensing into the television business, as opposed to Hollywood films, for example, was marked in 1998 with *Who Wants to Be a Millionaire*, when revenue from merchandise exceeded the value of sales of the programme format itself. The 'Millionaire' board game sold one million units in its first two years, and the personal computer version sold the same number in only seven weeks, becoming the biggest-selling game in Britain.) *Pop Idol* had the obvious attraction of a core audience of sixteen to thirty-four-year-old men and women, who comprised 72 per cent of the fourteen million viewers of the final programme in the first series. The programme's sponsor, the food company Nestlé, was not only able to feature its name at the opening and closing of the programme and its individual segments, but created animated chocolate characters representing pop singers performing songs in the advertising breaks. Viewers could vote for their favourite chocolate pop idol, merging the audience's relationship with the sponsor's products into the format of the programme as a whole.

Although it is not yet the case that television programmes have budgets based on the future income expected from merchandising and licensing, as is the case in the film industry, this development may happen in the near future as reality TV formats use the programme as a loss leader whose profitability depends on the merchandise and spin-offs it may generate. In the case of *Pop Idol* and other programmes that create celebrity performers, the very structure of the competition ensures that it will produce a person-commodity of one or more pop stars who have at least a partly guaranteed market appeal and the prospect of getting to number one in the charts and achieving major record sales. However, there is a significant risk of consumer

**format** the blueprint for a programme, including its setting, main characters, genre, form and main themes.

exhaustion with such a blanket product range, so when one of these series becomes a hit the companies rush to produce the next one, sometimes straight after or just a few months later, in order that the ball can be kept rolling for as long as the series has a prospect of being profitable. That is why there are so many quickly appearing sequels, like the various series of *American Idol* and *The X Factor*, for example, because the format can maintain momentum only for a limited time. New variations on the reality competition format have to be created to refresh the market. Especially among young adult viewers, programmes featuring 'ordinary people' in competitive reality TV formats were the flavour of the moment in British television at the turn of the century. On Channel 4's new satellite channel E4 and full interactive cable services, the most successful programme was not the expensive imported hospital drama *ER* or the long-running sitcom *Friends* but continuous footage of *Big Brother*.

---

## ACTIVITY 11.5

Why are talent competitions such as *The X Factor* attractive to young adult viewers? In what ways do programmes such as this have relationships to reality TV programmes in which 'ordinary people' become the focus of attention?

---

The audience for ITV's terrestrial programmes has been growing older for many years, and has a typically lower average income than the BBC's audience. ITV1 has made various attempts to attract younger viewers, and viewers with the higher disposable incomes that are attractive to advertisers. Paul Marquess – who had formerly been a story editor on *Coronation Street*, a producer of *Brookside* and the creator of the successful drama about the British football scene *Footballers' Wives* – was recruited by Thames Television and ITV to turn the police drama series *The Bill* into a serial:

> ITV and Thames had decided the serial bits were very successful and the audience research supported that. I arrived with a clear brief – to turn *The Bill* into a serial. They'd have serial elements, but they were mixed with stand-alone episodes, so you'd watch the story of Page and Quinnan's affair for six hours and then that six-parter would finish and the next time you saw them in a scene together, there'd be no eye-contact, no acknowledgement they'd ever had an affair. That dissatisfied me as a viewer.
>
> (Marquess quoted in McLean 2002: 8)

**soap opera** a continuing drama serial involving a large number of characters in a specific location, focusing on relationships, emotions and reversals of fortune.

**commodity** a raw material or product whose economic value is established by market price rather than the intrinsic qualities or usefulness of the material or product itself.

In the episodes produced by Marquess seven regular characters were swiftly killed off, to be replaced by actors with track records in **soap operas**, such as *EastEnders* and *Coronation Street*. Marquess's aim was to address a younger and more valuable audience for ITV: 'It still gets 7 million viewers as it is, but if you look at *The Bill*'s core demographic, it is white men over 50' (ibid.). The aim was not to increase the audience for *The Bill* but to change its composition to make it more valuable as a **commodity** that could be sold to advertisers.

Figure 11.1   Reg (Jeff Stewart) and Tony (Graham Cole) arrest Mark (Simon Williams) for assaulting a police officer in an episode of *The Bill*, one of ITV's longest-running dramas. © talkback THAMES

BARB and the broadcasters themselves use a standard breakdown of the population into groups according to their economic and social position. Highly paid professionals make up the 'A' group, lower-management and clerical workers form the 'B' group, while the 'C1' group consists of skilled manual workers. Less attractive groups to advertisers, such as people in temporary employment, those living on pensions and the unemployed, are represented by the codes 'C2', 'D' and 'E'. It is evidently very important for broadcasters that their audience contains a high proportion of the most economically and socially powerful people in the national audience. In 2001 the percentages of ABC1 viewers on four terrestrial channels (M. Brown 2001: 8–9) were:

- BBC1: 46
- Channel 4: 45
- BBC2: 44
- ITV: 38.

Watching television is important to ABC1s, and 22 per cent of the members of the elite AB social group relax by watching television, compared to 13 per cent who read and 8 per cent who listen to music. So the fact that 45 per cent of *EastEnders'* audience is ABC1 partly explains BBC1's decision to increase showings of the soap opera to four episodes per week, while ITV's police drama series *A Touch of Frost* gained a welcome 48 per cent share of ABC1s watching television in its time slot. Channel 4 has addressed this audience by buying American 'quality' programmes such as *ER* and *The West Wing*, and has commissioned original British drama and funded feature films addressed to the ABC1 audience.

## Attitudes to the audience

We have seen in this chapter how the television audience is conceived by broadcasters as a market and a commodity. This situation is made more complex by the requirement in British television for the audience to be informed and educated, as well as entertained. For the media theorist John Hartley, this conflict can be understood by analysing how broadcasters consider audiences in a way that is parallel to adults' control of children. Hartley (1992: 17) argues that 'there's a struggle between what are presumed to be *paedocratic* audience practices on the one hand (governed *by* childlike qualities), and *pedagogic* discourses on the other (government *over* childish tendencies)'. Although television viewers can be addressed in a range of ways – for example, as citizens, as working people or as members of ethnic, gender or class groups – Hartley argues that television in developed societies such as Britain is understood primarily as an entertainment medium. In this respect television focuses on the delivery of pleasure to its audience. Despite the fact that there are some genres of programme, such as news, that address the audience with information, and genres such as some children's programmes that aim to educate the audience, the majority of programmes either are entertainment or use entertainment forms in order to attract viewers, retain them on a channel and encourage viewing of future programmes. Hartley (1992: 111) claims that broadcasters

> appeal to the playful, imaginative, fantasy, irresponsible aspects of adult behaviour. They seek the common personal ground that unites diverse and often directly antagonistic groupings in a given population. What better, then, than a fictional version of everyone's supposed childlike tendencies which might be understood as predating such social groupings?

The argument is that treating the audience as children is a strategy of control. It is based on an assumption that television viewers, seeking pleasure and entertainment, unconsciously wish to regress to a childlike state.

The other side of Hartley's view is that television also aims to instruct television viewers, in parallel to the ways in which adults seek to instruct and train children. He is not referring only to programmes that have an explicit educational aim but to a much broader address to the audience. For example, the promotion of television programmes, trailers and reviews of programmes instruct the audience about what is available for them to watch, and how they might choose to watch it. The regulation of television both within the industry and by the official regulatory bodies can also be regarded as instructional in this way. The activities of regulatory bodies in controlling what viewers can and cannot see (see Chapter 10), and devising regulations about, for example, what kind of programme content can be viewed by children or at certain times of day, are, for Hartley, means of controlling and instructing the audience in the way in which adults seek to control the behaviour of children.

By discussing the television audience in this way Hartley draws our attention to the contradictory status of the audience in television culture. On one hand, the audience is very valuable to broadcasters. It is the group that they address, and the source of their income. Like the love that adults have for their children, broadcasters show care and interest in the audience. On the other hand, audiences can be hard to understand and difficult to communicate with, and it is difficult for broadcasters and regulators to gain control of viewers' attitudes and behaviour. Like children again, audiences can be unruly and undisciplined. Hartley draws attention to the way in which the institutions of television address an audience on which they depend, but whom they can also patronise and seek to control. He notes that the Annan report on broadcasting in Britain (Annan Committee 1977: 25) stated a child-centred view of television viewing, in which the identities of viewers are those of family members, defined in terms of their relation to children: 'The audience for a programme may total millions: but people watch and listen in the family circle, in their homes, so that violations of the taboos of language and behaviour, which exist in every society, are witnessed by the whole family – parents, children and grandparents – in each other's presence.' In this context it is worth remembering the arguments in the preceding chapter about television regulation. Regulators often draw on their anxiety about what children might see on television in order to frame the guidelines used by programme-makers. Although it is certainly the case that regulators worry about the influence of television on children, Hartley's argument can also remind us that this may be an ideological strategy unconsciously concealing assumptions about the audience as a whole, adults as well as children. In television culture audiences are always nebulous, distant and hard to understand.

In Television Studies audiences can be regarded as distant and unknowable, as objects rather than subjects or agents who act on their own initiative. Alternatively, they can be viewed as having an active agency and not simply being passive objects who are positioned by television texts so that they lap up a single '**preferred reading**'. By considering audiences as active, it is possible to take account of the complex social and cultural contexts in which television viewing takes place, and in which television programmes are made. As Bob Mullan (1997: 18) has argued,

> Viewers often, but not always, engage in meaning-making: they do not always sit there empty-minded awaiting edification. When a viewer watches television they do not leave their histories at the living-room door: neither do they abandon their cultural, class, racial, economic or sexual identities, nor do they forget either their media knowledge of comparable programmes, information in newspapers, and other aspects of the infrastructure of television viewing.

From this '**active audience**' perspective, audiences are not regarded as masses, crowds or mobs whose behaviour appears from the outside to be irrational and uncontrollable.

## Interactivity

Although interactive television, where viewers can respond directly to programme content through their remote-control handset, is a decisive and important development in contemporary television, viewers have always interacted with television. There are many genres of programme that invite the viewer to become involved and to participate remotely. For example, television coverage of sport routinely addresses the viewer as a witness watching the sport along with television commentators and spectators at the event. The spoken discourse of sports commentators also routinely invites viewers to make judgements about the performance of the sportspeople and to evaluate their success. The positioning of cameras in television coverage of sport

**preferred reading**
an interpretation of a text that seems to be the one most encouraged by the text; the 'correct' interpretation.

**active audience**
television audiences regarded not as passive consumers of meanings, but as negotiating meanings for themselves that are often resistant to those meanings that are intended or that are discovered by close analysis.

provides a much closer view of the action than is normally available to spectators at the event itself, and cutting between camera shots allows the television viewer to identify with the efforts and emotions of the competitors. The production and editing of television sport are designed to promote viewer involvement and to stimulate viewers' interaction with the event as it is taking place.

In a similar way television talk shows address the viewer as someone taking part in the discussion. Expert commentators – often professionals such as psychologists, therapists and lawyers – appear on television talk shows and provide specialist opinion, while studio audiences engage either by individual members making comments to the host or the guests, or simply by cheering, booing or laughing, for example. Television viewers are invited to identify at various points in the programme with the experts, their guests or the studio audience. Occasionally talk shows also include opportunities for viewers to phone in and speak directly to the host and ask questions or make comments. Although most of the time viewers of talk shows are involved only virtually, by responding to the programme solely within their own viewing space in the home, nevertheless, as with sport's progress on television, the format and staging of the programme address the viewer as someone interested and involved in an ongoing discussion. A space is 'hollowed out' for the viewer to occupy, in which an active response and involvement are required.

Strategies such as these are intended to stimulate active viewing of television programmes, where viewers give their full attention to what they are seeing and hearing, and where there may be opportunities for action by the viewer. It is generally supposed by advertisers that the greater the attention given by television viewers to programmes, the more chance there is that those viewers will also give their attention to advertisements. From an advertiser's point of view, of course, it is very important that viewers watch and remember the advertisements they have seen on television. Advertisements therefore often include opportunities for viewer activity. These may simply be invitations for the viewer to get a joke, to solve a puzzle or simply to figure out which product an advertisement is selling. Being intrigued by a visually interesting advertisement and enjoying its wit are in themselves kinds of activity that make the advertisement and its product more memorable. But there are further strategies that advertisers can use, such as providing telephone numbers and internet addresses that invite viewers to seek further information immediately about a product or service. A particular case in which the strategies of advertisements and programmes merge together is in television shopping channels. These of course address the viewer as a potential buyer of the products that are displayed, and the presenters of shopping programmes address the viewer directly when describing and recommending products. Displays of prices, availability and special offers appear in windows on the screen, along with the telephone number that the viewer can use to purchase a particular product. Shopping channels also sometimes use short segments in which viewers who have rung in to buy a product are interviewed briefly by the presenter about why they found it attractive, and whether they would recommend it.

**digital television** television pictures and sound encoded into the ones and zeros of electronic data. Digital signals can also be sent back down cables by viewers, enabling interaction with television programmes.

But true interactive television goes much further than this. **Digital television** systems allow television viewers to choose programmes from a menu available in an on-screen programme guide. Viewers can also call up additional information about programmes, and access brief television segments that support the programme they are watching. Wildlife programmes, for example, may have supporting material that gives further information about the animals seen in the programme, or provides further footage that was not included in the broadcast version. The technology of picture in picture allows this material to appear in smaller windows within the television screen, or for the viewer to see what is being shown on another channel. It has been suggested for a long time that it will also be possible for viewers to see alternative endings of drama programmes, or to change the relationship between narrative sequences, in a way that is already possible in retail DVD systems. The technological development that allows all of these opportunities to exist is digital television. By pressing buttons on a remote-control handset, viewers can control which stream of signals appears as picture and sound on their screen, and shift easily from one stream of digital information to another.

With up to 200 available channels, conventional listings publications are inadequate for viewers of interactive television. Instead, electronic programme guides are available on the television screen. These look similar to the grids that are already common in listings publications, such as *TV Guide*, in the United States. They are in effect lists of time slots where for a particular time period all of the programmes available on all the channels are shown. Interactive television viewers can then scroll through these lists, and view information about particular programmes. Electronic programme guides are easiest to use when programmes are of standard lengths, such as thirty minutes, one hour, or two hours for, say, films or football matches. In the multi-channel environment of the United States, even in terrestrial broadcasting the use of standard programme lengths makes it easier for viewers to hop between channels, and the introduction of interactive television more widely in Britain produced greater standardisation of programme lengths for this reason. It also seems that the broadcast of digital interactive programmes has disrupted the conventional pattern of television schedules. Because digital television makes it easy to choose to view a programme at a variety of different starting times (because the same programme is shown on perhaps three or four different channels, on different days and at different times, for example on Channel 4, E4 and E4+1), the viewer's chance to catch a programme is greatly increased. The power of television schedulers to control when audiences watch programmes is correspondingly diminished, and, in effect, viewers themselves become schedulers.

## Paying for interactive television

Half of the households in Britain had access to digital television in 2007, and thus could watch interactive television. From the perspective of the television broadcaster, interactive television is a 'premium service' which viewers can be charged additional money to use. It has been difficult, however, to find ways of making money from digital television in Britain. Shopping, voting and online betting can be provided through interactive television services, and the converged email and phone services on digital mean that viewers can enter phone competitions (on premium-rate phonelines) and post reviews of films. Digital television also allows games to be played over the line. But interactive shopping through the television set has attracted relatively small numbers of users, and it currently seems that only online betting or voting for competitors in game shows are profitable uses of the interactive technology for the companies that have invested in it.

In the case of *Big Brother* the relationship between the programme and its website is no longer one of an 'original' text and an add-on that enhances the programme or perpetuates audience interest in it beyond transmission. The two are fully integrated, planned at the same time, and interdependent. This makes *Big Brother* an important facet and example of convergence in media culture. The interactive services associated with the show were created by the Victoria Real agency. Endemol, the company which created *Big Brother*, originally owned a 50 per cent stake in the agency and bought it outright in 2003. *Big Brother* has been sponsored by the telephone companies $O_2$, Carphone Warehouse and, in 2007, Virgin Media. Mobile phone companies can offer instant text updates, and new technology opens up the possibility of broadcasting footage from the house to phone users. These sponsors have all sought to associate themselves with the programme to enhance the value of their own products and brands.

The new media community expects that convergence between media will not mean that programmes are made for broadcast over the internet, but that the convergence will provide vehicles for consumers to flow between media such as the internet, mobile telephones and television. Programmes will be able to perpetuate their life beyond the run of an individual series by encouraging their audiences to interact with them after they have finished. And production companies are also hoping to draw audiences into new programmes as soon as they begin since those programmes will already have had a presence in other media.

Channel 4 introduced interactive services accessible through E4, as well as on the internet, in the second series of *Big Brother* in 2001. Since the programme had established **brand recognition**, and viewers of the first series had been able to interact with the programme on the internet, Channel 4 was able to enhance the second series in ways that audiences already understood. *Big Brother* has a large audience among the eighteen to thirty-four age group, and this sector is more likely than others in the British population to have access to interactive television technology (and the internet). Viewers of *Big Brother* with the appropriate equipment were able to take part in interactive games using their remote controls, and could vote for the eviction of contestants, take part in quizzes and gain access to additional information and video coverage. So *Big Brother 2* and *3* had numerous benefits for Channel 4 in attracting and maintaining a valuable youth audience, stimulating the use of and demand for digital interactive services, and promoting the brand identity of a programme closely identified with the channel. For the 2004 series of *Big Brother*, Channel 4 changed its offerings to give greater priority to interactive services because this strategy had not been wholly successful. In 2003, interest from internet users had dropped by 50 per cent after the first week of screening, but in 2004 hits on the *Big Brother* website escalated sharply and managers in charge of interactivity at Endemol speculated that the revival in the use of interaction was a result of the casting of *Big Brother*, where more conflict and titillation were on offer. For the first time, the 2004 version of the website carried content that could be seen only there and had to be paid for by users. This content included behind-the-scenes documentaries and extended footage. The free streaming of coverage that marked the first series of *Big Brother* was no longer available. With its access to the families and friends of the contestants, the official website was able to present webchats and brief written reports that could extend the information available to users. The material on the site aimed also to divert its users to other services offered by Channel 4, such

**brand recognition**
the ability of audiences to recognise the distinctive identity of a product, service or institution and the values and meanings associated with it.

as its pages on cars and property. In a newspaper article about Channel 4's financial prospects, Maggie Brown (2004b) reported that the channel expected to lose 20 per cent of its audience by 2012 as the number of channels increase and secure some of its audience and advertising revenue.

Text messaging and interactive services brought in the relatively small amount of two million pounds in 2004, including *Big Brother*. In that year Channel 4's share of the audience was divided into:

- 13 per cent share of viewing in homes with only terrestrial television
- 11 per cent share in homes with the Freeview multi-channel set-top box
- 6 per cent share in homes subscribing to Sky.

The channel expected its overall share to fall to 8 per cent when terrestrial television is switched off. In this context, maximising the revenue from interactive services associated with programmes, and especially strong brands like *Big Brother*, may be crucial to the channel's continuing health.

So far it has not been profitable for television programme-makers to invest in interactivity in fiction programmes. The telecommunications and cable television company NTL announced in March 2000 that it had allocated a fund of five million pounds that would be spent over five years to develop interactive television drama programmes. This was planned to be a joint venture with Five, whereby the latter would screen the interactive drama and thereby persuade more viewers to purchase the hardware, such as digital television receivers and set-top boxes manufactured by NTL, that are necessary to view such programmes. The pilot programme that Five commissioned from the independent production company Leisure Time was to be a crime drama, but knowing that the only currently profitable use of interactive television was in betting, Five adjusted the specifications for the programme to include an element of competition. It would therefore be possible for viewers to place bets on the fates of the characters and increase the element of suspense in the narrative. However, in 2001 the project was abandoned as being too complex and expensive. Making a drama programme that has multiple simultaneous plot lines, each of them accessible to viewers making choices through their remote-control handsets and thus composing different programmes according to the choices they have made, is an extremely expensive and complicated business. The programme-makers are asked in effect to write and produce several different conventional programmes, and find ways of linking narrative segments, plot events and character development so that the choices made by the viewer would continue to result in a meaningful and enjoyable show.

But there are ways of introducing interactivity by more simple means, and over Christmas 2006 ITV tried an interesting experiment with its popular soap opera *Emmerdale*. The regular character Tom King was killed in mysterious circumstances and many of the programme's villagers were suspects in the murder. ITV set up a website in which viewers could take part in solving the crime, by providing a virtual tour of the village on which users could pick up items and look for clues in the pub and the farms where the serial is set. Written diaries, or 'blogs', appeared on the website in which regular characters gave their opinions on the crime and who might have committed it, and users could put questions to the character Shadrach, who was stationed in the Woolpack pub. Users who signed up on the website received emails each week, supposedly written by characters in the serial, where clues and hints gave new information that might lead to the identification of Tom King's killer. The first clue posted on the website was an anonymous letter, saying: 'You've lied. You've cheated. You've stolen. You've murdered. The law can't get you. So I will.' None of this requires the writing of multiple storylines in *Emmerdale*, since the solution to the puzzle of who killed Tom is not in the hands of the viewers and can be decided in advance by the production team. The only difficulty is keeping the identity of the killer secret until the producers are ready to reveal it.

In the digital television environment there are more broadcasting channels, and therefore smaller amounts of money per channel and per programme to spend because the audience sizes for programmes are correspondingly smaller than those of conventional terrestrial television. The costs of making programmes are therefore more difficult to recoup from advertisers, and need to be generated from the subscriptions paid by the viewers of interactive digital television channels, or from one-off payments made by viewers to see a particular programme. Subscription and **pay-per-view** are gradually becoming economically significant in Britain, and it seems likely that these modes of viewing will increase in importance.

Interactivity is bound to change the forms and formats of television programmes. If interactive betting or voting are the primary ways of generating revenue, increasingly programmes will be structured to include opportunities for competition among the people appearing in them, and the possibility of a range of different outcomes within programmes and at their conclusion, so that viewers are able to gamble or vote for the results. The ways in which audiences view programmes, identify with and relate to people appearing on television and follow storylines would also change.

Some of these changes can already be seen in programmes broadcast on terrestrial television and on cable and satellite in Britain. This is because new developments in technology of any kind are more likely to be adopted when they enhance a service that already exists or offer services that are linked to an established brand or property. As John Storey (1999: 125) has argued, people's media use is strongly influenced by their habits and routines, since 'cultural consumption is a practice of everyday life. Cultural commodities are not appropriated or used in a social vacuum; such usage and appropriation takes place in the context of other forms of appropriation and use, themselves connected to the other routines, which together form the fabric of everyday life.'

The prominence of betting as a means of gathering revenue for interactive television has important consequences for audiences' relationships with television, and more generally as an index of shifts in the **ideology** of television culture. As this section has argued, betting and voting are used in order to stimulate the involvement of the viewer in programmes, since putting the viewer's own money on the line or supporting a game-show contestant produces a tangible reason for him or her to focus exclusively on what is being watched. There are significant differences between this kind of involvement with television and the conventional ways in which Television Studies has discussed the viewer's relationship with programmes, which has been seen in terms of identification with the patterns and rhythms of narrative and identifications with characters and people represented in programmes, and in terms of an ebb and flow of attention across a period of watching time. If interactive viewers have sums of money at stake in programmes, then that money is a representation of the viewer themself. The transaction of placing a bet forms a link

**pay-per-view**
specific television programmes (such as sports events or films) offered to subscribers on payment of a fixed, one-off fee.

**ideology**
the set of beliefs, attitudes and assumptions arising from the economic and class divisions in a culture, underlying the ways of life accepted as normal in that culture.

between the space of viewing and the represented space in the television programme. Indeed, the bigger the bet that the viewer makes, the more, perhaps, the viewer is involved and interested in the programme that they are watching and the more connected is their space with the represented space of television. It is also important to remember that betting is about risk and probability. If interactive betting becomes widespread and socially significant, there is likely to be a change in the ways that people conceive of their reality. Society could be considered primarily in terms of success and failure, winners and losers, and the ability of individuals to take risks in order to succeed. In such a society it is necessary to speculate in order to accumulate, but there will always be risk factors that cannot be predicted. The forces of chance and fate, rather than planning, effort and consistency of action, may acquire increasing importance. The sense that society is a collective community may reduce in importance compared to individualism and competition. Ideological assumptions such as these give support to the increased short-term thinking, acceptance of risk and unpredictability and diminished social cohesion that are currently found in more capitalist societies, such as the United States, as compared to Western European nations.

## ACTIVITY 11.6

If you were trying to pitch an interactive programme to a broadcaster, which programme format and genre might you choose in order to include plenty of opportunities for viewer interaction? How would you respond to the broadcaster's concerns about the profitability of your programme (the balance between programme cost and potential income)?

## Case study: television scheduling

John Ellis (2000: 25) has argued that the composition of a television schedule is parallel to the operations involved in editing during the programme-making process: 'Instead of combining shots and sounds into a sequence and sequences into a programme, as an editor does, the scheduler combines whole programme units into an evening's flow, whole evenings into a week, whole weeks into a season, and whole seasons into a year.' Scheduling is therefore an activity of selection and combination, just as editing is, and schedulers aim to offer audiences a variety of programmes that have relationships between them of a similar kind to the relationships between the moments and sequences of an individual programme. Some programmes will have connections between them (in the same way that a current affairs programme may be scheduled after the news), while others will be placed next to programmes that have a quite different genre and format (a Hollywood film might follow Premiership football). Although in the early years of television production the lengths of programmes and their interrelationships with each other were subject to little overall planning, by the 1980s standard programme lengths, such as thirty minutes and one hour, had produced the grids of time slots that were already common in broadcasting in the United States.

*continued*

Schedules are planned on the basis of assumptions about the nature of the television audience and the ways in which it watches. Schedules have for a long time been planned around the ways that hypothetical family audiences organise their time. Children come home from school at the end of the afternoon, meals are usually eaten in the early or mid-evening, and children are expected to go to bed at around 9.00 p.m. In general, the early evening contains shorter and more diverse programmes, while the later evening offers adult viewers longer and more complex forms and formats. Over the year as a whole, new programmes are traditionally introduced around September, when the holiday season has finished and family routines get back to normal as school time begins. In the summer people watch less television because they are more likely to be outside in the warmer weather, so the summer period contains more repeated programmes and fewer programmes in which broadcasters have invested significant money or to which they attach great importance. At a particular point during the year, expected events such as the FA Cup final, the Eurovision Song Contest and Christmas celebrations will require the schedule to be rearranged and specially planned.

Of course, the schedulers for one channel will need to take account of what its competitors have planned. There are several possible responses to competition. The purpose of scheduling is to gain the highest audience share and ratings, with schedulers working in the interests of the broadcasting channel for which they work, not for the producers of individual programmes. Therefore, a programme which might seem to be worthy of a prominent place in the schedule might be moved to a much less attractive spot because of a strategic decision about the programming which a competing channel is offering at the same time. The schedulers for one channel might go 'head to head' with the competition and place a programme likely to attract large audiences against another high-rating programme on a competing channel. Or the scheduler might accept that the ratings battle is lost in that time slot, and schedule a programme that was never likely to be a ratings winner, thus conceding the battle to a stronger competitor.

British schedulers keep in contact with their competitors at other channels, under regulations which require them to exchange information about each other's programming one week beforehand. The power to commission new programmes is in the hands of the executives at broadcasting channels, but schedulers have an important role to play in identifying programmes which are likely to gain audiences, based on information they have about what audiences have watched in the past. So they provide recommendations to commissioning executives and thus have an important influence on which programmes are made. John Ellis (2000: 26) goes as far as to say that the schedule is 'the locus of power in television, the mechanism whereby demographic speculations are turned into a viewing experience. And it is more than that as well, for any schedule contains the distillation of the past history of a channel, of national broadcasting as a whole, and of the particular habits of national life.'

The scheduling of *Big Brother* in the summer has been successful for Channel 4, since television programming in that season is usually made at lower cost per hour and involves numerous repeats, because people are expected to be outside more than at other times of the year. *Big Brother* was initially shown in the late evening, but was shifted to an earlier time slot once the audience had sampled it and word of mouth began to increase the number of people interested in the programme. However, the critically acclaimed American drama series *The West Wing* was shifted from a 10.00 p.m. start to an 11.00 p.m. start after a few weeks because of initially small audiences, even though the programme had built a significant audience of ABC1 viewers and gathered widespread support in broadsheet newspapers. Many objections to the shift in *The West Wing*'s start time were made, further increasing the prominence of the programme and emphasising what was perceived as a scheduling error. While the scheduling of *Big Brother* in the summer turned out to be a risk that paid off for Channel 4, clearly its schedulers did not succeed in guessing correctly in the case of *The West Wing*. The problem arises in part from a vicious circle that affects schedulers' use of audience data:

> The success or failure of a particular scheduling strategy is measured by the same methodology that suggested it in the first place. A problem with audience size or composition produced by a particular programming policy is identified through using the BARB figures. This leads to changes in that policy, whose success is measured by using the same BARB data.
>
> (Ellis 2000: 35)

In 2001 the BBC had higher ratings per twenty-four-hour period than ITV for the first time in many years. The BBC needs to attract audiences large enough to justify the levying of the licence fee, and at the same time to provide **public service** programmes. The factors affecting ITV scheduling are somewhat different: decisions have commercial implications in terms of ITV's income from advertisers, which is based on the size and composition of audiences available to watch advertisements during programmes. Programmes about home improvement are likely to be shown at times when people are considering doing work on their houses, for example on Fridays and Saturdays, when major DIY superstores are most busy. ITV is unlikely to show DIY programmes on Sundays, when viewers will already have completed their shopping for materials. This British situation is different from that in the USA, where programmes are generally scheduled in **strips**: for example, soap operas in the afternoon, sitcoms in **prime time**, drama in the late evening. Each American network channel's schedule is similar to those of its competitors, with much less variety and unexpectedness than is found in Britain.

By re-evaluating audience figures, channel controllers and schedulers identify patterns of audience movement. For example, a 'pre-echo' is an audience group intending to watch a programme starting shortly, thus increasing the audience for the programme scheduled just before the one in which they are interested. 'Echoes' are audiences inherited from a programme that has just been broadcast. Now that British programmes tend to fit into the grid of half-hour and hour-long slots, there are more 'junction points' at which large numbers of viewers may switch from one channel to another. For example, over the years news has been broadcast on both BBC1 and ITV1 at 10.00 p.m., and the 9.00 p.m. watershed is a point at which programmes aimed at a more adult audience can begin, resulting in a tendency for all channels to change the kinds of programme available at 9.00 p.m. or 10.00 p.m., thus producing a junction where audiences may choose to move to one channel or another. 'Tent pole' programmes are those that can be relied on to gain a large audience, thus lifting up the trend line showing audience size, like the ridge pole of a tent. Schedulers might also position a programme with a relatively low audience between two popular ones, hoping to inherit audiences from the preceding programme and to pick up audiences expecting to see the following one, producing 'hammocking', whereby the viewing figures for the less popular programme are raised by those on either side.

News programmes fulfil the regulatory requirement for broadcasters to inform their audience about contemporary events, but can also be used to control the audience's patterns of viewing because they occur at junction points. An early-evening news programme may encourage viewers to remain watching that channel for subsequent entertainment programmes in mid-

**public service**
in television, the provision of a mix of programmes that inform, educate and entertain in ways that encourage the betterment of audiences and society in general.

**stripping**
in television scheduling, placing a programme or genre of programme at the same time on several days of each week.

**prime time**  the part of a day's television schedule when the greatest number of viewers may be watching, normally the mid-evening period.

*continued*

## ACTIVITY 11.7

Using information about programme ratings (which can be found in the weekly television newspaper *Broadcast*), look for examples of relationships between programmes on the same channel in the current television schedules that seem to represent 'tent-poling' and 'hammocking'. How important is it to broadcasters that they 'protect' less popular programmes by trying to inherit audiences for them by scheduling them next to more popular programmes?

evening prime time, while late-evening news occurs when adult-oriented programmes are shown. After the 9.00 p.m. 'watershed', when children are presumed not to be watching, the long late-evening news can persuade viewers to remain on the same channel for the programmes that follow. ITV's late-evening news, which was traditionally broadcast at 10.00 p.m. was rescheduled between 1999 and 2001 to air even later in the evening after ITV executives had campaigned for more than five years to shift its slot. The executives wanted the move to make room for relatively long-duration programmes, especially films and football matches, that could take up the whole mid-evening period and deny prime-time audiences to competing channels. However, in July 2000 the Independent Television Commission demanded that ITV return *News at Ten* to its 10.00 p.m. slot from early the following year. The Commission allowed that the programme could move to a later slot on Fridays and on one other day of the week, but it was always named *News at Ten*, regardless of when it was broadcast, because of viewers' high brand recognition for this name. The 2001 version of *News at Ten* was, however, shorter than before (at about twenty minutes), thus allowing ITV to add two and a half minutes of extra advertising time to the 10.00–10.30 p.m. slot, and twenty seconds of extra trails for forthcoming programmes. This increase in advertising and trailer time was economically important because news is watched by comparatively high numbers of viewers in the ABC1 social categories (professional, managerial and skilled workers), the viewers whom advertisers prefer to target with commercials for 'big-ticket items' that are both expensive and aspirational, such as cars. ITV had gained about seventy million pounds a year from moving its news to 11.00 p.m. and thus being able to schedule programmes with large audiences, such as football matches, in which advertisers would pay large sums to display their products. But with a shorter news programme in the 10.00 p.m. slot and more room for advertisements around it, the loss incurred from shifting the news back to its traditional time was largely offset. In 2003 the situation changed yet again. To avoid competition with the BBC's news at 10.00 p.m. and allow space for films and longer dramas, ITV replaced *News at Ten* with *ITV News* at 10.30. This was the latest move in the balancing act between commitment to news in fixed time slots and the desire to make best use of the valuable mid-evening viewing hours.

Scheduling is still hugely significant in British television, though some of the changes occurring in broadcasting in the present and near future may well change the ways in which it is done. This chapter has briefly discussed some of these changes, such as interactive digital television, the proliferation of channels and the threats to conventional terrestrial television from falling advertising revenues. The introduction of personal video recorders, such as the SkyPlus box, will also have an effect on scheduling, since viewers will in effect become schedulers themselves (see Chapter 2). The personal video recorder offers a searchable programme guide from which the viewer can choose up to eighty hours of programmes that will be stored digitally in the hard drive. Since all the programmes stored on the machine are there to be watched whenever the viewer wishes, and in any order, if this technology is widely adopted it will render much of the scheduling effort that currently takes place potentially redundant. Nevertheless, for the moment it seems likely that viewers will still want to see the free programmes which are available simply by switching on the television when the daily routines of life in British households allow them the opportunity to do so. Scheduling remains a crucial activity in shaping audiences.

## SUMMARY OF KEY POINTS

- The measurement of audiences and prediction of how they respond to television are important to television institutions' economic success and the planning of programmes.
- Not only audience size but the composition of the audience is measured on behalf of British television institutions by independent researchers.
- The increasing numbers of television channels, broadcasting hours and systems of delivery (such as Freeview, cable and satellite) have fractured television audiences into smaller niche groups.
- Some audience groups are more desirable than others, usually because of their economic or social status.
- To address and hold particular audiences, television producers change programmes, create new programmes, mix the genre conventions used in programmes and look for opportunities to increase viewers' involvement in programmes.
- Television schedules are designed to attract and hold audiences, so studying schedules reveals how television channels perceive their audiences.

## Further reading

Allen, R., 'Audience-oriented criticism and television', in R. Allen (ed.), *Channels of Discourse, Reassembled: Television and Contemporary Criticism* (London: Routledge, 1992), pp. 101–37.

Ang, I., *Living Room Wars: Rethinking Audiences for a Postmodern World* (London: Routledge, 1996.

—— *Desperately Seeking the Audience* (London: Routledge, 1991).

Bennett, J., 'The public service value of interactive television', *New Review of Film and Television Studies*, 4:3 (2006), pp. 263–85.

Bignell, J., *Big Brother: Reality TV in the Twenty-first Century* (Basingstoke: Palgrave Macmillan, 2005).

Corner, J., *Critical Ideas in Television Studies* (Oxford: Clarendon, 1999).

—— *Television Form and Public Address* (London: Edward Arnold, 1995).

Dickinson, R., R. Harindranath and O. Linné (eds), *Approaches to Audiences: A Reader* (London: Arnold, 1998).

Ellis, J., 'Scheduling: the last creative act in television', *Media, Culture & Society*, 22:1 (2000), pp. 25–38.

—— *Visible Fictions: Cinema, Television, Video* (London: Routledge & Kegan Paul, 1982).

Hartley, J., *Tele-Ology: Studies in Television* (London: Routledge, 1992).

Holmes, S., '"But this time *you* choose!": approaching the "interactive" audience in reality TV', *International Journal of Cultural Studies*, 7:2 (2004), pp. 213–31.

Jermyn, D. and S. Holmes, 'The audience is dead; long live the audience!: interactivity, "telephilia", and the contemporary television audience', *Critical Studies in Television*, 1:1 (2006), pp. 49–57.

Jhally, S. and B. Livant, 'Watching as working: the valorization of audience consciousness', *Journal of Communication*, 36:2 (1986), pp. 124–43.

Lewis, J., *The Ideological Octopus: An Exploration of Television and Its Audience* (London: Routledge, 1991).

Livingston, S. and P. Lunt, *Talk on Television: Audience Participation and Public Debate* (London: Routledge, 1994).

Lury, K., *British Youth Television: Cynicism and Enchantment* (Oxford: Oxford University Press, 2001).

Ruddock, A., *Understanding Audiences: Theory and Method* (London: Sage, 2001).

Seiter, E., H. Borchers, G. Kreutzner and E.-M. Warth (eds), *Remote Control: Television, Audiences and Cultural Power* (London: Routledge, 1989).

Storey, J., *Cultural Consumption and Everyday Life* (London: Arnold, 1999).

Tulloch, J., *Watching Television Audiences: Cultural Theories and Methods* (London: Arnold, 2000).

# Television in Everyday Life

# Television in Everyday Life

**code** in semiotics, a system or set of rules that shapes how signs can be used, and therefore how meanings can be made and understood.

**ideology** the set of beliefs, attitudes and assumptions arising from the economic and class divisions in a culture, underlying the ways of life accepted as normal in that culture. **discourse** in television, a particular usage of television's audio-visual 'language' (news programme discourse or nature documentary discourse, for instance).

**polysemia** the quality of having multiple meanings at the same time. Texts like this are called 'polysemic'.

**preferred reading** an interpretation of a text that seems to be the one most encouraged by the text; the 'correct' interpretation.

**negotiated reading** a viewer interpretation of a television text where the viewer understands meaning in relation to his or her own knowledge and experience, rather than simply accepting the meaning proposed by the text.

**resistance** the ways in which audiences make meaning from television programmes that is counter to the meanings thought to be intended, or that are discovered by close analysis.

## Introduction

Theorists of television have for a long time been interested in determining how audiences understand the **codes** of television programmes. An influential contribution to this, called the 'encoding–decoding' model, has been developed in order to connect the kind of detailed analysis of programmes discussed in Chapter 4 with research into the viewing practices of real audiences. This work by the media academic Stuart Hall (1980) argued that programmes contain dominant **ideological discourses** that are encoded in programmes through the production practices of programme-makers which result in conventional forms of narrative structure, invitations to the audience to identify with particular characters and the telling of stories that reflect taken-for-granted social meanings. Hall was interested in the factors that might affect the encoding of these meanings and also how audiences might decode them. Since the images and sounds of television are **polysemic**, it can never be guaranteed that audiences will make sense of the programme in a way that is consistent with the meanings encoded in it. Hall argued that each television programme contains a 'dominant' or **'preferred' reading**, and thus limits the range of ways in which audiences can interpret it.

However, three important criticisms can be made of the encoding–decoding model. First, it is easier to determine preferred meanings in programmes that are primarily intended to convey information, such as news programmes. Drama and other kinds of fiction tend to offer more alternative understandings of the action represented in them, and therefore a greater range of possible interpretations. Second, the encoding–decoding model does not make it clear whether preferred meanings are part of the television programme, something that can be identified after analysis by a media theorist, or actually in the minds of audiences. Third, the ideological values encoded in television programmes seem to be so powerful according to this model that they cannot be challenged. It is clear that some programme-makers produce radical and alternative programmes, so it remains to be explained how the conventions of communicating meaning in television leave a space for change.

In a study of how different audience groups made sense of *Nationwide*, a current affairs magazine programme from the 1970s, David Morley (1980) selected groups according to their social and economic background. He asked the different groups to watch selections from *Nationwide*, and tested Stuart Hall's encoding–decoding model against their responses. He found that many of their comments did not seem to justify the model. These viewers did not understand *Nationwide* primarily in the categories of 'dominant', **'negotiated'** and **'resistant'** readings. There were two main reasons for this:

- Characteristics of the groups that were not directly related to their social and economic position affected Morley's results. The gender and ethnic background of people seemed to be just as important as their economic status.
- Many of the viewers in Morley's groups found *Nationwide* irrelevant to them, or they were not able to make much sense of the programmes they had seen.

The conclusion that Morley drew from this was that audience research should pay much more attention to the knowledge and experience that viewers brought with them to watching television. This knowledge and experience are termed the viewer's 'cultural competence' or 'cultural capital'. On the basis of what viewers already know and understand, they have reactions to television that are as much to do with pleasure and frustration as with the issues of social and political position on which Morley had focused. Much of the audience research that is discussed in this chapter proceeds from the two problems that Morley identified in his studies.

## Attention and involvement

Aiming to provide a way of distinguishing between the different levels of attention that television viewers give to the programmes they watch, Jeremy Tunstall (1983) distinguished between primary, secondary and tertiary involvement with media. He terms the most concentrated kind of attention 'primary involvement'. This is where the viewer concentrates closely on what he or she sees and hears on television, to the exclusion of any other activity. Of course, many television viewers are doing something else while they are watching television. The kind of attention where viewers are sometimes distracted is categorised as 'secondary involvement'. In a situation like this, the viewer is watching the television screen some of the time, and listening to most of the sound, but they might also be flicking through a magazine, darning socks or keeping an eye on the children, for example. The lowest level of attention is called 'tertiary involvement'. Here, the viewer is paying only momentary attention to the television while being engaged in another activity that demands concentration. For instance, the viewer might be cooking a meal while a television set in the kitchen is switched on, so that he or she scarcely sees any of the images on the screen and tunes in only occasionally to the sound. Clearly, the level of involvement in television makes a great deal of difference to the meanings that viewers can make of what they see and hear. Television in contemporary culture is so deeply embedded in the routines of everyday life that the viewer's involvement with it can vary enormously. When studying television it is important to remember that there will be a spectrum of ways in which viewers engage with programmes.

### ACTIVITY 12.1

Think about your own television viewing in relation to concepts of primary, secondary and tertiary involvement. How is the range of ways that you watch television affected by your daily routines? What kinds of programme succeed in gaining primary involvement from you, and why?

Some television programmes are constructed in order to attract viewers to engage with them at the level of primary involvement. This is the case, for example, with news programmes. Main evening news bulletins are scheduled at fixed points such as 7.00 p.m. and 10.00 p.m. Their **scheduling** already carries the connotation that news programmes are important, and that viewers could and should make an appointment to view them. They begin with loud and dramatic opening music, calling the viewer's attention to the television set and announcing that something important is about to be broadcast. The implication is that viewers should stop what they are doing and pay attention, granting primary involvement to the programme. Once the programme begins, the opening shot is normally a head-on address to the viewer by the presenter, who welcomes the viewer by saying, 'Good evening.' A dialogue is constructed by this address to the viewer, and the viewer is invited to take up the position of someone being spoken to directly, someone who is paying attention to what is being said.

News programmes are complex television texts, in which a large number of segments are linked together. There are likely to be:

- sequences in which the news presenter is speaking directly to the viewer
- sequences of news reportage
- dialogue between the presenter and experts in the studio or reporters live on location where a news story is occurring
- displays on the screen of graphics, maps, statistics and diagrams.

News is a very rich **semiotic** text that is constructed to demand attention from the viewer. That attention is rewarded by allowing the viewer to gain information from a variety of viewpoints and by means of myriad semiotic codes that convey meanings in different ways.

Some of the time, it is likely that the complex television texts of news programmes succeed in attracting and rewarding primary involvement from their viewers. But it is also likely that the density of news programmes often passes the viewer by. A few hours after watching the news, or even a few minutes after watching it, many viewers will find it very difficult to remember all of the news stories that were presented, let alone the nuances of the different points of view and fragments of information that the programme offered. Instead, they will construct a sense of what is important in the news, often based as much on their existing knowledge of ongoing news stories, and on other information sources such as newspapers and gossip, as on the news programme itself. Some of this cultural knowledge of news must be shared among large numbers of people, since it is this shared but specific news knowledge which enables news quizzes such as *Have I Got News for You* (a **satirical** television programme based on current affairs) and phone-in radio programmes to be both comprehensible and entertaining.

The embedding of programmes in a **flow** of television over a period of time and the distractions present during viewing, as well as a complex of factors that predispose viewers to be interested in some news items and not others, are all factors that tend to dissolve the detail of what is seen on television into the diffuse fabric of everyday life. This could be seen as a failing, in that television has to struggle so hard against the other aspects of people's lives that it has in many ways a relatively weak power to shape and inform. Yet, on the other hand, this criticism is based on the

**schedule**
the arrangement of programmes, advertisements and other material into a sequential order within a certain period of time, such as an evening, day or week.

**semiotics**  the study of signs and their meanings, initially developed for the study of spoken language, and now used also to study the visual and aural 'languages' of other media, such as television.

**satire**  a mode of critical commentary about society or an aspect of it, using humour to attack people or ideas.

**flow**  the ways that programmes, advertisements, etc. follow one another in an unbroken sequence across the day or part of the day, and the experience of watching the sequence of programmes, advertisements, trailers, etc.

assumption that television *should* shape and affect its audiences in a dramatic way. Audience researchers have been more sceptical about the role of television in society. They have argued that television should be regarded as only one of many ways in which people make sense of their reality. Although it is important, it needs to be understood as part of everyday life.

## Broadcasters' audience research

Television programme-makers devise new programmes not simply on the basis of ideas that they are interested in but in order to target and attract particular audiences. The information provided to them about existing programmes by **BARB** gives them some basis for understanding that particular kinds of **format** are attractive to certain audiences (for example, significant numbers of young adults enjoy **observational documentary** programmes with strong continuing characters, which leads to a wave of **docusoaps**). But this information is not always reliable, so single pilot programmes of new formats are routinely made and shown to **focus groups** comprising carefully selected individuals of a certain age, gender and social background. Moderators are employed to lead the discussions in the focus group, in a similar way to how teachers ask questions and lead the discussion in a classroom. Drama programmes are an exception to this practice, since making a single programme from an intended series is expensive and may not provide a representative sample for the focus group to discuss. But even they are shown to focus groups once they have been completed. The results of the focus group discussions give the broadcasters a sense of the elements of a programme that should be emphasised in trailers and other advertising, and suggest how and when a new programme might be scheduled.

The aim of a focus group discussion conducted for a broadcaster is not only to learn whether audiences might enjoy a planned programme. It is important for the broadcaster to fit the programme into the existing habits and routines of audiences' television viewing. For example, participants might be asked whether they would prefer to watch the new programme at 7.00 or 8.00 p.m., and whether it would be best placed on a weekday or at the weekend. Finding out whether viewers might prefer the new programme to a competitor on another channel can enable schedulers to make decisions about whether the new show should aim to inherit the same audience as a similar competing programme, and whether to place it directly against its competitor. Since the majority of viewers watch television accompanied by other members of their household, participants in the focus group might also be asked whether they would be embarrassed to watch the new programme with their children, their parents or their spouse. Or participants might be asked whether this would be a programme that would attract the whole family to watch at the same time, perhaps during a mealtime.

Clearly, focus groups represent very small samples of the total viewing audience, and the results derived from such studies can therefore be unreliable. A further problem with using this methodology is that viewers tend to make judgements based on what they already know. It is very difficult for people to give an opinion on something that is really new without comparing and contrasting it unfavourably with programmes they already like. It is for this reason that broadcasters are criticised for producing a diet of television that seems always the same. Once a particular **genre**

**BARB (Broadcasters Audience Research Bureau)** the independent body that gathers and reports viewing statistics on behalf of UK television institutions.

**format** the blueprint for a programme, including its setting, main characters, genre, form and main themes.

**observational documentary** a documentary form in which the programme-maker aims to observe neutrally what would have happened even if he or she had not been present.

**docusoap** a television form combining documentary's depiction of non-actors in ordinary situations with soap opera's continuing narratives about selected characters.

**focus groups** small groups of selected people, representing larger social groupings, such as people of a certain age group, gender or economic status, who take part in discussions about a topic chosen for investigation.

**genre** a type of programme. Programmes of the same genre have shared characteristics.

or format has been successful (such as docusoap, police or hospital drama) there is a tendency for programme-makers to keep delivering more of the same, since they know it works.

---

### ACTIVITY 12.2

Think about the trailers you have seen for new programmes recently, and, if possible, videotape two or three so you can analyse them in detail. What aspects of the trailers (their visual and aural signifiers, signs of genre and their placing between particular current programmes) seem calculated to address a certain audience, and a certain mode of viewing?

---

Because of the difficulty of obtaining reliable information from focus groups, consultancy companies have begun to undertake what they call 'reality research'. This involves a researcher living full time with, and filming, a selected family or household, and employing several researchers doing this simultaneously with different households, such as a group of young professionals sharing a house, a family with several children and a retired couple. This is 'participant research', in which the researcher aims to become embedded in the lives of the subjects and thus understand how media use fits into the context of their lives. This research reveals that people use media technology in ways which had not been envisaged by its creators, such as leaving a television set on all day as a deterrent to burglars when all the occupants of the house are out, and that, because most households have only one **digital television**, collective family viewing is more likely in digital households than in **analogue** households.

The procedures of focus group discussion and participant observation are commonly used by researchers in academic Television Studies, and the remainder of this chapter discusses the methods, findings and problems in audience research carried out by those researchers rather than the television industry.

## Audience power

The rise of audience research in Television Studies, beginning around the end of the 1970s, has some connections with the theories of **postmodernism** that were discussed in Chapter 7. Television Studies theorists began to regard the television audience not as a relatively uniform mass but instead as a complex set of overlapping groups with different allegiances, backgrounds and interests. The effect of this was to shift the object of study from the television programme, as a text, to the television audience responding to this text. The key concepts in the discourse of Television Studies of plurality and difference were still in use, but now applied not to the many meanings of programme texts themselves but to the many different ways in which audiences might interpret programmes. It could be argued that earlier critical methodologies focusing on the text privileged the role of the critic in determining the correct meaning of television programmes, assuming that the programme meanings discovered through analysis were those that the audience was taking. By

**digital television**
television pictures and sound encoded into the ones and zeros of electronic data. Digital signals can also be sent back down cables by viewers, making possible interaction with television programmes.

**analogue**
broadcasting signals in waves of varying frequency. Analogue signals require greater space or 'bandwidth' than digital signals, and do not allow interactive response from viewers.

**postmodernism**
the most recent phase of capitalist culture, the aesthetic forms and styles associated with it, and the theoretical approaches developed to understand it.

focusing on the audience, often by setting up situations in which the researcher listens in person to viewers, Television Studies granted more power and authority to ordinary viewers and undercut, to some extent, the mastery of academic discourse over the subject that it aimed to discuss. In undertaking these new methods of research, Television Studies also paid much more attention than it had done previously to groups of people excluded from study. In particular, television viewers belonging to ethnic subcultures, women viewers, children and the elderly began to be the subjects of research, and their responses to television were taken seriously. As in theories of postmodernism, marginalised groups and marginalised forms of popular culture became central to the debate. Because the researchers working in Television Studies are generally critical of the power relationships operating in contemporary society, audience studies also provided an opportunity to find new sources of potential resistance to the ways in which the television business is organised, and to the conventional and ideological meanings that are discovered in the majority of programmes by close **textual analysis**. Rather than looking for instances of television programmes that could be held up as examples of resistant texts, researchers looked for groups among the television audience that could be characterised as resistant viewers.

The case study at the end of this chapter discusses audience research on soap opera. Landmark studies frequently conducted by **feminist** Television Studies academics showed how programmes often regarded as of low quality (such as soap opera) could be central to the everyday experience of women viewers, who themselves were in a position of relatively low social power in comparison to men. The results of these studies were important for redirecting attention from television texts to television audiences, and making approaches to the decoding of the meaning of television much more sophisticated. It became possible to see how the **polysemic** range of meanings in a television text might be actualised in practice by viewers constructing a wide range of meanings from the television programmes they watch. The political context of this issue is connected to the feminist political agenda which states that 'the personal is political': in other words, the everyday experiences of ordinary people can both reveal much about how society is organised and suggest possibilities for change and models of resistance. The primary emphasis of research on soap opera, and of much audience research by Television Studies academics in general, has been on the viewer's pleasure in television. But it is worth considering the alternatives to pleasure as well, such as boredom, frustration and denigration.

The appearance of new media formats seems to proclaim a realignment between the audience and the text, and *Big Brother* has been at the forefront of the exploitation of young audiences' familiarity with technology, such as the internet and **interactive** technologies where the users are able to choose and change what they watch. When interactive users are able to influence and reconfigure texts, this can have the effect of producing a greater sense of authenticity and belief in the liveness of the material. Research by Janet Jones (2004) suggests that these interactive formats reduce viewers' suspicion that what they are seeing is being mediated by programme-makers, building on the convergence of new media with television in order to produce a sense of immediacy by drawing on the apparent authenticity of live and interactive material.

Authenticity is often produced by the relationship between the live and the mediated, which exist in tension with each other. Jones's research on how people

**textual analysis** a critical approach which seeks to understand a television text's meanings by undertaking detailed analysis of its image and sound components, and the relationships between those components.

**feminism** the political and theoretical thinking which in different ways considers the roles of women and femininity in society and culture, often with the aim of critiquing current roles and changing them for the better.

**interactive** offering the opportunity for viewers to respond to what is broadcast, by sending signals back to the broadcaster (along a cable or phone-line, for example).

remember actuality after experiencing something through different levels of mediation offered by different media platforms shows that the first encounter creates a frame for subsequent memories of that moment. In *Big Brother* the media platforms are the broadcast signal, either live or edited, received on Channel 4, the internet or interactive television channels, and automatic messaging systems that send notification of significant events to the user's mobile telephone. Where there is less mediation because of a live broadcasting context, such as on E4 or a web broadcast, this produces a more detailed memory of a moment than in a more mediated form. Audiences for less mediated material show a greater diversity of remembered moments, and more personalised recollection of those moments.

There are significant differences between the technological platforms in which viewers encounter **reality TV** programmes that may be broadcast live, broadcast in the form of recorded highlights, streamed over the internet, or disseminated by short messages to mobile phones. The live broadcast on E4 has low mediation in that although there is some editing for taste, decency and legality, it is marked as live with a caption 'live' on the screen, and the material itself is visual, audio and graphic. The relatively unmediated live broadcast gives the opportunity for the viewer to interpret the material actively and create meanings for himself or herself. By contrast, the messages broadcast to mobile phones have comparatively high mediation, since they consist only of short text similar to newspaper headlines, and very brief descriptions of events. However, these messages are sent within twenty minutes of the occurrence of an event, so despite their high mediation they are close to the temporality of live broadcasting. They provide viewers with only a limited set of interpretive possibilities as the input is restricted to the written form of verbal messages. The broadcasts of recorded highlights in the evening Channel 4 schedule exhibit a high degree of mediation, since any event is enfolded within voice-over, editing of visual material, and the use of graphics on the screen. The recorded programmes have much less temporal closeness to the events, since they usually catalogue events that occurred in the *Big Brother* house on the previous day. Viewers are provided with primarily visual information, which frames events using a varied range of points of view mixed with information presented in graphical or caption form. These evening broadcasts restrict the opportunities for viewer interpretation, though to a lesser extent than is the case with the mobile-phone messages.

This recent work by Jones suggests that the viewer's emotional engagement is restricted by a high degree of mediation. Overall, watching live television appears to present opportunities for interaction that are not present in recorded programmes.

**reality TV** programmes where the unscripted behaviour of 'ordinary people' is the focus of interest.

## ACTIVITY 12.3

Make a list of five programmes that you think are low in quality: programmes that you might not admit to liking, or even watching at all. Are there any common threads linking the programmes on your list (are they daytime television, programmes of a certain format or genre or programmes aimed at a certain audience)? Are the programmes on your list addressed by academic writing about television you have read, and if so how?

Cultures are, of course, located specifically in time and space, and although much of the research discussed in this chapter has taken place in relation to programmes made in Britain, based on research on audiences living here, it is important to note how reactions to television can differ in different local contexts.

*Big Brother Africa* ran for 106 days and was broadcast across that continent in 2003, drawing an average audience of over thirty million (about two-thirds of Africa's 900 million population saw the programme at some point). It was accessible primarily to English-speaking Africans, and its audiences consisted not only of individual viewers but communal groups watching in bars or in the homes of the 4 per cent of the continent's population who owned television sets. The South Africa-based satellite television company M-Net co-produced *Big Brother Africa* and broadcast it to more than forty African countries. M-Net attracts its relatively wealthy subscribers by broadcasting formats familiar to audiences in the developed world, such as soap operas and football in addition to the African versions of reality TV series (an African *Pop Idol* is another popular programme). *Big Brother Africa* was also broadcast in early-evening terrestrial highlights episodes, in a similar way to its scheduling in Britain.

It seems likely that, for Africans, the appeal of this kind of programme mix, and of *Big Brother* in particular, was that it represented an African-originated programme whose focus was not on the international news agenda's usual representations of the continent, which centre on war and natural disasters. *Big Brother Africa* in 2003 was the first pan-continental version, following two earlier series that contained only South African contestants and where the winners in each case were white men. The 2003 series included contestants from Angola, Botswana, Ghana, Kenya, Malawi, Namibia, South Africa, Tanzania, Uganda, Zambia and Zimbabwe. It began with an equal number of male and female contestants, and was won by a twenty-four-year-old Zambian woman who collected the $100,000 prize. Later, she met Nelson Mandela, and in common with several fellow contestants became a celebrity. As in other versions worldwide, the housemates secured contracts as product-endorsers in advertising, as actors and as television presenters.

The series achieved a significant fan base, organised in some cities into semi-formal clubs. But among the political elites of some African countries, *Big Brother Africa* raised moral and political questions. The parliament in Malawi banned the series for two weeks until the High Court declared this unconstitutional and required the national broadcaster to carry it again. In July 2003 President Sam Nujoma of Namibia asked the state-owned Namibian Broadcasting Corporation to cease broadcasting the programme, though his appeal was ignored and Namibian audiences continued to view the programme on NBC, as well as live coverage on satellite television. In Uganda, religious and women's groups, members of parliament and commentators denounced the series for immorality, but it continued to be shown there, too. Similarly in Zambia, *Big Brother Africa* was declared immoral by a pressure-group of the country's churches, but they failed in their attempt to have it taken off air. The Nigerian media regulator sought legal grounds for prosecuting the channels broadcasting *Big Brother Africa* but the case collapsed. (These controversies were not confined to Africa, incidentally, since the Arabian version of *Big Brother* was suspended after just two weeks because of its alleged un-Islamic content, while in Italy the channel broadcasting its version of the show, Canale 5, was fined for infringing standards of **taste and decency**). In Africa the

**taste and deceny** conformity to standards of good taste and acceptable language and behaviour represented on television, as required by regulations.

attempts to ban the show arose because of what was perceived as non-African, Western immorality among the contestants, who were, as a group, relatively educated and liberal. After only twenty-nine days of broadcasting two housemates had sex quite openly.

*Big Brother Africa* demonstrated the shared standards of personal ethics prevalent among younger, educated Africans from the participating nations, thus drawing public attention to generational differences between 'traditional' and 'liberal' social groups, and the impact of Western culture as one of the causes of that social differentiation across the continent. Thus, *Big Brother Africa* demonstrated the differences within contemporary African culture, in terms of both the mixing of contestants of several nationalities and the use of the format itself as a Western one made specific to its region of broadcast. The visits by non-Africans to the house, notably a housemate from the British version of *Big Brother*, and the exchange programme whereby one of the African housemates went to Britain's *Big Brother* house in return, drew attention to national, regional and global differences. Reality TV became a public space in which these similarities and differences could be played out by ordinary people, and it seems that viewers in Africa were using television in order to work through problems with which they were consciously or unconsciously concerned. Ordinary viewers and powerful interest groups were discussing and evaluating not only the issues in *Big Brother* itself but those in their own lives.

---

### ACTIVITY 12.4

How does the cross-cultural example of *Big Brother Africa* affect the concept of 'preferred meaning': if the meanings of television are so different in different cultures, why should we continue to study television programmes as texts?

---

## Limitations of ethnography

**ethnography**
the detailed study of how people live, conducted by observing behaviour and talking to selected individuals about their attitudes and activities.

**Ethnographic** studies of television audiences take their methodology from the academic discipline of **anthropology**. This began in the nineteenth century, and involves the study of humankind. It was part of the expansion of the methods of the experimental physical sciences (such as biology and chemistry) into the arena of human activity, and initially focused on the study of 'primitive' peoples living in the underdeveloped territories controlled by the empires of Western European nations. The ideology underlying these early anthropological studies was a belief in the possibility of human progress, from tribal cultures to the industrial and technologically developed societies from which the anthropological researchers themselves came. It was assumed by anthropologists that over time all human societies would evolve in more or less the same way, into industrial, democratic and bureaucratic cultures.

**anthropology**
the study of humankind, including the evolution of humans and the different kinds of human society existing in different times and places.

However, anthropology has since questioned some of these assumptions, and argued that there is no necessary forward movement of human societies towards a particular form. The underdeveloped, non-technological societies that still exist in some parts of the world are no longer regarded as in some way 'behind the times' or as throwbacks to an earlier phase in the development of the human race. But anthropologists still seek to understand how different cultures function, and whether there are consistent structures that underlie human culture, family relationships and ways of organising work, leisure and identity.

Research on television audiences addresses some of the same issues by seeking to understand how television functions in relationships between people, and how it affects the ways in which people's daily lives and understanding of themselves are formed. Yet one of the legacies that remains from the history of the discipline of anthropology is that the researcher has normally been in a much more socially powerful position than the respondents that he or she interviews and studies. Ordinary television viewers are interesting to researchers because they are different, even exotic, rather like the 'primitive' tribal people who were the subjects for early anthropological projects.

Television audience researchers aim for what the anthropologist Clifford Geertz (1967) called a 'thick description' of audience behaviour. This involves discovering 'a stratified hierarchy of meaningful structures in terms of which [social behaviours] are produced, perceived and interpreted, and without which they would not . . . in fact exist' (Geertz 1967: 7). The observation must be interpreted in relation to the cultural frameworks which make it meaningful, so that the ethnographer can interpret what he or she observes. The television ethnographer's results are therefore interpretations of the subjects' interpretations of his or her own actions and thoughts, and often those of other people, too.

Figure 12.1   Engraving showing the 'Principal Varieties of Mankind' by John Emslie, 1850. Courtesy of the Science Museum, Science & Society Picture Library

Ethnography is a form of textual analysis, and interpreting audiences reveals the intricate, singular and different ways in which people make interpretations of their world and think about their own cultural behaviour. Layer on layer of interpretation is produced, and the best kinds of audience research explore not only the results obtained from the research but the constructed quality of the ethnographer's text. Ethnographic researchers are writers, and the observing, transcribing and interpreting functions involved in their work are not as separate as the 'scientific' history of the discipline might imply; in fact, the different functions that researchers perform contaminate each other. Doing audience research requires the ethnographer to adopt several identities at different times, or simultaneously, being:

- participant
- observer
- recorder
- author
- interpreter
- theorist.

Commonly, researchers reflect on their agendas but try to present viewers as sharing either the same enthusiasms or the same political views as themselves. But television audience researchers, who often say that they themselves belong to the subcultures they study, have to remember that what they do is a cultural practice itself which will inevitably alter and affect the behaviour which they observe.

Academic studies of television audiences using ethnographic methods are difficult to evaluate. They are most often carried out by talking to respondents who have voluntarily put themselves forward as research subjects, and who are therefore likely to have something they want to say about television. The methods used to find respondents can give rise to a number of problems in the design of audience research studies. Some researchers have used the method called 'snowballing', in which one person takes on the responsibility to find another who will participate in the study, then that person finds another volunteer, and so on. While this methodology is less artificial than trying to select a panel of respondents who are representative in some way, it inevitably produces a self-selected group. Other researchers have placed advertisements in magazines, for example, and reviewed the responses they receive. Here, of course, those people who respond have something that they wish to communicate, and they also communicate in writing. The formalities of writing letters, such as the need to organise material, to be polite and to choose a language that may distort information by formalising it, are problems that this methodology has to address. When writing down their reactions, viewers may consciously or unconsciously modify their responses by putting them into the disciplined forms that are conventional in letters to people whom we do not know personally. Interviews can present some of the same problems, when respondents can tailor what they say in order to give the answers that they think may be most interesting to the researcher, or that present them in the most interesting light, for example.

Ethnographic research on television viewers is still relatively recent in the discipline of Television Studies, and few of the academics who have carried it out have been trained in the methodologies of anthropology or sociology from which ethnography derives. But researchers have become increasingly conscious of these problems, and books and articles presenting their findings now almost always contain explanations of their methodology and draw attention to the limitations of their results.

---

## ACTIVITY 12.5

If you wanted to design an ethnographic study of how elderly viewers respond to daytime drama programmes, how would you go about selecting a sample of viewers, deciding on the questions you wanted to ask, and analysing your results? What problems might you encounter in conducting your study, and how could you minimise or solve these problems?

---

Specific cultural groups, such as the resistant television audience groups studied in media audience research, are imaginary communities. While some media audience cultures can claim a degree of cultural unity, this is sustained in distinction to national and global media cultures that they cannot change. The theorist of fan cultures Henry Jenkins (Tulloch and Jenkins 1995) conducted studies of the attitudes to *Star Trek* of a range of different groups, including science students at the Massachusetts Institute of Technology (MIT) and members of a gay *Star Trek* fan group, the Gaylaxians. Jenkins points out that MIT students largely share the ideological values of the programme, such as faith in human progress, the ability of science to solve social problems, and value attributed to the technology represented in *Star Trek* and the technology used to represent it in special effects. Members of this group are hardly a resistant audience because they are highly educated middle-class males who are destined to be among the professionals who wield social power.

In his study of the Gaylaxians, Jenkins (Tulloch and Jenkins 1995: 264) notes that

> Resistant reading can sustain the Gaylaxians' own activism, can become a source of collective identity and mutual support, but precisely because it is a subcultural activity which is denied public visibility, resistant reading cannot change the political agenda, cannot challenge other constructions of gay identity, and cannot have an impact on the ways people outside the group think about the issues which matter to the Gaylaxians.

The more that an audience is identified by researchers as an emblem of resistance to the dominant norms of television and contemporary society, the less likely it is that this audience group will be able to exert any actual power to create change in either television or society.

But some of the television audiences studied by ethnographic researchers do not have a constituted identity at all, except for when an identity is attributed to them by the researcher doing the ethnographic work. In a discussion of some of the many studies of women viewers of soap opera, for example, Ien Ang and Joke Hermes (1996) have pointed out that researchers have a tendency to assume that the responses of particular research respondents are representative of the larger group made up of women viewers in general. The results of talking to one small sample of women can be made to stand for all women (often restricted to those of a certain social class or race) in order to make an argument about how this entire group is likely to understand and enjoy television. The impetus behind much audience research is to value the voices of viewers in a dominant television broadcasting culture which largely excludes them, and thus to claim the agency of the audience, and that audience research itself can have political agency as a way of intervening in the discussion of the politics of contemporary culture. The British television academics Julia Hallam and Margaret Marshment (1995) made a study of women viewers of the British three-part BBC television serial *Oranges Are not the Only Fruit* (1989, based on the novel of the same name by Jeanette Winterson). After completing interviews with their sample of viewers, Hallam and Marshment (1995: 14) concluded that the diversity of viewers' responses 'remained within a recognizable "we" of common experiences and pleasures which seemed to owe much to our common positions as women'. The researchers (1995: 3) claimed that

> we were not "looking for" negotiated or resistant readings among the respondents . . . but our feminist standpoint does need to be taken into account. We hoped to find that they did like [the serial] and did interpret it in line with the preferred reading because . . . it would . . . thus constitute a significant feminist anti-homophobic intervention in popular culture.

Since research is always carried out with an explicit or implicit research agenda, or at least a set of research questions, there is a tendency for academic publication of audience research to find the answers that it aimed to find. After all, it is much more interesting to read about research findings where positive results have been obtained rather than studies where the research subjects had little coherent to say, or where the design and methodology of the research were found to be flawed.

## Fan audiences

Viewers who regard themselves as fans of particular programmes are a special subgroup of television audiences who reveal some of the strengths and weaknesses of ethnographic audience research. As with the other research discussed in this chapter, the main emphasis has been on how fans gain pleasure from their close relationship with television programmes, and how their relationships with television provide them with kinds of social identity that are desirable to them. The way that fans actively appropriate television culture can be regarded as an unusually extreme but revealing instance of how all television viewers take possession of the programmes they watch, and assimilate the meanings of those programmes into their own lives. Fan communities are self-selected, groups of people who have decided to identify themselves closely with programmes and with fellow television viewers who also devote special attention to the same programme. Prominent programmes whose fan cultures have been investigated by television researchers include *Star Trek* and its sequels, *The X Files*, *Doctor Who* and *Buffy the Vampire Slayer*. It is notable that these programmes all fall into the category of science-fiction or fantasy television, since one of the arguments of audience research on their fan communities is that being a fan is itself crucially tied up with constructing fantasies that provide the scenario for fans to reimagine themselves and to experiment with the possibilities and limits of their interests and desires.

The range of ways in which fans take possession of a television programme for themselves, and redirect its components and meanings for themselves, has been described by the media theorist Henry Jenkins (1992) as 'textual poaching'. Drawing the analogy with poachers who illegally capture game from land that is owned by someone else, Jenkins argues that fans invade the territory of television programmes that are created, controlled and owned by the 'official' television culture of professional programme-makers. Rather than viewing programmes according to the preferred readings encoded by their creators, the fans pick out the elements that are of interest to them and make them function in new ways. For some audience researchers, there is a heroic aspect to this, whereby fans are considered as a resistant audience that refuses to adopt the conventional position laid out for it by a television programme, and instead reappropriates programmes in ways that contradict the aims of their creators and owners. Indeed, fans operate in similar ways to the creators of television programmes, producing alternative products that supplement or take the place of industrially produced shows. For example, fans:

- create websites about their favourite programme
- set up and distribute magazines and newsletters
- organise collective cultural events such as conventions.

These activities can be regarded as resistant, in that they promote ways of viewing, talking about and restaging programmes that take possession of the original and change it in interesting ways. But on the other hand, fan culture reproduces many of the ways in which 'official' television production culture works. Fans discriminate between insiders (who belong to the world of fan culture) and outsiders (who do not), just as television professionals seek to preserve their elite position within the industry and normally deny access to members of the audience. Fans produce and circulate texts and products, in parallel with the ways in which programme-makers produce and circulate texts and products. The cultural competence that fans seek to possess (such as detailed knowledge about their favourite programme) is a form of capital that gives them status within their community. In a similar way television programme-makers accumulate insider knowledge about their business and also accumulate financial capital and profit for themselves and the broadcasting organisations for which they work.

The growth of the internet has provided television fans with extensive possibilities for communicating with each other. To take the example of *Doctor Who*, this British science-fiction adventure series began in 1963 and ran until 1996. Nevertheless, six years after the last series was broadcast, in 2002, there were still more than forty newsgroups and chat forums running on the internet, despite the lack of new programmes for its fans to discuss. These web resources consisted of fictional stories written by fans, websites devoted to actors who had appeared in the programme, fan magazines and sites offering non-professional films of *Doctor Who* made by fans. Eventually one of the show's more illustrious fans, the writer and producer Russell T. Davies, resurrected the series, and it returned to great success on British screens in 2005.

John Tulloch (Tulloch and Jenkins 1995: 145) describes the central fan activity as 'the power to gloss', meaning the power of television fans to interpret and re-interpret programmes for themselves and to engage in dialogue and debate with each other around questions of interpretation. Henry Jenkins (1992: 86) argues that 'Organised fandom is, perhaps first and foremost, an institution of theory and criticism, a semi-structured space where competing interpretations and evaluations of common texts are proposed, debated and negotiated and where readers speculate about the nature of the mass media and their own relationship to it.' By engaging in such debates, fans are able to display their cultural capital of knowledge about the programme, and the debates and discussions themselves constitute a fan community. The possibility of potentially endless debate about interpretation enables the fan community and its activities to continue indefinitely, even when (as in the case of another science-fiction series, *Blake's 7*, for instance) there are no new programmes to discuss. Series television, such as the long-running programmes that have tended to be the focus of fan interest, is normally written by a wide range of writers, may feature different actors who join and leave over the period of a programme's run, and the narrative structure, thematic concerns and settings (the components of the programme format) may change. These discontinuities allow broad scope for fan interpretation, and for making value judgements about the success or failure of particular episodes or groups of episodes.

**merchandising**
the sale of products associated with a television programme, such as toys, books and clothing.

The overwhelming majority of comments posted to newsgroups on television programmes consists of opinions of the broadcast episodes. The majority of fans are interested in the official productions associated with television programmes and the **merchandising** products produced under licence that are connected to them. So, although the internet provides a virtual community for television fans, only a very small proportion of fan activity has to do with media production itself, and

Figure 12.2  David Tennant as the Doctor and Billie Piper as Rose in *Doctor Who*. © BBC Photograph Library.

instead it is concerned with consumption. As John Fiske (1992b: 44) notes, 'the emphasis is not so much on acquiring a few good (and thus expensive) objects as accumulating as many as possible'. Being a fan means acquiring the cultural capital of knowledge about television programmes, and also amassing the commercial objects, such as videos and DVDs, that make possible possession of the programmes. Being a fan is a means not only of resisting the dominant interpretations shaped by programme-makers and taking possession of the meanings of television programmes for oneself but of positioning oneself as a consumer of the commodities that programme producers now increasingly use as valuable streams of income to fund further programme-making. Knowing that fans are likely already to have amassed videotape copies of programmes, it is currently common for the owners of franchises such as *Star Trek* and *Doctor Who* to re-release programmes on DVD with tempting extras, such as interviews with cast members and producers, so that fans will buy the original programmes all over again. The desire for a complete collection of programmes in the highest-quality format stimulates the desire to amass commercial objects among the fan community.

So, although television fans are in a sense the heroes of audience research in Television Studies, since they are the viewers who most actively respond to television programmes and engage most consciously in alternative and resistant practices prompted by television programmes, they are also complicit with the television industry and the structures and assumptions that underlie it. Indeed, fan culture is a response to a cultural disempowerment that derives from being a member of the audience rather than a producer of programmes. No matter how active, resistant, knowledgeable or interested a television fan may be, his or her activities and those of the fan community have little effect on the ways in which the television industry works or on the television programmes that are produced.

## Children and television

Television Studies academics have worked on how television viewing relates to wider social behaviour. As this chapter has shown, this includes how different kinds of audience watch different kinds of programme, and how social groups of different age and status watch different programmes. Children watching television have been a focus of study for several decades. In the 1950s and 1960s, for example, researchers in the United States attempted to devise experiments in which the **effects** of television on children could be discovered (Bandura 1977 and Himmelwhite *et al.* 1958, for example). This kind of research has since been heavily criticised, because the settings in which it took place, the kinds of television shown to children and the methods used by the researchers were very artificial and distant from the ways in which children normally watch television. Despite the flaws in the research, in any case very few increases in aggressive or antisocial behaviour were observed in the children the researchers studied. Nevertheless, work such as this provided sufficient material to support campaigns for the regulation of children's television in order to protect what were seen as vulnerable audiences from programmes that might turn them into antisocial adults (see Chapter 10). Another result of this research was the launch of a campaign for the teaching of '**media literacy**' in schools, on the assumption that if children understood how television representations were

**effects** measurable outcomes produced by watching television, such as becoming more violent or adopting a certain opinion.

**media literacy** the skills and competence that viewers learn in order to understand easily the audio-visual 'languages' of media texts.

constructed, and were equipped with the study skills to analyse narrative and character, for example, they would be better able to negotiate the meanings of television for themselves.

More recently, the developing strands of work described in this chapter, in which more sophisticated methods of studying audiences were devised using interviews conducted at home or in more real-world settings, have been used to attempt to find out how children make meanings from their television viewing, and how their television experience fits into their broader social lives.

Several books have been published by the media academic David Buckingham (1993a, 1993b, 1996), who draws on the range of audience research techniques discussed in this chapter to explore both parents' and children's reactions to television. Some of this work focuses on cognitive issues, in other words what adults and children understand from television consciously, while other strands of the research focus on children's emotional and unconscious responses to television. The results show that both watching television and talking about programmes play a significant role in the process by which children learn to understand themselves, other people and society. Some of children's interaction with television involves learning and using knowledge of television codes and conventions (media literacy), such as the differences between television genres, narrative forms and placing programmes in context by deploying knowledge about the production processes involved in their making. It appears that the more children know about television codes, conventions and production processes, the more they are able to control the emotional reactions that are provoked by programmes. This seems to support the arguments made by academics and educators that the teaching of television and media in schools performs a useful social function. But, interestingly, some of the more controversial aspects of children's viewing of television also seemed to be both useful and important to them.

It is known that children sometimes consciously seek out disturbing programmes containing violence or sex, and programmes in the genres of horror or action adventure from which broadcasting regulations seek to protect them. Buckingham (1996) found that the function of watching these programmes for children was to test their own maturity in coping with troubling emotions. In other words, watching programmes that could be disturbing was part of a child's effort to grow up, to understand the adult world and to anticipate being part of it. A key concept in understanding this process is **modality**. Adults use the recognition of modality in order to judge whether representations are realistic, fantastic or comic, for example. Children watch violent, sexual or otherwise potentially disturbing programmes in order to learn how to deploy an understanding of modality, and thus to share the viewing practices of adults. Indeed, children's television programmes commonly feature central characters who are childlike even though they may be adults, thus representing the negotiations that real children in the audience make about their difference or similarity to adults and their place in the adult world. Characters in children's television programmes who are actually children are also commonly active in the narrative because adults fail to deal with a problem, or are incompetent.

Academic research on child viewers seems to confirm that, for children, the most important aspect of watching television is that it provides a resource for working through conscious and unconscious understandings of their identity, and their social position in relation to adults. Watching television is pleasurable for children, but it is also an essential part of their gradual integration into society as a whole.

**modality** the fit between a fictional representation and the conventional understanding of reality. High modality describes a close fit, and weak modality a distant one.

## ACTIVITY 12.6

To what extent do adults (like children) watch television not only in order to enjoy it but to test their reactions to disturbing issues such as violence or sex? How might modality be useful in explaining adults' use of the concept of realism as a standard against which to judge and evaluate programmes?

## Case study: soap opera audiences

In 1982 Dorothy Hobson produced an important study of women's relationship to television soap opera. Hobson's work focused on the original incarnation (1964–88) of ITV's soap opera *Crossroads*, in which the main characters worked in a motel in the Midlands, and which was screened in the early evenings in competition with the current affairs magazine *Nationwide* that David Morley (1980) studied (see above). Her concern was that the family environment could be regarded from a feminist point of view as a place in which women were subordinate. She wanted to learn how watching television fitted into the patterns of behaviour in the household, in particular how watching television might provide a space of pleasure and resistance for women at home.

For women at home, television provides a contact with the outside world, and watching television, Hobson found, was not a spare-time activity but rather an important part of women's daily routines. She found that women did not watch programmes that had connotations of masculinity, such as:

- news
- current affairs
- documentary
- sport.

Instead, they watched:

- comedy series
- soap opera
- light entertainment
- quiz programmes.

Television was perceived in gendered terms, with some formats and genres regarded as **feminine** and others as **masculine**. The programmes perceived as feminine were those that had connections with the personal and emotional concerns of everyday family life, or offered an escape through fantasy from the dreary routine of everyday life. Of course, these are precisely the programmes that are conventionally criticised as being trivial, trashy and lightweight. Hobson's research aimed to give value to these programmes and to the experiences of the women who watched them. In this respect it is part of a larger tradition of feminist work on television which seeks to redress the balance of power in society that tends to render women's experience less significant than that of men.

**feminine** having characteristics associated with the cultural role of women and not men.

**masculine** having characteristics associated with the cultural role of men and not women.

*continued*

Much of the work carried out in the 1980s on the domestic context of ordinary viewing focused on women viewers, and on programmes attractive to female audiences. Indeed, the genre of soap opera in particular became a focus of attention because the textual characteristics of the genre were argued to map closely on to traits recognised in society as feminine. The narrative structure of the soap opera is multi-layered and open ended. It is constructed in short segments, following a range of storylines, and does not come to an end. Whereas it might seem that nothing happens in soap opera, this is the result of attention being directed to the wrong things. Soap opera works primarily through dialogue, both between the characters in the programme and between members of the audience, who are invited to speculate about what will happen and to make judgements about the moral and emotional problems experienced by the characters. Talk and gossip are recognised by sociologists as important components of women's lives, as ways of constructing community and shared experience. Soap operas provide both a representation of this community and material that actual women can discuss with each other. Furthermore, since narrative information is conveyed largely through dialogue in soap opera, it is possible to watch soaps with what Tunstall (1983) called 'secondary involvement', getting on with other tasks and looking occasionally at the screen, while following the action by listening to the sound. Hobson (1982: 112) reported, 'the woman with whom I had gone to watch the programme [*Crossroads*] was serving the evening meal, feeding her five and three year old daughters and attempting to watch . . . on a black-and-white television situated on top of the freezer opposite the kitchen table'. *Crossroads* was constructed in the segmented form and with information conveyed primarily by dialogue that are characteristic of soap opera. Despite being scheduled at a time when women were often very busy, it could therefore be watched effectively by the distracted viewer. Commenting on Hobson's research, Storey (1999: 109) noted:

> Television is usually watched in the midst of other everyday activities. As Hobson discovered, domestic routines and responsibilities and the expectations of other family members ensured that most of the women with whom she watched *Crossroads* were not allowed the luxury of the detailed concentration expected and enjoyed by staff and students watching in darkened rooms on media-studies courses.

**prime time** the part of a day's television schedule when the greatest number of viewers may be watching, normally the mid-evening period.

The American **prime-time** soap opera *Dallas* became the subject of important studies by television theorists in the 1980s. This hour-long drama was set among the families of the oil barons of Texas, and focused on the struggles for power among the executives of the oil companies, and the family disputes, romantic affairs and personal problems that preoccupied them. The central characters of *Dallas* are the members of the Ewing family, and the storyline focuses on the sudden reversals of fortune, emotional crises and the relationships between business deals and personal allegiances that make up the daily life of its characters. While male characters, including J. R. Ewing and his brother Bobby, are significant to the narratives, J. R.'s wife Sue Ellen and other women are also central. The programme gained extraordinary popularity in the United States, Britain and worldwide, being shown in over ninety countries, including Turkey, Hong Kong, Australia and Morocco.

The most significant study of *Dallas* was by the Dutch media theorist Ien Ang, who published a book on the programme in 1985 (revised in 1989). Ang's aim was to understand how the predominantly female audience of *Dallas* fitted the programme into the texture of their daily lives, and to research the kind of pleasure and displeasure that they gained from it. In her native Netherlands *Dallas* was watched in the early 1980s by half of the population. At the time of her research three-quarters of that audience were women.

Ang placed an advertisement in the Dutch women's magazine *Viva*, asking people to write to her giving their reactions to the programme. She received forty-two replies, and her study analysed episodes of the programme. However, more significantly, it also analysed the discourses in the letters of the women who wrote to her. Since *Dallas* focuses largely on the emotional relationships between characters, Ang argued that the programme has a 'tragic' **structure of feeling**. By this, she meant that *Dallas* is structured so that any temporary resolution to the characters' problems gives rise to further narrative complication and emotional suffering. Ang argued that in order to gain this understanding of *Dallas*, its viewers must possess a cultural competence that she called a 'melodramatic imagination' (Ang 1989: 78). This was an orientation to everyday life in which ordinary problems could be granted the emotional significance and moral weight that are found in theatre **melodrama** or tragedy, thus giving enhanced value to events and experiences that could otherwise seem trivial. Ang found these characteristics in the performance style of the actors in *Dallas*, and showed that the behaviour of the characters formed a system of signs that communicated powerful inner feelings through external behaviour. For example, J. R. Ewing's wife Sue Ellen became an alcoholic, and her extreme behaviour functioned as a sign of her emotional disturbance provoked by the aggressive actions of her husband and his unfaithfulness to her.

The main conclusion of Ang's analysis was that its predominantly women viewers decoded and found pleasure in *Dallas* through a melodramatic imagination because of their ideological position in culture. Different decodings are produced by viewers who occupy different social positions in a particular society, as well as by viewers who live in different nations and cultures. Women in Western societies such as the Netherlands are expected to be emotional, caring and community-forming (as opposed to the masculine characteristics of adventurousness, aggression and individualism). The negotiation of the meanings of television programmes is affected not only by membership of a national culture but by the social status of the viewer in that culture. Ang found that there was a fit between the conventional meanings of femininity among the audience and the fictional moral and emotional world of *Dallas*. As well as finding the emotional and communal values of femininity in the programme itself, Ang noted that viewers' pleasure in the programme also depended on the sharing of its meanings with fellow women viewers. Audience responses to *Dallas* were determined not only by the text but by the social environment in which talk about the programme among women friends, workmates and family members took place. As in Hobson's analysis of *Crossroads*, Ang's semiotic analysis of *Dallas* showed that it conforms in its structure to the cultural competences that its female audience held. *Dallas* has few action sequences, and is primarily occupied with dialogue. The characters interact extensively with each other, and the giving and withholding of information through gossip is significant to the story. Viewers wrote about the realism of *Dallas*, but Ang (1989: 45) interpreted this as meaning *emotional* realism: 'the realism experience of the *Dallas* fans quoted . . . is situated at the emotional level: what is recognized as real is not knowledge of the world, but a subjective experience of the world'. This emotional realism is conveyed by a performance style in which characters say what they do not mean, and mean what they do not say, so that it is not only dialogue that conveys meaning but, for example, close-up shots of characters' reactions to events, which show how to read the meanings of the action.

Ang's study of *Dallas* is important in Television Studies for several reasons. It took seriously a very popular programme that had little credibility as 'quality television', suggesting that television theorists should direct their attention not only to prestigious programmes but to popular drama. Her work was written from a feminist point of view, putting on the critical

**structure of feeling**
the assumptions, attitudes and ideas prevalent in a society, arising from the ideologies underpinning that society.

**melodrama**
a form of drama characterised by exaggerated performance, a focus on reversals of fortune and extreme emotional reactions to events.

*continued*

agenda questions of gender and the politics of everyday life that contrasted with the emphasis of earlier critics on economics, social class and occupation. By making extensive use of the words of actual viewers, Ang sought to combine the analysis of a television programme from a textual point of view with evidence about how the decoding of meaning was carried out in ordinary, everyday circumstances.

We can compare this research from two decades ago with a more recent study of the viewers of *Big Brother* by Annette Hill (2002). She found that while 30 per cent of the males in her representative sample of eight thousand viewers watched reality TV programmes like *Big Brother* either regularly or occasionally, 48 per cent of the females watched them. So *Big Brother* had a significant appeal for women, and Hill suggests that viewers were probably drawing on their understanding of the 'emotional realism' that Ang discussed in soap operas. Viewers watched it because everyone else was watching it and it enabled them to join social groups and conversations, especially among young people or when older adults wished to connect with younger adults and children. The content that audiences most prized was the moment of revelation of the self: 'audiences look for the moment of authenticity when real people are "really" themselves in an unreal environment' (Hill 2002: 324). Many respondents mentioned 'Nasty' Nick and Mel in *Big Brother 1* in relation to this, and especially the moment when Nick cried when confronted by the fact that he had been cheating. But different categories of viewers interpreted the signs of performance versus authenticity differently:

> Young boys thought no adult would cry on camera unless they were genuinely upset, while some more cynical adults believed that crying to camera was a clear sign of performance. Thus, viewers judge the moment of authenticity in a gamedoc such as *BB* by referring to their knowledge of the contestants coupled with knowledge of themselves, and how they would react in a similar situation.
>
> (Hill 2002: 335)

The appeal of *Big Brother*, especially for women, was focused on emotion, and was judged by viewers in relation to their own experiences, which varied according to their gender and age group. Sixteen to thirty-four-year-olds were twice as likely as older viewers to watch it. And adults were twice as likely to watch it if they had children in their households, so the adults watched with their children, who were on school holidays at the time.

We can see that this emphasis on emotion, talk among viewers about the programme, and integrating the watching of *Big Brother* into family life all match the results that emerged from feminist work on soap opera, and show how more recent television genres, such as reality TV, have borrowed some of the characteristics, attractions and viewer responses that are found in the 'feminine' form of television soap opera.

Viewing context, such as watching television with other members of a family or with your best friends, affects viewing experience. People watching with their families will often be persuaded to watch something they do not enjoy, whereas watching a favourite programme with a group of friends might help confirm a person's shared relationships with members of that group. John Storey (1999: 114) summarises this social role of television viewing by arguing that:

> Watching television is always so much more than a series of acts of interpretation; it is above all else a social practice. That is, it can be a means to isolate oneself . . . or to make contact with other family members . . . In these ways, the cultural consumption of

television is as much about social relationships as it is about interpretations of individual programmes.

While women watching television might use it as a reward for work done in the home, their reasons for watching and the pleasures they gain might be quite different from, for instance, those of teenage girls watching MTV with their friends. Audience researchers have also studied people's talk about television. Information about who talks about television, to whom, where and how (for example, in the school playground, at work, in pubs, or when meeting other people for the first time) reveals the different roles television can play in making, breaking and maintaining social relationships. Researchers have looked at how 'television viewing is generally a somewhat busy activity, interrupted by many other activities and routinely accompanied by talk, much of it having nothing to do with the programme being watched' (Storey 1999: 16).

For the discipline of Television Studies in general, the shift of interest on to viewers and audiences rather than on television programmes as texts has focused on 'active' rather than 'passive' viewing, and provided good reasons to value kinds of viewing and kinds of television programme which have traditionally been considered of low quality. Rather than being passively positioned by the semiotic codes of a television programme, viewers can now be understood as makers of meaning. Watching television requires viewers to draw on their personal histories and their cultural, class, racial, economic or sexual identities, and to use their cultural competence, gained from media knowledge of comparable programmes and the various information sources available to them, to construct a relationship with the television programme in the context of their cultural lives.

## ACTIVITY 12.7

How might the watching of certain television programmes cement relationships between, for example, parents and young children, a group of *Doctor Who* fans or a group of teenage girls? Which programmes might be the most productive in cementing relationships, and what role would be played by talk among the viewers in these collective viewing situations?

## SUMMARY OF KEY POINTS

- Television Studies has developed ways of understanding how audiences make meanings from television, and debated the significance of television in everyday life.
- The television audience is considered not as a uniform mass but instead as a collection of diverse groups whose personal and social experiences shape their responses to television.

- Television Studies has taken a particular interest in audiences from groups with relatively little social power (such as children, fans of cult programmes and women at home), and their use of television to express their identities and form social networks.
- Studies of television audiences in different regions and countries have shown that television is understood differently in different social contexts.
- The methods used to study audiences range from the statistical methods used by television institutions to detailed and lengthy personal interviews with small groups of viewers in ordinary settings.
- Television Studies researchers have sought to reduce the distance between themselves and the ordinary viewers they study, in order to understand and value everyday television viewing.

## Further reading

Allen, R., 'Audience-oriented criticism and television', in R. Allen (ed.), *Channels of Discourse, Reassembled: Television and Contemporary Criticism* (London: Routledge, 1992), pp. 101–37.

Ang, I., *Living Room Wars: Rethinking Audiences for a Postmodern World* (London: Routledge, 1996.

—— *Watching Dallas: Soap Operas and the Melodramatic Imagination*, trans. D. Couling, revised edition (London: Routledge, 1989).

Ang, I. and J. Hermes, 'Gender and/in media consumption', in I. Ang, *Living Room Wars: Rethinking Audiences for a Postmodern World* (London: Routledge, 1996), pp. 108–29.

Bruhn Jensen, K. (ed.), *News of the World: World Cultures Look at Television News* (London: Routledge, 1998).

Buckingham, D., *Moving Images: Understanding Children's Emotional Responses to Television* (Manchester: Manchester University Press, 1996).

—— *Children Talking Television: The Making of Television Literacy* (London: Falmer, 1993a).

—— *Reading Audiences: Young People and the Media* (Manchester: Manchester University Press,1993b).

—— *Public Secrets: EastEnders and Its Audience* (London: BFI, 1987).

Dickinson, R., R. Harindranath and O. Linné (eds), *Approaches to Audiences: A Reader* (London: Arnold, 1998).

Dovey, J., *Freakshow* (Cambridge: Polity, 2000).

Dowmunt, T. (ed.), *Channels of Resistance: Global Television and Local Empowerment* (London: BFI, 1993).

Drummond, P. and R. Patterson (eds), *Television and Its Audience: International Research Perspectives* (London: BFI, 1988).

Geraghty, C., 'Audiences and "ethnography": questions of practice', in C. Geraghty and D. Lusted (eds), *The Television Studies Book* (London: Arnold, 1998), pp. 141–57.

—— *Women and Soap Opera: A Study of Prime Time Soaps* (Cambridge: Polity Press, 1991).

Gray, A., *Video Playtime: The Gendering of a Leisure Technology* (London: Routledge, 1992).

Hall, S., 'Encoding/decoding', in S. Hall, D. Hobson, A. Lowe and P. Willis (eds), *Culture, Media, Language* (London: Hutchinson, 1980), pp. 128–38.

Hallam, J. and M. Marshment, 'Framing experience: case studies in the reception of *Oranges Are not the Only Fruit*', *Screen*, 36:1 (1995), pp. 1–15.

Hill, A., *Big Brother*: the real audience', *Television and New Media*, 3: 3 (2002), pp. 323–41.

Hobson, D., *Crossroads: The Drama of a Soap Opera* (London: Methuen, 1982).

Holmes, S. and S. Redmond, *Framing Celebrity: New Directions in Celebrity Culture* (London: Routledge, 2006).

Jancovich, M. and J. Lyons (eds), *Quality Popular Television: Cult TV, the Industry and the Fans* (London: BFI, 2005).

Jenkins, H., *Textual Poachers: Television Fans and Participatory Culture* (London: Routledge, 1992).

Jermyn, D. and S. Holmes, 'The audience is dead; long live the audience!: Interactivity, "telephilia", and the contemporary television audience', *Critical Studies in Television*, 1:1 (2006), pp. 49–57.

Jones, J., 'Emerging platform identities: *Big Brother* UK and interactive multi-platform usage', in E. Mathijs and J. Jones (eds), *Big Brother International: Formats, Critics and Publics* (London: Wallflower, 2004), pp. 210–31.

Lewis, L. (ed.), *The Adoring Audience: Fan Culture and Popular Media* (London: Routledge, 1991).

Liebes, T. and Katz, E., *The Export of Meaning: Cross-cultural Readings of 'Dallas'* (New York: Oxford University Press, 1990).

Lull, J. (ed.), *World Families Watch Television* (London: Sage, 1988).

Morley, D., *Television, Audiences and Cultural Studies* (London: Routledge, 1992).

Petrie, D. and J. Willis (eds), *Television and the Household: Reports from the BFI's Audience Tracking Study* (London: BFI, 1995).

Ruddock, A., *Understanding Audiences: Theory and Method* (London: Sage, 2001).

Storey, J. *Cultural Consumption and Everyday Life* (London: Arnold, 1999).

Tulloch, J., *Watching Television Audiences: Cultural Theories and Methods* (London: Arnold, 2000).

Tulloch, J. and H. Jenkins, *Science Fiction Audiences: Watching Doctor Who and Star Trek* (London: Routledge, 1995).

# Glossary of key terms

**180-degree rule** the convention that cameras are positioned only on one side of an imaginary line drawn to connect two performers in a scene. This produces a coherent sense of space for the viewer.

**active audience** television audiences regarded not as passive consumers of meanings but as negotiating meanings for themselves that are often resistant to those meanings that are intended or that are discovered by close analysis.

**actuality footage** television pictures representing an event that was filmed live. The term usually refers to pictures of news events.

**adaptation** transferring a novel, theatre play, poem, etc. from its original medium into another medium, such as television.

**aesthetic** a specific artistic form. Aesthetics means the study of art and beauty.

**affiliates** local television stations (normally in the USA) that have made agreements (affiliations) with a network to broadcast programmes offered by that network rather than another.

**analogue** broadcasting signals in waves of varying frequency. Analogue signals require greater space or 'bandwidth' than digital signals, and do not allow interactive response from viewers.

**Annan Committee** a committee reporting in 1977 to government on the future of broadcasting. It supported public service broadcasting, the funding of the BBC by licence fee, and the planned introduction of a fourth television channel.

**anthology** a series of separate, unconnected programmes broadcast under a shared title.

**anthropology** the study of humankind, including the evolution of humans and the different kinds of human society existing in different times and places.

**art video** the use of video technology in artistic work intended for gallery exhibition.

**audience share** the percentage of viewers estimated to have watched one channel as opposed to another channel broadcasting at the same time.

**authorship** the question of who an author is, the role of the author as creator and the significance of the author's input into the material being studied.

**avant-garde** work aiming to challenge the norms and conventions of its medium, and the group of people making such work.

**back lighting** lighting the subject of a shot from behind to provide depth by separating the subject from the background.

**balance**  the requirement in television news and current affairs to present both sides of an argument or issue.

**BARB (Broadcasters Audience Research Bureau)**  the independent body that gathers and reports viewing statistics on behalf of UK television institutions.

**binary opposition**  two contrasting terms, ideas or concepts, such as inside/outside, masculine/feminine or culture/nature.

**blooper**  a mistake by a performer in a programme, or a technical error. The term often refers to humorous mistakes.

**bourgeoisie**  the middle class, who are owners of property and businesses.

**brand recognition**  the ability of audiences to recognise the distinctive identity of a product, service or institution and the values and meanings associated with it.

**broadcasting**  the transmission of signals from a central source which can be received by dispersed receivers over a large geographical area.

**budget**  the money allocated to the making of a particular programme or series of programmes, which is controlled by the producer.

**cable television**  originally called Community Antenna Television (CATV). Transmission of television signals along cables in the ground.

**capitalism**  the organisation of an economy around the private ownership of accumulated wealth, involving the exploitation of labour to produce profit that creates such wealth.

**censorship**  the omission of sensitive, prohibited or disturbing material at any stage in the production process from the initial idea to its transmission.

**class**  a section of society defined by their relationship to economic activity, whether as workers (the working class) or possessors of economic power (the bourgoisie), for example.

**classic serial**  the dramatisation in serial form of literature written in the past, most often in the nineteenth and early twentieth centuries, where the literary source already has high cultural status.

**close-up**  a camera shot where the frame is filled by the face of a person or a detail of a face. Close-ups may also show details of an object or place.

**closed-circuit television (CCTV)**  a small-scale television system where the images and sound are not intended for broadcast: for example, a network of security cameras.

**CNN**  Cable News Network, the first international satellite news channel, operating from the United States.

**code**  in semiotics, a system or set of rules that shapes how signs can be used, and therefore how meanings can be made and understood.

**commercial television**  television funded by the sale of advertising time or sponsorship of programmes.

**commissioning** the process by which an idea for a programme is selected to go into production.

**committed** a term used in the study of the politics of culture, implying that a person or a text has a commitment to positive and progressive social change.

**commodity** a raw material or product whose economic value is established by market price rather than the intrinsic qualities or usefulness of the material or product itself.

**computer generated imaging (CGI)** the creation of images by programming computers with mathematical equations that can generate realistic two-dimensional pictures.

**connotations** the term used in semiotic analysis for the meanings that are associated with a particular sign or combination of signs.

**consensus** a shared and accepted opinion or attitude among a certain group of people.

**conventions** the frameworks and procedures used to make or interpret texts.

**convergence** the process whereby previously separate media technologies merge. For example, computers can now send faxes, show DVD films and play music.

**copyright** the legal right of ownership over written, visual or aural material, including the prohibition on copying this material without permission from its owner.

**couch potatoes** a derogatory term for television viewers supposedly sitting motionless at home watching television passively and indiscriminately.

**cultural imperialism** the critical argument that powerful nations and regions (especially those of the Western world) dominate less developed nations and regions by exporting values and ideologies.

**Cultural Studies** the academic discipline devoted to studying culture, involving work on texts, institutions, audiences and economic contexts.

**culture** the shared attitudes, ways of life and assumptions of a group of people.

**cut** the moment at which one camera shot ceases and another begins, where no transitional visual effect (such as a fade or a dissolve) is used.

**cutaway** in fictional dialogue or interviews, shots that do not include people speaking. Cutaways often consist of details of the setting or of interviewees (such as hands).

**demography** the study of population, and the groupings of people (demographic groups) within the whole population.

**denotation** in semiotics, the function of signs to portray or refer to something in the real world.

**deregulation** the removal of legal restrictions or guidelines that regulate the economics of the television industry or the standards to which programmes must adhere.

**dialectic** a term associated especially with Marxist theories, meaning a struggle between two opposing ideas.

**diegesis** the telling of events as narrative. Diegetic sound is sound emanating from the represented environment, and extra-diegetic sound comes from outside that environment.

**digital television** television pictures and sound encoded into the ones and zeros of electronic data. Digital signals can also be sent back down cables by viewers, making possible interaction with television programmes.

**director** the person responsible for the creative process of turning a script or idea into a finished programme, by working with a technical crew, performers and an editor.

**discourse** a particular use of language for a certain purpose in a certain context (such as academic discourse or poetic discourse), and similarly, in television, a particular usage of television's audio-visual 'language' (news programme discourse or nature documentary discourse, for instance).

**documentary** a form aiming to record actual events, often with an explanatory purpose or to analyse and debate an issue.

**docusoap** a television form combining documentary's depiction of non-actors in ordinary situations with soap opera's continuing narratives about selected characters.

**dolly** a wheeled camera platform. A 'dolly shot' is a camera shot where the camera is moved forward or back using this platform.

**drama-documentary** a television form combining dramatised storytelling with the 'objective' informational techniques of documentary. Abbreviated as 'dramadoc' or 'docudrama'.

**dubbing** replacing the original speech in a programme, advertisement, etc. with speech added later, often to translate speech in a foreign language.

**dumbing-down** the notion that television has declined in quality when compared to an earlier period, showing programmes that are more 'dumb' or stupid and addressing its audience as if they were stupid.

**effects** measurable outcomes produced by watching television, such as becoming more violent or adopting a certain opinion.

**electronic news-gathering (ENG)** the use of lightweight cameras and digital technology such as portable satellite transmission dishes to record and transmit news pictures and sound.

**ethnicity** membership of a group with a specific identity based on a sense of belonging, such as British-Asian or Italian-American.

**ethnography** the detailed study of how people live, conducted by observing behaviour and talking to selected individuals about their attitudes and activities.

**fan culture** the activities of groups of fans, as distinct from 'ordinary' viewers.

**Federal Communications Commission (FCC)** the government body in the USA which regulates the operations and output of television companies and other broadcasters.

**feminine** having characteristics associated with the cultural role of women and not men.

**feminism** the political and theoretical thinking which in different ways considers the roles of women and femininity in society and culture, often with the aim of critiquing current roles and changing them for the better.

**final cut** the final edited version of a programme that is delivered to the television institution for broadcast.

**flashback** a television sequence marked as representing events that happened in a time previous to the programme's present.

**flow** the ways in which programmes, advertisements, etc. follow one another in an unbroken sequence across the day or part of the day, and the experience of watching the sequence of programmes, advertisements, trailers, etc.

**fly-on-the-wall** a documentary form where the subject is observed without the programme-maker's intervention.

**focus groups** small groups of selected people representing larger social groupings, such as people of a certain age group, gender or economic status, who take part in discussions about a topic chosen for investigation.

**format** the blueprint for a programme, including its setting, main characters, genre, form and main themes.

**found footage** television or film sequences 'found' in previously made programmes or films, and which can be incorporated unchanged into the programme being made.

**franchise** the right to broadcast on the terrestrial ITV channel for a set number of years, secured by paying a fee to government.

**Frankfurt School** a group of theorists in the mid-twentieth century who worked on theories of contemporary culture from a Marxist perspective. Key members, notably Theodor Adorno and Max Horkheimer, left Nazi Germany in the 1930s to work abroad.

**free market** a television market place where factors such as quotas and regulations do not restrict the free operation of economic 'laws' of supply and demand.

**free-to-air** television programming for which viewers make no direct payment.

**gallery** the enclosed room in a television studio where production staff observe the shooting of a programme and control the activities of camera operators, sound technicians, performers and other personnel.

**gatekeepers** the critical term used for the people and institutions (such as commissioning producers and regulatory bodies) who control access to television broadcasting.

**gender** the social and cultural division of people into masculine or feminine individuals. This is different from sex, which refers to the biological difference between male and female bodies.

**genre** a type of programme. Programmes of the same genre have shared characteristics.

**globalisation** the process whereby ownership of television institutions in different nations and regions is concentrated in the hands of international corporations, and whereby programmes and formats are traded between institutions around the world.

**hegemony** a term deriving from Marxist theories of society, meaning a situation where different social classes or groups are persuaded to consent to a political order that may be detrimental to them.

**hype** publicity and public relations effort aiming to raise interest in a television programme or an aspect of one.

**iconic sign** in semiotics, a sign which resembles its referent. Photographs, for example, contain iconic signs resembling the objects they represent.

**identification** a term deriving from psychoanalytic theories of cinema, which describes the viewer's conscious or unconscious wish to take the place of someone or something in a television text.

**idents** the symbols representing production companies, television channels, etc., often comprising graphics or animations.

**ideology** the set of beliefs, attitudes and assumptions arising from the economic and class divisions in a culture, underlying the ways of life accepted as normal in that culture.

**independent production companies** businesses making television programmes which can be sold to television networks that transmit and distribute them.

**Independent Television Authority (ITA)** the first official body set up to regulate commercial television in Britain.

**indexical sign** in semiotics, a sign which is the result of what it signifies, in the way that smoke is the result of fire.

**information society** a contemporary highly developed culture (especially Western culture) where the production and exchange of information is more significant than conventional industrial production.

**interactive** offering the opportunity for viewers to respond to what is broadcast, by sending signals back to the broadcaster (along a cable or phone-line, for example).

**intertextuality** how one text draws on the meanings of another by referring to it, by allusion, quotation or parody, for example.

**licence fee** an annual payment by all owners of television sets, which is the main source of income for the BBC.

**location** any place in which television images are shot, except inside a television studio.

**long shot** a camera shot taking in the whole body of a performer, or more generally a shot with a wide field of vision.

**long take** an imprecise term denoting a longer than usual uninterrupted camera shot.

**market research** the collection of information about consumers and their preferences, used to identify products that can be advertised to consumers likely to buy them.

**Marxism** the political and economic theories associated with the German nineteenth-century theorist Karl Marx, who described and critiqued capitalist societies and proposed communism as a revolutionary alternative.

**masculine** having characteristics associated with the cultural role of men and not women.

**media imperialism** the critical argument that powerful nations and cultures (especially the USA) exert control over other nations and cultures through the media products they export.

**media literacy** the skills and competence that viewers learn in order to understand easily the audio-visual 'languages' of media texts.

**MediaWatch** previously the National Viewers' and Listeners' Association, an organisation devoted to monitoring the activities of British broadcasters, with a special interest in upholding standards of taste and decency.

**melodrama** a form of drama characterised by exaggerated performance, a focus on reversals of fortune and extreme emotional reactions to events.

**merchandising** the sale of products associated with a television programme, such as toys, books and clothing.

**metaphor** the carrying-over from something of some of its meanings on to another thing of an apparently different kind. For example, a television narrative about life aboard ship could be a metaphor for British social life (the ship as metaphor for society).

**metonymy** the substitution of one thing for another, either because one is part of the other or because one is connected with the other. For example, 'the Crown' can be a metonym for the British state.

**microwave link** the transmission across large distances of digital signals carried by high-frequency microwaves, to ground stations or to satellites.

***mise-en-scène*** literally meaning 'putting on stage', all the elements of a shot or sequence that contribute to its meanings, such as lighting, camera position and setting.

**modality** the fit between a fictional representation and the conventional understanding of reality. High modality describes a close fit, and weak modality a distant one.

**monopoly** control over the provision of a service or product by one institution or business.

**multi-accentuality** the situation where meanings are able to be read in different ways by different groups of viewers because a text offers multiple meanings at the same time.

**narration** the process of telling a story through image and sound. Narration can also refer to the spoken text accompanying television images.

**narrative** an ordered sequence of images and sound that tells a fictional or factual story.

**natural break** a vague term meaning a point at which a programme can be interrupted without causing undue disruption to the ongoing flow.

**naturalism** originally having a very specific meaning in literature and drama, this term is now used more loosely to denote television fiction that adopts realistic conventions of character portrayal, linear cause-and-effect narrative, and a consistent and recognisable fictional world.

**negotiated reading** a viewer interpretation of a television text where the viewer understands meaning in relation to his or her own knowledge and experience, rather than simply accepting the meaning proposed by the text.

**network** a television institution that transmits programmes through local or regional broadcasting stations that are owned by or affiliated to that institution.

**news agency** a media institution that gathers news reports and distributes them to its customers (who include television news broadcasters).

**news value** the degree of significance attributed to a news story, where items with high news value are deemed most significant to the audience.

**niche audiences** particular groups of viewers defined by age group, gender or economic status, for example, who may be the target audience for a programme.

**noddy shot** in television interviews, shots of the interviewer reacting silently (often by nodding) to the interviewee's responses to questions.

**observational documentary** a documentary form in which the programme-maker aims to observe neutrally what would have happened even if he or she had not been present.

**Ofcom** the Office of Communications, a government body responsible for regulating television and other communications media in Britain.

**off-line editing** the first stage of editing a completed programme, where the sequence of shots, sounds and music is established.

**online editing** the final stage of editing a completed programme, where effects are added and a high-quality version of the programme is produced.

**outside broadcast** the television transmission of outdoor events such as sport or ceremonial occasions, using equipment set up in advance for the purpose. Abbreviated as OB.

**outsourcing** obtaining services from an independent business rather than from within a television institution, usually as a means of cutting costs.

**outtake** a shot or sequence which was omitted from a finished programme because of a mistake during production or an artistic decision.

**PAL** Phased Alternate Line transmission of television pictures, a German technical standard introduced in the 1960s making possible improved picture quality and colour pictures.

**pan** a shot where the camera is turned to the left or to the right. The term derives from the word 'panorama', suggesting the wide visual field that a pan can reveal.

**pan-and-scan** capturing a section of an image and enlarging it to fill the television frame, a technique used to fit wide film images into the square television screen.

**pastiche** the imitation of forms or conventions in another text. The term can convey a negative view that the imitation is less effective or valuable than the original.

**patriarchy** a social system in which power is held by men rather than women, and masculine values dominate.

**pay-per-view** specific television programmes (such as sports events or films) offered to subscribers on payment of a fixed, one-off fee.

**people meter** a device resembling a television remote control, used in sample households to monitor what viewers watch. Viewers record which channels they watch and for how long.

**period drama** television fiction set in the past, most often the nineteenth or early twentieth centuries.

**personal video recorder (PVR)** a device that records digital television onto a microchip for storage and replay, and can automatically record programmes it thinks the viewer will enjoy.

**personalities** people appearing on television who are recognised by audiences as celebrities with a media image and public status beyond the role they play in a particular programme.

**Pilkington Report** the report of a government committee chaired by Lord Pilkington (1960) whose recommendations included the setting up of a second BBC television channel.

**pitch** a very short written or spoken outline for a programme, perhaps only a few sentences, often used to persuade a commissioning producer to commission the programme.

**point of view shot** a camera shot where the camera is placed in, or close to, the position from where a previously seen character might look.

**polysemia** the quality of having multiple meanings at the same time. Texts like this are called 'polysemic'.

**pool system** in journalism, grouping journalists together to share information so that all of them need not be present at a news event.

**popular culture** the texts created by ordinary people (as opposed to an elite group) or created for them, and the ways these are used.

**Postmaster General** the person appointed by government to regulate communications institutions such as the Post Office, radio and television.

**postmodernism** the most recent phase of capitalist culture, the aesthetic forms and styles associated with it, and the theoretical approaches developed to understand it.

**preferred reading** an interpretation of a text that seems to be the one most encouraged by the text; the 'correct' interpretation.

**prime time** the part of a day's television schedule when the greatest number of viewers may be watching, normally the mid-evening period.

**private sphere** the domestic world of the home, family and personal life.

**privatisation** the policy of placing industries or institutions in the hands of privately owned businesses, rather than state ownership.

**producer** the person working for a television institution who is responsible for the budget, planning and making of a television programme or series of programmes.

**production values** the level of investment in a television production, such as the amount spent on costumes, props, effects and sets.

**progressive** encouraging positive change or progress, usually implying progress towards fairer and more equal ways of organising society.

**psychoanalysis** the study of human mental life, including not only conscious thoughts, wishes and fears but unconscious ones. Psychoanalysis is an analytical and theoretical set of ideas as well as a therapeutic treatment.

**public service** in television, the provision of a mix of programmes that inform, educate and entertain in ways that encourage the betterment of audiences and society in general.

**public sphere** the world of politics, economic affairs and national and international events, as opposed to the 'private sphere' of domestic life.

**public television** television funded by government or by private supporters, rather than solely by advertising.

**quality** in television, kinds of programme that are perceived as more expensively produced and, especially, more culturally worthwhile than other programmes.

**quota** a proportion of television programming, such as a proportion of programmes made in a particular nation.

**ratings** the number of viewers estimated to have watched certain programmes, as compared to the numbers watching other programmes.

**realism** the aim for representations to reproduce reality faithfully, and the ways this is done.

**reality TV** programmes where the unscripted behaviour of 'ordinary people' is the focus of interest.

**reflexivity** a text's reflection on its own status as a text: for example, drawing attention to generic conventions, or revealing the technologies used to make a programme.

**register** a term in the study of language for the kinds of speech or writing used to represent a particular kind of idea or to address a certain audience.

**regulation** the control of television institutions by laws, codes of practice or guidelines.

**resistance** the ways in which audiences make meaning from television programmes that is counter to the meanings thought to be intended, or that are discovered by close analysis.

**satellite television** television signals beamed from a ground transmitter to a stationary satellite that broadcasts the signal to a specific area (called the 'footprint') below it.

**satire** a mode of critical commentary about society or an aspect of it, using humour to attack people or ideas.

**schedule** the arrangement of programmes, advertisements and other material into a sequential order within a certain period of time, such as an evening, day or week.

**semiotics** the study of signs and their meanings, initially developed for the study of spoken language, and now used also to study the visual and aural 'languages' of other media such as television.

**serial** a television form in which a developing narrative unfolds across a sequence of separate episodes.

**series** a television form in which each programme in the series has a different story or topic, though settings, main characters and performers remain the same.

**set-top box** the electronic decoding equipment connected to home television sets that allows access to digital television signals.

**shooting ratio** the number of minutes of film used to film a scene or complete programme as compared to the screen-time of the finished scene or programme.

**shot-reverse-shot** the convention of alternating a shot of one character and a shot of another character in a scene, producing a back-and-forth movement which represents their interaction visually.

**sign** in semiotics, something which communicates meaning, such as a word, an image or a sound.

**simulation** a representation that mirrors an aspect of reality so perfectly that it takes the place of the reality it aims to reproduce.

**slot** the position in a television schedule where a programme is shown.

**soap opera** a continuing drama serial involving a large number of characters in a specific location, focusing on relationships, emotions and reversals of fortune.

**sociology** the academic study of society, aiming to describe and explain aspects of life in that society.

**spectacle** a fascinating image which draws attention to its immediate surface meanings and offers visual pleasure for its own sake.

**spin-off** a product, television programme, book, etc. that is created to exploit the reputation, meaning or commercial success of a previous one, often in a different medium from the original.

**sponsorship** the funding of programmes or channels by businesses, whose names are usually prominently displayed in the programmes or channels as a means of advertising.

**status quo** the ways in which culture and society are currently organised.

**storyboard** a sequence of drawn images showing the shots to be used in a programme.

**strand** a linked series of programmes, sharing a common title.

**stripping** in television scheduling, placing a programme or genre of programme at the same time on several days of each week.

**structure of feeling** the assumptions, attitudes and ideas prevalent in a society, arising from the ideologies underpinning that society.

**subject** in psychoanalysis, the term for the individual self whose identity has both conscious and unconscious components.

**subscription** payment to a television broadcaster in exchange for the opportunity to view programmes on certain channels that are otherwise blocked.

**subtitle** written text appearing on the television screen, normally to translate speech in a foreign language.

**symbol** a representation which condenses many meanings together and can stand for those many meanings in a certain context. For example, a brand-new car could be a symbol of wealth, social status and masculine prowess.

**symbolic sign** in semiotics, a sign which is connected arbitrarily to its referent rather than because the sign resembles its referent. For example, a photograph of a cat resembles it, whereas the word 'cat' does not: the latter is a symbolic sign.

**syndication** the sale of programmes for regional television broadcasters to transmit within their territory.

**syntagm** in semiotics, a linked sequence of signs existing at a certain point in time. Written or spoken sentences and television sequences are examples of syntagmas.

**taste and decency** conformity to the standards of good taste and acceptable language and behaviour represented on television, as required by regulations.

**teaser** a very short television sequence advertising a forthcoming programme, often puzzling or teasing to viewers because it contains little information and encourages curiosity and interest.

**telenovela** a fictional continuing melodrama on television that lasts for a specific number of episodes. Telenovelas are particularly associated with South American television.

**terrestrial** broadcasting from a ground-based transmission system, as opposed to broadcasting via satellite.

**text** an object such as a television programme, film or poem, considered as a network of meaningful signs that can be analysed and interpreted.

**textual analysis** a critical approach which seeks to understand a television text's meanings by undertaking detailed analysis of its image and sound components, and the relationships between those components.

**title sequence** the sequence at the opening of a television programme in which the programme title and performers' names may appear along with other information, accompanied by images, sound and music introducing the programme.

**tracking shot** a camera shot where the camera is moved along (often on a miniature railway track) parallel to a moving subject of the shot while photographing it.

**trailer** a short television sequence advertising a forthcoming programme, usually containing selected 'highlights' from the programme.

**treatment** a short written outline for a programme, usually written for a commissioning producer to read, specifying how the programme will tell its story or address its subject.

**uplink** the electronic system which beams television signals from the ground to a satellite for onward transmission to a television institution elsewhere.

**uses and gratifications** a theoretical approach that assumes people engage in an activity because it provides them with a benefit of some kind.

**utopia** an ideal society.

**variety programmes** entertainment programmes containing a mix of material, such as songs and comedy sketches.

**vertical integration** the control by media institutions of all levels of a business, from the production of products to their distribution and means of reception.

**voice-over** speech accompanying visual images but not presumed to derive from the same place or time as the images.

**vox pop** literally meaning 'the voice of the people', short television interviews conducted with members of the public, usually in the street.

**voyeurism** gaining sexual pleasure from looking at someone or something surreptitiously.

**watershed** the time in the day (conventionally 9.00 p.m.) after which programmes with content that may disturb children can be shown.

**whip-pan** a very rapid panning shot from one point to another.

**zapping** hopping rapidly from channel to channel while watching television, using a remote control (a 'zapper').

# Select bibliography

Addley, E., 'Why the cameras love us', *Guardian* Big Brother supplement, 14 September 2002, pp. 14–16.

Allen, J., 'The social matrix of television: invention in the United States', in E. A. Kaplan (ed.), *Regarding Television: Critical Approaches – An Anthology* (Los Angeles: AFI, 1983), pp. 109–19.

Allen, R. (ed.), 'Audience-oriented criticism and television', in R. Allen (ed.), *Channels of Discourse, Reassembled: Television and Contemporary Criticism* (London: Routledge, 1992a), pp. 101–37.

—— *Channels of Discourse, Reassembled: Television and Contemporary Criticism* (London: Routledge, 1992b).

—— *Speaking of Soap Operas* (Chapel Hill, S.C.: University of South Carolina Press, 1985).

Allen, S., G. Branston and C. Carter (eds), *News, Gender and Power* (London: Routledge, 1998).

Alleyne, M., *News Revolution: Political and Economic Decisions about Global Information* (Basingstoke: Macmillan, 1997).

Alps, T., 'Is it make or break time for TV ads?', *Guardian* Media section, 11 November 2004, p. 8.

Althusser, L., 'Ideology and ideological state apparatuses: notes towards an investigation', in *Lenin and Philosophy* (London: New Left Books, 1971), pp. 121–73.

Alvarado, M. and J. Thompson (eds), *The Media Reader* (London: BFI, 1990).

Amadiegwu, M., 'Don't shoot this messenger', *Guardian* Media section, 3 July 2006, p. 7.

Ang, I., 'Melodramatic identifications: television fiction and women's fantasy', in C. Brunsdon, J. D'Acci and L. Spigel (eds), *Feminist Television Criticism: A Reader* (Oxford: Oxford University Press, 1997), pp. 155–66.

—— *Living Room Wars: Rethinking Audiences for a Postmodern World* (London: Routledge, 1996).

—— *Desperately Seeking the Audience* (London: Routledge, 1991).

—— *Watching Dallas: Soap Operas and the Melodramatic Imagination*, trans. D. Couling, revised edition (London: Routledge, 1989).

Ang, I. and J. Hermes, 'Gender and/in media consumption', in I. Ang, *Living Room Wars: Rethinking Audiences for a Postmodern World* (London: Routledge, 1996), pp. 108–29.

Annan Committee, *Report of the Committee on the Future of Broadcasting* (London: HMSO, 1977).

Armstrong, S., 'Go figure: Black viewing', *Guardian* Media section, 22 May 2006, p. 9.

Badsey, S., 'The influence of the media on recent British military operations', in I.

Stewart and S. Carruthers (eds), *War, Culture and the Media: Representations of the Military in Twentieth-Century Britain* (Trowbridge: Flicks Books, 1993), pp. 5–21.

Balnaves, M., J. Donald and S. Hemelryk Donald, *The Global Media Atlas* (London: BFI, 2001).

Bandura, A., *Social Learning Theory* (London: Prentice Hall, 1977).

Barker, C., *Global Television: An Introduction* (Oxford: Blackwell, 1997).

Baudrillard, J., 'The reality gulf', *Guardian*, 11 January 1991, reprinted in P. Brooker and W. Brooker (eds), *Postmodern After-Images: A Reader in Film, Television and Video* (London: Arnold, 1997), pp. 165–7.

—— *In the Shadow of the Silent Majorities*, trans. P. Foss, J. Johnson and P. Patton (New York: Semiotext(e), 1983a).

—— *Simulations* (New York: Semiotext(e), 1983b).

Bayes, S., *The Avid Handbook*, third edition (Woburn, Mass.: Butterworth-Heinemann, 2000).

Bazalgette, C. and D. Buckingham (eds), *In Front of the Children: Screen Entertainment and Young Audiences* (London: BFI, 1995).

BBC, *Producers' Guidelines* (London: BBC, 1993).

Benjamin, W., 'The work of art in the age of mechanical reproduction', in *Illuminations*, ed. H. Arendt, trans. H. Zohn (New York: Schocken Books, 1969), pp. 219–54.

Bennett, J., 'The public service value of interactive television', *New Review of Film and Television Studies*, 4:3 (2006), pp. 263–85.

Bertens, H., *The Idea of the Postmodern: A History* (London: Routledge, 1995).

Bignell, J., 'Seeing and knowing: reflexivity and quality', in J. McCabe and K. Akass (eds), *Contemporary American TV Drama: The Quality Debate* (London: I. B. Tauris, 2007).

—— *Big Brother: Reality TV in the Twenty-first Century* (Basingstoke: Palgrave Macmillan, 2005).

—— 'Sex, confession and witness', in K. Akass and J. McCabe (eds), *Reading 'Sex and the City'* (London and New York: I. B. Tauris, 2004), pp. 161–76.

—— *Media Semiotics: An Introduction*, second edition (Manchester: Manchester University Press, 2002a).

—— 'Writing the child in media theory', *Yearbook of English Studies*, 32 (2002b), pp. 127–39.

—— 'Docudrama as melodrama: representing Princess Diana and Margaret Thatcher', in B. Carson and M. Llewellyn-Jones (eds), *Frames and Fictions on Television: The Politics of Identity within Drama* (Exeter: Intellect, 2000a), pp. 17–26.

—— *Postmodern Media Culture* (Edinburgh: Edinburgh University Press, 2000b).

Bignell, J., S. Lacey and M. Macmurraugh-Kavanagh (eds), *British Television Drama: Past, Present and Future* (Basingstoke: Palgrave, 2000).

Billingham, P., *Sensing the City through Television* (Exeter: Intellect, 2000).

Born, G., *Uncertain Vision: Birt, Dyke and the Reinvention of the BBC* (London: Vintage, 2005).

Boyd-Barrett, O. and T. Rantanen, *The Globalization of News* (London: Sage, 1998).

Boyle, R. and R. Haynes, *Power Play: Sport, the Media and Popular Culture* (Harlow: Pearson, 2000).

Brandt, G. (ed.), *British Television Drama in the 1980s* (Cambridge: Cambridge University Press, 1993).

Branston, G. and R. Stafford, *The Media Student's Book*, second edition (London: Routledge, 1999).

Briggs, A. and P. Cobley (eds), *The Media: An Introduction* (Harlow: Addison Wesley Longman, 1998).

Broadcasting Standards Commission, *Codes of Guidance* (London: BSC, 1998).

Brooker, P. and W. Brooker (eds), *Postmodern After-Images: A Reader in Film, Television and Video* (London: Arnold, 1997).

Brown, I., 'TV in the Englishman's castle', *BBC Year Book 1951* (London: BBC, 1951), pp. 17–19.

Brown, M., 'Swapping success', *Guardian* Media section, 4 October 2004a, p. 10.

—— 'The £100m crisis at Channel 4', *Guardian* Media section, 11 November 2004b, pp. 8–9.

—— 'Vying for VIPs', *Guardian* Media section, 5 March 2001, pp. 8–9.

Brown, M. and M. Wells, 'How did it rate?', *Guardian* Media section, 27 August 2001, pp. 2–3.

Bruhn Jensen, K. (ed.), *News of the World: World Cultures Look at Television News* (London: Routledge, 1998).

Brunsdon, C., *The Feminist, the Housewife, and the Soap Opera* (Oxford: Oxford University Press, 2000).

—— 'Structure of anxiety: recent British television crime fiction', *Screen*, 39:3 (1998a), pp. 223–43.

—— 'What is the television of Television Studies?', in C. Geraghty and D. Lusted (eds), *The Television Studies Book* (London: Arnold, 1998b), pp. 95–113.

—— 'Problems with quality', *Screen*, 31:1 (1990), pp. 67–90.

—— '*Crossroads* – notes on soap opera', *Screen*, 22:4 (1981), pp. 32–7.

Brunsdon, J., J. D'Acci and L. Spigel, 'Introduction', in C. Brunsdon, J. D'Acci, and L. Spigel (eds), *Feminist Television Criticism: A Reader* (Oxford: Oxford University Press, 1997), pp. 1–16.

Bruzzi, S., *The New Documentary: A Critical Introduction* (London: Routledge, 2000).

Bryant, S., *The Television Heritage: Television Archiving Now and in an Uncertain Future* (London: BFI, 1989).

Buckingham, D., *Moving Images: Understanding Children's Emotional Responses to Television* (Manchester: Manchester University Press, 1996).

—— *Children Talking Television: The Making of Television Literacy* (London: Falmer, 1993a).

—— *Reading Audiences: Young People and the Media* (Manchester: Manchester University Press, 1993b).

—— *Public Secrets: EastEnders and Its Audience* (London: BFI, 1987).

Burton, G., *Talking Television: An Introduction to the Study of Television* (London: Arnold, 2000).

Calabrese, A., 'The trade in television news', in J. Wasko (ed.), *A Companion to Television* (Malden, Mass., and Oxford: Blackwell, 2005), pp. 270–90.

Campion, M. J., *Look Who's Talking: Cultural Diversity, Public Service Broadcasting and the National Conversation* (Oxford: Nuffield, 2005).

Carson, B. and M. Llewellyn-Jones (eds), *Frames and Fictions on Television: The Politics of Identity within Drama* (Exeter: Intellect, 2000).

Caughie, J., *Television Drama: Realism, Modernism, and British Culture* (Oxford: Oxford University Press, 2000).

—— 'Television criticism: a discourse in search of an object', *Screen*, 25:4–5 (1984), pp. 109–20.

—— 'Progressive television and documentary drama', *Screen*, 21:3 (1980) pp. 4–35.

Clarke, A., '"You're nicked!": television police series and the fictional representation of law and order', in D. Strinati and S. Wagg (eds), *Come on Down? Popular Media Culture in Post-war Britain* (London: Routledge, 1992), pp. 232–53.

Coles, G., 'Docusoap: actuality and the serial format', in B. Carson and M. Llewellyn-Jones (eds), *Frames and Fictions on Television: The Politics of Identity within Drama* (Exeter: Intellect, 2000), pp. 27–39.

Collins, J., 'Postmodernism and television', in R. Allen (ed.), *Channels of Discourse, Reassembled: Television and Contemporary Criticism* (London: Routledge, 1992), pp. 327–53.

Cook, G., *The Discourse of Advertising* (London: Routledge, 1992).

Cooke, L., *British Television Drama: A History* (London: BFI, 2003).

Corner, J., '"A fiction (un)like any other"?', *Critical Studies in Television*, 1:1 (2006), pp. 89–96.

—— *Critical Ideas in Television Studies* (Oxford: Clarendon, 1999).

—— *Studying Media: Problems of Theory and Method* (London: Arnold, 1998).

—— *The Art of Record: A Critical Introduction to Documentary* (Manchester: Manchester University Press, 1996).

—— *Television Form and Public Address* (London: Edward Arnold, 1995).

—— *Popular Television in Britain* (London: BFI, 1991).

Corner, J. and S. Harvey (eds), *Television Times: A Reader* (London: Arnold, 1996).

Corrigan, P., 'On the difficulty of being sociological (historical materialist) in the study of television: the "moment" of English television, 1936–1939', in T. Syvertsen (ed.), *1992 and after: Nordic Television in Transition* (Bergen: University of Bergen, 1990), pp. 130–60.

Cottle, S. (ed.), *Ethnic Minorities and the Media* (Oxford: Oxford University Press, 2000).

Creeber, G. (ed.), *The Television Genre Book* (London: BFI, 2001).

Creeber, G., *Serial Television: Big Drama on the Small Screen* (London: BFI, 2005).

Crisell, A., *An Introductory History of British Broadcasting* (London: Routledge, 1997).

Cumberbatch, G., S. Gauntlett and V. Lyne, *Minority Group Representation on British Terrestrial Television: Key Findings, 1993–2003* (London: BBC/Ofcom, 2004).

Curran, J. and J. Seaton (eds), *Power without Responsibility: The Press and Broadcasting in Britain*, fifth edition (London: Routledge, 1997).

Dahlgren, P., *Television and the Public Sphere* (London: Sage, 1995).

Dajani, N., 'Television in the Arab East', in J. Wasko (ed.), *A Companion to Television* (Malden, Mass., and Oxford: Blackwell, 2005), pp. 580–601.

Dickinson, R., R. Harindranath and O. Linné (eds), *Approaches to Audiences: A Reader* (London: Arnold, 1998).

Dominick, J., B. Sherman and G. Copeland, *Broadcasting/Cable and Beyond: An Introduction to Modern Electronic Media*, third edition (New York: McGraw-Hill, 1996).

Dovey, J., *Freakshow* (Cambridge: Polity, 2000).

Dowmunt, T. (ed.), *Channels of Resistance: Global Television and Local Empowerment* (London: BFI, 1993).

Drummond, P. and R. Patterson (eds), *Television and Its Audience: International Research Perspectives* (London: BFI, 1988).

Dyer, R., *Light Entertainment* (London: BFI, 1973).

Dyer, R., C. Geraghty, M. Jordan, T. Lovell, R. Paterson and J. Stewart, *Coronation Street* (London: BFI, 1981).

Eco, U., 'Interpreting serials', in *The Limits of Interpretation* (Bloomington, Ind.: Indiana University Press, 1990), pp. 83–100.

—— 'A guide to the neo-television of the 1980s', *Framework*, 25 (1984), pp. 18–25.

Eden, J., 'Caruso control', *Radio Times*, 5–11 August 2006, pp. 11–12.

Eldridge, J. (ed.), *Glasgow Media Reader*, vol. 1: *News Content, Language and Visuals* (London: Routledge, 1995).

Ellis, J., 'Scheduling: the last creative act in television', *Media, Culture & Society*, 22:1 (2000), pp. 25–38.

—— *Visible Fictions: Cinema, Television, Video* (London: Routledge and Kegan Paul, 1982).

Eyre, P., 'Taboo television', *Guardian* Media section, 24 July 2006, p. 2.

Fairclough, N., *Media Discourse* (London: Arnold, 1995).

Feuer, J., 'Genre study and television', in R. Allen (ed.), *Channels of Discourse, Reassembled: Television and Contemporary Criticism* (London: Routledge, 1992), pp. 138–60.

Fiske, J., *Media Matters* (Minneapolis, Minn.: University of Minnesota Press, 1994).

—— 'British cultural studies and television', in R. Allen (ed.), *Channels of Discourse, Reassembled: Television and Contemporary Criticism* (London: Routledge, 1992a), pp. 284–326.

—— 'The cultural economy of fandom', in L. Lewis (ed.), *The Adoring Audience: Fan Culture and Popular Media* (London: Routledge, 1992b), pp. 30–49.

—— *Television Culture* (London: Routledge, 1992c).

—— 'Postmodernism and television', in J. Curran and M. Gurevitch (eds), *Mass Media and Society* (London: Edward Arnold, 1991), pp. 55–67.

—— *Introduction to Communication Studies* (London: Routledge, 1990).

Fiske, J. and J. Hartley, *Reading Television* (London: Methuen, 1978).

Flitterman-Lewis, S., 'Psychoanalysis, film, and television', in R. Allen (ed.), *Channels of Discourse, Reassembled: Television and Contemporary Criticism* (London: Routledge, 1992), pp. 203–46.

Franklin, B. (ed.), *British Television Policy: A Reader* (London: Routledge, 2001).

Freedman, L. and E. Karsh, *The Gulf Conflict 1990–1991: Diplomacy and War in the New World Order* (London: Faber, 1993).

Frost, V., 'The press toe the line on the Iraq War', *Guardian* Media section, 13 November 2006, p. 7.

Galtung, J. and M. Ruge, 'Structuring and selecting news', in S. Cohen and J. Young (eds), *The Manufacture of News: Social Problems, Deviance and the Mass Media* (London: Constable, 1973), pp. 62–72.

Garber, M., J. Matlock and R. Walkowitz (eds), *Media Spectacles* (London: Routledge, 1993).

Garnett, T., 'Contexts', in J. Bignell, S. Lacey and M. Macmurraugh-Kavanagh (eds), *British Television Drama: Past, Present and Future* (Basingstoke: Palgrave, 2000), pp. 11–23.

Geertz, C., *The Interpretation of Cultures: Selected Essays* (London: Fontana, 1967).

Geraghty, C., 'Audiences and "ethnography": questions of practice', in C. Geraghty and D. Lusted (eds), *The Television Studies Book* (London: Arnold, 1998), pp. 141–57.

—— *Women and Soap Opera: A Study of Prime Time Soaps* (Cambridge: Polity Press, 1991).

Geraghty, C. and D. Lusted (eds), *The Television Studies Book* (London: Arnold, 1998).

Gibbs, J., *Mise-en-Scène: Film Style and Interpretation* (London: Wallflower, 2002).

Gibson, O., 'Every year, it's the most extreme ever', *Guardian*, 5 June 2006, p. 5.

Giddens, A., *The Consequences of Modernity* (Cambridge: Polity, 1990).

Gillespie, M., 'Ambivalent positionings: the Gulf War', in P. Brooker and W. Brooker (eds), *Postmodern After-Images: A Reader in Film, Television and Video* (London: Arnold, 1997), pp. 172–81.

Glasgow Media Group, *War and Peace News* (Milton Keynes: Open University Press, 1986).

—— *More Bad News* (London: Routledge and Kegan Paul, 1980).

—— *Bad News* (London: Routledge and Kegan Paul, 1976).

Goodwin, A., 'MTV', in J. Corner and S. Harvey (eds), *Television Times: A Reader* (London: Arnold, 1996), pp. 75–87.

—— *Dancing in the Distraction Factory: Music, Television and Popular Culture* (London: Routledge, 1993).

Goodwin, A. and G. Whannel (eds), *Understanding Television* (London: Routledge, 1990).

Goodwin, P., 'The role of the state', in J. Stokes and A. Reading (eds), *The Media in Britain: Current Debates and Developments* (Basingstoke: Macmillan, 1999), pp. 130–42.

Gray, A., *Video Playtime: The Gendering of a Leisure Technology* (London: Routledge, 1992).

Gray, H., *Watching Race: Television and the Struggle for 'Blackness'* (Minneapolis, Minn.: University of Minnesota Press, 1995).

Gripsrud, J., 'Television, broadcasting, flow: key metaphors in TV theory', in C. Geraghty and D. Lusted (eds), *The Television Studies Book* (London: Arnold, 1998), pp. 17–32.

—— *The Dynasty Years: Hollywood Television and Critical Media Studies* (London: Routledge, 1995).

Grossberg, L., 'The in-difference of television', *Screen* 28 (1987), pp. 28–45.

Grossberg, L., C. Nelson and P. Treichler, with L. Baughman and J. Macgregor Wise (eds), *Cultural Studies* (New York: Routledge, 1992).

Gurevitch, M., 'The globalization of electronic journalism', in J. Curran and M. Gurevitch (eds), *Mass Media and Society* (London: Edward Arnold, 1991), pp. 178–93.

Habermas, J., *The Theory of Communicative Action*, vol. 2: *Lifeworld and System: A Critique of Functionalist Reason* (Cambridge: Polity, 1987).

Hall, S. (ed.), *Representation: Cultural Representations and Signifying Practices* (London: Sage, 1997).

—— 'Black and white television', in D. Morley and K. Chen (eds), *Remote Control: Dilemmas of Black Intervention in British Film and TV* (London: BFI, 1996), pp. 13–28.

—— 'Encoding/decoding', in S. Hall, D. Hobson, A. Lowe and P. Willis (eds), *Culture, Media, Language* (London: Hutchinson, 1980), pp. 128–38.

Hallam, J. and M. Marshment, 'Framing experience: case studies in the reception of *Oranges Are not the Only Fruit*', *Screen*, 36:1 (1995), pp. 1–15.

Hammond, M. and L. Mazdon (eds), *The Contemporary Television Series* (Edinburgh: Edinburgh University Press, 2005).

Harbord, J. and J. Wright, *Forty Years of British Television* (London: Boxtree, 1992).

Harrison, J., *Terrestrial Television News in Britain: The Culture of Production* (Manchester: Manchester University Press, 2000).

Hart, C., *Television Program Making* (Oxford: Focal Press, 1999).

Hartley, J., *Tele-ology: Studies in Television* (London: Routledge, 1992).

—— *Understanding News* (London: Routledge, 1982).

Harvey, S., 'Channel 4 television from Annan to Grade', in S. Hood (ed.), *Behind the Screens* (London: Lawrence and Wishart, 1994), pp. 102–29.

Havens, T., '"The biggest show in the world": race and the global popularity of *The Cosby Show*', *Media Culture & Society*, 22:4 (2000), pp. 371–91.

Herman, E. and R. McChesney, *The Global Media: The New Missionaries of Global Capitalism* (London: Cassell, 1997).

Hill, A., *Big Brother*: the real audience', *Television and New Media*, 3:3 (2002), pp. 323–41.

Hill, J. and M. McLoone (eds), *Big Picture Small Screen: The Relations between Film and Television* (Luton: University of Luton Press, 1997).

Himmelwhite, H. T. *et al.*, *Television and the Child: An Experimental Study of the Effect of Television on the Young* (London: Nuffield Foundation and Oxford University Press, 1958).

Hobson, D., 'From *Crossroads* to *Wife Swap*: learning from audiences', *Critical Studies in Television*, 1:1 (2006), pp. 121–8.

—— *Crossroads: The Drama of a Soap Opera* (London: Methuen, 1982).

Hollingsworth, M. and R. Norton-Taylor, *Blacklist: The Inside Story of Political Vetting* (London, Hogarth, 1988).

Holmes, S., '"But this time *you* choose!": approaching the "interactive" audience in reality TV', *International Journal of Cultural Studies*, 7:2 (2004), pp. 213–31.

Holmes, S. and D. Jermyn (eds), *Understanding Reality Television* (London: Routledge, 2004).

Holmes, S. and S. Redmond, *Framing Celebrity: New Directions in Celebrity Culture* (London: Routledge, 2006).

Hood, S. (ed.), *Behind the Screens: The Structure of British Television in the Nineties* (London: Lawrence and Wishart, 1994).

Hutcheon, L., 'The politics of postmodernism, parody, and history', *Cultural Critique*, 5 (1986–7), pp. 179–207.

Huyssen, A., *After the Great Divide: Modernism, Mass Culture and Postmodernism* (London: Macmillan, 1986).

Independent Television Commission, *The ITC Programme Code* (London: ITC, 1998).

Jacobs, J., *Body Trauma TV: The New Hospital Dramas* (London: BFI, 2003).

Jacobson, R., *Television Research: A Directory of Conceptual Categories, Topic Suggestions and Selected Sources* (Jefferson: McFarland, 1995).

Jameson, F., *Postmodernism, or the Cultural Logic of Late Capitalism* (London: Verso, 1992).

—— 'Reading without interpretation: postmodernism and the videotext', in D. Attridge and N. Fabb (eds), *The Linguistics of Writing: Arguments between Language and Literature* (Manchester: Manchester University Press, 1987), pp. 199–233.

Jancovich, M. and J. Lyons (eds), *Quality Popular Television: Cult TV, the Industry and the Fans* (London: BFI, 2005).

Jenkins, H., *Textual Poachers: Television Fans and Participatory Culture* (London: Routledge, 1992).

Jermyn, D. and S. Holmes, 'The audience is dead; long live the audience!: interactivity, "telephilia", and the contemporary television audience', *Critical Studies in Television*, 1:1 (2006), pp. 49–57.

Jhally, S. and J. Lewis, *Enlightened Racism: The Cosby Show, Audiences, and the Myth of the American Dream* (San Francisco, Calif.: Westview, 1992).

Jhally, S. and B. Livant, 'Watching as working: the valorization of audience consciousness', *Journal of Communication*, 36:2 (1986), pp. 124–43.

Johnson, C. and R. Turnock (eds), *ITV Cultures: Independent Television over Fifty Years* (London: Open University Press, 2005).

Jones, J., 'Emerging platform identities: *Big Brother* UK and interactive multi-platform usage', in E. Mathijs and J. Jones (eds), *Big Brother International: Formats, Critics and Publics* (London: Wallflower, 2004), pp. 210–31.

Juluri, V., 'Music television and the invention of youth culture in India', *Television and New Media*, 3:4 (2002), pp. 367–86.

Kaplan, E. A., *Rocking around the Clock: Music Television, Postmodernism and Consumer Culture* (London: Methuen, 1987).

Katz, E. and Liebes, T., 'Mutual aid in the decoding of *Dallas*: preliminary notes from a cross-cultural study', in P. Drummond, *Television in Transition* (London: BFI, 1985), pp. 187–98.

—— 'Once upon a time in Dallas', *Intermedia*, 12:3 (1984), pp. 28–32.

Kauffmann, S., *Avid Editing* (Woburn, Mass.: Butterworth-Heinemann, 2000).

Kellner, D., *Media Culture: Cultural Studies, Identity and Politics between the Modern and the Postmodern* (London: Routledge, 1995).

Kidd-Hewitt, D. and R. Osborne (eds), *Crime and the Media: The Postmodern Spectacle* (London: Pluto, 1995).

Kilborn, R. and J. Izod, *An Introduction to Television Documentary: Confronting Reality* (Manchester: Manchester University Press, 1997).

Kirkham, S., '*Big Brother* in trouble over sex shock (again)', *Guardian*, 4 August 2005, p. 3.

Kozloff, S., 'Narrative theory and television', in R. Allen (ed.), *Channels of Discourse, Reassembled: Television and Contemporary Criticism* (London: Routledge, 1992), pp. 67–100.

Lacan, J., 'The mirror stage', in *Ecrits: A Selection*, trans. A. Sheridan (London: Tavistock, 1977), pp. 1–7.

Lacey, N., *Narrative and Genre: Key Concepts in Media Studies* (Basingstoke: Macmillan, 2000).

Lacey, S., *Tony Garnett* (Manchester: Manchester University Press, 2007).

Langer, J., *Tabloid Television: Popular Journalism and 'Other News'* (London: Routledge, 1998).

Leal, O., 'Popular taste and erudite repertoire: the place and space of television in Brazil', *Cultural Studies*, 4:1 (1990), pp. 19–29.

Lewis, J., *The Ideological Octopus: An Exploration of Television and Its Audience* (London: Routledge, 1991).

—— 'Decoding television news', in P. Drummond and R. Paterson (eds), *Television in Transition* (London: BFI, 1985), pp. 205–34.

Lewis, L. (ed.), *The Adoring Audience: Fan Culture and Popular Media* (London: Routledge, 1991).

—— *Gender Politics and MTV: Voicing the Difference* (Philadelphia, Pa.: Temple University Press, 1990).

Liebes, T. and Katz, E., *The Export of Meaning: Cross-cultural Readings of 'Dallas'* (New York: Oxford University Press, 1990).

Lindof, T. (ed.), *Natural Audiences: Qualitative Research of Media Uses and Effects* (Norwood: Ablex, 1987).

Lister, M. (ed.), *The Photographic Image in Digital Culture* (London: Routledge, 1995).

Livingston, S. and P. Lunt, *Talk on Television: Audience Participation and Public Debate* (London: Routledge, 1994).

Lorimer, R., with P. Scannell, *Mass Communications: A Comparative Introduction* (Manchester: Manchester University Press, 1994).

Lull, J. (ed.), 'Critical response: the audience as nuisance', *Critical Studies in Mass Communication* 5 (1988a), pp. 239–43.

—— *World Families Watch Television* (London: Sage, 1988b).

Lury, K., *Interpreting Television* (London: Hodder Arnold, 2005).

—— *British Youth Television: Cynicism and Enchantment* (Oxford: Oxford University Press, 2001).

Lusted, D., 'The popular culture debate and light entertainment on television', in C. Geraghty and D. Lusted (eds), *The Television Studies Book* (London: Arnold, 1998), pp. 175–90.

Lyotard, J.-F., 'Answering the question: what is postmodernism?', in T. Docherty (ed.), *Postmodernism: A Reader* (Hemel Hempstead: Harvester Wheatsheaf, 1993), pp. 38–46.

—— *The Postmodern Condition*, trans. G. Bennington and B. Massumi (Manchester: Manchester University Press, 1984; first published 1979).

McCracken, E., *Decoding Women's Magazines: From Mademoiselle to Ms.* (Basingstoke: Macmillan, 1993).

Macdonald, M., *Representing Women: Myths of Femininity in the Popular Media* (London: Arnold, 1995).

MacGregor, B., *Live, Direct and Biased? Making Television News in the Satellite Age* (London: HodderHeadline, 1997).

Mackay, H. and T. O'Sullivan (eds), *The Media Reader: Continuity and Transformation* (London: Sage, 1999).

McLean, G. 'CSI: Tarantino', *Guardian* New Media section, 11 July 2005, p. 12.

—— 'Corner shop to cop shop', *Guardian* Media section, 18 February 2002, pp. 8–9.

McLuhan, M., *Understanding Media: The Extensions of Man* (London: Ark, 1987).

McNair, B., *News and Journalism in the UK: A Textbook* (London: Routledge, 1994).

McQueen, D., *Television: A Media Student's Guide* (London: Arnold, 1998).

Mader, R., 'Globo village: television in Brazil', in T. Dowmunt (ed.), *Channels of Resistance: Global Television and Local Empowerment* (London: BFI, 1993), pp. 67–89.

Marris, P. and S. Thornham (eds), *Media Studies: A Reader* (Edinburgh: Edinburgh University Press, 1999).

Masterman, L., *Television Mythologies: Stars, Shows and Signs* (London: Comedia, 1984).

Mathijs, E. and J. Jones (eds), *Big Brother International: Formats, Critics and Publics* (London: Wallflower, 2004)

Meech, P., 'Advertising', in J. Stokes and A. Reading (eds), *The Media in Britain: Current Debates and Developments* (Basingstoke: Macmillan, 1999), pp. 25–40.

Messenger Davies, M., 'Production studies', *Critical Studies in Television*, 1:1 (2006), pp. 21–30.

Millerson, G., *Video Production Handbook*, third edition (Oxford: Focal Press, 2001).

Mills, B., 'Comedy verité: contemporary sitcom form', *Screen*, 45:1 (2004), pp. 63–78.

Modleski, T., *Loving with a Vengeance* (Hamden, Conn.: Shoe String Press, 1982).

Moores, S., *Interpreting Audiences* (London: Sage, 1993).

Morley, D., *Television, Audiences and Cultural Studies* (London: Routledge, 1992).

—— *The 'Nationwide' Audience* (London: BFI, 1980).

Morris, M., 'Feminism, reading, postmodernism', in T. Docherty (ed.), *Postmodernism: A Reader* (Hemel Hempstead: Harvester Wheatsheaf, 1993), pp. 368–89.

—— 'Banality in cultural studies', *Block*, 14 (1988), pp. 15–25.

Mort, F., *Cultures of Consumption: Masculinities and Social Space in Late Twentieth Century Britain* (London: Routledge, 1996).

Mosely, R., 'Makeover takeover on British television', *Screen*, 41:3 (2000), pp. 299–314.

Moss, S., 'New kids on the block', *Guardian* Media section, 28 January 2002, pp. 2–3.

Mullan, B., *Consuming Television* (Oxford: Blackwell, 1997).

Mundy, J., *Popular Music on Screen: From Hollywood Musical to Music Video* (Manchester: Manchester University Press, 1999).

Murdoch, G., 'Authorship and organization', *Screen Education*, 35 (1980), pp. 19–34.

Myers, G., *Ad Worlds: Brands, Media, Audiences* (London: Arnold, 1999).

Neale, S. and F. Krutnik, *Popular Film and Television Comedy* (London: Routledge, 1990).

Neale, S. and G. Turner, 'Introduction: what is genre?', in G. Creeber (ed.), *The Television Genre Book* (London: BFI, 2001), pp. 1–7.

Nelson, R., *TV Drama in Transition: Forms, Values and Cultural Change* (Basingstoke: Macmillan, 1997).

Newcomb, H., 'The development of television studies', in J. Wasko (ed.), *A Companion to Television* (Malden, Mass., and Oxford: Blackwell, 2005), pp. 15–28.

—— *TV: The Most Popular Art* (New York: Anchor, 1974).

Nichols, B., *Introduction to Documentary* (Bloomington, Ind.: Indiana University Press, 2001).

—— *Blurred Boundaries: Questions of Meaning in Contemporary Culture* (Bloomington, Ind.: Indiana University Press, 1994).

—— *Representing Reality: Issues and Concepts in Documentary* (Bloomington, Ind.: Indiana University Press, 1991).

Norris, C., '"Postscript": Baudrillard's second Gulf War article', in P. Brooker and W. Brooker (eds), *Postmodern After-Images: A Reader in Film, Television and Video* (London: Arnold, 1997), pp. 168–71.

Orlebar, J., *Digital Television Production* (London: Arnold, 2002).

O'Sullivan, T., 'Television, memories and cultures of viewing 1950–65', in J. Corner (ed.), *Popular Television in Britain: Studies in Cultural History* (London: BFI, 1991), pp. 159–81.

O'Sullivan, T., B. Dutton and P. Rayner, *Studying the Media: An Introduction* (London: Edward Arnold, 1994).

Paget, D., *No Other Way to Tell It: Dramadoc/Docudrama on Television* (Manchester: Manchester University Press, 1998).

Petley, J., 'The regulation of media content', in J. Stokes and A. Reading (eds), *The Media in Britain: Current Debates and Developments* (Basingstoke: Macmillan, 1999), pp. 143–57.

Petrie, D. and J. Willis (eds), *Television and the Household: Reports from the BFI's Audience Tracking Study* (London: BFI, 1995).

Philips, D., 'Medicated soap: the woman doctor in television medical drama', in B. Carson and M. Llewellyn-Jones (eds), *Frames and Fictions on Television: The Politics of Identity within Drama* (Exeter: Intellect, 2000), pp. 50–61.

Philo, G., 'Missing in action', *Guardian* Higher Education section, 16 April 2002, pp. 10–11.

—— (ed.), *Glasgow Media Reader*, vol. 2: *Industry, War, Economy and Politics* (London: Routledge, 1995).

—— 'Whose news?', *Media, Culture & Society*, 9:4 (1987), pp. 397–406.

Piper, H., 'Reality TV, *Wife Swap* and the drama of banality', *Screen* 54:4 (2004), pp. 273–86.

Poster, M., *The Second Media Age* (Cambridge: Polity, 1995).

Purser, P., 'Dennis Potter', in G. Brandt (ed.), *British Television Drama* (Cambridge: Cambridge University Press, 1981), pp. 168–93.

Rolinson, D., *Alan Clarke* (Manchester: Manchester University Press, 2005).

Rose, B. (ed.), *TV Genres: A Handbook and Reference Guide* (Westport, Conn.: Greenwood, 1985).

Ruddock, A., *Understanding Audiences: Theory and Method* (London: Sage, 2001).

Saussure, F. de, *Course in General Linguistics*, ed. C. Bally, A. Sechehaye and A. Riedlinger, trans. W. Baskin (London: Fontana, 1974).

Scannell, P., 'Television and history', in J. Wasko (ed.), *A Companion to Television* (Malden, Mass., and Oxford: Blackwell, 2005), pp. 51–66.

—— 'Public service broadcasting: the history of a concept', in A. Goodwin and G. Whannel (eds), *Understanding Television* (London: Routledge, 1990), pp. 11–29.

Schlesinger, P., *Putting 'Reality' Together: BBC News* (London: Constable, 1978).

Sears, J., '*Crimewatch* and the rhetoric of verisimilitude', *Critical Survey*, 7:1 (1995), pp. 51–8.

Seiter, E., 'Semiotics, structuralism, and television', in R. Allen (ed.), *Channels of Discourse, Reassembled: Television and Contemporary Criticism* (London: Routledge, 1992), pp. 31–66.

Seiter, E., H. Borchers, G. Kreutzner and E.-M. Warth (eds), *Remote Control: Television, Audiences and Cultural Power* (London: Routledge, 1989).

Selby, K. and R. Cowdery, *How to Study Television* (Basingstoke: Macmillan, 1995).

Shattuc, J., *The Talking Cure: TV Talk Shows and Women* (London: Routledge, 1997).

Sheen, E. and R. Giddings (eds), *The Classic Novel: From Page to Screen* (Manchester: Manchester University Press, 1999).

Shubik, I., *Play for Today: The Evolution of Television Drama* (London: Davis-Poynter, 1975).

Simpson, J., 'What comfort zone?', *Guardian* Media section, 29 May 2006, p. 6.

Sinclair, J., 'Latin American commercial television: "primitive capitalism"', in J. Wasko (ed.), *A Companion to Television* (Malden, Mass., and Oxford: Blackwell, 2005), pp. 503–20.

Sinclair, J., E. Jacka and S. Cunningham, 'New patterns in global television', in P. Marris and S. Thornham (eds), *The Media Reader* (Edinburgh: Edinburgh University Press, 1999), pp. 170–90.

—— (eds), *Peripheral Vision: New Patterns in Global Television* (Oxford: Oxford University Press, 1996).

Smith, A., *Television: An International History*, second edition (Oxford: Oxford University Press, 1998).

Sobchack, V., 'Democratic franchise and the electronic frontier', in Z. Sardar and J. Ravetz (eds), *Cyberfutures* (London: Pluto, 1996), pp. 77–89.

Sparks, R., *Television and the Drama of Crime* (Buckingham: Open University Press, 1992).

Sreberny-Mohammadi, A. with K. Nordenstreng, R. Stevenson and F. Ugboajah (eds), *Foreign News in the Media: International Reporting in 29 Countries* (Paris: UNESCO, 1985).

Sreberny-Mohammadi, A., D. Winseck, J. McKenna and O. Boyd-Barrett (eds), *Media in Global Context: A Reader* (London: Arnold, 1997).

Stewart, I. and S. Carruthers (eds), *War, Culture and the Media: Representations of the Military in 20th Century Britain* (Trowbridge: Flicks Books, 1996).

Stokes, J. and A. Reading (eds), *The Media in Britain: Current Debates and Developments* (Basingstoke: Macmillan, 1999).

Storey, J. *Cultural Consumption and Everyday Life* (London: Arnold, 1999).

Thornham, S. and T. Purvis, *Television Drama: Theories and Identities* (Basingstoke: Palgrave Macmillan, 2005).

Thussu, K. D. (ed.), *Electronic Empires: Global Media and Local Resistance* (London: Arnold, 1998).

Tolson, A., *Mediations: Text and Discourse in Media Studies* (London: Arnold, 1996).

Tulloch, J., *Watching Television Audiences: Cultural Theories and Methods* (London: Arnold, 2000).

—— *Television Drama: Agency, Audience and Myth* (London: Routledge, 1990).

Tulloch, J. and H. Jenkins, *Science Fiction Audiences: Watching Doctor Who and Star Trek* (London: Routledge, 1995).

Tunstall, J. (ed.), *Media Occupations and Professions: A Reader* (Oxford: Oxford University Press, 2001).

—— *Television Producers* (London: Routledge, 1993).

—— *The Media in Britain* (London: Constable, 1983).

UNESCO, *Many Voices, One World: Towards a New, More Just, and More Efficient World Information and Communication Order* (Paris: UNESCO, 1980).

Uricchio, W., 'Rituals of reception, patterns of neglect: Nazi television and its postwar representation', *Wide Angle*, 11:1 (1989), pp. 48–66.

Vahimagi, T., *British Television: An Illustrated Guide* (London: BFI, 1994).

Wagg, S. (ed.), *Because I Tell a Joke or Two: Comedy, Politics and Social Difference* (London: Routledge, 1998).

Walker, I., 'Desert stories or faith in facts?', in M. Lister (ed.), *The Photographic Image in Digital Culture* (London: Routledge, 1995), pp. 236–52.

Wasko, J. (ed.), *A Companion to Television* (Malden, Mass., and Oxford: Blackwell, 2005).

Wayne, M., *Dissident Voices: The Politics of Television and Cultural Change* (London: Pluto, 1998).

Webster, F., *Theories of the Information Society* (London: Routledge, 1995).

Whannel, G., *Fields in Vision: Television Sport and Cultural Transformation* (London: Routledge, 1992).

Whitaker, B., 'Same news, different perspective', *Guardian* Media section, 6 February 2006, pp. 1–2.

Whitehouse, M., *Cleaning up TV: From Protest to Participation* (London: Blandford, 1967).

Wicke, J. and M. Ferguson, 'Introduction: feminism and postmodernism; or, The way we live now', in M. Ferguson and J. Wicke (eds), *Feminism and Postmodernism* (London: Duke University Press, 1994), pp. 1–9.

Williams, R., *Television, Technology and Cultural Form* (London: Collins, 1974).

—— *Drama in Performance* (London: C. A. Watts, 1968).

Winship, J., *Inside Women's Magazines* (London: Pandora, 1987).

Winston, B., *Media Technology and Society: A History* (London: Routledge, 1998).

—— *Claiming the Real: The Documentary Film Revisited* (London: BFI, 1995).

Woods, T., *Beginning Postmodernism* (Manchester: Manchester University Press, 1999).

Zhou, Y. and Z. Guo, 'Television in China: history, political economy, and ideology', in J. Wasko (ed.), *A Companion to Television* (Malden, Mass., and Oxford: Blackwell, 2005), pp. 521–39.

# Index

Note: Page numbers in *italics* refer to illustrations